THE
AFRIC

This *Companion* provides a comprehensive overview of African American theatre, from the early nineteenth century to the present day. Along the way, it chronicles the evolution of African American theatre and its engagement with the wider community, including discussions of slave rebellions on the national stage, African Americans on Broadway, the Harlem Renaissance, African American women dramatists, and the "New Negro" and "Black Arts" movements. Leading scholars spotlight the producers, directors, playwrights, and actors whose efforts helped to fashion a more accurate appearance of black life on stage, and reveal the impact of African American theatre both within the United States and further afield. Chapters also address recent theatre productions in the context of political and cultural change and ask where African American theatre is heading in the twenty-first century.

HARVEY YOUNG is an associate professor at Northwestern University, where he holds appointments in African-American Studies, Performance Studies, and Theatre.

A complete list of books in the series is at the back of this book.

THE CAMBRIDGE
COMPANION TO
AFRICAN AMERICAN
THEATRE

EDITED BY
HARVEY YOUNG
Northwestern University

CAMBRIDGE
UNIVERSITY PRESS

CAMBRIDGE UNIVERSITY PRESS
Cambridge, New York, Melbourne, Madrid, Cape Town,
Singapore, São Paulo, Delhi, Mexico City

Cambridge University Press
The Edinburgh Building, Cambridge CB2 8RU, UK

Published in the United States of America by Cambridge University Press, New York

www.cambridge.org
Information on this title: www.cambridge.org/9781107017122

First published 2013

Printed in the United Kingdom by the MPG Books Group

A catalog record for this publication is available from the British Library

Library of Congress Cataloging in Publication data
The Cambridge companion to African American theatre / edited by Harvey Young.
pages   cm. – (Cambridge companions to literature)
Includes bibliographical references and index.
ISBN 978-1-107-01712-2 (hardback) – ISBN 978-1-107-60275-5 (paperback)
1. African American theater–History.   2. American drama–African American authors–
History and criticism.   3. African Americans in the performing arts.
I. Young, Harvey, 1975–
PN2270.A35C36 2012
792.089'96073–dc23
2012018843

ISBN 978-1-107-01712-2 hardback
ISBN 978-1-107-60275-5 paperback

For my parents,
Harvey Young, Sr.
and
Regina Huff Young

CONTENTS

ILLUSTRATIONS

CONTRIBUTORS

FAEDRA CHATARD CARPENTER is Assistant Professor in the School of Theatre, Dance, and Performance Studies at the University of Maryland, College Park. Her interests include the study of race, sexuality, and gender in contemporary performance. She has published work in *Review*, *Theatre Topics*, *Women & Performance*, *Text and Performance Quarterly*, and *Callaloo*.

SOYICA DIGGS COLBERT is Assistant Professor of English at Dartmouth College. She is the author of *The Black Theatrical Body: Reception, Performance, and the Stage*, and the editor of a special issue of *African American Review* on black performance. She has published articles on James Baldwin, Alice Childress, and August Wilson.

HARRY J. ELAM, Jr. is the Freeman-Thornton Vice Provost for Undergraduate Education and Olive H. Palmer Professor in the Humanities at Stanford University. He is the author of *Taking It to the Streets: The Social Protest Theater of Luis Valdez and Amiri Baraka* and *The Past as Present in the Drama of August Wilson*, and coeditor of four books.

NADINE GEORGE-GRAVES is Professor of Theatre and Dance at the University of California, San Diego. She is the author of *The Royalty of Negro Vaudeville: The Whitman Sisters and the Negotiation of Race, Gender, and Class in African American Theater, 1900–1940*, and *Urban Bush Women: Twenty Years of Dance Theater, Community Engagement and Working It Out*.

DOUGLAS A. JONES, Jr. is Cotsen Fellow in the Society of Fellows at Princeton University. His book, *The Captive Stage: Black Exception, Performance, and the Proslavery Imagination of the Antebellum North*, is forthcoming from University of Michigan Press. In fall, 2013, he will join the faculty of the Department of English at Rutgers University.

ADRIENNE MACKI BRACONI is Assistant Professor at the University of Connecticut, where she holds appointments in Dramatic Arts and the Institute for African American Studies. Her current book project focuses on the relationship between African American theatrical performance and interracial and intraracial community-building in Harlem during the interwar Depression era through the mid twentieth century.

HEATHER S. NATHANS is Professor of Theatre at the University of Maryland. She is the author of *Early American Theatre from the Revolution to Thomas Jefferson* and *Slavery and Sentiment on the American Stage, 1781–1861*. Her articles have appeared in *Theatre History Studies*, *New England Theatre Journal*, *Journal of American Drama and Theatre*, *Early American Studies*, and *Pennsylvania History Journal*.

MONICA WHITE NDOUNOU is Assistant Professor of Theatre at Tufts University. Her most recent publications include articles in *Consciousness, Theatre, Literature and the Arts*; *New England Theatre Journal*; and *Theatre Topics*.

SAMUEL O'CONNELL is Assistant Professor in Theatre and Interdisciplinary Arts in the Visual and Performing Arts Department at Worcester State College. His research interests focus on the intersections of media technology and live performance in popular culture.

SANDRA L. RICHARDS is Professor of African American Studies and Theatre at Northwestern University. She has published numerous articles on African American and Nigerian dramatists and is the author of *Ancient Songs Set Ablaze: The Theatre of Femi Osofisan*.

JONATHAN SHANDELL is Assistant Professor of Theatre Arts at Arcadia University. His scholarship is in American theatre history, with a focus on race and interracial collaboration on the mid-twentieth-century American stage. He has published in *African American Review*, *Maroon: The Yale Journal of African American Studies*, *African American National Biography*, *Theatre Topics*, *Theatre Journal*, and *American Theatre*.

SANDRA G. SHANNON is Professor of Dramatic Literature and Criticism in the Department of English at Howard University. Her prolific publication record includes two book-length studies: *The Dramatic Vision of August Wilson* and *August Wilson's Fences: A Reference Guide*, an edited collection: *August Wilson and Black Aesthetics*, and a significant number of additional publications in notable refereed journals.

HARVEY YOUNG is Associate Professor of Theatre at Northwestern University. He is the author of *Embodying Black Experience: Stillness, Critical Memory, and the Black Body*, and coeditor of *Performance in the Borderlands: A Critical Anthology* and *Reimagining* A Raisin in the Sun: *Four New Plays*.

AIMEE ZYGMONSKI is Assistant Professor of Theatre at the University of Nevada, Las Vegas. Her research focuses on the interstices between stereotypes and contemporary African American drama. Her publications include essays in *Theatre Journal* and *Theatre Research International*.

ACKNOWLEDGEMENTS

An edited collection brings together an array of voices and talents for a common purpose. In addition to those whose names appear in the table of contents, the editor would like to acknowledge the following individuals whose presence and efforts were instrumental to the completion of this book. Vicki Cooper, Fleur Jones, and Rebecca Taylor at Cambridge University Press saw the potential in this project and served as the book's earliest advocates. Project manager Emma Wildsmith at Out of House Publishing Solutions arranged for copy-editing, typesetting, and proofreading. Robert Whitelock copy-edited this manuscript. Christine Simonian Bean at Northwestern University and Katie Zien at McGill University provided general (but vital) editorial assistance, including reformatting chapters and reading chapter drafts. Zeke Young, an always smiling and often singing three-year-old, provided the soundtrack as his father edited this book.

CHRONOLOGY

1529	First enslaved Africans arrive in North America.
1741	Enslaved Africans allegedly attempt to kill the white men of Manhattan, known as "The Great Negro Plot."
1807	Birth of Ira Aldridge.
1818	Birth of Frederick Douglass.
1821	William Alexander Brown opens the African Theatre (also known as the Minor Theatre, African Grove, or the African Company), the first African American theatre in New York City.
1823	Brown's *The Drama of King Shotaway* produced; thought to be the first African-American-authored play produced in the United States. Charles Mathews performs *A Trip to America* in London.
1827	The first African-American-owned and operated newspaper, *Freedom's Journal*, published.
1830	Thomas Dartmouth Rice (a white blackface performer) makes the Jim Crow character his signature act.
1833	Ira Aldridge performs at Covent Garden in London.
1831	Nat Turner leads a slave rebellion in Virginia; known as Nat Turner's Rebellion or the Southampton Insurrection.
1839	Enslaved African revolt on the *Amistad*.
1850	Congress passes the 1850 Fugitive Slave Act.
1852	Harriet Beecher Stowe's *Uncle Tom's Cabin* published.
1859	John Brown launches attack on Harpers Ferry.

1861	Civil War begins.
1863	Abraham Lincoln signs the Emancipation Proclamation.
1865	Civil War ends. Ku Klux Klan forms.
1867	Death of Ira Aldridge.
1868	Birth of W. E. B. Du Bois.
1873	Birth of George W. Walker.
1874	Birth of Egbert "Bert" Williams.
1876	First Jim Crow laws enacted.
1878	Birth of Charles Gilpin.
1894	Birth of Eulalie Spence.
1895	Death of Frederick Douglass.
1896	*The Gold Bug* opens; George Walker and Bert Williams become the first African Americans on Broadway.
1902	Birth of Langston Hughes. *In Dahomey* opens as the first full-length musical written and performed by African Americans on Broadway.
1903	W. E. B. Du Bois publishes *The Souls of Black Folk*.
1909	Formation of the National Association for the Advancement of Colored People (NAACP). Bert Williams stars in the Ziegfeld Follies, becoming the first African American to receive top billing.
1911	Death of George W. Walker.
1912	The Lafayette Theatre becomes the first New York City theatre to desegregate.
1914	The Great War (World War I) begins.
1915	Anita Bush founds the Anita Bush Stock Company (later renamed the Lafayette Players), becoming the first major professional black dramatic company in the USA. The NAACP forms a Drama Committee. The Playhouse Settlement (later the Karamu Theatre of Cleveland) founded.

1916	Angelina Weld Grimké's *Rachel* opens. Birth of Alice Childress. Harlem Renaissance begins.
1918	The Great War ends.
1920	Eugene O'Neill's *The Emperor Jones* opens on Broadway, starring Charles Gilpin.
1921	Birth of Errol Gaston Hill.
1922	Death of Egbert "Bert" Williams. Ethiopian Art Theatre of Chicago opens.
1923	Willis Richardson's one-act *The Chip Woman's Fortune* opens: the first drama by an African American playwright on Broadway.
1925	Garland Anderson's *Appearances* opens: the first full-length drama by an African American on Broadway. Georgia Douglas Johnson founds the S Street Salon.
1926	W. E. B. Du Bois founds the Krigwa Players.
1929	US stock market crash, indicating the start of the Great Depression. The Negro Experimental Players founded. The Harlem Experimental Theatre founded.
1930	Birth of Lorraine Hansberry. Death of Charles Gilpin.
1931	Nine black teenage boys ("The Scottsboro Boys") accused of and tried for rape in Alabama. The Harlem Players founded.
1932	Birth of Adrienne Kennedy.
1934	Birth of LeRoi Jones (Amiri Baraka).
1935	Birth of Ed Bullins. Langston Hughes's *Mulatto* premieres on Broadway. The Federal Theatre Project created by the New Deal Works Progress Administration: includes "Negro Units."
1938	Langston Hughes and Louise Thompson form The Harlem Suitcase Theatre.
1939	World War II begins.
1940	Frederick O'Neal and Abram Hill found the American Negro Theatre in Harlem.

1945	World War II ends. Birth of August Wilson.
1948	President Harry Truman signs Executive Order 9981, declaring equal treatment for all in the armed services. Birth of Ntozake Shange.
1952	Ralph Ellison's *Invisible Man* published.
1954	*Brown v. Board of Education of Topeka, Kansas* Supreme Court ruling, declares segregation in public schools unconstitutional. Birth of George C. Wolfe.
1959	Lorraine Hansberry's *A Raisin in the Sun* debuts on Broadway: the first play staged on Broadway by an African American woman playwright. Lloyd Richards, the director of *A Raisin in the Sun*, becomes the first African American director of a Broadway play.
1961	Ellen Stewart founds Café La Mama (later La MaMa Experimental Theatre Club).
1963	March on Washington; Martin Luther King, Jr. delivers his "I Have a Dream" speech. Birth of Suzan-Lori Parks. Death of W. E. B. Du Bois.
1964	President Lyndon Johnson signs the Civil Rights Act of 1964. Birth of Lynn Nottage.
1965	Congress passes the Voting Rights Act of 1965. Black Arts Movement begins. Amiri Baraka opens the Black Arts Repertory and School. Assassination of Malcolm X. Death of Lorraine Hansberry.
1966	Black Panther Party forms.
1967	Robert Macbeth opens the New Lafayette Theatre. Douglas Turner Ward founds the Negro Ensemble Company. Death of Langston Hughes.
1968	Assassination of Martin Luther King, Jr. Barbara Ann Teer founds the National Black Theatre.
1969	James Earl Jones wins Tony Award for Best Actor for *The Great White Hope*.
1970	Woody King, Jr. starts the New Federal Theatre.

1971   Melvin Van Peebles's *Ain't Supposed to Die a Natural Death* opens on Broadway.

1974   Joseph Walker wins Tony Award for Best Play for *The River Niger*.

1975   Charlie Small's *The Wiz* opens on Broadway and wins Tony Award for Best Musical.

1976   Ntozake Shange's choreopoem *for colored girls who have considered suicide / when the rainbow is enuf* opens on Broadway. James V. Hatch and Ted Shine publish *Black Theatre USA*.

1981   *Dreamgirls* opens on Broadway. Death of Eulalie Spence.

1982   Charles Fuller receives Pulitzer Prize for Drama for *A Soldier's Play*.

1984   Jawole Willa Jo Zollar founds Urban Bush Women.

1986   Black Theatre Network founded. Margaret Wilkerson publishes *Nine Plays by Black Women*.

1987   August Wilson receives Pulitzer Prize for Drama for *Fences*. James Earl Jones receives Tony Award for Best Actor for *Fences*.

1989   Larry Leon Hamlin founds the National Black Theatre Festival.

1990   August Wilson receives Pulitzer Prize for Drama for *The Piano Lesson*.

1991   Pomo Afro Homos premiere *Fierce Love: Stories from Black Gay Life*.

1992   Los Angeles Uprising (also known as Los Angeles Riots).

1994   Anna Deveare Smith's *Twilight: Los Angeles, 1992* opens on Broadway.

1996   Suzan-Lori Parks's *Venus* premieres at the Yale Repertory Theatre.

1997   Djanet Sears's *Harlem Duet* premieres in Toronto.

1999   Hiphop Theatre Junction formed in Washington, DC.

2002   Suzan-Lori Parks receives the Pulitzer Prize for Drama for *Topdog/Underdog*. Kenny Leon and Jane Bishop found True Colors Theatre Company. Paul Carter Harrison publishes *Black Theatre*.

2003   Errol G. Hill and James V. Hatch publish *A History of African American Theatre*.

2004   Phylicia Rashād wins Tony Award for Best Actress for revival of *A Raisin in the Sun*.

2005   Death of August Wilson. Hurricane Katrina strikes New Orleans, killing approximately 1,800 people.

2008   Barack Obama elected president of the United States. Death of Barbara Ann Teer.

2009   Lynn Nottage wins Pulitzer Prize for Drama for *Ruined*.

2010   Denzel Washington and Viola Davis win Tony Awards for Best Actor and Best Actress for Broadway revival of *Fences*.

2011   Plays by three African American women appear on Broadway: Katori Hall's *The Mountaintop*, Lydia Diamond's *Stick Fly*, and *The Gershwins' Porgy and Bess*, a musical revival adapted by Suzan-Lori Parks. Death of Ellen Stewart.

2012   Audra McDonald wins Tony Award for Best Actress in Parks's adaptation of *Porgy and Bess*.

HARVEY YOUNG

Introduction

In June, 1996, playwright August Wilson delivered a keynote address at the biennial gathering of the Theatre Communications Group (TCG), a professional organization of theatre artists and scholars. Arriving at the podium, the two-time Pulitzer Prize winner, who was widely considered to be the most influential voice active in the American theatre, surveyed the assembled audience. He saw the leaders of prominent regional theatres in the country, emerging young artists eager to take their places, and critics whose pens had the power to attract (or drive away) corporate and governmental funding. There were several hundred attendees. The vast majority of them were white. Wilson was not surprised by the composition of his audience. Having developed his seven history plays on the African American experience, which were part of a planned ten-play cycle, at regional theatres across the country en route to Broadway, the accomplished playwright was well aware of the complexion of American theatre. His success, his standing at the podium on that day and, more generally, as one of the world's greatest living playwrights, was aided by many of the people who sat before him. Now, they were awaiting his remarks.

Wilson's "provocative" and "passionate" address,[1] which would later be published under the title "The Ground on which I Stand,"[2] triggered a national conversation, within the arts, about race, multiculturalism, and cultural separatism. It catalyzed a series of debates, including a couple featuring August Wilson and his primary antagonist, theatre critic Robert Brustein. It inspired scholars to interrogate the relevance of the "color line" at the end of the twentieth century and within the theatre. Standing at the podium, Wilson asserted that more opportunities needed to be made available to non-white artists to create and engage in work that reflects their unique cultural experiences and history. He criticized colorblind casting practices for not acknowledging cultural difference. He called for the creation of ethnic theatres whose missions would be to champion the work of and create opportunities for artists of color.

What made Wilson's remarks so controversial was that the playwright's own career ascendance seemed to suggest that American theatre had achieved not only racial diversity but also racial syncretism. The TCG address was a celebratory occasion. It was a chance for August Wilson and his collaborators and supporters (his TCG audience) to reflect upon how much the theatre industry had progressed. One hundred years earlier, theatre audiences were segregated by race, and blackface minstrelsy remained popular on vaudeville stages. A century later, the most critically acclaimed and commercially viable dramatist in the country was a mixed-race playwright who identified as African American.

Wilson was not in a celebratory mood. He maintained that the contemporary theatre industry had done little to support, encourage, appreciate, and preserve the distinct voices, expressions, and experiences of artists of color. Offering evidence, he pointed to the League of Resident Theatres (LORT), the largest professional association of non-profit and not-for-profit theatres in the United States. Although not every major regional theatre is a LORT member, the seventy-five-member organization is often considered to be synonymous with American theatre. In 1996, only one of the then sixty-seven LORT theatres could be identified as "African American," meaning that its mission was to cultivate and produce the work of (or relating to) African Americans. The lack of producing venues and sponsoring institutions with a sustained commitment to the development of Black theatre suggested to Wilson that the future of African American theatre was at risk and that the value of black experiences expressed on stage remained underappreciated.

This book opens with August Wilson's address in 1996 to demonstrate that the work of building African American theatre remains both incomplete and controversial. These themes – an ongoing desire *to build* and *create* spaces to stage African American experiences, and the *challenges* that attended these efforts – recur throughout the following pages. It was the lack of opportunities for African American artists and the absence of stages for their work that prompted William Alexander Brown to found the African Theatre in New York City in 1821. The venue where Ira Aldridge, the often-celebrated interpreter of Shakespeare's plays, made his theatrical debut, the African Theatre attracted the ire of white theatre impresarios who actively campaigned for its closure. The theatre would succumb to these outside pressures and permanently shut its doors after only three years of operation. The fact that Wilson would lament the paucity of theatres 175 years after the opening of Brown's theatre hints at the challenges, difficulties, and obstacles that have accompanied efforts to build and maintain African American theatre.

The Cambridge Companion to African American Theatre centers the struggle to create a uniquely African American theatre. It offers an introduction to significant moments, topics, and themes that influenced the development of Black theatre over the past two centuries. The book begins in the nineteenth century, when slavery was legal and when African Americans who were "free" lacked basic citizenship rights, such as the right to vote. It ends approximately two centuries later, after August Wilson's premature death and during the presidency of Barack Obama, the first African American President of the United States. With each passing decade, African American actors, playwrights, directors, and producers actively employed the theatre not only to comment upon the events and concerns of their present but also to record and preserve their experiences and everyday realities for future consideration.

The complexion of America

It is difficult to discuss American cultural production, particularly within the area of the expressive arts, without acknowledging the significant influence of African Americans. Unlike most other racial and ethnic groups in the United States, the majority of African Americans arrived not by choice but by force. African captives were shipped as cargo across the Atlantic Ocean and sold as property throughout the Americas. Once on the continents (North and South America), families were repeatedly broken and fragmented as parents, children, and close relatives were sold to different buyers. The brutality of slavery, which lasted over many generations (approximately 300 years), severed most ties to the languages, cultures, and customs of the captives' ancestral homelands. As the influence of African practices faded with the passage of time, a new culture and set of customs were developed to replace them. They were premised upon experiences within the Americas. This new, distinctly American culture was unlike anything seen or heard elsewhere in the world.

African American music was one of the first widely recognized and uniquely American cultural forms. In 1892 – before black spirituals evolved into the blues, jazz, and, later, inspired the creation of rock 'n' roll music – famed Czech composer Antonín Dvořák predicted "that the future music of [the United States] must be founded on what are called Negro melodies ... They are the folk songs of America and your composers must turn to them."[3] These melodies, which had been performed across Europe as well as other parts of the world thanks to the travels of African American "jubilee" singers, contained, in song, the experiences of black folk. They detailed the harsh reality of slavery and occasionally expressed an African American optimism that a better life, perhaps even in death, awaited those who toiled and struggled. African American innovations in the area of music would continue: blues in the 1920s, jazz in the 1930s and 1940s, rhythm and blues in the 1950s and 1960s, and, more recently, rap and hip-hop music in the opening decades of the twenty-first century. Black musical expression became a metonym for American culture.

African American autobiographies, as a literary form, similarly formed the core of a distinctive and uniquely American culture. Although such creations were limited during the years when slavery was legal as a result of concerted efforts to prevent African Americans from becoming literate, the few existing narratives were widely circulated by abolitionists for their ability to offer an intimate, first-person glimpse into the hardships of slavery and an individual's ability to overcome extreme adversity. While it could be argued that the dominant strain of American autobiography is the depiction of the United States as the "last best hope,"[4] where immigrants can arrive penniless and fashion a more prosperous future for their families than they could in their homelands, the African American narratives are distinct in their depictions of the unparalleled hardships that the protagonist survived. For example, Frederick Douglass in his best-selling autobiography recalls the "shrieks and piteous cries"[5] of his aunt who was whipped for attempting to date a fellow captive. The struggles and sufferings of African Americans, as remembered and recounted in literature, contributed toward the fashioning of the belief that America was the place where a person's fortune could be radically reversed.

The widespread popularity of black music as well as the orations of prominent African American abolitionists in the early-to-mid nineteenth century fueled a desire to see African Americans represented on theatrical stages. Charles Mathews, the famed white English solo performer, developed a crowd-pleasing performance with his one-man show *A Trip to America* (1823), which consisted of his impersonations of the various American character types that he encountered during a visit to the country. Among those impersonated, caricatured, and, arguably, stereotyped by Mathews were African Americans who labored as porters and, in one instance, as an actor, presumably at Brown's African Theatre. Mathews's depiction of the porters and the unnamed actor as seemingly dim-witted would set (white) audience expectations for the appearance and the behavior of the African American character. When Ira Aldridge performed at Covent Garden in London in 1833, his performances of Shakespeare's plays were consistently panned by critics possibly as a consequence of their having been primed by Mathews. Around the same time, T. D. Rice, who is widely rumored to be the individual who started the phenomenon of blackface minstrelsy, achieved international fame for his seeming ability to channel blackness in his performances of the Jim Crow character, a blackface figure dressed in tattered rags who spoke in broken English and sang and danced before audiences. Rice's performances, which toured throughout the United States and Europe, particularly the United Kingdom, inspired a number of imitators who, like Rice, proceeded to introduce minstrelsy to international audiences throughout the remainder of the nineteenth century, and transformed blackface performance into, arguably, the most significant theatrical form to emerge from the Americas. Novelist and satirist Mark Twain enthusiastically identified blackface minstrelsy as "the show which to me had no peer and whose peer has not yet arrived, in my experience."[6]

It is notable that these early representations of the African American character on stage were imagined and devised by non-African American artists. They were not designed with the aim of accurately reflecting the black experience. Instead, they placed a spotlight on white privilege relative to assumptions of blackness. Mathews's performances were less about the porters and the African Theatre actor and more about the movements of an English thespian in the particular environment of the early-nineteenth-century United States. His performances sought to relay to his audiences the feeling of being an outsider or tourist in the strange but exciting new nation that had developed since the American colonies had won their independence forty years earlier. Rice was less interested in representing African American song and dance and more interested in developing an appealing but extreme character type. The rumor that he developed his Jim Crow character by exaggerating the street performance of an African American street musician with a physical disability supports this contention. In each of these instances, the staging of a caricatured or stereotypical version of the African American character was employed to push an agenda and, frequently, a racial politics that were unconcerned with the actual, lived experiences of African Americans. Such stereotypes and caricatures are part of the larger history of African American theatre. This book engages with their legacy but elects to spotlight critically the work of black artists who succeeded in overcoming arguably racist assumptions of blackness rather than those who created and popularized them.

The Cambridge Companion to African American Theatre centers dramatic and musical works that explicitly aim to offer an honest and recognizably real portrayal of African American cultural and historical experiences. It explores the long history of American theatrical production and spotlights the activities of those individuals whose efforts helped to fashion a more accurate appearance of black life on stage. Along the way, this book chronicles the evolution of African American theatre, from the days of legalized

African captivity, to the "New Negro" and "Black Arts" movements, to contemporary "post-race" and "post-black" campaigns. In addressing such a large period of time, this book champions an elastic conception of African American theatre that accounts for the changing conceptions of blackness as a result of the radical social and political events that occurred over the past two centuries. Although their definitions of African American theatre vary, the theatre artists featured in this book – from producer William Alexander Brown to playwright Lynn Nottage – share the belief that the everyday concerns and experiences of African Americans are important and worthy of being expressed on the stage.

Defining African American theatre

In this book, thirteen prominent historians and critics of African American theatre offer engaged and engaging close readings of specific theatrical movements, genres, and plays that were instrumental to the development of Black theatre. Within their individual chapters, the authors attend to the issues that were particular to a historical moment. The subtle shifts in the evolution of Black theatre appear in their discussions of the differing perspectives of contemporaries, such as the contrasting viewpoints on the utility of theatre held by Alain Locke and W. E. B. Du Bois, or the unique ways in which Barbara Ann Teer and Ntozake Shange embraced an Africanist presence within their plays. The chapters inform one another and, together, offer a full and detailed chronological mapping of African American theatre from the 1800s to today.

The expansive period covered within this book can be divided into four temporal periods: antebellum and Reconstruction, the New Negro, the Black Arts Movement, and the post-black. Although each is formally addressed in individual chapters, it is worthwhile briefly to consider them in order to appreciate better the historical development of African American theatre. In the antebellum and, later, Reconstruction periods, the years preceding and immediately following the Civil War (1861–1865), African Americans were legally denied citizenship (and, in the earlier period, personhood) rights. Theatrical advocates, like Brown, succeeded – albeit briefly – in creating theatre companies and leisure gardens for the entertainment of black customers. The creation of venues, like the African Theatre, and the presence of audiences, particularly black audiences, who were eager to see performances occasionally penned by black playwrights and performed by black artists, launched the first wave of African American theatrical production. By the end of the Reconstruction era and the dawn of the twentieth century, African American theatre troupes toured across the country and began to appear on

Broadway. Bob Cole, J. Rosamond Johnson, Bert Williams, George Walker, and Aida Overton Walker were among the innovators who, through their performances, slowly revised and refashioned the popular representations of blackness as designed by Rice and his imitators into something that was more recognizable to African American audiences.

Although the concept of the "New Negro" was popularized and given new cultural relevance by Alain Locke, and is most closely associated with the locale of Harlem, the authors in this collection who address this period emphasize the influence of the writings of W. E. B. Du Bois and the space of Washington, DC on theatre. Du Bois championed the creation of African American theatre in the 1920s as a bold and powerful act of self-determination. Using the theatre as a tool to engage black communities, he asserted that playwrights among other artists could articulate the experience of blackness. Audiences could gather to see themselves, their stories, their culture, and their lives represented on the stage. This mirroring function rested at the very heart of his conception of African American theatre. Indeed, Du Bois insisted that theatre artists had an obligation to present, in a recognizable manner, the concerns of black folk.

> The plays of a real Negro theatre must be: 1. About us. That is, they must have plots which reveal real Negro life as it is. 2. By us. That is, they must be written by Negro authors who understand from birth and continual association just what it means to be a Negro today. 3. For us. That is, the theatre must cater primarily to Negro audiences and be supported and sustained by their entertainment and approval. 4. Near us. The theatre must be in a Negro neighborhood near the mass of ordinary Negro people.[7]

It is not surprising that Du Bois, who famously identified "the color-line" as the central "problem" of the twentieth century,[8] would craft a definition of Black theatre that would be informed by its presence. Writing during the segregationist period when neighborhood associations vigorously, forcibly, and *legally* worked to maintain the whiteness of their communities, he understood the necessity of creating a distinctive and unique art form that could exist within black neighborhoods.

For Du Bois, African American theatre reflects the embodied experience of being black. The author of *The Souls of Black Folk* asserted the value of a phenomenal, a body-based, "understand[ing] from birth and continual association just what it means to be a Negro today." The theatre for which he advocates reveals the experience of black folk living at a moment when not only racial segregation was legal but also the murders of African Americans by white lynch mobs usually went unprosecuted. It reflects the efforts of artists who challenged widely popular Jim Crow stereotypes and caricatures by creating characters who more accurately resembled – in look, mannerism, and everyday concerns – the folks who resided in black neighborhoods. Most importantly, it, according to Du Bois, unifies black audiences by creating and emboldening a sense of community. The frequent "us" refrain in his definition reveals this.

When playwright Amiri Baraka offered a definition of "Black theatre," he extended Du Bois's about/by/for/near formulation and added a fifth feature: it must be "liberating."

> It is a theater that actually functions to liberate Black people. It is a theater that will commit Black people to their own liberation and instruct them about what they should do and what they should be doing, will involve them emotionally. It will also, hopefully, involve them programmatically in their liberation and should not only be utilizing the so-called Black lifestyle or the lifestyle of African people in America but it should also be an act of liberation.[9]

For Baraka, African American theatre needed to be more than a reflection of "us." Active in the decades *following* the end of legal segregation in 1954, the celebrated production of Lorraine Hansberry's play *A Raisin in the Sun* on Broadway in 1959, and the most active years of the Civil Rights Movement (1955–1965), the playwright yearned for the creation of theatre that would re-energize and reactivate the social and political consciousness of black folk. Theatre could (and should) encourage audiences not to be complacent with the successes of the Civil Rights Movement. It should motivate and mobilize audiences toward continuing the Movement to bring about social change.

Arguably short-lived, the Black Arts Movement inspired artists to think critically about the political potential of African American theatre. Beginning in the mid 1960s and ending a decade later, the Movement spurred the creation of hundreds of theatre companies that sought to revise stereotypes of blackness, emphasize the beauty of black culture, and engage the social and political concerns of African American communities. Despite the fact that the majority of these companies would fold within a decade, the legacy of the Black Arts Movement lived on thanks to the ongoing influence of surviving companies, such as Penumbra Theatre in Minneapolis, and artists, such as August Wilson, whose voices were nurtured within them. Wilson, in his TCG address, refers to the Black Arts Movement as the "kiln in which [he] was fired."[10]

Toward the close of the twentieth century and into the dawn of the twenty-first century, artists and scholars increasingly began to trouble the received, historical definitions of blackness and to deny the "color line" a place in the new century. For example, in a 2005 essay, playwright Suzan-Lori Parks

responded to the "What is a Black play?" question in the following manner: "A black play is blacker than black. A black play is written by a black
person. A black play has black actors. A black play is written by a white
person and has white actors. A black play doesnt have anything to do with
black people. Im saying *The Glass Menagerie* is a black play. SAY WHAT?
EXCUSE ME?!?!"[11] This excerpt, which is part of a more extensive list of
the many possibilities of a black play, signals a generational shift in thinking about and conceptualizing blackness. Parks's perspective connects with
a post-black and post-race perspective that does not seek to erase race but
rather looks to other experiences *in addition* to race that define a person's
sense of self. Admittedly, the "post" can feel like a misnomer in that the goal
is not to bound blackness – to develop an end point that can then be moved
beyond – but rather to expand understandings of blackness. Post-black is
additive, blackness plus. In her definition, Parks denies African American
theatre its exclusivity by reading it not as something to be possessed by a
particular group of people within a given community. She rejects the "us"
and, by extension, "them" binary in favor of a universalism that sees the
influence of blackness everywhere. African American theatre is indivisible
from American theatre. They are one and the same.

An orientation map

The Cambridge Companion to African American Theatre centers the efforts
of mostly African American artists who worked to revise the stereotypes
and negative images of blackness and to bring a more accurate and recognizable representation of African American experiences to the stage. These
men and women understood that expressive art has the capacity to enable
self-determination, to record and preserve historical experiences, and to
fashion community. Producers established venues that bolstered a sense of
African American community by providing audiences with opportunities to
see themselves and their stories enacted on stage. Playwrights literally took
pen in hand to write characters and plot lines that offered insight into the
everyday reality of being African American within the United States. Actors
infused their roles with a sensibility that revised historical stereotypes and
caricatures of black folk and gave the African American character a new
face. This book centers the work, the labor, and effort of artists to script and
share African American experiences on stage from the nineteenth century to
the present day.

Douglas A. Jones, Jr. looks at performance in the antebellum period and
casts a critical spotlight on the ambivalent nature of African American theatre. He looks at both the coerced performances of black captives – such as

their singing and dancing during the transatlantic crossing of slave ships and preceding their still stands on auction blocks – and those voluntarily created acts, such as the "wild songs" on plantations and, later, the productions at Brown's African Theatre, to interrogate the multiple purposes to which black performance could be employed. He demonstrates that Black theatre in itself is not inherently liberating. It has been used to reinforce the condition of oppression. However, it has also been infused with the potential to create an "oppositional culture" capable of challenging the status quo.

Heather Nathans centers the representation of slave rebellions and rebellious black characters on the theatrical stage "from the colonial era through the beginning of the twentieth century." She reveals how dramatic representations of captive uprisings were influenced by actual events. For example, the revolution in Haiti (formerly Saint Domingue), which was led by Toussaint L'Ouverture in 1791, inspired the scripting of numerous plays about unrest and revolution in "Hayti," among other places. Nathans reveals that plays, penned by both white and black playwrights, frequently depicted the unjust conditions to which black men and women were subjected. They framed rebellion and revolt as justifiable acts.

Monica White Ndounou focuses on Bert Williams, George Walker, and Langston Hughes. Through a close reading of their seminal productions, she reveals how the artists attempted to challenge existing theatrical stereotypes and caricatures of blackness. Ndounou reads these figures as trailblazers, paving the path for future artists who were able to present more accurate depictions of African American life on the Broadway stage. The author covers more than fifty years of theatre history, from the emergence of Williams and Walker in the late nineteenth century to the premiere of Hughes's *The Barrier* on the Great White Way in 1950.

Jonathan Shandell offers an overview of the Negro Little Theatre Movement, the twenty-year period between the 1910s and 1930s that witnessed the flourishing of small, independent theatres across the country. As Shandell notes, these theatres "took root in library auditoriums, churches, community centers, universities, and anywhere else a platform could be built and artists and audiences might gather." This chapter spotlights a handful of these theatres – the Anita Bush Stock Company, the Ethiopian Art Theatre, the Krigwa Players, the Harlem Suitcase Company, and the Karamu Theatre of Cleveland – and discusses both their evolution and lasting impact. Along the way, Shandell chronicles the efforts of several individuals, including W. E. B. Du Bois, Alain Locke, and Charles Gilpin, who were instrumental to their creation. The chapter ends with a brief account of the Federal Theatre Project's "Negro units" and their aesthetic similarity to African American little theatres.

Covering the same temporal period as Shandell, Soyica Diggs Colbert explores the dramas of the Harlem Renaissance, which were usually nurtured in Washington, DC, to reveal how dramatists such as Angelina Weld Grimké, Georgia Douglas Johnson, Willis Richardson, Zora Neale Hurston, and Marita Bonner, among others, created dramas that asserted the "value" of African American life. Writing not only during a period in which the lynchings of black men and women were common but also rarely punished, these artists' assertion of black respectability demanded a reassessment and, indeed, a revaluation of blackness.

Adrienne Macki Braconi challenges critics who assert that the plays of Eulalie Spence, Alice Childress, and Lorraine Hansberry were either apolitical or not sufficiently political. In her chapter, Braconi reintroduces the playwrights, who were active between 1930 and 1960, and chronicles the vital roles that they played in opening the doors for black women to have their work staged regionally as well as on Broadway. Furthermore, she makes a convincing case that their plays feature "self-actualized black characters fighting against oppression and consumption while struggling to maintain racial and gender subjectivity."

Aimee Zygmonski provides a close reading of Amiri Baraka's play *Dutchman* followed by a study of the creation of his Black Arts Repertory Theatre to provide an insider perspective into the development of the Black Arts Movement. Her study of Baraka's racial and political awakening as represented in the increasing self-awareness of his character Clay allows her to identify emergent themes that would eventually inform "the Movement." Although the Black Arts Movement did not last long, Zygmonski asserts that the awakened consciousness that resulted from this flurry of activity "reverberate[s]" in the works of more contemporary and present-day artists.

In his chapter, Samuel O'Connell reads a single case study, Melvin Van Peebles's 1971 Broadway musical *Ain't Supposed to Die a Natural Death*. Beginning with an overview of the relevant critical writings related to whether black music can reflect cultural and racial experiences, O'Connell contends that the genre of soul music, which Van Peebles incorporates within his stage play, succeeds in capturing the rhythm and politics of late 1960s and early 1970s Harlem. A theatrical innovator, Van Peebles challenged the accepted format of the integrated musical, a musical with a unified (and thematically related) book and music, and pioneered a new type of black musical form, the fragmented musical, which was better equipped to reflect the racial and political frictions that were occurring in the midst of the Black Power and the Black Arts movements.

Faedra Chatard Carpenter centers the representation of theatrical whiteness within her chapter through analyses of the plays of four playwrights: Adrienne Kennedy, Douglas Turner Ward, Lydia Diamond, and Suzan-Lori Parks. Although the dramas studied by Carpenter chronologically range from *Funnyhouse of a Negro* (1964) to *The Bluest Eye* (2006), which reveal a contemporary engagement with ideas of race and embodiment, the author opens her chapter by noting that critical whiteness studies has a long history within African American communities. She memorably writes, "black folks have been analyzing white folks for quite some time." The novel contributions of her chapter are her emphasis on how the critical evaluation of whiteness by black artists is part of African American theatre, and her reminder of the power of theatrical spectacle to engage with issues of race.

Nadine George-Graves discusses the vital role that theatre plays in engaging, healing, and transforming African American communities within her account of the theatrical contributions of producer Barbara Ann Teer, playwright Ntozake Shange, and choreographer Jawole Willa Jo Zollar. She addresses the unifying and recuperative power of theatre and how Teer, Shange, and Zollar embrace Africanist practices with the intent of reaching and elevating the "spirit" of their audiences. The recognition of one's affinity with others exists as a step toward developing a social activist movement.

Sandra G. Shannon celebrates Lynn Nottage, Adrienne Kennedy, Lorraine Hansberry, Alice Childress, and Shirley Graham Du Bois for their ability "to expand their worldview beyond the United States' borders and to inspire, through their dramas, an emotional affinity with the sufferings of people from cultures other than their own." She bridges these theatrical innovators both by highlighting their interest in Africa and by demonstrating how they were able to employ the theatre to comment upon world politics and with the intent of effecting social change.

Sandra L. Richards shares a hemispheric approach to understanding African American theatre. Centering the writings of Canadian, US, and Caribbean playwrights, she not only moves across the Americas but also the twentieth century. Richards identifies the similar concerns of geographically and temporally separated playwrights as markers of African Diaspora drama. Among the salient features of this category, which includes dramatic works by Amiri Baraka, Djanet Sears, August Wilson, and Aimé Césaire, among others, are plays that retain African cultural elements, depict resistance to colonial governing, and circulate a common or shared understanding of the operations of blackness within a particular political moment.

Harry J. Elam, Jr. temporally locates his chapter in the "age of Obama," the period following the election of Barack Obama as the first black president of the United States. Following the 2008 election, he notes a shift in the way that critics and scholars talked about race, particularly blackness. Quoting art curator Thelma Golden, Elam investigates, through four case studies, whether the "post-black" is "the new black." He looks at the 2009 Broadway revival of August Wilson's *Joe Turner's Come and Gone*, Branden Jacobs-Jenkins's *Neighbors*, Eisa Davis's *Bulrusher*, and Fred Ebb and John Kander's musical *The Scottsboro Boys* to address race politics, the re-emergence of blackface, and the topic of mixed-race identity within the contemporary theatre.

The Cambridge Companion to African American Theatre provides critical and historical frameworks with which to understand better the scores of authors, plays, and movements introduced in the pages that follow. It offers fresh perspectives on African American theatre written by leading theatre critics and scholars. In addition, this book features a chronology, a timeline of key events in African American theatre history, and a further reading list for additional information related to Black theatre. Readers are encouraged to adopt whichever reading strategy best suits their needs and interests. A conventional approach, exploring the book from the first page to the last, offers a chronological overview of the emergence of African American theatre. In addition, it reveals a gradual shift from archive-based historical criticism to theoretically informed critical analysis. The chapters could be read independently of one another in order to gain a focused understanding of a particular moment or movement. Whichever approach is taken, an in-depth engagement with the history of African American theatre is what awaits.

NOTES

1   May Joseph, "Alliances across Margins," *African American Review*, 31.4 (1997): 595; Jacqueline Petropoulos, "'The Ground on which I Stand': Rewriting History, African Canadian Style," in *Signatures of the Past*, ed. Marc Maufort and Caroline De Wagner (New York: Peter Lang, 2008), 73.

2   August Wilson, "The Ground on which I Stand," *Callaloo*, 20.3 (1998): 493–503.

3   Antonín Dvořák, "The Real Value of Negro Melodies," *New York Herald*, May 21, 1893.

4   Abraham Lincoln, "Second Annual Message," December 1, 1862, in *The American Presidency Project*, ed. Gerhard Peters and John T. Woolley, www.presidency. ucsb.edu/ws/?pid=29503 (last accessed February 20, 2012).

5   Frederick Douglass, *My Bondage, My Freedom* (New York: Miller, Orton, & Mulligan, 1855), 87.

6   Mark Twain, *Mark Twain's Own Autobiography*, ed. Michael J. Kiskis (Madison: University of Wisconsin Press, 1924), 175.

7   W. E. B. Du Bois, "Krigwa Player Little Negro Theatre," *The Crisis*, 32 (July, 1926): 135.

8   W. E. B. Du Bois, *The Souls of Black Folk* (New York: Dover, 1994), v.

9 Quoted in Mike Coleman, "What is Black Theater?," in *Conversations with Amiri Baraka*, ed. Amiri Baraka and Charlie Reilly (Jackson: University Press of Mississippi, 1994), 84.

10 Wilson, "The Ground on which I Stand," 494.

11 Suzan-Lori Parks, "New Black Math," *Theatre Journal*, 57.4 (2005): 580.

I

DOUGLAS A. JONES, JR.

Slavery, performance, and the design of African American theatre

On the evening of June 28, 1849, Frederick Douglass attended a performance by Gavitt's Original Ethiopian Serenaders, one of the few all-black minstrel troupes before the Civil War. In spite of his "disgust" at minstrelsy's racist grotesqueries, Douglass decided to go to the theatre because of his "love of music" and "curiosity to see persons of color exaggerating the peculiarities of their race," as he put it in his review that ran in his newspaper, *The North Star*, the following day.[1] Midway through the review, Douglass turned from his assessment of the Serenaders' act to reflect on the political potential of black performance in general. He writes: "It is something gained, when the colored man in any form can appear before a white audience; and we think that even this company, with industry, application, and a proper cultivation of their taste, may yet be instrumental in removing the prejudice against our race."[2] In other words, if African Americans controlled the means of production – even if they appropriated the form of blackface minstrelsy, which by the late 1840s was virulently anti-black – their aesthetic and cultural efforts could help redress racial inequality. Much to Douglass's dismay, however, Gavitt's Original Ethiopian Serenaders simply "exaggerate[d] the exaggerations of our enemies" and "cater[ed] to the lower elements of the baser sort."[3]

In his brief review, Douglass articulated a profound degree of ambivalence regarding the use of performance in the work of black uplift. His ambivalence was born of the decidedly fraught relation that enslaved Africans and their descendants have had with cultural performance since the time of their earliest arrivals in the early seventeenth century. Simply put, Douglass perceived how dominant performance practices entrenched sociopolitical norms such as slavery and white supremacy, but he also recognized how slaves and free people of color used performance to fashion modes of protest and pleasure. What, therefore, to do? This essay traces performance's conflictive functionality in colonial and antebellum black life. The resultant conceptual ambivalence toward performance preoccupied the antebellum black public sphere and affected the design of black sociocultural institutions. One of those institutions was the theatre, and the critical discourse concerning black performance that emerged during the time of slavery continues to inform how we imagine the form and function of the African American theatre and, more generally, black cultural production.[4]

Theorizations of the shape and substance of black performance began with North American black life itself, "not in Africa or America but in the netherworld between the two continents ... as a product of the momentous meeting of Africans and Europeans and then their equally fateful rendezvous with the peoples of the New World."[5] Indeed, European captors often forced the African captive to sing and dance on the decks of slave ships in order to preserve the health – and therefore value – of their human cargo. Alexander Falconbridge, a surgeon who worked in the late-eighteenth-century slave trade and frequented the western coast of Africa, described the form and function of this practice:

> Exercise being deemed necessary for the preservation of their health, they are sometimes obliged to dance, when the weather will permit their coming on deck. If they go about it reluctantly, or do not move with agility, they are flogged ... Their music, upon these occasions, consists of a drum, sometimes only with one head; and when it is worn out, they do not scruple to make use of the bottom of one of the tubs before described. The poor wretches are frequently compelled to sing also; but when they do so, their songs are generally, as may naturally be expected, melancholy lamentations of their exile from the native country.[6]

This account outlines a system of coerced performance in which the slave, regardless of his degree of participation, contributed to his own abjection: if he danced, he increased his marketability as human commodity because he sustained his health; if he refused to dance, his captors whipped him into submission. Resistance in this system, therefore, was almost impossible.

Almost. Given the bare and brutal circumstances of the Middle Passage, slaves had to work across clan and tribal lines in order to create and survive their starkly efficient performances. These embodied efforts forged bonds of *African* solidarity, as slaves quashed interethnic rivalries in order to endure, and eventually resist, the wretchedness of their captivity. Notwithstanding its underlying structure of coercion, the on-deck performance constituted one of the "simple but *cooperative* efforts ... [that] may be viewed as the true beginnings of African-American culture and society."[7] Indeed, slaves turned the oppressive conditions of their netherworld performances into a *crucible of collective possibility.*

To consider the possible within the regimes of chattel slavery was, first and foremost, to take stock of the actuality of one's condition. African captives on slave ships, for example, rallied around the fact of their shared blackness because race accounted for their shared enslavement. In this way, they embraced what intellectual historian Eddie S. Glaude, Jr. terms "the pragmatic view of race," that is, "the recognition that social and political conditions make racial solidarity an important political and social strategy."[8] The medium of cultural performance was crucial to the formation of racial solidarity among slaves because it allowed them to assess their condition in communal and expressive terms. These performative reflections made plain the commonality of their condition and, as such, fostered the racial oneness that was necessary for survival, redressive action, and pragmatic problem solving.[9]

Thus the "melancholy lamentations" such as those Falconbridge witnessed enacted slaves' collective sense of pain and longing. This seems obvious, that slaves would lament their condition in mournful tones. But what I am after here is the ways that performance fostered racial solidarity in the face of captivity and across ethnic, linguistic, and geographical lines of difference. That is, in their "melancholy lamentations" slaves communed through rhythm, tone, and gesture; the specificity of the word was frequently less important to the composition, both musical *and* social.[10] For instance, aboard the *Hudibras*, as it traveled from the southern coast of Nigeria to the West Indies in 1786–7, slaves "universally esteemed" one of their female counterparts who, as an onlooking captor put it, was their "oracle of literature," "orator," and a "songstress." According to this seaman, the female captives in particular loved her "slow airs, of a pathetic nature," even though the majority of them did not speak her language; they were Igbo, she was not.[11] In other words, most of the admiring women revered their songstress because they were drawn to the ways her plaintive tones, corporeality, and supra-linguistic performatives expressed the existential depths of their shared condition.

Frederick Douglass's consideration of plantation "wild songs" also stressed how performance fostered slave collectivity, in spite of the strictures of language and music theory. He writes: "[Slaves] would compose and sing as they went along, consulting neither time nor tune. The thought that came up, came out – if not in the word, in the sound … [Such songs] they would sing, as a chorus, to words which to many would seem unmeaning jargon, but which, nevertheless, were full of meaning to themselves."[12] Douglass's assessment suggests an animating, structural continuation from the musical performances on slave ships to the "wild songs" on the plantation. In both practices, and in slave performance in general, the "unmeaning jargon" of "rude and apparently incoherent songs" was the phonic material by which slaves grappled with the incomprehensibility of their very condition: from the perspective of the captive, these nonsensical modes of expression articulated the nonsensicality of chattel slavery itself.[13]

This phonic material marked the concurrent objectification and humanization of the slave. It was what Stephen Best and Saidiya Hartman term "black noise." Black noise is the product of the "shuttling between grief and grievance" that the captive and his descendants undertake, and it "represents the kinds of political aspirations that are inaudible and illegible within the prevailing formulas of political rationality; these yearnings are illegible because they are so wildly utopian and derelict to capitalism."[14] Black noise was slavery's performative double, perfectly synchronous with, and thoroughly oppositional to, the institution. Douglass credited black noise with animating his drive for freedom: "To those [wild] songs I trace my first glimmering conception of the dehumanizing character of slavery. I can never get rid of that conception. Those songs still follow me, to deepen my hatred of slavery, and quicken my sympathies for my brethren in bonds."[15] This stirring meditation on the aurality of slave performance suggests that black noise carried captives' originary desire – freedom – from the abyssal netherworld of the slave ship to the laborious fields and factories of the New World. Thus performance archived slave experience and thereby maintained bonds of (racial) solidarity across time and space.

Despite his appreciation of the wild songs' expressive provocations, however, Douglass also knew that his ideological opponents used the medium of performance against the social and political interests of the slave. He condemned how slaves on plantations "engaged in such sports and merriments as playing ball, wrestling, running foot-races, fiddling, dancing, and drinking whiskey" during Christmas celebrations. Douglass believed these doings were "among the most effective means in the hands of the slaveholder in keeping down the spirit of insurrection" because they acted "as conductors, or safety-valves, to carry off the rebellious spirit of enslaved humanity."[16] In this view, masters temporarily loosened normative constraints during the holiday season and at other times throughout the year because they sought to shape the slave's interiority, namely, attenuate any building sense of resistance and sap his "wildest desperation" for freedom.

Performance also allowed masters to mold the slave's exteriority to their political and economic advantage. In her slave narrative, *Incidents in the Life of a Slave Girl*, Harriet Jacobs describes how her master compelled his slaves to act pleased with their enslavement and extol the master's benevolence to outside observers. Such performances, Jacobs writes, worked to defend the "beautiful 'patriarchal institution'" because they concealed the quotidian brutalities that were necessary to slavery's operation, rendering the plantation a pastoral utopia where slaves were free to revel in the simple, Christian pleasures that their master's protection afforded them.[17] These scenes of ventriloquism and manipulation convinced northern observers such as influential Boston minister Nehemiah Adams that "there are elements in [slaveholding] fitted to promote the highest happiness and welfare, temporal and spiritual, of the negro."[18] In fact, Adams argued that slavery was a positive good because it engendered performance practices that brought man closer to God. At the end of his widely circulated apologia, *A South-Side View of Slavery*, Adams writes: "If the nations of the earth celebrate in heaven their national experiences under the providence and grace of God, Africa's song will probably do as much as any to illustrate them. But who will write Africa's hymn? ... No man can learn that song, no man can write it, but some African slave."[19] In this romantic racialist view, slavery benefits both captive and captor because its cultural formations, particularly the "African hymn," nourish their spiritual well-being and Christian resolve.[20]

Along with Adams's comparatively benign view of the function of the "African hymn" and the performative deceptions of plantation life that Jacobs outlined, William Wells Brown's account of singing and dancing in the pens of the New Orleans slave market also attests to the pro-slavery potentiality of slave performance. In one of the many profitable transactions available to slave owners, Wells Brown's master rented him to a slave speculator for a year. This "soul-driver," as slaves commonly termed speculators, required Wells Brown to ready his fellow slaves for purchase. Wells Brown described his method of preparation, which was common in the bustling slave pens of New Orleans:

> Before slaves were exhibited for sale, they were dressed and driven out into the yard. Some were set to dancing, some to jumping, some to singing, and some to playing cards. This was done to make them appear cheerful and happy. My business was to see that they were placed in those situations before the arrival of the purchasers, and I have often set them to dancing when their cheeks were wet with tears.[21]

Similar to the performances Falconbridge observed on slave ships bound for the New World, the trader made slaves sing and dance to manipulate their corporeality and affectivity. In both instances, captors relied on performance to increase the captive's marketability and utility as human chattel.

Saidiya Hartman has written compellingly on the pro-slavery elasticity and structures of subjection that pervaded slave performance. Because of the multiple and contradictory uses of black song, dance, and theatricality,

Hartman finds that a conceptual "problematic of enjoyment in which pleasure is inseparable from subjection, will indistinguishable from submission, and bodily integrity bound to violence" inhered within slave performance.[22] Enjoyment here extended beyond the theatrical frame and into the "audience" of white spectators who, directly and indirectly, benefited from the political and economic gains that slave performance created. For whites to enjoy the performing black slave was to produce the white self; that is, white spectatorship was *performative* in that watching was an enactment of white mastery, will, and domination. These affirmations of free whiteness were both personal and communal. When the speculator compelled his slaves to perform for potential buyers in the markets of New Orleans, for instance, he displayed his chattel *and* his power for his onlooking peers. At the same time, his peers' identity as discerning and prospective buyers allied them as one. As historian Walter Johnson explains, "Through shared communion in the rites of the slave market – the looking, stripping, touching, bantering, and evaluating – white men confirmed their commonality with the other men with whom they inspected the slaves."[23] Indeed, white interest in slave performances was an investment in the fashioning of white subjectivity itself.

But in spite of these mechanisms of white domination and spectatorship, slaves articulated their own forms of individual and communal possibility, making political use of performance's excess. That is, slaves crafted their own modes of psychic relief and corporeal restoration in performances aboard decks, on plantations, and in pens. To the dominant gaze, an effusive gesture frequently registered as evidence of the slave's satisfaction with bondage.[24] But these movements, and the broader acts that framed them, were not signs of black approval of black captivity; instead, they were gestures of transient but necessary relief from the quotidian injuries of chattel bondage. As Hartman puts it, such acts were "fraught with utopian and transformative impulses" that made "allegorical claims for emancipation, redress, and restitution."[25] These claims articulated a collectivist yearning for liberation that fueled black resistance to enslavement, which, tautologically, is "the performative essence of blackness … [and] of black performance."[26] Within the frame of performance, coerced or otherwise, slaves fashioned aesthetic and epistemological material that animated the freedom movements of black politics and of black subjectivity.

Thus a kind of interarticulation between performing slave and gazing master emerged that enacted and entrenched the ontological antinomy of African life in the New World: the simultaneity of black liberation and black abjection. This existential discordance and its performative frames also produced theoretical consequences, namely, the structure of ambivalence that shaped black thinking on the utility of cultural performance in African American life. Frederick Douglass's ruminations on slave song and dance and the (often class-based) disagreements regarding the propriety of public parades and festive celebrations among antebellum African Americans, for example, both signal the vexed conceptualization of black performance before the Civil War.[27] As African Americans gained the latitude to act on their own terms, they pondered how embodied cultural practices could signify as counter-narratives to dominant understandings of blackness and facilitate the actualization of racial equality. Or, would the everyday forms of racial terror and the anti-black figures of the white cultural imagination overdetermine the meaning of the performing black body? Or, did interracial societal politics even matter if performance offered personal and communal pleasure, release, and self-awareness?

The debate over performance as a politicized mode of ideological desire, as opposed to performance as an aestheticist mode of phenomenological pleasure, gripped the antebellum black public sphere. Even if something of a false dichotomy, the propagandistic and the aesthetic constitute an extraordinarily productive dialectic that has calibrated the course of black cultural theory and production.[28] This dialectic was borne of the theoretical ambivalence that was itself borne of the ever-refractive primal scenes (of subjection) in which slaves sang, danced, and acted. Put simply: since performance sustained slavery *and* freedom it could not be trusted *nor* neglected.

Reading the performative materials that (re)produced and reflected this conundrum, Hartman considers their role in the constitution of slave life. She explains how performance acts such as plantation wild songs in and of themselves did not constitute slaves' "oppositional culture," but evidenced the affective and cognitive conditions that made such a culture realizable. Hartman writes:

> Yet these songs insufficiently meet the requirements of an oppositional culture, one capable of combating ostensibly beneficial diversions and poised to destroy these designs for mastery. While every tone testifies against slavery, sorrow rather than resistance characterizes such songs ... Above all, these songs are valued as dirges expressive of the social death of slavery and inchoate expressions of a latent political consciousness.[29]

In this view, a politicized "culture" is a collection of strategies that is intentional and teleological. But before that culture is organized, its charge must first be seen, heard, and felt as necessary and possible – hence the importance of the performance act. Indeed, performance *articulates* interiority and desire, albeit in excessive and deficient form.[30] "The thought that

Figure 1.1 Frederick Douglass, *c.* 1870.

came up, came out," Douglass wrote.[31] Even if the wild songs were not an "oppositional culture," they were performative vessels that enacted and made sensible the political unconscious upon which that culture would eventually be built.

Put another way, slave performances such as plantation wild songs or the on-deck "lamentations" helped facilitate the transformation of black grief to black grievance, what in Hartman's terms might be called the move

from "sorrow" to an "oppositional culture." Performance's ability to cata-
lyze ideological formations and political and social action – not to mention
its function as a medium of experiential articulation, community building,
and identity formation for both captor and captive – betrays its centrality to
chattel slavery and the history of blackness.[32] That history, during the time
of slavery and beyond, has largely been a history of (performed) resistance
against captivity, physical and conceptual. When organized around method,
relationships, and objective, these acts of resistance have constituted oppositional cultures. To be sure, there is in my claim a certain structuralist
insistence that stresses, following Raymond Williams, that "the significance
in an activity must be sought in terms of the whole organization, which is
more than the sum of its separable parts. What we are looking for, always, is
the actual life that the whole organization is there to express."[33] This "whole
organization" is an apparatus of *culture*; when a culture resists dominant
ideologies, values, and action, it is *oppositional*.

One of the first oppositional cultures that molded the "inchoate expressions of a latent political consciousness" of slave performance into its own
kind of "whole organization" was the African American theatre. William
Alexander Brown, a retired ship steward who worked on a Liverpool-based
transatlantic vessel and who theatre and social historians believe was from
the Caribbean, opened the first African American theatre in New York City
in 1821.[34] Brown's theatre first emerged as part of his pleasure garden, a
retreat for New Yorkers to escape the bustle of city life and combat the heat
of the summer with cold food and drink. African Americans operated other
pleasure gardens that served exclusively white patrons, but Brown's was
the first to cater to a black clientele; it was especially appealing to (aspiring) middle-class African Americans who avoided the dance halls and oyster
cellars of their working-class counterparts. As social historian Leslie Harris
notes, Brown's pleasure garden "provide[d] entertainment for a wider range
of black New Yorkers [and] ... offered blacks one of the few permanent recreation spots not affiliated with a church or mutual aid society."[35] Brown's
theatre was the most conspicuous form of entertainment he offered and it
was known over its three-year history as the Minor Theatre, the American
Theatre, or the African Company. In his theatrical efforts, Brown was committed to creative and social democracy, and he left "a blueprint for an
inclusive national theatre," as one theatre historian argues.[36]

Perhaps more than anything else, Brown's practices of inclusivity –
namely, his welcoming of all New Yorkers as spectators, fostering comely
representations of black, white, and Native American identities, and staging
works by white and non-white playwrights – made his theatre an oppositional culture.[37] These practices, materially and symbolically, countered the

dominant racial assumption that blacks were unfit for political, social, and economic equality. This belief and its ideological derivatives undergirded the ever-forming modes of legal and extralegal white supremacy. For instance, the very year that Brown opened his pleasure garden theatre, New York ratified a new state constitution that executed universal male suffrage for white men but disenfranchised almost all black men.[38] At the time, New York was also in the midst of the Gradual Manumission Act of 1799 and its 1817 amendment, both of which outlined protracted processes of general emancipation.[39] Although the vast majority of black New Yorkers in 1821 were legally free, most of them had at some point been slaves or indentured servants. And perhaps more to the point, provisions such as those outlined in the 1821 State Constitution and the exclusion of African Americans from nearly all occupations except the most menial of jobs severely circumscribed the exercise of black freedom in any case. Brown's theatrical formations, indeed his socio-cultural politics in general, must be read as oppositional responses to these "limits of emancipation," to use Harris's succinct phrase.[40] That is to say, the efforts of Brown and his cohort were a *politicized design* of racial inclusivity that combated a *politicized design* of racial exclusivity, namely, white supremacy.[41] The *Spectator* journal put it best in 1822: "Thus it seems that these descendants of Africa are determined to carry into full practice the doctrine of *liberty and equality*, physically by acting plays and mentally by writing them."[42]

Brown's oppositional design, however, was not static. While the essential charge remained the same – namely, counteract white supremacy – the relationships and particulars of his way of cultural life varied. That is, Brown was always in the process of reforming and revising his work, even as he held firm to the principles of racial inclusivity and equality. This process, which theatre historian Marvin McAllister calls Brown's "institutional becoming," was reflected in the various names Brown used for his company, the 1822 relocation of his theatre to Park Row where he willfully competed with one of the city's leading theatres, and his actors' and patrons' assumption of various racial and national identities, which included all-black productions of Shakespearean tragedy.[43] McAllister writes, "Brown's multifaceted, ever evolving institutional journey was partly a product of an incredibly fluid early national theatre … [and it] mirrored the young nation's struggle with plurality and its difficult sojourn through a defining period."[44] Indeed, Brown's theatrical efforts reflect the instability of the fledgling nation and its struggle to define itself during this most formative period.

But Brown also built his theatre, and perhaps more consequentially so, on the institutional foundation that enslaved Africans laid for their descendants. His theatre was very much a *black thing*, borne of the ideological paradigms of community building forged in West and Central Africa and maintained in the captives' passage from western Africa. I want to focus on how Brown's theatre was a product of this conceptual legacy – a relationship that scholars have mostly ignored – because it clarifies the organic forms of opposition, rather than the derivative or learned, that regulated the originary design of African American theatre.[45]

The most critical of these organic determinations was slaves' and their descendants' practice of collectivism. In his valuable study of antebellum black voluntary and mutual aid societies, *In the Company of Black Men*, historian Craig Steven Wilder explains the distinctiveness of African American collectivism. He writes:

> [The] African American community has its basis in collectivism: a behavioral and rhetorical tendency to privilege the group over the individual. Collective cultures arose as enslaved Africans unleashed the potential for group action and mass resistance in familiar West African relationships. That does not mean that West African cultures were, by deduction or rule, collectivist, but rather that Africans entered the Americas equipped with intellectual traditions and sociological models that facilitated a communitarian response to oppression.[46]

This view of black collectivism sheds light on the ways in which Brown's efforts were conceptually homologous with contemporaneous black voluntary and mutual relief societies. To be sure, Brown's theatre did not operate under a constitution, a roll of officers, and other conventional trappings of antebellum benevolent societies; nevertheless, the (theatrical) community Brown created was a collectivist social space that helped black New Yorkers withstand oppression and endure their existentially precarious transition from slavery to freedom. The affective and psychological relief Brown's entertainment offered his patrons was a necessary complement to the material aid that associations such as the New York African Society of Mutual Relief (NYASMR) provided.[47] Because of the ethic of collectivism, African Americans across class, occupation, religion, and all other categories of personal difference profited from these forms of relief.

In *In the Company of Black Men*, Wilder demonstrates that the design of the voluntary associations "has been misconstrued as the arrogant stamp of a tiny, elite class, when in reality the African societies' members were quite varied and their charges included the impoverished, fugitives, and orphans."[48] Similarly, all types of black New Yorkers – free and slave, middle-class and working-class – patronized Brown's pleasure garden and theatre. Playwright and newspaper editor Mordecai Noah, who was also Brown's most vocal and spiteful public detractor, published an account of who were either slaves or indentured servants relaxing at the "African Grove," which was Noah's appellation for Brown's pleasure garden.[49] Using money earned from labor performed outside the terms of their service or that their masters gave them for recreation, these patrons communed with other black New Yorkers with higher degrees of freedom and greater economic means. This cross-condition, cross-class sociality was not simply a reflection of the fact that free blacks in the antebellum North lived a "relative uniformity of ... social experience."[50] More importantly, black New Yorkers continuously embraced that experience to reaffirm and re-employ their collectivist (cultural) politics that positioned the group over the individual.

Thus even if Brown originally imagined a retreat for an "esteemed class" of "economically privileged" ship stewards, as McAllister suggests, the socioeconomic realities and the ideological commitments of black New Yorkers, not to mention those of Brown himself, meant his theatre would always be collectivist.[51] For one, those in maritime trades were frequently away from the city with their wages. To stay afloat, Brown knew he had to serve other groups.[52] Furthermore, McAllister mischaracterizes black stewards as "early Afro-America's elite class." Rather, stewards were working-class sailors who waited on passengers and officers.[53] Bourgeois reformees frequently conceptualized (black) stewardship as another form of slavery, not least because stewards suffered floggings.[54] These characterizations coupled with the transient nature of seafaring meant an unstable position for the majority of black stewards in African American community formations. As historian W. Jeffrey Bolster explains in his groundbreaking study of colonial and antebellum black sailors, *Blackjacks: African American Seamen in the Age of Sail*: "The values inculcated by maritime work rarely promoted the responsibility and respectability so important to free black society in its formative stage. Seafaring remained a pillar of early-nineteenth-century northern free black society, but its perilous nature and meager wages made it a precarious one."[55] Not elite but exclusive, the class of black stewards never reached the social status of those in the professional and artisan classes, but they remained important providers for their working-class families and the community at large.

If anything, haunts like Brown's pleasure garden and theatre allowed stewards and other members of the African American working class to *perform* "elite." In his remembrance of Brown's theatre, radical abolitionist and physician James McCune Smith notes that as a steward, Brown "belonged to a class ... [that] occupied a respectable and responsible position." McCune Smith then goes on to describe how the steward, who "next to the captain, [was] the most important person on the ship," greeted passengers in resplendent clothing and competed with other stewards over matters of style.[56]

Although McCune Smith vastly overstates where stewards ranked on ships, he rightly draws our attention to the forms of everyday pleasure and politics that self-making afforded black stewards.[57] Similarly, in his sardonic review of the opening of the "African Grove," Noah provided a kind of thick description of Brown's patrons and detailed their sartorial choices and discourse.[58] Beneath Noah's layer of racial derision ("Thus they run the rounds of fashion; ape their masters and mistresses in everything ...") and minstrelized transcript (replete with the customary lexicon of "eber," "de," and "dat," among them), we can spot black social actors, many of them working-class, who, like black stewards, performed their own scripts of respectability as both personal articulation and sociopolitical intervention. These scripts were far less top-down and alienating than the moral and behavioral dictates that bourgeois-minded African American leaders prescribed with more force beginning in the 1830s.[59] The community Brown established was therefore a collectivist one in that it allowed black workers *and* (aspiring) black professionals to rehearse a shared ethics and social culture. In this way, Brown's institution was doubly theatrical: the extra-theatrical performances of respectable free blackness complemented the on-stage entertainments.

In the main, performing respectability in black antebellum institutions was not a capitulary embrace of bourgeois norms but rather a community-affirming *deconstruction* of those norms. As performance historian Tavia Nyong'o puts it, respectability "was not based in a defense of extent social relations but enacted through a mimetic performative intervention into those relations, upon terms ... that claimed respect in the face of its quotidian denial."[60] Antebellum African Americans honed the intervention of black respectability in Brown's theatre, mutual relief societies, and other institutions. Thus sartorial élan, fancy promenades, and elevated discourse not only constituted a "question of style" but also a question of politics.[61] The originary design of black institutions, including the African American theatre, was to provide the space where oppositional performative tactics such as respectability could be forged and eventually deployed. Indeed, Brown's theatre was not only the place where an eventual world-class actor like Ira Aldridge launched his professional career, but also a cultural training ground for everyday African Americans to cultivate "everyday forms of resistance": black style, black leisure, and black collectivism.

James C. Scott argues that "there is rarely any dramatic confrontation" between such forms of resistance and representatives of the state.[62] In the case of Brown's theatrical community, however, black respectability and solidarity triggered a series of physical and discursive attacks from the dominant public sphere.[63] For instance, the police forced Brown to cancel a production of *Richard III* in 1822 because it distressed a rival white theatre and the white community at large. Theatre historian Joyce Green MacDonald argues this episode was "an early example of the use of Shakespeare as a tool for enforcing cultural and political hegemony ... By aspiring to play Shakespeare publicly for a paying audience, the actors of the African Company exacerbated existing white ill-ease about the possibility of maintaining prevailing constructions of the relative positions and natures of the races."[64] Yes, but much more: the police and their applauding white publics attacked the oppositional culture that Brown and his patrons had maintained over the past year, of which all-black Shakespeare was only an element. Allied under the performative frame of respectability and the pragmatic ethic of collectivism, this culture of free black men and women flouted the assumptions of racial inequality and challenged white supremacy. In response, the dominant public sphere rioted against Brown's theatrical community and the ideological assumptions upon which it rested.

Thus Brown, his performers, and his public left a critical blueprint for African American theatre that, in its first building, nurtured black collectivity and provoked white rancor and violence. Indeed, when African Americans participated in antebellum black institutions, their performances of respectability worked to eradicate personal differences just as performances aboard ship decks, on plantations, and in trading pens fostered bonds of slave solidarity across ethnic and linguistic lines. Antebellum black theatre and performance sustained the critical strategy of racial solidarity by returning black people to the "single common theme that overpowered whatever differentiated them: they were African men [and women] – enslaved, once enslaved, or the sons [or daughters] of the enslaved."[65] At the same time, there was significant political, social, and personal risk involved in black theatre and performance: for free African Americans it exposed them to violent reprisals from their white counterparts, and for slaves it frequently entrenched their objectification as human chattel. Ambivalence abounded: What, therefore, to do?

NOTES

1 Frederick Douglass, "Gavitt's Original Ethiopian Serenaders," *The North Star*, June 29, 1849.
2 *Ibid.*
3 *Ibid.*
4 See *Theatre Journal*, 57.4 (2005), the journal's special issue on black performance.
5 Ira Berlin, *Many Thousands Gone: The First Two Centuries of Slavery in North America* (Cambridge, MA: Harvard University Press, 1998), 17.

6 Alexander Falconbridge, *An Account of the Slave Trade on the Coast of Africa* (London: J. Phillips, 1788), 23.

7 Sidney Mintz and Richard Price, *The Birth of African-American Culture: An Anthropological Perspective* (Boston, MA: Beacon Press, 1992 [1976]), 43.

8 Eddie S. Glaude, Jr., *Exodus! Religion, Race, and Nation in Early Nineteenth-Century Black America* (Chicago: University of Chicago Press, 2000), 147.

9 See Saidiya Hartman, *Scenes of Subjection: Terror, Slavery, and Self-Making in Nineteenth-Century America* (New York: Oxford University Press, 1997), 59–61.

10 Of course, the sung word *could* be an important form of communication among slaves. For example, historian Marcus Rediker notes that song was "a way of finding one's kin, fellow villagers, and countrymen and -women, and identifying which cultural groups were on board the ships." See Marcus Rediker, *The Slave Ship: A Human History* (New York: Penguin, 2007), 282.

11 William Butterworth, *Three Years Adventures, of a Minor, In England, Africa, the West Indies, South Carolina and Georgia* (Leeds, 1822), quoted in Rediker, *The Slave Ship*, 279–82. British sailor Henry Schroeder, who published under the pseudonym "William Butterfield," spoke Igbo but did not understand her songs. Furthermore, this particular vessel traded on the Bight of Biafra, meaning "the dominant group on board were the Igbo" (Rediker, *The Slave Ship*, 279).

12 Frederick Douglass, *Narrative of the Life of Frederick Douglass, an American Slave*, ed. David Blight (Boston, MA: Bedford Books of St. Martin's Press, 2003 [1845]), 46–7.

13 *Ibid.*

14 Stephen Best and Saidiya Hartman, "Fugitive Justice," *Representations*, 92 (2005): 9. Best and Hartman list "'forty acres and a mule,' the end of commodity production and restoration of the commons, the realization of 'the sublime ideal of freedom,' and the resuscitation of the socially dead" as examples of the "yearnings" that black noise articulates. For a discussion of the relation of black performance to the simultaneity of objecthood and humanity, see Fred Moten, *In the Break: The Aesthetics of the Black Radical Tradition* (Minneapolis: University of Minnesota Press, 2003), 1–24.

15 Douglass, *Narrative*, 47.

16 *Ibid.*, 80. Masters and observers also regarded slave performances during Pinkster, the late-eighteenth- and early-nineteenth-century celebration of the change of seasons usually affiliated with North American Dutch communities, as "safety valves." In these festivals of misrule, slaves acted as "kings" and frequently served as authority figures. Historian Shane White argues that despite Pinkster's normativizing function, the embodied and material practices slaves produced in the festival were early forms of African American culture. See Shane White, *Somewhat More Independent: The End of Slavery in New York City, 1770–1810* (Athens: University of Georgia Press, 1991), 95–106.

17 Harriet Jacobs, *Incidents in the Life of a Slave Girl* (New York: Norton, 2001 [1861]), 62. Jacobs writes that masters hid the "half-starved wretches toiling from dawn till dark," the "mothers shrieking for their children, torn from their arms by slave traders," the "young girls dragged down into moral filth," the

"pools of blood around the whipping post," the "hounds trained to tear human flesh," and the "men screwed into cotton gins to die."

18 Nehemiah Adams, *A South-Side View of Slavery; or, Three Months at the South, in 1854* (Boston, MA: Marvin and Mussey, 1854), 97.

19 *Ibid.*, 213.

20 Historian George M. Frederickson famously coined the term "romantic racialism" in his classic study of nineteenth-century racism, *The Black Image in the White Mind*. Romantic racialism describes the ideology and representation of the African/black as inherently virtuous and docile and therefore vital to the nation's moral constitution. See George M. Frederickson, *The Black Image in the White Mind: The Debate on Afro-American Character and Destiny, 1817–1914* (Hanover, NH: Wesleyan University Press, 1987 [1971]), 97–129.

21 William Wells Brown, *Narrative of William W. Brown, a Fugitive Slave* (Boston, MA, 1847), in *Slave Narratives*, ed. William L. Andrews and Henry Louis Gates, Jr. (New York: Penguin, 2002), 392.

22 Hartman, *Scenes of Subjection*, 33.

23 Walter Johnson, *Soul by Soul: Life inside the Antebellum Slave Market* (Cambridge, MA: Harvard University Press, 1999), 149–50.

24 Hartman, *Scenes of Subjection*, 35–8.

25 *Ibid.*, 63.

26 Moten, *In the Break*, 16.

27 On African American freedom celebrations before the Civil War, see Glaude, *Exodus!*, 82–104, 122–5.

28 During the Harlem Renaissance, for example, these questions captivated African American cultural theorists who framed the question in terms of "art or propaganda." In his 1928 essay, "Art or Propaganda," Alain Locke objected to performative and literary propaganda because "apart from its besetting sin of monotony and disproportion, [propaganda] perpetuates the position of group inferiority even in crying out against it. For it leaves and speaks under the shadow of a dominant majority whom it harangues, cajoles, threatens or supplicates. It is too extroverted for balance or poise or inner dignity and self-respect." Locke's espousal of "art" is a clear rejoinder to W. E. B. Du Bois's call for propaganda throughout the period. In his classic essay, "Criteria for Negro Art" (1926), Du Bois argued "all Art [i.e., true art] is propaganda and ever must be, despite the wailing of the purists ... I do not care a damn for any art that is not used for propaganda." Both Locke and Du Bois understood the theatre as a primary site for the creation and expression of art or propaganda. See Alain Locke, "Art or Propaganda," *Harlem: A Forum for Negro Life*, 1.1 (November, 1928), in *Voices from the Harlem Renaissance*, ed. Nathan Irvin Huggins (Oxford: Oxford University Press, 1995 [1976]), 312; W. E. B. Du Bois, "The Criteria of Negro Art," *The Crisis*, 32 (October, 1926), in *The Oxford W. E. B. Du Bois Reader*, ed. Eric J. Sundquist (New York: Oxford University Press, 1996), 324–8.

29 Hartman, *Scenes of Subjection*, 48.

30 See Peggy Phelan's extremely useful summary of the economy of representation, where she explains how representation "always conveys more than it intends; and it is never totalizing." Peggy Phelan, *Unmarked: The Politics of Performance* (London: Routledge, 1993), 2–4.

31 Douglass, *Narrative*, 46.

32 Performance tactics like imitation and mimicry also offered slaves some moments of relief from the diurnal operation of slavery. As Paul Gilroy writes, "Survival in slave regimes or in other extreme conditions intrinsic to colonial order promoted the acquisition of what we might now understand to be performance skills, and refined the appreciation of mimesis by both dominant and dominated." He notes the "everyday triumphs" that "mimicking and in a sense mastering" the master afforded slaves. Paul Gilroy, "'... To Be Real': The Dissident Forms of Black Expressive Culture," in *Let's Get It On: The Politics of Black Performance*, ed. Catherine Ugwu (Seattle: Bay Press, 1995), 14.

33 Raymond Williams, *The Long Revolution* (London: Chatto & Windus, 1961), 49. Many thanks to La Marr Bruce, literary and performance theorist and friend, for recalling my attention to Williams's classic essay, "The Analysis of Culture."

34 Errol Hill and James Vernon Hatch, *A History of African American Theatre* (Cambridge; New York: Cambridge University Press, 2003), 25; Marvin Edward McAllister, *White People Do Not Know How to Behave at Entertainments Designed for Ladies & Gentlemen of Colour: William Brown's African & American Theater* (Chapel Hill: University of North Carolina Press, 2003), 1–9.

35 Leslie M. Harris, *In the Shadow of Slavery: African Americans in New York City, 1626–1863* (Chicago: University of Chicago Press, 2003), 78.

36 McAllister, *White People Do Not Know How to Behave*, 9.

37 Brown staged Shakespeare's *Richard III* as one of the company's first productions, and shortly thereafter, in January, 1822, he staged his own play, *Shotaway; or, The Insurrections of the Caribs of St. Domingo*. Although no script remains, *Shotaway* seems to have been the first produced black-authored play in the United States. See McAllister, *White People Do Not Know How to Behave*, 67–101.

38 Article II, Section 1 of the 1821 New York Constitution read: "... but no man of colour, unless he shall have been for three years a citizen of this state, and for one year next preceding any election, shall be seized and possessed of a freehold estate of the value of two hundred and fifty dollars, over and above all debts and incumbrances charged thereon; and shall have been actually rated, and paid a tax thereon, shall be entitled to vote at any such election." Thus only those African Americans who were not slaves three years within the time of an election *and* who were extraordinarily wealthy could vote in state and local elections.

39 The 1799 Act freed slave children born after July 4, 1799 once they had served their mothers' owners for a lengthy period of time: twenty-eight years for males and twenty-five years for females. But in 1817, the state legislature made important changes: *all* slaves born before July 4, 1799 would be free in 1827, and those born after March 31, 1817 would be free at twenty-one years old; slave children born between July 4, 1799 and March 31, 1817, however, would continue to serve under the conditions of the original law. See Harris, *In the Shadow of Slavery*, 64–71, 94. Harris points out that under the terms of the 1817 law, "slave masters [potentially] retained access to the labor of blacks as late as 1848, when the last black children, if born to slave women before July 4, 1827, would be free of indenture." *Ibid.*, 94.

40 *Ibid.*, 96–133.

41 My emphasis on "design" throughout this chapter comes from Hartman's insightful description of the work of an "oppositional culture," that it is "poised to destroy … designs for mastery" (Hartman, *Scenes of Subjection*, 48). Williams's notion of culture as "whole organization" also suggests the importance of design. See Williams, *The Long Revolution, passim.*

42 *Spectator* (New York), January 16, 1822.

43 McAllister, *White People Do Not Know How to Behave*, 39–51.

44 *Ibid.*, 3.

45 McAllister's study, by far the most thorough treatment of Brown and his pleasure garden and theatre, is primarily concerned with the Du Boisean "twoness" (the sense of being both American and black) that Brown and his fellow Afro-New Yorkers felt – that is, how "Brown's institutional 'becoming'… [was] shaped by powerful forces from the dominant culture." He does admit that Brown's institution "personified Old World African Values" but quickly moves to understand those values in terms of their "metaphoric" presence (*ibid.*, 1–14, *passim*). I want to stress the material – indeed, *embodied* – presence of those values and its effect on the formation of African American theatre and black institutional life.

46 Craig Steven Wilder, *In the Company of Black Men: The African Influence on African American Culture in New York City* (New York: New York University Press, 2001), 3.

47 For more on the NYASMR, see *ibid.*, 83–96, 125–40.

48 *Ibid.*, 81.

49 Mordecai Noah, "Africans," *National Advocate*, August 3, 1821, in *A Documentary History of the African Theatre*, ed. George Thompson, Jr. (Evanston, IL: Northwestern University Press, 1999), 58–9.

50 Patrick Rael, *Black Identity and Black Protest in the Antebellum North* (Chapel Hill: University of North Carolina Press, 2002), 25; 12–53. For a classic explanation of the distinctiveness of free African Americans in the North, see Ira Berlin, "The Structure of the Free Negro Caste in the Antebellum United States," *Journal of Social History*, 9 (1976): 297–318.

51 McAllister, *White People Do Not Know How to Behave*, 29.

52 W. Jeffrey Bolster, *Blackjacks: African American Seamen in the Age of Sail* (Cambridge, MA: Harvard University Press, 1997), 158–89; Harris, *In the Shadow of Slavery*, 80–2, 100. For more on black occupations and economics in early-nineteenth-century New York, see White, *Somewhat More Independent*, 156–71.

53 There were a few African Americans who acquired wealth in the shipping business. The most famous was the Massachusetts-based shipping magnate, Paul Cuffe, who publicly advocated for African Americans to move to Africa to create their own independent nation. See Bolster, *Blackjacks*, 171–6; and Paul Cuffe, *Captain Paul Cuffe's Logs and Letters, 1808–1817: A Black Quaker's "Voice from within the Veil,"* ed. Rosalind Cobb Wiggins (Washington, DC: Howard University Press, 1996).

54 Bolster, *Blackjacks*, 69–77.

55 *Ibid.*, 159.

56 James McCune Smith, "Ira Aldridge," *The Anglo-African Magazine*, January 2, 1860, in Thompson, *A Documentary History*, 213–14.

57 See Bolster, *Blackjacks*, *passim*; Thomas C. Buchanan, "Rascals on the Antebellum Mississippi: African American Steamboat Workers and the St. Louis Hanging of 1841," *Journal of Social History*, 34 (2001): 797–816.

58 Noah, "Africans," 58–9.

59 Glaude, *Exodus!*, 115–42; Evelyn Brooks Higginbotham, "The Politics of Respectability," in *Righteous Discontent: The Women's Movement in the Black Baptist Church, 1880–1920* (Cambridge, MA: Harvard University Press, 1993), 185–230.

60 Tavia Nyong'o, *The Amalgamation Waltz: Race, Performance, and the Ruses of Memory* (Minneapolis: University of Minnesota Press, 2009), 118.

61 See White, *Somewhat More Independent*, 185–206.

62 James C. Scott, *Weapons of the Weak: Everyday Forms of Peasant Resistance* (New Haven: Yale University Press, 1985), 36.

63 McAllister, *White People Do Not Know How to Behave*, 131–66.

64 Joyce Green MacDonald, "'Othello,' 'Othello' Burlesques, and the Performance of Blackness," *Theatre Journal*, 46 (1994): 234–6.

65 Wilder, *In the Company of Black Men*, 131.

2

Slave rebellions on the national stage

A wolf by the ears

On August 22, 1831, a slave named Nat Turner unleashed a bloody uprising in Southampton County, Virginia that terrified white Southerners, galvanized white abolitionists, and inspired generations of black revolutionaries.[1] After his capture, Turner recounted tales of butchering women and children, and of hacking to death the white owners who had oppressed slaves for decades. Turner's rebellion ignited an equally vicious backlash among whites who tortured slaves suspected of complicity in the plot. Even slaves who had no prior knowledge of Turner's plans were regarded with suspicion and often harshly treated as a pre-emptive measure against any future stirrings of revolt – as the *Richmond Enquirer* noted, "Rumors are sufficient to keep alive the vigilance of the people."[2]

Yet in the midst of the panic and terror, the one emotion that seemed noticeably absent was surprise. While some newspapers professed puzzlement that a slave who had been taught to read and write, and who had received no "cause or provocation," would rebel,[3] those accounts highlight the widespread understanding that slavery was an inherently violent system and that slave rebellions were "not isolated and infrequent events."[4] By underscoring Turner's gentle treatment prior to the rebellion, the newspapers tacitly acknowledged that there were masters who behaved brutally toward their slaves. As their tone suggests, whites realized on some level that the violence embedded in the state of slavery was only held in check by a kind of mutual compact between blacks and whites. Whites understood that black subjugation had to be enforced with a measure of violence, but not to such an extent that blacks would rebel.[5] Blacks understood that they could express dissent through various ritualized behaviors such as Pinkster festivals or licensed singing and dancing celebrations on the plantation during holiday seasons,[6] but that beyond a certain point whites would respond with punishments that could result in sale to the Deep South (a virtual death

34

sentence), maiming, or murder. Yet, despite masters' threats of retribution, a "tradition of hemispheric resistance to slavery" beyond ritual enactments continued up to the Civil War.[7]

Even after Emancipation, the threat of violence kept black and white relations in a state of constant tension, and resistance to oppression continued to flash across the culture. The mass migration of freed slaves to the North and West meant that the tentative treaties negotiated between master and slave would have to be rewritten in new terms and by new participants whose legal status (if not their socioeconomic or political one) had undergone a total transformation. Additionally, the failure of radical Reconstruction and the rapid political and economic transformation of the white South in the post-Civil War period fundamentally changed the meaning of racially motivated violence in that region, particularly with the rise of the Ku Klux Klan.

Throughout this chapter, I explore the performance of racial violence on the American stage from the colonial era through the beginning of the twentieth century. I focus particularly on the legacy of slave rebellions, a specter that haunted the white imagination from the inception of American slavery. As the transatlantic slave trade and abolitionist movement gained momentum, the menace of slave revolt took on even more complex political and social meanings. Narratives, rumors, newspaper reports, and political pamphlets fueled not only the white panic about possible slave uprisings, but the black imagination as well. As Herbert Aptheker notes in his foundational study, *American Negro Slave Revolts*, "The unearthing of the history of Negro slave rebellions is peculiarly subject to difficulties arising from exaggeration, distortion, and censorship."[8] However, it is precisely that pattern of exaggeration, distortion, and censorship that fascinates me and that plays such a significant role in transforming these stories of rebellion for consumption in the theatre. Which rituals were concealed in the shift from cultural practice to theatrical performance? How were slave uprisings and rebel leaders interpolated into popular culture? Without an element of "surprise," how could authors create dramatic tension? How were characters and narratives reimagined to suit the tastes and needs of the various audiences for whom they were staged? Whose voices were heard and whose were silenced? How did the stories change with Emancipation as new narrative voices took control?

Dangerous inspiration

Although Turner's rebellion marked a turning point in the history of American slavery, the representation of slave rebellions in transatlantic culture dated back more than a century before his 1831 uprising, and the menace of racial violence had found its way into American drama long before. For example, in the winter of 1741 white New Yorkers trembled as fire after fire raced through the city. The fires burned amidst strange rumors that all the slaves planned to rise up and kill the white men of Manhattan, seizing their wives and their property. While it was never completely clear whether there had been a specific plot to massacre the city's white populations, or, if such a plot had existed, how many people were involved, dozens of blacks and whites were questioned in the trials that followed. Thirty slaves were put to death for their alleged roles in this plot.

Jill Lepore's compelling study, *New York Burning: Liberty, Slavery, and Conspiracy in Eighteenth-Century Manhattan*, chronicles the "Great Negro Plot" of 1741 and focuses on the highly performative nature of both the plot and the trial. As Lepore notes, the plot's outline, as framed by the trial's white judges, conforms neatly to traditional European dramatic conventions of the period.[9] She notes the ways in which suspects linked the origins of the conspiracy to a ritual celebration held in a tavern, during which black plotters swore allegiance to each other and vengeance against their white oppressors. As the story unfolded in the trial testimony, allegations arose that the plotters had planned to make a black man "king" of New York City – a notion that white judges found both absurd and terrifying, little imagining that the term had ritual meaning for the black community.[10]

I draw three points from Lepore's work that are significant to this chapter. First, Lepore suggests that in crafting their own narratives of the supposed plot whites were largely insensible to the meaning of black cultural rituals, such as Pinkster (also known sometimes as "Nigger 'Lection Day") in which traditional power roles were reversed as a black "king" or "governor" was ushered into power as a Lord of Misrule.[11] Thus, whites who heard rumors about a black man becoming "king" of New York (as happened in the 1741 plot) might not recognize the symbolic nature of that language. Or, as Dale Cockrell notes, even if they understood that these rituals were simulated rather than real rebellions, they still harbored suspicions about Africans' real intentions. For example, some whites in Massachusetts expressed anxiety that blacks were "assembling together, beating drums, using powder and having guns and swords" as part of their Pinkster or Election Day celebrations.[12] Clearly whites were primed to see the potential for violent uprising in black cultural performance – a subtext that was almost certainly there to be read.

Second, Lepore details the extent to which hints of a plot in one city conjured memories of plots elsewhere – such as the uprising in New York

City led by Coromantees on April 6, 1712, and the rebellions in St. John's (1733) and Antigua (1736).[13] Whites witnessing the events of 1741 had read newspaper accounts of the 1739 Stono Rebellion in South Carolina, led by Congolese-Angolan slaves.[14] Over time, these stories of rebellion assumed a familiar structure, so that each successive narrative began to conform to similar plot points in the white imagination.

Third, Lepore highlights whites' inability to credit blacks with the ingenuity and inspiration to plan and carry out riots on their own. Suggestions of fiendish "instigators" peppered accounts of slave rebellions all the way up until the Civil War.[15] Crediting blacks with the ability to devise a successful uprising meant revising oft-repeated rhetoric about African American intelligence and courage, and it also gave credence to the notion that blacks might have ample justification for rebelling.

While early British plays on the colonial stage did not depict outright slave rebellion, they nevertheless hinted at the potential for violence by black/ African characters. *Othello, Cato, Oroonoko,* and *The Padlock* offer four examples of plays popular in the colonial era featuring strong and rebellious black characters who all display a willingness to challenge white authority. Shakespeare's *Othello* had its first production in the British colonies on December 26, 1751.[16] The play remained a fixture on the colonial stage and also made its way into colonial culture, appearing variously as a name for slaves, horses, and ships.[17] Thomas Southerne's *Oroonoko* (1695), based on Aphra Behn's popular novel of the same name, tells the story of a captured black prince who leads a revolt against his masters. After his plot is foiled, he is tortured to death – a process he endures with no complaint. Joseph Addison's 1712 tragedy *Cato* became a colonial favorite – particularly on the eve of revolution – for its message of republican virtue. It features a warlike black prince named Juba.[18] Isaac Bickerstaffe's 1768 comedy *The Padlock* includes the complex black character Mungo. Mungo challenges his master's right to beat him and helps his master's intended fiancée romance another man. Mungo became a popular figure with British abolitionists, and he was included in a 1793 American cartoon in which Thomas Jefferson, Satan, and various American political figures touted the glorious promise of the French Revolution. In the image, Mungo's character gleefully proclaims that it will be his "turn" next – a claim that links him to France's bloody Reign of Terror.[19]

The French Revolution helped to inspire a new wave of African-led violence that was eventually translated onto the American stage. The year 1791 witnessed the outbreak of the Haitian Revolution. White refugees from Saint Domingue (also called St. Domingo) poured into the United States, carrying terrifying tales of violence. Rebel leaders Toussaint L'Ouverture,

Jean-Jacques Dessalines, and Henri Christophe all assumed mythic status in both the black and the white imagination.

In 1794 a Philadelphian named John Murdock penned *The Triumphs of Love; or, Happy Reconciliations*, which featured two young refugees from St. Domingo: Beauchamp and his sister Clementina. Murdock contrasts the plight of the whites forced to flee St. Domingo, leaving possessions and homes behind, with his white hero, George Friendly, Jr. George, following the lessons of the American Revolution and the dictates of sentimental culture, chooses to free his slave Sambo. This anti-slavery play shows Americans extending friendship to former slaveholders (George marries Clementina), but only after they have all been converted to the cause of universal emancipation – whether by choice or by force.[20]

As I have suggested, the voices that remained unheard are equally important in considering how the violence of slavery was or was not represented on the American stage. The year 1796 brought an English translation of August von Kotzebue's *The Negro Slaves* to Britain (and a version of the work had reached America by 1799). William Dunlap, playwright and frequent translator of Kotzebue's dramas, dismissed this story set in Jamaica as "a piece of exaggerated, overstrained, nauseous, sentimentality."[21] New York's *Monthly Magazine and American Review* noted that although the play had been translated into English it was doubtful it would ever be produced.[22] Given Kotzebue's enormous popularity on the American stage, these assessments may seem surprising. Yet this play, endorsed in London by abolitionist William Wilberforce, would have been virtually unproducible in the eighteenth-century American playhouse. It recounts horrific descriptions of the Middle Passage, depicts slaves (including some wearing muzzles and iron collars) brutally treated by overseers and owners, and shows a slave rebelling against the white men who attack his father and lay claim to his wife.[23]

Other unstaged but widely circulated dramas of the early national period reminded readers of the potential for African-led violence against whites. Jon H. Nichols's 1802 closet play *The Essex Junto* cast John Adams as the evil duke of Braintree who beats his slaves when they bemoan having been stolen from their families. The duke exclaims, "I've no slave who's not infidel or jacobin." Labeling slaves as Jacobins allied them not only with the violence of the French Revolution, but with Thomas Jefferson (who had sympathized with the French and was often tarred with the Jacobin label). In Act III, scene 5, the character Monticello (Jefferson) arms his slaves and tells them to help him fight Braintree.[24] In Act IV, scene 3, General Creole (Alexander Hamilton) confesses to having had secret correspondence with Toussaint L'Ouverture, "Hispaniola's sooty chief."[25] As Nichols's play suggests, the challenge of how to deal with a state led by black military forces baffled

America's fledgling government, particularly given their seeming inability to control the African-descended peoples within their own borders.

Another more fleeting mention of the ongoing political disruption in Haiti appears in the 1819 play *The Sea Serpent*. Written by Charleston lawyer and theatre critic William Crafts, the play premiered in Charleston, but drew notices from newspapers as far away as Philadelphia; New York; Boston; and Portsmouth, NH. While the play does not focus on African American slave rebellions, there is a scene in which some of the sailors sing about their valor in the face of grave danger, mentioning "Dessalines, that scoundrel black."[26] The line is significant because American sailors would have been well aware of the ongoing tumult in Haiti, since they regularly brought not only news but refugees from the island.

While these mentions of L'Ouverture and Dessalines are brief in Nichols's and Crafts's plays, they suggest the extent to which images of black rebel leaders had infiltrated both American culture and the American playhouse. Reading or hearing these names, black and white audience members might recall not only Jefferson's and Monroe's disastrous dealings with the black leaders in Haiti, but perhaps recent slave rebellions in the United States as well, including Gabriel Prosser's planned attack in August of 1800; the Chatham Manor attack in Virginia in 1805; the German Coast uprising in the Louisiana Territory in 1811;[27] and the George Boxley plot in Virginia in 1815.[28] As one white observer described the conspirators in the Prosser rebellion, "The accused have exhibited a spirit, which, if it becomes general, must deluge the Southern country in blood. They manifested a sense of their rights, a contempt of danger, and a thirst for revenge which portend unhappy consequences."[29] As this succession of uprisings suggests, that deluge was already well underway.

Kill and spare not

By 1831, the year that Robert Montgomery Bird's *The Gladiator* debuted on the American stage, the nation had witnessed more slave uprisings than could be counted. Every threatened rebellion had brought stricter laws and greater anxiety about how the country's ever-growing population of blacks could be controlled. Yet in one of the most puzzling cases of willful blindness in American theatre history, critics and audiences largely failed to link the violent rhetoric of Bird's tragedy with the Turner rebellion. While the play tells the story of a Roman slave revolt, some of the most well-known lines of the tragedy seem as though they might have been drawn directly from any of the numerous slave uprisings that had already terrified white Americans, well before Nat Turner's plot:

> Ho slaves, arise! It is your hour to kill!
> Kill and spare not – For wrath and liberty!
> Freedom for bondmen – freedom and revenge![30]

Although it was written in April of 1831, the play premiered on September 26 of that year, less than five weeks after Turner's uprising – indeed, Turner was still eluding his pursuers when the play opened at New York's Park Theatre. As Tice Miller notes, Turner was not the only rebel figure terrifying white spectators. Nine years earlier, Denmark Vesey had planned a rebellion in Charleston, and in 1829, David Walker's efforts to rouse slaves and free blacks prompted many Southern states to pass laws "to make inciting slaves to rebellion a serious crime."[31] Bird himself seemed attuned to the resonances between his play and the events unfolding in Southampton. As he noted in his diary, "Armed negroes marching through Southampton County, murdering, ravishing, and burning ... If they had but a Spartacus among them – to organize the half million of Virginia ... and lead them on in the Crusade of Massacre, what a blessed example might they not give the world of the excellence of slavery!"[32] Bird's ironic exclamation reflected his anti-slavery sentiments – beliefs more explicitly expressed in his earlier, unproduced play, *The City Looking Glass* (1828). In that play, Bird describes slavery as "A system abhorrent to the general principles of morality and justice, and disgraceful to the character of our country."[33]

Peter Reed suggests that white audiences constructed a kind of "classical blackness" in order to frame characters such as Spartacus outside the real-life parallels of Nat Turner and other African American rebels. Yet despite efforts to realign Spartacus with either classical tragic heroes, contemporary class rivalries, or overseas revolutions (Poland's struggle for freedom), "Bird's Roman revolt subtly presents stage forms of blackness."[34] Reed argues that the body of star performer Edwin Forrest, who played Spartacus, invited audiences to "experiment with the spectacles of underclass and interracial mutualities masked behind the dominating presence of Forrest's heroic, muscular performance."[35] He cites not only the allusions to Spartacus that proliferated in black culture or plays with black characters (such as *Obi; or, Three Finger'd Jack*), but also the fact that Forrest had, earlier in his career, played African characters in blackface. Yet for many white Americans, Forrest could "simultaneously embody and erase blackness."[36] Forrest's metaphorical blackness inoculated his white audience against other types of racial identification and sympathy.

But what of black audiences? How had they incorporated these lessons and characters into their culture? In 1822, New York's short-lived African

Grove Theatre announced a production of the now lost play, *Shotaway; or, The Insurrection of the Caribs of St. Domingo*. Newspapers at the time noted, "These descendants of Africa are determined to carry into full practice the doctrine of *liberty and equality*, physically by acting plays and mentally by writing them."[37] Marvin McAllister notes that the theatre's choice "could not have been more defiant or progressive."[38] James Hewlett and Ira Aldridge, the two well-known black stars who launched their careers at the African Grove Theatre, would go on to play militant black characters elsewhere after the theatre closed its doors in 1823. Aldridge had a particularly successful career, appearing in the following plays: *The Castle Spectre*; *Christophe, King of Hayti*; *The Ethiopian*; *Othello*; *Oroonoko*; *The Padlock*; *Pizarro*; *The Revenge*; and *The Slave*.[39] Each of these dramas features a black/Moorish/colored character that rebels against white authority.

After the closing of the African Grove Theatre and pleasure gardens, black New Yorkers opened a new venue: the Haytian Retreat.[40] While little is known of the fate of this enterprise or the entertainments offered within, its creation (two years after emancipation in New York state) and its name are highly suggestive of African Americans' intention to claim the legacy of Haiti and to incorporate it (literally and figuratively) into the American landscape.[41] The development of African American newspapers such as *Freedom's Journal*, and later *The Colored American*, and Frederick Douglass's various papers, helped African Americans recontextualize the legacy of slave uprisings (whether contemporary or classical) outside a white frame of reference.

In July of 1839, a group of slaves led a revolt onboard the *Amistad* – a rebellion that would generate a long and highly publicized court case over whether the slaves were the legal property of Spain, or had been illegally kidnapped and transported from Africa.[42] The case and the character of Cinque (the rebel leader) aroused lively interest among many white Northerners who hastened to romanticize the slaves and demonize their Spanish captors. For example, the *New Hampshire Sentinel* described Cinque as "A young prince perhaps, torn from his kindred and country by kidnappers ..."[43] Within just a few months of the rebellion, the Bowery Theatre debuted *The Black Schooner; or, The Private Slaver "Amistad."*[44] While many white spectators compared Cinque and his compatriots to Othello, perhaps imagining this as a compliment to the rebels, black newspapers such as *The Colored American* adamantly rejected this label. Instead, *The Colored American* placed Cinque in a different lineage that included Nat Turner, claiming that "God may have cast this chieftain on our shore in this crisis to aid in the delivery of his people."[45]

Seven months after the opening of *The Black Schooner*, New York theatres featured another play about a revolutionary black leader: *Christophe, King of Hayti* (also known as *The Death of Christophe, King of Hayti*). First produced on February 3, 1840 at the New Chatham Theatre, the play opened one month after the theatre's production of *Obi; or, Three Finger'd Jack*, featuring William Wood in the lead role.[46] The play reappeared at Burton's Theatre in New York in 1852.[47] Christophe (also known as King Henri I) offered an intriguing character for American audiences. Unlike many of the other rebel leaders in Hayti, Christophe had tried to re-establish relations with the English (and had even sought to eradicate the French language from the country). He killed himself on October 8, 1820 during a siege by more radical factions on the island. This combination helped to make him a more sympathetic and tragic figure. He could perhaps even approach Reed's notion of "classical" blackness for his white audiences – a blackness the significance of which resided not in racial representation, but in metaphorical meaning.

Two years after *Christophe*, the theme of slave rebellions surfaced again on the American stage – once in a fleeting mention as part of a minstrel parody, and the other in a more serious form. Irish playwright and performer John Brougham was known for his irreverent satires of European high culture. On June 12, 1842, he staged a parody of *Othello*. Advertisements for the production described Othello as "an independent Nigger from the republic of Hayti."[48] Although black newspapers had resisted identifying black leaders with Othello, Brougham's minstrel adaptation suggests that, at least in the white imagination, *any* strong African male figure fit this kind of militant stereotype. Popular cartoons of the 1830s and 1840s ridicule Haitian leaders, casting them as grotesque shadows of white generals such as George Washington.[49]

A second, more unusual representation of a slave uprising appeared in 1842. *Zamba; or, The Insurrection* by Mrs. Elizabeth Stryker Ricord centers on a slave uprising in the West Indies. In her prologue to the play Ricord claimed,

> The piece, having been imagined, and even traced out, at least twenty years ago ... has no relation to the sentiments on the subject of slavery, that, of late, have excited such interest in our republic. My design ... is to exhibit the influence that Evangelical Christianity might exercise over all classes of society, from the highest station of arrogant affluence, to the lowest stage of degraded poverty.

Ricord suggested that without the benefit of a moralizing Christian influence, "These poor degraded people, as may well be supposed, are superstitious and often very corrupt. Those who are from Africa, sometimes mingle their Fetish or heathen customs with false notions of the Christian religion."[50] Indeed, Ricord's note about the "Fetish" customs echoed contemporary American newspapers, which described black Haitians making "preparations for the attack [of 1791]" by having "their Obies perform the *Oangah*, or mysterious rite to their demons," indicating that the "women and children danced an accompaniment to the ceremony, with howlings and outcries that savored of Pandemonium."[51] Both Ricord's preface and the newspaper story suggest that many white Americans continued to find black religious and cultural rituals alien and disturbing. The escalation of black celebrations in the 1830s and 1840s included the development of what Geneviève Fabre describes as an "alternate calendar" of rituals commemorating L'Ouverture's triumph in Haiti or Nat Turner's birthday.[52] The fact that some of these rituals celebrating revolutionaries might be a precursor to attacks only heightened whites' fear.[53]

What narrative strategy might offer white audiences a way out of the dire fate that apparently awaited them at the hands of the budding revolutionaries around them? Christian sentiment held the key. Zamba, the lead character in Ricord's play, overcomes his pagan roots and desire for revenge, and saves his master from a threatened slave uprising, demonstrating both his Christian charity and his fitness for freedom.[54] Although Ricord's play never received a full production, it was published and circulated among white Northerners. It bears some resemblance to a play with which many American theatregoers would already have been familiar: Thomas Morton's controversial opera, *The Slave* (which had debuted at New York's Park Theatre on July 4, 1817). Like *Zamba*, Morton's *The Slave* tells the story of a slave uprising thwarted by a noble African character, Gambia, whose sense of moral duty eventually triumphs over his passion for vengeance. Although *The Slave* remained in the American repertoire for more than thirty years, it is worth noting that some white audiences found Gambia's heroic conduct hard to credit – a cynical, but perhaps understandable point of view from an Anglo-European society that had witnessed so many slave uprisings over the years.[55] Similarly, readers of Ricord's play might have seen Zamba as an archetype of a faithful Christian slave who bore little resemblance to reality. Those suspicions might have been understandable, particularly in light of a speech given on August 16, 1843 by black abolitionist Henry Highland Garnet. Garnet's "An Address to the Slaves of the United States of America" rejected the gradualist approach of many white abolitionists, insisting on immediate action and invoking the rebel leaders of the past as examples of slaves who had done their *duty* in trying to free themselves: "IT IS YOUR SOLEMN AND IMPERATIVE DUTY TO USE EVERY

MEANS, BOTH MORAL, INTELLECTUAL, AND PHYSICAL, THAT PROMISE SUCCESS [*sic*]."[56] Garnet invoked Vesey as a "martyr to freedom," Turner as one whom "future generations will number ... with the noble and the brave," and Cinque as "The hero of the Amistad."[57] While controversial at the time, Garnet's speech was published in 1848 along with David Walker's *Appeal to the Coloured Citizens of the World*. No less a figure than John Brown "helped to finance the publication."[58]

Leaps for freedom

The 1850s marked a watershed decade in the representation of slavery-related violence on the American stage. *Uncle Tom's Cabin* (both the novel by Harriet Beecher Stowe and the stage version created by George L. Aiken)[59] shows the struggle among African Americans as to whether liberty should be achieved through violent or peaceful means. Intriguingly, Aiken's stage adaptation of *Uncle Tom's Cabin* showed freedom realized through rebellion *and* through Christian compliance, using the characters of George Harris and Uncle Tom to contrast the two perspectives. As the play opens, Eliza's husband, George Harris, declares his intention to escape from an increasingly cruel and arbitrary master. George proclaims, "Master will find out that I'm one whipping won't tame ... I can't trust in heaven." In Act II, scene 6, as George, Eliza, and their son Harry make their way to free territory with slave catchers in hot pursuit, George draws his pistol and shoots at the men trying to drag him back into bondage: "We have arms to defend ourselves, and we mean to do it. You can come up if you like, but the first one that comes within range of our bullets is a dead man!"[60] Tom, by contrast, is sold from master to master, until he winds up in the custody of the evil Simon Legree. Yet Tom refuses to harm his master, although in the same breath he denies Legree's rights over him: "My soul an't yours, mas'r; you haven't bought it – ye can't buy it; it's been bought and paid for by one that is able to keep it, and you can't harm it!"[61] Eventually beaten to death by Legree, Tom finds his reward in the afterlife; the final tableau of the stage shows Tom kneeling at Little Eva's feet in Heaven.

If *Uncle Tom's Cabin* staged somewhat ambiguous sentiments about the relationship between African-American-led violence and slavery, Stowe's *Dred* left little to the imagination. The H. J. Conway adaptation presented in 1856 deals openly with the threat of slave rebellion (as does the novel), and compares Dred to Denmark Vesey. As one character comments:

> There's a fine specimen of your educated nigger. Religious, too; can find you half a dozen warrants in Scripture for cutting the same number of white

Figure 2.1 *Uncle Tom's Cabin*, lithograph, 1899.

people's throats. He's a true son of his father, Denmark Vesey, who headed the bloody insurrection of the niggers in South Carolina; like him, he's a religious enthusiast, and like him, I doubt not, is in communication with other educated niggers on plantations not a hundred miles from here.[62]

Tellingly the dialog invokes not only the fearsome rebel leader, but calls upon the standard white narrative that indicates slaves were often guided (or misguided) by religious beliefs into rebellion, as well as the ever-present white Southern anxiety that slaves were always plotting in communication with each other.

As the nation drew closer to war, the invocation of rebel leaders in public speeches and dramas escalated. Back when Garnet had challenged black Americans to embrace their African and American birthrights to claim their freedom, few white leaders had been willing to echo his calls for physical resistance to slavery. Years later, the passage of the 1850 Fugitive Slave Act and a succession of legal cases such as Anthony Burns (1854), Dred Scott (1857), and others, had persuaded anti-slavery activists that armed resistance or even aggression might hold the key to abolishing slavery. Some activists invoked familiar rebel leaders through their rhetoric and others through action. On February 1, 1859, white abolitionist speaker Wendell Phillips lectured on Toussaint L'Ouverture at the Brooklyn Mercantile Library.[63] On October 16, 1859, John Brown launched his ill-fated attack on Harpers Ferry. Though Brown's efforts failed, they galvanized the national press, instantly recalling memories of Nat Turner's rebellion. For example, the *New York Herald* ran an article on Brown with the headline "Old Brown and Nat Turner, The Colored Men's Heroes." The essay described Brown's raid and announced that there would be a talk on Nat Turner on November 1 at the Shiloh Church.[64] The paper provided a description of the talk in its November 3 issue. Henry Highland Garnet introduced the speaker, Reverend Stella Martin, known as the "Lion of the West." After praising Turner and Brown, and claiming Brown as the inheritor of Turner's legacy, Martin added that the time had come to end slavery by any means necessary: "If it can only be done by the bloody sword and the leaden ball, then I say let revolution raise its head and let fire and sword devastate the land."[65] The same evening that Martin lectured on Brown and Turner to the black congregation of the Shiloh Church, Wendell Phillips lectured on Brown to the pro-abolitionist congregation at Henry Ward Beecher's Brooklyn Church. According to Baltimore's paper, *The Sun*, Phillips's speech was a "glowing eulogy on Old Brown, fully justifying his course in Kansas and at Harper's Ferry."[66]

Less than two weeks after Brown's execution, his story made it to the stage as *Ossawattomie Brown; or, the Insurrection at Harpers Ferry*. Penned by Katherine Swayze, the play focuses on abstract concepts of right and wrong, rather than a specific call to violent revolution. It is interesting to contemplate whether the actor playing Brown performed the same kind of "classical blackness" for his audience that Edwin Forrest had for his almost thirty years before.[67] John Brown would become the stuff of legend – the song "John Brown's Body" was chorused on both the battlefield and the stage. One particularly subversive use of the song appears in Boston playwright Benjamin Woolf's 1861 farce *Off to the War!* As Mr. and Mrs. Doddlewobble contemplate the coming conflict, their black servant Cæsar enters singing "John Brown's Body." Cæsar's choice of song deliberately underscores the provocation he had given his employer in the first scene of the play:

CÆSAR: Ready for you breakfast yet, sah?

DODD: Ready for my breakfast yet, sah? No! I shall never be ready for my breakfast again, you black scoundrel!

CÆSAR: Don't call names, massa; don't call names. Niggers is riz. Niggers is somebodies now. Dey musn't be called names. You hab heard ob de impending crisis, – eh, massa?

DODD: Impending crisis! Yes: I've heard of nothing else these thirty years.

CÆSAR: Well, den, it am impended. Niggers is de crisis. Yes, dey is. I'se one ob de criseses. Yah, yah! *(Laughs)* Niggers is de war and de crisis bofe. Lor, massa, dis heah war ain't about any ob yar common white folks and your rights. No: it ain't a-goin' to do you any good. It's about de niggers. Niggers is de war, massa.

DODD: How dare you stand there, and talk in that way?

CÆSAR: *(Grinning)* Kase niggers is de war.[68]

Caesar's taunt that "Niggers is riz" perfectly – if crudely – captures the sentiments of both black and white Americans on the eve of the Civil War. New dramatic structures would have to be created to encompass the "crisis" of the war and the change in African American status in white American culture. John Ernest argues that before the Civil War, African Americans "recognized that the clear incoherence and sheer chaos of African American experience exposed the instabilities of the white nationalist 'text' of history, indicating a history uncontained and unaccountable by the existing narratives."[69] After the war, blacks faced the challenge of rescripting that history into new models.

Rights of memory

In 1865, Henry Highland Garnet preached a funeral oration for the institution of slavery. Yet that same year Frederick Douglass reminded his followers that the work of the abolitionists was far from over and that the war to win equality had ended neither with emancipation nor with Lincoln's assassination. How would the heroes of the prewar rebellions be remembered in this new era? L'Ouverture, Vesey, Turner, Cinque, Brown, and countless others had provided poignant inspiration to millions of enslaved people of color, while inspiring dread in millions of whites. How would African Americans incorporate the heritage of heroism into their new status as citizens?

In his 1903 work *The Souls of Black Folk*, W. E. B. Du Bois described "two classes of colored Americans." He described one class as "spiritually descended from Toussaint the Savior, through Gabriel, Vesey, and Turner." Yet, he noted that this group was limited in its goals because "they hate the white South blindly and distrust the white race generally."[70] Could the spiritual descendants of these rebel leaders create a space for themselves in American culture, and how would stage images of African American rebels shift once black authors assumed greater control of the narrative?

The spectacles of racial violence that played out across the United States in the wake of the war were no less horrifying than the ones that had plagued the nation during more than two centuries of slavery. Yet they had a different dynamic, based on the power shifts that had taken place during the war. Change had begun when black soldiers started enlisting in the Union army. While many whites (Southern and Northern alike) feared the consequences of arming free blacks and Southern slaves willing to join Northern forces, others marveled, "Nobody knows anything about these men who has not seen them in battle ... There is a fierce energy about them beyond anything of which I have ever read."[71] After the legal end of slavery and the close of the war, those whites struggling to subordinate blacks would have to devise new measures to intimidate and persecute them. Some white Southerners continued old patterns of negotiation combined with intimidation that they had used before the war. While they no longer retained legal rights over their former slaves, they created more laws to control black behavior (with voting and property rights).[72] Others turned to violence: the birth of the Klan in 1865 ignited new waves of terrorist activities directed against blacks seen as demanding too many rights or presuming equality with whites. Many white Northerners found themselves confused in the aftermath of the war. The failure of Reconstruction left the Union with a decimated and angry population in the South, and with thousands of newly freed slaves pouring into Northern cities seeking jobs and new opportunities. Moreover, many Northern whites now had to cope with both new economic pressures and a black population eager to assert its rights (including desegregated schools and streetcars, and the right to vote). Blacks were developing new forms of resistance and rebellion. Whereas they had once been forced to operate outside the law to win their freedoms, they now embraced their role as citizens working *within* the American legal framework.

For example, on March 25, 1871, a group of African American citizens in Frankfort, Kentucky presented a petition to the state senate, praying for the state's intervention in escalating Klan attacks. The petition included a list of 116 incidents going back to 1867, ranging from the burning of black schools to public whippings of black citizens to numerous murders and lynchings.[73] Twenty-eight years after the Kentucky residents had submitted this petition, violence against blacks continued unabated. Harvey Young describes the lynching of Kentucky citizen Richard Coleman – a spectacle witnessed by thousands of white men, women, and children, who, after Coleman's death, carried away parts of his body and his teeth as souvenirs of the occasion.[74] Sixty years before Coleman's murder, many white Americans might have been able simultaneously to "embody and erase" the threat of blackness through stage spectacles such as Forrest's Spartacus, seeing Spartacus's rebellion as a metaphor for their own struggles for freedom. By the turn of the twentieth century, that ability to interpret blackness in a metaphorical way seemed to have vanished, obliterated by the need literally to "erase" the flesh of black victims.

On October 26, 1881, Steele MacKaye premiered his adaptation of Albion Tourgée's successful novel *A Fool's Errand* at Philadelphia's Arch Street Theatre. The play presents Klan characters, a black patriarchal leader, and a series of romantic partnerships that offer the keys to reconciling quarreling factions. The text offers a fascinating glimpse into how Klan violence was being constructed and interpreted in white American culture. One Klan member, Burleson, describes the "compact" that he and his compatriots made with the Klan: "When we made our compact with the Klan – its sole purpose was to frighten niggers from the polls, and so prevent nigger rule in the South. But the scum of our state have crept into our ranks, prostituting its power to murder for mere personal revenge!"[75] Burleson regards the violent intimidation of blacks as a perfectly acceptable justification for the Klan. Indeed, in one scene he threatens the community's black patriarch, Uncle Jerry Hunt:

> BURLESON: If you wish to keep your people out of trouble, teach them to keep their places and have civil tongues in their heads.
> JERRY: Sartin Massa sartin. Dats what I tries ter do.
> BURLESON: You niggers are getting too infernally free.
> JERRY: De Lo'd has made us free Massa!
> BURLESON: You mean the Yanks have made you free to work and take care for yourselves – but not to lie around and loaf and brag as if you were the equals of white folks! ... Look here Uncle, you've been tryin' to spoil my niggers lately – enticing them off to school as you call it. This won't do – Don't try it again – dy'e hear?
> JERRY: Massa Burleson, I hears – but all de same I'se boun' ter do it. I means ter lead my peple out ob de darkness fo' de glory ob de Lo'd!

BURLESON: Oh, hang your cant. If you don't leave my niggers alone I'll make you!

JERRY: Yo' can't do dat. Nuffin ull eber stop ole Jerry from a' doin' his dooty to his peple sah! *(Raises cane solemnly)* An' yo'd better take ca'r Massa Burleson, an' not stan' in de way ob de Lo'd. Mind yer – He's de Lo'd Almighty an' 'll grind yer ter powdah ef yo' do![76]

Intriguingly, critics focused less on the play's controversial racial sentiments and more on what one reviewer described as the "best scene in the piece," which was a "song and dance by a party of negroes, most of them genuine colored children." The review fails to mention that this song takes place just before the Klan launches an attack.[77] MacKaye's version also omits the lynching of Uncle Jerry. Tourgée writes that Uncle Jerry

> forgot his accustomed prudence, and moved by a very unreasonable anger at the impotence of the law, which could not punish those who could not be clearly identified, he openly and boldly declared the monstrous doctrine that the colored people ought to defend themselves and each other. That he should entertain such ideas was in itself a misfortune; that he should give expression to such incendiary notions was a fatal error.[78]

As Tourgée observes, Uncle Jerry is not killed for any violent *action* he takes. He is lynched merely for stating that violence was a legitimate option in the war against racial oppression. By excising Uncle Jerry's murder and inserting jubilees and dancing children, MacKaye's production downplayed the serious threat facing post-Civil War black Americans who became too visible for their own good.

Another incident in 1900 New York points to the constant danger that menaced blacks who became too visible in white culture. Errol Hill and James Hatch describe a race riot that erupted at the funeral of a white police officer stabbed by a black man when the black man tried to stop the officer from harassing his wife. During the course of the riot, enraged whites attacked blacks on the streets, and at one point began yelling to get several black performers (including Williams and Walker) then appearing in New York theatres. The actors barely escaped with their lives. The episode is telling not only for what it reveals about the lunatic level of racial violence sweeping the nation, but for what it suggests about how the role of rebel had been reconstituted in black culture. Simply by appearing on the public stage, Walker, Williams, Hogan, Cole, and Johnson were defying white rules for black conduct.[79]

With some white Americans bent on the destruction of any black efforts at self-improvement, how could African Americans effectively stage their resistance? Would appearing onstage be enough, or could they take things further?

As Errol Hill, James Hatch, David Krasner, and other outstanding scholars of African American theatre have chronicled, the end of the nineteenth century and the beginning of the twentieth transformed the ways in which African Americans represented themselves in American drama and popular culture. Whether they presented subversive revolutionaries, as in the hit musical *In Dahomey* (1902), *Abyssinia* (1906), or *Bandana Land* (1907), or serious pageants such as Du Bois's *The Star of Ethiopia* (1913), they enacted a kind of performative historiography that reclaimed black rebels from "the exaggeration, distortion, and censorship" with which white historians had continually surrounded them.[80] This is not to suggest that these plays were intended to represent an objective "truth," but rather that they shifted ownership of the history. Black playwrights frequently invoked black revolutionary history as an inspiration for moral strength and courage.[81] For example, *The Star of Ethiopia* presents L'Ouverture and Turner as part of the same legacy of rebellion; beating tom-toms and singing mark their appearances. The play closes with a crowd of children– a new generation – emerging onstage to claim the legacy of Benezet, L'Ouverture, Walker, Turner, Garrison, Douglass, Truth, Brown, Lincoln, and all those who fought for African American freedom.[82] As the Washington newspaper *The Bee* commented, the play "combined historic accuracy and symbolic truth."[83]

In 1919, *The Crisis* published an essay marking the 300th anniversary of the arrival of African slaves on North American shores. The author asked his readers: "Why must we remember? Is this but a counsel of Vengeance and Hate? God forbid. We must remember because if once the world forgets evil, evil is reborn."[84] With the coming of the Harlem Renaissance, black dramatists rushed to reclaim the heroes of the past. Many playwrights and artists called on black revolutionary history in the first decade of the twentieth century: Clarence Muse's silent film, *Toussaint L'Ouverture* (1921);[85] Katherine Tillman's *The Spirit of Allen* (1922); Randolph Edmonds's *Denmark Vesey* (1929); Ronald Gow's *John Brown* (1934); Randolph Edmonds's *Nat Turner* (1935); May Miller's *Harriet Tubman* (1935); Georgia Douglas Johnson's *Frederick Douglass* (1935); Langston Hughes's *Emperor of Haiti* (1936); Theodore Ward's *Even the Dead Arise* (1938); Gus Edwards's *Frederick Douglass* (1938); and Owen Vincent Dodson's *Amistad* (1939).[86]

While it may seem odd to end the chapter with a list in lieu of a final argument, perhaps no other form is more appropriate for this topic than a ritual calling-forth of the ancestors who stirred, inspired, and guided generations of black Americans to freedom. The theatrical transformation of black rebels – from the ghosts that taunted white audiences to the spirits that shaped a newly freed people – was a troubled process that spanned more than two centuries. During that time, the stage helped to fuel debates on black citizenship while helping the nation come to terms with slavery's violent past and fearful legacy.

NOTES

1 The heading refers to Thomas Jefferson, who once likened the problem of leaving slavery an unresolved issue in American society to trying to hold a wolf by the ears.

2 Kenneth S. Greenberg (ed.), *Nat Turner: A Slave Rebellion in History and Memory* (New York: Oxford University Press, 2003); *Richmond Enquirer*, September 2, 1831. New York's *Watch-Tower* republished a letter from North Carolina, printed in a Norfolk, Virginia newspaper, claiming that, "The negroes have risen against the white people, and the whole country is in an uproar. We have to keep guard night and day. We have had no battle yet, but it is expected every hour." *The Watch-Tower*, September 5, 1831.

3 *Ithaca Journal and General Advertiser*, September 7, 1831.

4 Greenberg, *Nat Turner*, xiii. Greenberg is describing the theory propounded by Herbert Aptheker in what would become his landmark 1963 study, *American Negro Slave Revolts*. As Greenberg notes, Aptheker shifted the discourse on slave rebellions away from the theory that they were aberrant occurrences in antebellum culture.

5 Indeed, the *Richmond Enquirer* suggested that the key to preventing future uprisings was a combination of "humane and just treatment" by owners, a "rigid enforcement of the laws" governing slaves, and a constant exhibition of "a military force always prepared for prompt action." *Richmond Enquirer*, September 30, 1831.

6 Roger D. Abrahams has described slaves' subversive performance rituals in his *Singing the Master: The Emergence of African American Culture in the Plantation South* (New York: Pantheon Books, 1992).

7 Greenberg, *Nat Turner*, xiv.

8 Herbert Aptheker, *American Negro Slave Revolts* (New York: International, 1963), 150.

9 Jill Lepore, *New York Burning: Liberty, Slavery, and Conspiracy in Eighteenth-Century Manhattan* (New York: Alfred A. Knopf, 2005). Lepore invokes *The Beaux' Stratagem* as her dramatic model, although numerous other Restoration and early-eighteenth-century tragedies and comedies revolve around intricate disguises and efforts to hoodwink or overthrow authority figures.

10 Lepore, *New York Burning*, 158–9.

11 *Ibid.*, 159–60; Dale Cockrell, *Demons of Disorder: Early Blackface Minstrels and Their World* (New York: Cambridge University Press, 1997), 37–9.

12 *Ibid.*, 38.

13 For example, Philadelphia's *American Weekly Mercury* reported on December 2, 1736 that, "We are informed from Antigua that the Negroes there are largely combin'd to rise and destroy the White people ... The design was, on a Ball Night ... to have blown up the Ball House ... and at the same time, four companies

of Negroes, consisting for 400 each ... were to have entered the Town with Cutlasses, &c."

14 Lepore, *New York Burning*, 159–60; Michael A. Gomez, *Exchanging Our Country's Marks: The Transformation of African Identities in the Colonial and Antebellum South* (Chapel Hill: University of North Carolina Press, 1998), 136. Gomez notes that the Stono Rebellion had a substantial impact on slavery in South Carolina. It temporarily reduced the slave trade, but ultimately, as the need for slave labor grew, the memory of the uprising encouraged traders to capture slaves from different regions of Africa than those where the rebels had originated.

15 For example, one report of the Turner uprising, reprinted in the *Newburyport Herald* of Massachusetts, claimed that three whites had been complicit in the plot, along with the slaves. See *Newburyport Herald*, September 2, 1831. A white man planned the Boxley plot in 1815, and whites were often named or investigated in pre-Civil War plots. This pattern persisted well into the twentieth century, as opponents to the Civil Rights Movement attacked the "outside agitators" who were supposedly encouraging peaceful Southern blacks to protest white oppression.

16 *New-York Gazette; or, The Weekly Post-Boy*, December 12, 1751. Also see Hugh F. Rankin, *The Theater in Colonial America* (Chapel Hill: University of North Carolina Press, 1965), 33–6.

17 For examples, see the *Pennsylvania Gazette*, June 29, 1758 for the first listing of a ship called *Othello* (the ship's name appears ten additional times in various colonial newspapers up until 1776). Articles about a horse named Othello appear beginning on April 17, 1766 in the *Pennsylvania Gazette*, and continue up until 1776. Sixty articles and advertisements for the horse and his descendants appear in papers from Pennsylvania to Rhode Island. For the 103 articles that mention the name "Othello" published in American newspapers between 1700 and 1776, see *Infoweb Newsbank*, http://infoweb.newsbank.com (last accessed June 25, 2011).

18 *Cato* was so popular that masters often borrowed names from the play for their slaves (such as Cato, Utica, and Juba). Peter Reed argues that Juba became part of white Atlantic culture's depiction of "classical blackness" (see the discussion of *The Gladiator*, below, pp. 39–41).

19 Heather S. Nathans, *Slavery and Sentiment on the American Stage, 1787–1861: Lifting the Veil of Black* (Cambridge; New York: Cambridge University Press, 2009), 6.

20 John Murdock, *The Triumphs of Love; or, Happy Reconciliations* (Philadelphia: R. Folwell, 1794). The play received one performance on the Philadelphia stage in 1795. See Nathans, *Slavery and Sentiment*, 43–8.

21 William Dunlap, *A History of the American Theatre from Its Origins to 1832*, ed. Tice L. Miller (Urbana: University of Illinois Press, 2005), 261.

22 *Monthly Magazine and American Review*, April, 1799.

23 August von Kotzebue, *The Negro Slaves*, translated from the German (London: T. Cadell, Jr. and W. Davies, 1796).

24 J. Horatio Nichols, *The Essex Junto; or, Quixotic Guardian* (Salem, MA: Coverley, 1802).

25 *Ibid.* Also see Michelle Granshaw, "General Creole: Jon H. Nichols's Political Plays in the Early American Republic," *New England Theatre Journal*, 21 (2010): 3–23.

26 William Crafts, Jr., *The Sea Serpent; or, The Gloucester Hoax*, http://gateway.proquest.com.proxy-um.researchport.umd.edu/openurl/openurl?ctx_ver=Z39.88-2003&xri:pqil:res_ver=0.2&res_id=xri:ilcs-us&rft_id=xri:ilcs:ft:amdram:Z000614207:0 (last accessed June 4, 2011). Also see William Stanley Hoole, *The Antebellum Charleston Theatre* (Tuscaloosa: University of Alabama Press, 1946), 18–19.

27 A free black supposedly led this uprising from St. Domingo.

28 For accounts of these uprisings and *hundreds* of other incidents of slave rebellions during the antebellum period, see Aptheker, *American Negro Slave Revolts.*

29 *Ibid.*, 223. In some cases, white audiences borrowed narratives and characters from the stage to define their experience with rebellious slaves. This was the case in Wake County, North Carolina, where citizens were menaced throughout much of 1819 by a gang of maroons, one of whom became known as "Abaellino," from the popular drama *Abaellino, The Great Bandit.*

30 Robert Montgomery Bird, *The Gladiator*, in *Early American Drama*, ed. Jeffrey H. Richards (New York: Penguin, 1997), 198.

31 Tice L. Miller, *Entertaining the Nation: American Drama in the Eighteenth and Nineteenth Centuries* (Carbondale: Southern Illinois University Press, 2007), 70–1.

32 Quoted in *ibid.*, 70.

33 Quoted in Nathans, *Slavery and Sentiment*, 71.

34 Peter P. Reed, *Rogue Performances: Staging the Underclasses in Early American Theatre Culture* (New York: Palgrave, 2009), 162.

35 *Ibid.*, 152.

36 *Ibid.*, 163.

37 *Spectator*, quoted in Marvin Edward McAllister, *White People Do Not Know How to Behave at Entertainments Designed for Ladies & Gentlemen of Color: William Brown's African and American Theater* (Chapel Hill: University of North Carolina Press, 2003), 50.

38 McAllister, *White People Do Not Know How to Behave*, 50. McAllister notes that Brown's company also produced Kotzebue's *Pizarro*, which tells of an Indian rebellion against Spanish invaders.

39 Bernth Lindfors, "'Nothing Extenuate, nor Set Down Aught in Malice': New Biographical Information on Ira Aldridge," *African American Review*, 28.3 (Fall, 1994): 457–72.

40 The Haytian Retreat opened in 1829. The scant records of its existence have been thoroughly and expertly canvassed by Naomi Stubbs, "The Pleasure Gardens of Antebellum America and the Performance of American Identities," Ph.D. dissertation (Graduate Center, CUNY, 2011).

41 New York's Haytian Retreat was far from the only example of this name being used by black communities throughout the United States in the nineteenth century. Cities as large as Boston and towns as small as Rockville, Maryland boasted small "Haytis" in the years before the Civil War.

42 This high-profile case eventually involved former President John Quincy Adams, as well as a host of prominent abolitionists. It dragged on for more than two years until the captives of the *Amistad* were eventually returned to Africa.

43 *New Hampshire Sentinel*, September 4, 1839.

44 Not surprisingly, some Southern newspapers regarded this glorification of the *Amistad* story with disfavor. For example, see the various articles on the *Amistad* case and the staging of the rebellion in Charleston's *Southern Patriot*, September, 1839.

45 *The Colored American*, September 28, 1839, quoted in Nathans, *Slavery and Sentiment*, 188.

46 Joseph N. Ireland, *Records of the New York Stage from 1750 to 1860*, 2 vols. (New York: Benjamin Blom, 1966 [1866]), Vol. II, 324.

47 To date I have not been able to locate any reviews of the production of *Christophe, King of Hayti* (or of any similarly titled productions of the play during this period).

48 George C. D. Odell, *Annals of the New York Stage*, 15 vols. (New York: Columbia University Press, 1927–49), Vol. IV, 622. Haiti received substantial news attention in 1842 for a massive earthquake that shook Cape Hayti (also known as Cape François).

49 Philadelphia's Arch Street Theatre presented a play by T. D. English entitled *The Empire of Hayti; or, Kingcraft in 1852* on October 2, 1849. I have not been able to locate a script for this production, though it is listed as a farce. See Arthur Herman Wilson, *A History of the Philadelphia Theatre, 1835–1855* (New York: Greenwood Press, 1968).

50 Elizabeth Stryker Ricord, *Zamba; or, The Insurrection* (Cambridge: John Owen, 1842).

51 "Notes of Life in Hayti: Number Eight. The Ill-Fated City," *The Knickerbocker; or, New York Monthly Magazine*, August 1, 1842, 153, available online at www.proquest.com/docview/137120618?accountid=14696 (last accessed May 1, 2011).

52 Geneviève Fabre, "African American Commemorative Celebrations," in *History and Memory in African American Culture*, ed. Geneviève Fabre and Robert O'Meally (New York: Oxford University Press, 1994), 86–7.

53 It should also be noted that throughout the 1830s and 1840s, black presence in Election Day celebrations and other liberty or temperance activities continued to escalate. Thus white urban Americans in the North would also have seen blacks parading in the streets, playing music, or wearing costumes that might have seemed equally as disturbing as the images depicting slave uprisings.

54 See the description of Zamba's actions in Zoe Detsi-Diamanti, *Early American Women Dramatists, 1775–1860* (New York: Garland, 1998), 205.

55 For a more complete discussion of *The Slave*, see Nathans, *Slavery and Sentiment*, 171–5. The year 1847 brought another play set in Haiti: *The New World*, by Harriet Fanning Read of Jamaica, Massachusetts. Read was a playwright and performer on the Boston stage. *The New World* brings together Native Americans, slaves, and Spaniards in a civil conflict. It seems to lack the same kind of overt anti-slavery message as Ricord's or Morton's plays boast.

56 Henry Highland Garnet, "An Address to the Slaves of the United States of America," included in William Wells Brown, *Clotel; or, The President's Daughter*, ed. Robert S. Levine (Boston: Bedford St. Martin's, 2000), 476.

57 *Ibid.*, 478–9.

58 *Ibid.*, 471.

59 Aiken's adaptation is one of the most enduring versions of Stowe's novel (though she never sanctioned it). Other widely circulated versions of the story altered it substantially, including some retellings that allowed Uncle Tom to live, or that reframed the George and Eliza plot and George's threat to kill any slave catchers who tried to pursue him. For more on these numerous adaptations see Sarah Meer, *Uncle Tom Mania: Slavery, Minstrelsy, and Transatlantic Culture in the 1850s* (Athens: University of Georgia Press, 2005).

60 George L. Aiken, *Uncle Tom's Cabin*, in *Early American Drama*, ed. Jeffrey H. Richards (New York: Penguin, 1997), 376, 404.

61 *Ibid.*, 428.

62 H. J. Conway, *Dred: A Tale of the Dismal Swamp* (New York: John Amerman, 1856), 12.

63 On February 4, 1860, the Cincinnati *Daily Atheneum* announced the following performance at Wood's Theatre: "Last Night of the New play called Toussaint L'Ouverture, or the Insurrection of Hayti," on a double bill with *A Glance at New York*. The Toussaint play was advertised as featuring "Negroes, Plantation slaves, Dancers, Musicians, Negro Soldiers, Women, Children, &c, &c." The newspaper noted that the play depicted the:

> wondrous incidents and thrilling history of the greatest of all Africans known to history ... Toussaint was a native African son of one of the kings; some say that he was born in Africa, others that he was brought to St. Domingo in infancy ... He took no part whatever in inciting the insurrection, but immediately upon the rising of the blacks, and the general carnage that ensued, he felt himself to be the only man able to direct and control the people, and by his wondrous talents he became the head and front of the movement.

Two days after the play's closing, the Cincinnati *Enquirer* observed that the piece had:

> generated nothing but a black, ominous cloud of empty benches ... The author probably expected that in these days of negro worship, the mere name of a negro rebel would draw, without the ... aid of dramatic and literary merit ... We felt no little sympathy for the handsome Road, whose admiration for female beauty is well known ... when we saw him forced to look with sympathetic eye on faces whose charms were veiled with a coating of calcined cork.

The play was attributed to Cincinnati native and actor Joshua Silsbee. The material on this production appears in James Francis Dunlap, "Queen City Stages: Professional Dramatic Activity in Cincinnati, 1837–1861," Ph.D. dissertation (Ohio State University, 1954), 1703. This dissertation is in eight volumes and is over 2,000 pages long. It contains a daybook for all the playbills of the Cincinnati theatres.

64 *New York Herald*, October 29, 1859.

65 *Ibid.*, November 3, 1859.

66 *The Sun*, November 3, 1859.

67 For more on Brown's performance of blackness see John Stauffer, *The Black Hearts of Men: Radical Abolitionists and the Transformation of Race* (Cambridge, MA: Harvard University Press, 2002).

68 Benjamin Edward Woolf, *Off to the War!* (Boston: William V. Spencer, 1861), 2, 6.

69 John Ernest, *Liberation Historiography: African American Writers and the Challenge of History, 1794–1861* (Chapel Hill: University of North Carolina Press, 2004), 342.

70 W. E. B. Du Bois, *The Souls of Black Folk*, in *Crossing the Danger Water: Three Hundred Years of African-American Writing*, ed. Deirdre Mullane (New York: Doubleday, 1993), 377.

71 Leon F. Litwack, *Been in the Storm So Long: The Aftermath of Slavery* (New York: Vintage Books, 1980), 69. It is important to note that some white dramatists after the Civil War represented black soldiers as being afraid to fight. See Laura Downing's 1894 *Defending the Flag* and the discussion of the play in Leo Hamalian and James Vernon Hatch, *The Roots of African American Drama* (Detroit: Wayne State University Press, 1991), 21–2.

72 *Ibid.*, 223–447.

73 "Petition from Kentucky Citizens on Ku Klux Klan Violence," in Mullane, *Crossing the Danger Water*, 318–23. The withdrawal of Union troops from the South in 1876 left Southern blacks even more vulnerable to attacks.

74 Harvey Young, *Embodying Black Experience: Stillness, Critical Memory, and the Black Body* (Ann Arbor: University of Michigan Press, 2009), 167–8.

75 Steele MacKaye, *A Fool's Errand* (1881), available online at http://gateway.proquest.com.proxy-um.researchport.umd.edu/openurl/openurl?ctx_ver=Z39.88–2003&xri:pqil:res_ver=0.2&res_id=xri:ilcs-us&rft_id=xri:ilcs:ft:amdram:Z000781486:0 (last accessed May 1, 2011).

76 *Ibid.*

77 *Philadelphia Inquirer*, October 27, 1881.

78 Cited in Jeffrey W. Miller, "Redemption through Violence: White Mobs and Black Citizenship in Albion Tourgée's *A Fool's Errand*," *The Southern Literary Journal*, 35.1 (2002): 23.

79 Hill and Hatch, *A History of African American Theatre*, 187.

80 Aptheker, *American Negro Slave Revolts*, 150.

81 Some of the early-twentieth-century plays included William Easton's *Christophe* (1914), and Alice Dunbar-Nelson's *Mine Eyes Have Seen* (1918).

82 W. E. B. Du Bois, *Star of Ethiopia* (Episodes 5 and 6), available online at http://gateway.proquest.com.proxy-um.researchport.umd.edu/openurl/openurl?ctx_ver=Z39.88–2003&xri:pqil:res_ver=0.2&res_id=xri:ilcs-us&rft_id=xri:ilcs:ft:amdram:Z000781422:0 (last accessed May 1, 2011).

83 *The Bee*, September 18, 1915.

84 "Three Hundred Years", *The Crisis*, 00 (August, 1919); excerpted in Mullane, *Crossing the Danger Water*, 466.

85 Cedric J. Robinson, *Forgeries of Memory and Meaning: Blacks and the Regimes of Race in American Theater and Film before World War II* (Chapel Hill:

University of North Carolina Press, 2007), 233. Note that Robinson questions whether the film was ever released.

86 See Errol Hill, "The Revolutionary Tradition in Black Drama," *Theatre Journal*, 38.4 (December, 1986): 408–26; Errol Hill (ed.), *Black Heroes: Seven Plays* (New York: Applause Theatre, 1989).

3

MONICA WHITE NDOUNOU

Early black Americans on Broadway

You put me in *Macbeth* and *Carmen Jones*
And all kinds of *Swing Mikados*
And in everything but what's about me—
But someday somebody'll
Stand up and talk about me.
And write about me—
Black and beautiful—
And sing about me.
And put on plays about me!
I reckon it'll be
Me Myself!
Yes, it'll be me.

Langston Hughes,
"Note on Commercial Theatre" (1940)[1]

Toward the end of the twentieth century, several black theatre artists with Broadway experience articulated conflicting views of "the Great White Way." In 1972, Woodie King, Jr. and Ron Milner jointly declared, "Broadway ... is a contented fat white cow. If you slip in and milk her for a minute – well, then more black power to you, brother ... it's a weird price she's asking. She wants you to be a singing hyena, dancing on the graves of yourself and everyone you know."[2] A decade later, Lloyd Richards, the first black director on Broadway (*A Raisin in the Sun*, 1959), observed that "[Broadway] still has the connotation of Mecca. Who doesn't want to go to Mecca?"[3] Over the past 200 years, countless black American artists have contributed to the development of American theatre in direct and indirect ways. Those with a Broadway pedigree tend to be more readily remembered than those who also have had a major influence on theatre even in their absence or exclusion from Broadway.

The following analysis considers the presence of early black American artists who paved the path and opened the doors to Broadway for future African Americans. Performers like George W. Walker (1873–1911); his partner,

Bert A. Williams (1874–1922); and the prominent Harlem Renaissance poet and Broadway playwright, Langston Hughes (1902–67) were conscious of the limited and often subservient representations of black folk in the theatre. These artists actively challenged what Miles M. Jefferson refers to as the "Eternal Menial" in the migration of their work from the theatrical margins to Broadway.[4]

Walker's "The Real 'Coon' on the American Stage,"[5] Williams's "The Comic Side of Trouble,"[6] and Hughes's "A Note on the Commercial Theatre" express concerns regarding the limitations and possibilities of black cultural representation on the American stage. Each recognizes and challenges the "darky" image circulated via the minstrel show in its three-part structure (*Part I* – series of songs, jokes, and dances by performers in blackface seated in a semi-circle onstage with interlocutor at the center and two "end men" named for their instruments: Tambo [tambourine] and Bones [dried animal bones]; *Part II/The Olio* – a variety of specialty acts, comic skits, and monologues; and *Part III/The Afterpiece* – the entire company performs a short farce, Shakespearean burlesque, political lampoon, or comic parody of a contemporary fad or high cultural event performed with full costume and exaggerated style).[7] Their necessary interventions challenged existing forms and characterizations on Broadway, creating both new possibilities onstage and in the consciousness of audiences and future artists.

The first black Americans on Broadway arrived at the turn of the twentieth century. Studies by David Krasner, Camille Forbes, Gerald Bordman, Hugh F. Rankin, Bernard L. Peterson, Jr., and Henry T. Sampson, among others, identify numerous talented black American nineteenth-century performers, including Walker and Williams, who became the first black Americans on Broadway when they premiered in Victor Herbert's *The Gold Bug* (1896).[8] The predominantly white-cast, three-act, musical farce proceeded *In Dahomey* (1902), the first full-length musical written and played by blacks to be performed at a major Broadway theatre.[9]

Musical and comic representations of black Americans continued to dominate the Broadway stage, from *The Gold Bug* to *The Shoo-Fly Regiment* (1907), *The Red Moon* (1909), *Androcles and the Lion* (1915), and the Ziegfeld Follies, which featured Bert Williams from 1909 to 1919. White American playwright Eugene O'Neill's *The Emperor Jones* (1920) was the first non-musical play featuring a black lead character on Broadway.[10] O'Neill's subject matter – a black American man who becomes the leader of black natives on an island – had received prior comic treatment by Williams in *Mr. Lode of Koal* (1909). Hughes would later parody O'Neill's production in *The Em-Fuehrer Jones* (1920).[11] The first wave of black American playwrights (including Garland Anderson, Frank Wilson, Wallace Thurman,

Hall Johnson, Langston Hughes, and Hughes Allison) did not arrive on Broadway until the 1920s and 1930s.[12] These black American theatre artists understood the historical constructions of blackness, and challenged them with varying degrees of success.

An examination of the work and careers of Walker, Williams, and Hughes reveals that to "make it to Mecca" during this period was to access an aspect of the American Dream denied early black Americans in society and the entertainment industry. Following a brief overview of early representations of "blackness" on the American stage through the mid twentieth century, I identify the relevant themes, dramatic structures, characterizations, and intertextual references that indicate an increasingly progressive transformation of black representation on Broadway initiated by Williams and Walker and carried on by Langston Hughes. I begin with *In Dahomey*, *Abyssinia* (1906), and *Bandana Land* (1907), and then conclude with Langston Hughes's *Mulatto: A Tragedy of the Deep South* (1935),[13] *The Barrier* (1950),[14] and *Simply Heavenly* (1957).[15] Collectively, these creative works expose the limitations of black theatrical development on the Great White Way in the years preceding the 1959 Broadway premiere of Lorraine Hansberry's *A Raisin in the Sun*, which would symbolize the coming of a new era but not necessarily the end of an old one.

New York City's reputation as the place to see theatre grew in the eighteenth century, beginning around the 1750s. The move to midtown, the iconic space currently known as Broadway, would not occur until approximately 1850.[16] During this 100-year period, plays by William Shakespeare (especially in the 1750s and 1860s), ballad operas, and ballad farces were performed in venues like Mr. and Mrs. Lewis Hallam's New Theatre in Nassau Street near Wall Street.[17] Gradually, theatre moved uptown. Union Square became the heart of Broadway by the 1870s. The first black Americans began to appear in Broadway productions when theatres emerged in Times Square in the 1900s and, later, consolidated in the 1920s and 1930s. Upon arrival, they found themselves competing with depictions of blackness by white actors portraying Negro comic characters. Characterizations of the "Negro" in these plays reinforced stereotypes of a clownish, lazy, ignorant, and worthless subhuman group. Examples include the pseudonymous Andrew Barton's *The Disappointment* (1767), the first professionally produced American play with a Negro comic character,[18] and white actor Lewis Hallam in the role of Mungo, a black caricature of a servant from the West Indies, in a New York production of Isaac Bickerstaffe's *The Padlock* (1769).[19] The minstrel tradition emerged in the 1820s, gained popularity in the 1830s, and continued well into the early twentieth century as vaudeville increased in popularity. [20] According to Camille Forbes, blacks became "the principal comic character[s]" in the 1880s and 1890s, despite the prevalence of a variety of other ethnic stereotypes. [21]

In 1816, the first black performers had not yet appeared on Broadway but were notably present in New York City, where they established the first black theatre company, and later its resident theatre (the African Company and the African Grove Theatre) in 1821. [22] They gained significant recognition for their productions of Shakespearean texts at the time. Historically the burnt-cork artists and blackface minstrel performers overshadow the contributions to American theatre by performers like James Hewlett (1778–1836), the lead actor of the company. He openly challenged white comedian Charles Mathews when he satirized the African Company's Shakespearean performances and mocked their blackness in one of his comic routines. [23] The most famous black Shakespearean of the era, Ira Aldridge (1807–67), became an involuntary exile, and "traveled farther, was seen by more people in more nations and won a greater number of prestigious honors, decorations and awards than any other actor in the nineteenth century." [24] He played a variety of roles on the British stage where he also endured racist responses by audiences and critics owing to ongoing debates about the abolition of slavery. [25]

Building on the legacy of these early nineteenth-century performers – albeit within the context of minstrelsy and vaudeville – Walker and Williams paved the way for black playwrights and performers who accomplished significant Broadway milestones in the 1920s through the 1940s. Willis Richardson's one-act play *The Chip Woman's Fortune* (1923) is the first drama by a black American on Broadway, while Garland Anderson's *Appearances* (1925) is the first full-length drama by a black American to appear on Broadway. Frank Wilson, known for playing the title role in *Porgy* by Dorothy and DuBose Heyward (1927), opened *Meek Mose* on Broadway in 1928, the year before Wallace Thurman coauthored *Harlem* (1929) with white writer William J. Rapp. The 1930s saw the Broadway production of the following plays by black playwrights: Hall Johnson's *Run, Little Chillun* (1933), Langston Hughes's *Mulatto*, and Hughes Allison's *The Trial of Dr. Beck* (1937). However, in the following decade, significant black employment on Broadway happened only in shows with all-black casts: *Carmen Jones* (1943); *St. Louis Woman* (1946); and *Anna Lucasta* (1944), which ran for nearly 1,000 performances. [26] The select few who made it to Broadway were still in the uncomfortable position of having their plays and performances critiqued by white critics whose standard for measuring their effectiveness privileged familiar, stereotypical constructions of blackness.

Williams and Walker

Williams and Walker developed strategies to revise, reinvent, and eradicate the evolving "darky" image by perfecting a formula for Broadway production that incorporated black cultural sensibilities. Born in Lawrence, Kansas in 1873, George W. Walker was a child performer in a company of colored minstrels in his hometown before he began his transition from minstrel man to manager and performer of one of the most prolific black American duos in the history of American theatre. Walker moved from Lawrence to San Francisco in "easy stages," traveling from town to town, giving shows on the back of wagons for "quack doctors" attempting to gain an audience for the presentation of their medicinal products. Walker's strengths as an early performer included storytelling, singing, dancing, face-making, beating the tambourine, and rattling the bones. Through these experiences, Walker observed, "white people are always interested in what they call 'darky' singing and dancing, and the fact that I could entertain in that way as no white boy could, made me valuable."[27] His simultaneous recognition of the value of his blackness and his skills (along with the unique acting style of Williams) contributed to the success of the duo.

Bert A. Williams was born in 1874 in Nassau, Bahamas to a Danish father and a mother of Spanish and African ancestry. Leaving the West Indies as a child, his family migrated to Panama and eventually San Pedro, California. Unlike Walker, whose ambition toward entertainment began in childhood, Williams's primary goals were to pursue an education, more specifically in engineering at Stanford University. As a young adult, Williams and three white boys started a touring show through small towns on the West Coast, trying to earn easy money. The failed expedition ended in San Francisco, where Williams eventually met Walker while looking for stage work. The experience of the failed tour taught Williams a great deal about entertainment and race prejudice.[28] The duo eventually became the first black Americans on Broadway in the short-lived production of *The Gold Bug* and the more successful *In Dahomey*. Along the way, they developed their own business and creative strategies that led to *Abyssinia* and *Bandana Land*, establishing a tradition of black Americans on Broadway.[29]

Williams and Walker carefully studied the craft, the industry, audience expectations, and human nature. They earned $7 per week on their first job, and experienced several ups and downs. They frequented performances, especially those by blackfaced, white performers, billing themselves as "coons." Walker explains, "Bert and I watched the white 'coons,' and were often amused at seeing white men with black cork on their faces trying to imitate black folks. Nothing about these white men's actions was natural, and therefore nothing was as interesting as if black performers had been dancing and singing their own songs in their own way."[30] These observations represent one of the first steps that inspired Walker and Williams's nuanced approach to popular entertainment.

Walker's early realization is also indicative of Walker and Williams's emerging theory and practice of black performance, which began as a reappropriation but evolved into an innovative approach to black representation. Walker explains, "We thought there seemed to be a great demand for black faces on the stage, we would do all we could to get what we felt belonged to us by the laws of nature. We finally decided that as white men with black faces were billing themselves as 'coons,' Williams and Walker would do well to bill themselves the 'Two Real Coons,'" thereby attracting the attention of managers and making their way into an entertainment industry plagued by racial and color prejudice and petty jealousies.[31] They moved from Los Angeles to Denver, Colorado and eventually to Chicago, where they performed in their first large black production, a musical farce called *The Octoroons* (1895). Although *The Octoroons* maintained the three-part structure of the minstrel show, it also revised the form by discarding the end men and adding a chorus line. The *Dramatic Mirror* called *The Octoroons* "a Gorgeous, Spectacular Opera Comique," with six female leads and a line-up of beautiful women who sang and performed in variety sketches, ending the show with a chorus-march finale.[32] Walker and Williams joined the show only to be fired because of negative audience reception to their act. Fortunately, they developed and maintained lasting friendships with others from the show, including but not limited to performers Bob Cole and Jesse Shipp, as well as Will Marion Cook, whom they would later work with on their Broadway shows. Their failure in this production led the duo to explore other options and possibilities for success, one of which included Williams's decision to blacken his face and sing a song.[33] The successful alteration had the double-edged effect of paving the way for black performers and entrepreneurs in American entertainment, while also reinforcing the very 'darky' stereotypes they were attempting to thwart.

According to Walker, New York was the logical next step for the duo. Following a good run at the Midway Theatre in San Francisco, they succeeded in getting booked east, finally landing in New York and the production of *The Gold Bug*. This story of racial intermixing told in two acts was one of Victor Herbert's few failures. Owing to various difficulties, opening night was postponed numerous times.[34] Williams and Walker were required to audition for producer George Lederer and others, in spite of the fact that they were invited to join the cast. The show only lasted for one week (September 21–6), and Williams and Walker were not even listed in the program.[35] The path to Broadway could only be accomplished through working with white artists, writers, producers, and directors with resources and access to the venues.[36]

The science of their success is well documented in their essays and embedded in their work. They created an incubator for black talent that was admittedly male-centered, including Will Marion Cook, Harry T. Burleigh, Bob Cole, Billy Johnson, Jesse A. Shipp, Will Accoo, and Paul Laurence Dunbar, among others.[37] Williams developed an often imitated yet unduplicated acting style that Walker also attributed to their success.[38] In reference to Williams in *Senegambian Carnival* (1898), one reviewer exclaims, "Bert Williams is one of the cleverest delineators of negro characters on the stage, and has no trouble at all keeping his audience in roars of laughter."[39] In an interview published in *Soil* in 1916, Williams described his process:

> I try to portray the darky, the shiftless darky, to the fullest extent, his fun, his philosophy. Show this shiftless darky a book and he won't know what it's about. He can't read or write. But ask him a question and he'll answer it with a philosophy that has something in it ... there is nothing about the fellow I *work* that I don't know. I have studied him, his joys and sorrows. *Contrast is vital.*[40]

He also distinguishes himself from the character he performs, noting that white audiences often fail to see the difference between the performer and the character owing to their monolithic notions of blackness. In "The Comic Side of Trouble," Williams elaborates on the problem, explaining that (white) Americans "know very little about the unconscious humor of colored people and negroes because they do not come in contact with them."[41] Williams's technique of emphasizing "vital contrast" complements Walker's larger goals. According to Walker, "the one hope of colored performers must be in making a radical departure from the old 'darky' style of singing and dancing,"[42] which the duo accomplished in several ways. The two most prominent methods include strategic collaboration and careful study of music, comedy, dance, performance, and varied audience expectations. *Senegambian Carnival*,[43] *A Lucky Coon* (1898–9), *The Policy Players* (1899–1900), *Sons of Ham* (1900–2), *In Dahomey, Abyssinia*, and *Bandana Land* document their attempts.

The first four productions revolve around low-comedic plot situations.[44] *Senegambian Carnival* was an all-black revue written by Paul Laurence Dunbar and Will Marion Cook. Afterwards, Williams and Walker toured with Cook's *Clorindy, the Origin of the Cakewalk* (1898), which incorporated scenes from *Senegambian Carnival*. Both shows failed commercially, but Williams and Walker were able to rework the material in their next two touring shows: *A Lucky Coon* and *The Policy Players*, both of which center on a lottery windfall. Their next show, *The Sons of Ham*, featured two dead-beats (Williams and Walker) attempting to con a dying old man into giving them his fortune by pretending to be his children who are expected to arrive from boarding school. The actual twins arrive, thereby exposing the impostors. The production played for a short run at the Grand Opera House in New York City after an extensive tour around the country.[45] It proved an excellent vehicle for showcasing Williams and Walker. Despite this early success, the intertextuality and use of language and dialect as a technical device in their final three productions are the most demonstrative of their impact on Broadway and black theatre.

Developed through the collaborative efforts of Williams, Walker, Shipp, Cook, and Dunbar, *In Dahomey: A Negro Musical Comedy* draws character names from minstrelsy, while combining low comedy, ethnic jokes, and references to current social and political events within its three-act structure.[46] Whereas white comics were able to access a range of ethnic stereotypes (i.e., Irish, Hebrew, and Dutch), black performers could only play variations of the "darky" and the Chinese.[47] *In Dahomey* features these constrained representations of ethnic identity, while building on models established in previous shows. The storyline follows two conmen from Boston who plan to colonize Dahomey with poor American blacks. Shylock Homestead (Williams) and Rareback Punkerton (Walker) fall on hard times and are sent to Florida to con Cicero Lightfoot, president of a colonization society. Initially thought to be impoverished, Shylock Homestead is discovered to be rich. Punkerton determines to become his trustee in order to gain access to Homestead's wealth. Upon accomplishing this task, Walker as Punkerton struts around as a dandy, a leading figure in black society. Once Homestead realizes he is being swindled, he refuses to continue to support Punkerton's schemes, and the show ends in an extravagant cakewalk.[48]

The politics of Broadway production and performance are evident in early responses to the show. *In Dahomey* was "the first African American show that synthesized successfully the various genres of American musical theatre popularized at the beginning of the twentieth century – minstrelsy, vaudeville, comic opera, and musical comedy."[49] The novel idea of an entirely African American Broadway musical was met with hostility, according to a *New York Times* report of a potential race war.[50] *In Dahomey* opened at the New York Theatre on February 18, 1903 without incident. The script documents the variety of black performance during the period, as many of the members of the cast performed their specialty acts within the context of the narrative.[51]

However problematic, Williams and Walker portrayed native Africans several years before they utilized African identity and conceptions of Africa in *Senegambian Carnival* (in name only), *In Dahomey*, and *Abyssinia* (with principal African characters and/or extras). In "The Real 'Coon'" Walker describes the encounter:

> In 1893, natives from Dahomey, Africa were imported to San Francisco to be exhibited at the Midwinter Fair. They were late in arriving in time for the opening of the fair, and Afro-Americans were employed and exhibited for native Dahomians. After the arrival of the native Africans, Afro-Americans were dismissed. Having free access to the Fair grounds, we were permitted to visit the natives from Africa. It was there, for the first time, that we were brought into close touch with the native Africans, and the study of those natives interested us very much. We were not long in deciding that if we ever reached the point of having a show of our own, we would delineate and feature native African characters as far as we could, and still remain American, and make our acting interesting and entertaining to American audiences.[52]

None of *In Dahomey*'s principal characters are African, but the script calls for "Colonists" and "Natives" to appear in Act III. Walker goes on to boast, "we were the first to introduce Americanized African songs: for instance 'my Zulu Babe,' 'My Castle on the Nile,' 'My Dahomian Queen.'"[53] He attributes the increased popularity of Williams and Walker specifically, and of the colored performer in general, directly to the infusion of African themes into American performance tradition – in other words, the Americanization of African themes and music by black performers.

Williams and Walker portrayed native Dahomians in the exhibit at the fair, but continued to portray variations of the American "darky" in *In Dahomey* and *Abyssinia*. One wonders how their initial study of the Dahomians may have influenced their portrayal of African characters in production. Music seems the strongest indicator of the revolutionizing influence of the encounter. The song "Broadway in the Jungle" incorporates African iconography in its vision of the Great White Way, but in a more subversive way than Williams and Walker may have been credited with in their lifetime. They speak not of bringing Dahomians to Broadway but instead of building a Broadway for colored people in Dahomey.[54] They sing:

> If we went to Dahomey. Suppose the King would say
> We want a Broadway built for us, we want it right away.

They call for a space in which blacks control production and performance. Stereotypical references to Africa throughout, however, detract from the revolutionary idea (for instance, using a crocodile or "crock-o-dial" on the face of the Broadway clock, getting gorillas to use as the police and a hippopotamus for Justice of the Peace, etc.).[55] They fail to improve African representation, but succeed in the use of dialect and other devices.[56]

While "darky"-type dialect is used to represent the status of the "New Negro" in the opening of Act I, songs like "My Dahomian Queen," which appears in Act III, utilize high language. This is still problematic in terms of equating upper class and whiteness as ideal, but serves the purpose of creating the vital contrast Williams finds necessary to unsettle monolithic notions of blackness. Hatch and Shine provide the following example, which is not included in the play text as published in their anthology, but may have been in the English score:

> Swing along chillun, swing along de lane,
> Lif' yo' head an' yo' heels mighty high.
> Swing along chillun, 'tain't a goin' to rain,
> Sun's as red as de rose, in de sky,
> Come along Mandy, come along Sue,
> White fo'ks awatchin' an' seein' what you'
> Do
> White fo'ks jealous when you'se walkin'
> Two by two.[57]

This dialect is reminiscent of the minstrel type that Walker critiqued. It stands in stark contrast to "My Dahomian Queen," which reads:

> In Dahomey so grand,
> Just along side the strand,
> Lives a Moorish maid so near and dear to
> Me.
> When I sought her heart and hand,
> She made me understand
> That if I wish'd my little bride she'd be.
> ...
>
> My Dahomian Queen,
> My dusky turtle dove,
> What a beautiful scene,
> Me and my lady love.
> She's so sweet and serene,
> Fresh from the jungle green,
> She is my Kai-o-ka-lo-nian,
> Royal Dahomian queen.[58]

This passage offers the "vital contrast" in the music Williams implemented in performance. The language is more reflective of the high art lyrics attributed to the educated daughter of Cicero Lightfoot.[59] References to the black woman as a "Moorish maid," "bride," and "queen" contest the image promoted in minstrel shows. Likewise, references to Kai-o-ka-lo-nian represent a subversive use of well-known political events. The subtle equation of the "Dahomian queen" with the queen of Hawaii would have been recognizable to the audience of the play familiar with the Hawaiian queen deposed by American planters in 1893; she remained in the news owing to her lawsuit against the federal government for property losses.[60] The subversive undertones of this observation comment on the European "scramble for Africa" as well as the paradox of poor blacks colonizing African nations, as in the case of Liberia. This subtle commentary gets lost in the extravagant music, movement, and comic elements of the production.[61]

The story of *Abyssinia* revises the plot of African descendants from the United States returning to Africa. The story concerns Rastus Johnson (Williams) and his friend Jasmine Jenkins (Walker) who travel to Africa when Johnson wins a $15,000 lottery jackpot and decides to visit the land of his ancestors in Abyssinia with his winnings. While experiencing a series of adventures and missteps, the climax of the plot occurs when Rastus steals a vase and attempts to save his arm, which is threatened by virtue of Ethiopian justice. Rastus is saved from punishment without any assistance from Jasmine.

Abyssinia's innovation on a familiar theme from *In Dahomey* reflects the evolving consciousness of the duo. For instance, the language in *Abyssinia* demonstrates a similar philosophy regarding the African, which has been noted by scholars like Gerald Bordman. In regard to the lyrics (Alex Rogers) and libretto (Jesse A. Shipp), Bordman notes that they "wanted to suggest that coming to America marked a falling away from grace, if not perfection. The Africans speak the King's English. Indeed some of their dialogue and lyrics are so stilted they smack of parody."[62] The Africans' use of the king's English is reflected in refrains like:

> Soldiers of the King are we,
> We bow to his supremacy.
> We know naught of disloyalty,
> Hence cannot spare an enemy.

Such lines starkly contrast with the dialog exchanged between Williams and Walker:

JASMINE: And you's a philosophy?
RASTUS: Philosopher.
JASMINE: What's the duty of a philoso-, philoso- *(Finally add* pede)
RASTUS: To look on the bright side of other people's troubles when you haven't any of your own.

The vital contrasts represent a deliberate attempt to use language as a technical device to situate the African in an elevated status, as opposed to the degrading images of Africa and the American "darky." *Abyssinia* improved on the apparent limitations of its predecessor, but only succeeded in thirty-one performances in New York before its successful touring run. It was still unable to match the success of the revival of *In Dahomey*.[63]

In *Bandana Land*, their final show together, the duo abandoned the theme of Africa and African characterizations. *Bandana Land* opened at the Majestic Theatre in New York on February 3, 1908, with music by Will Marion Cook and lyrics and libretto by Bert A. Williams and Jesse A. Shipp. With a storyline capitalizing on the stars' specialties, the story concerns Mose Blackstone (Alex Rogers) and the syndicate he organizes in order to purchase Amos Simmons's farm, which a streetcar company also needs. In order to obtain more cash, the culprits con Skunkton Bowser (Bert Williams), the well-off businessman and owner of a minstrel show stranded in town. Once the farm is purchased, Blackstone sells half to the streetcar company and turns the other half into a park for Negroes, which serves as a device to blackmail the railway company to purchase the other half of the farm at a ridiculously expensive rate under threat of troublesome, noisy Negroes. The traditional happy ending to the all-black musical is maintained as Skunkton and his guardian Bud Jenkins (played by George Walker and eventually his wife, Aida Overton Walker) withdraw from the scheme, bringing it to an end.[64] The play's comic reference to gentrification offers the "vital contrast" by showing how those in empowered positions profit from the "darky" types in the popular imagination in entertainment, real estate, and other modes of business.

The power of these productions became painfully obvious after *Bandana Land* and the death of George Walker. Williams had trouble finding suitable material to display his talents. Yet he continued to perform professionally as the singular black presence in mainstream American theatre, becoming the first black American to receive top billing when he appeared in the Ziegfeld Follies from 1909 to 1919.[65] The legacies and strategies of the Williams and Walker duo were carried on (and carried out) by the next generation of playwrights and performers, represented by Langston Hughes.

Langston Hughes

Langston Hughes was born in Joplin, Missouri, the same year that *In Dahomey* appeared on Broadway. He graduated from Lincoln University in Pennsylvania before going on to become a columnist at several newspapers,

Figure 3.1 Gordon Parks, portrait of Langston Hughes, 1943.

and eventually a poet, writer, playwright, scriptwriter, librettist, lyricist, historian, and founder of theatre companies.[66]

Hughes's Broadway works *Mulatto*, *The Barrier*, and *Simply Heavenly* expose the limitations of existing dramatic structure and performance style for early black Americans. Each work establishes a "vital contrast" to explore the diversity of black American experiences. Set in Depression-era Georgia, *Mulatto: A Tragedy of the Deep South* and its operatic adaptation,

The Barrier, tell the story of Robert, a young, mixed-race man who identifies as black yet attempts to access the same rights and privileges as white
people, like his father Colonel Thomas Norwood. Robert's black mother,
Cora, lives with Colonel Norwood, the father of her four children. She fears
that Robert's headstrong ideas about his position in society will lead to his
demise. Unlike his siblings, Robert confronts their white father, who refers to
them as "nigger-children" even in the presence of their mother, his in-house
lover and housekeeper. When the unruly white mob corners him after he
kills his father, Robert narrowly escapes lynching by taking his own life.

The dramatic structure of *Mulatto* (first written in 1930 and produced
in 1935)[67] contrasts with Hughes's other work, especially his political plays
The Em-Fuehrer Jones and *Don't You Want to Be Free?* (1937). The latter
marks Hughes's departure from conventional play structure, representing a
style that became "loose-limbed and improvisational in effect, montage-like
rather than static and monumental, always strongly lyrical and rhythmic.[68]
Mulatto's more conventional European structure signifies on the theme of
miscegenation, as the first of his many works to appear on Broadway: *Street
Scene* (1947), a musical drama; *The Barrier*, an opera; *Simply Heavenly*,
a musical comedy; *Tambourines to Glory* (1963), the first gospel musical;
Mule Bone (1991), an original play and collaboration with Zora Neale
Hurston; and *Lovemusik* (2007), a musical drama featuring songs by
Langston Hughes. His plays cover a broad range of dramatic structures and
themes sharing the common focus on diverse black American experiences,
especially in regard to empowering representations of the folk. *Mulatto*, *The
Barrier*, and *Simply Heavenly* best exemplify Hughes's impact as an early
black American on Broadway, as well as the shifting tastes and expectations
of Broadway audiences and critics, and the historical moments in which
they premiered.

According to Leslie Catherine Sanders, Hughes may have developed the
idea for *Mulatto* as a result of white playwright Paul Green's *In Abraham's
Bosom* (1927).[69] He saw a rehearsal of the Pulitzer-Prize-winning play
while staying with the director Jasper Deter at the Hedgerow Theatre in
Rose Valley, Pennsylvania. The three-act play's self-righteous protagonist of
mixed-race heritage reminded Hughes of his own father, who "disliked poor
Black people and found white people intolerable."[70] Robert's self-righteous
behavior as the protagonist in *Mulatto* and *The Barrier*, and his embodiment of double consciousness, is reflected in a statement to his brother:
"Besides you and me's only half coons, anyhow, big boy. And I'm gonna act
like my white half, not my Black half." William responds, "Well, you ain't
gonna act like it long here in the middle o' Georgy. And you ain't gonna act
like it when de Colonel's around, either." They both prove to be correct as

the story continues.[71] According to Harry J. Elam, Jr. and Michelle Elam, Hughes wanted to manage the image of these characters by including detailed stage directions about how the mulatto actors who portrayed the characters should look and interact (i.e., the specification of the darker-skinned William and the near-white Robert, though clearly "Negroid").[72]

The choice to cast Rose McClendon as Cora Lewis in *Mulatto* supports Hughes's reworking of the miscegenation theme; McClendon appeared in Green's *In Abraham's Bosom*. Also considered a tragedy, Green's play opened on Broadway on December 30, 1926, continuing for 200 performances. It was revived on September 6, 1927 with a total of 88 performances. The story is set in North Carolina in the summer of 1885, almost two decades after the abolition of slavery. McClendon played the role of Goldie McAllister, the protagonist's wife. In *Mulatto*, she plays Cora. Hughes revises previous treatments of the miscegenation theme by repositioning "the suffering Black woman character" that Goldie and Cora represent at the center of the conflict.[73] For example, he constructs Cora as a woman who loves the white father of her children, yet fears for their safety in the unjust system that privileges their father and other white landowners.

Cora's conflicted positioning is best represented in two passages from *Mulatto*. The first occurs at the end of Act I when Colonel Norwood and Robert's altercation escalates into physical violence. Cora begs Robert to behave as a Negro is expected to for the sake of peace. As Robert prepares to exit the house through the front door of his father's plantation mansion, Cora continues to plead with him:

ROBERT: ... *(As* CORA *crosses hurriedly left,* ROBERT *goes toward the front door)* The Ford is parked out in front, anyway.

CORA: *(At the door left to the rear of the house)* Robert! Robert! *(As* ROBERT *nears the front door,* COLONEL NORWOOD *enters, almost runs into the boy, stops at the threshold and stares unbelievingly at his son.* CORA *backs up against the door left)*

NORWOOD: Get out of here! *(He points toward the door to the rear of the house where* CORA *is standing)*

ROBERT: *(Half smiling)* Didn't you want to talk to me?

NORWOOD: Get out of here!

ROBERT: Not that way. *(The* COLONEL *raises his cane to strike the boy.* CORA *screams.* ROBERT *draws himself up his full height, taller than the old man and looking very much like him, pale and proud. The man and the boy face each other.* NORWOOD *does not strike)*

NORWOOD: *(In a coarse whisper)* Get out of here. *(His hands trembling as he points)*

CORA: Robert! Come on, son, come on! Oh, my God, come on. *(Opening the door left)*

ROBERT: Not that way, ma. (*ROBERT walks proudly out the front door. NORWOOD, in an impotent rage, crosses the room to a small cabinet right, opens it nervously with a key from his pocket, takes out a pistol, and starts toward the front door. CORA overtakes him, seizes his arm, stops him*)

CORA: He's our son, Tom. (*She sinks slowly to her knees, holding his body*) Remember, he's our son.[74]

The father–son conflict and rising racial tension in the play converge in Robert's confrontation with Colonel Norwood in this pivotal scene. Cora's presence exemplifies her characterization as a strategic device that elevates the melodramatic tendency of the miscegenation narrative into the realm of tragedy. Robert's refusal to obey his parents, reflected in the stage directions and dialog, places Cora in the center of the conflict between her white lover and mixed-race, adult son. She is not the protagonist but becomes a significant point of identification for the audience. In this way, Hughes's tragic strategy illuminates the problems of racism and the second-class citizenship imposed upon black Americans.

To reiterate racism, not miscegenation, as the problem, Hughes softens the Norwood character in various ways in *The Barrier*. For example, in Act II, scene I of the opera, Hughes dramatizes a scene of Colonel Norwood in his study, following his initial altercation with Robert; it is referenced but not staged in *Mulatto*, Act II, scene I. In *The Barrier*, Colonel Norwood sings about his conflicted feelings for his son Robert, "who is so *damn much* like me," "flesh of my flesh, and bone of my bone." Norwood laments "the steel of the Norwoods, now darkened by Africa," and the fact that the boy is still a bastard, which prevents him from loving his son.[75] Dramatizing this scene, which was initially presented in *Mulatto* with Norwood behind closed doors brooding while Cora tries to talk sense into Robert, represents Norwood as a tragic figure as opposed to a villain.

In terms of Broadway audience appeal, Hughes's treatment of Cora in *Mulatto* appears to be more successful than the revised treatment of Norwood in *The Barrier*. Through McClendon's performance of "the suffering Black woman" in *Mulatto*, the character type becomes less a plot device and more of an identifiable character for audiences who can empathize with Cora's dual and conflicting sense of duty to her lover and their mixed-race child. This distinguishes Hughes's tragedy from the melodrama staged on Broadway when white producer Martin Jones optioned and rewrote Hughes's play and enforced segregationist policies in terms of seating and the treatment of the cast and writer. For example, *Mulatto* was put into rehearsal without Hughes's participation and opened on Broadway before Hughes had an opportunity to rewrite it. Jones even replaced the mulatto actors playing Robert and Sallie with white actors, in spite of Hughes's detailed instructions regarding the characterizations.[76] Jones also corrupted Hughes's original version by including a gratuitous rape scene, thereby changing the play from a poetic tragedy to a melodrama with more emphasis on sex.[77]

Mulatto's 373 performances on Broadway in 1935 made it the longest-running of any play by a black playwright until Lorraine Hansberry's *A Raisin in the Sun*, in spite of negative and mixed reviews.[78] Rose McClendon's performance as Cora Lewis, a critical point of entry into the narrative, most likely contributed to its success and overshadowed many of the shortcomings for which Hughes was criticized. As Brooks Atkinson explains, *Mulatto* "offers the combination of Rose McClendon and a playwright flaming with sincerity." He finds Hughes lacks

> the dramatic strength of mind that makes it possible for a writer to tell a coherent, driving story in the theatre ... As for Cora Lewis, she has the honor to be played by Rose McClendon who is an artist with a sensitive personality and a bell-like voice. Plays are not very numerous for Miss McClendon, but it is always a privilege to see her adding fineness of perception to the parts she takes. [79]

Here, McClendon, like Williams, exemplifies the powerful potential of the relationship between the early black performers and writers. The vehicles in which they performed may have smothered their talents in some cases (i.e., Williams in *Mr. Lode of Koal* and *Under the Bamboo Tree*). Yet most often, the strength of their skills prompted new work by perceptive writers like Hughes in terms of dramatic structures, characters, and scenarios that could better accommodate their powerful performances.[80]

Hughes's commitment to developing a nuanced miscegenation narrative could not overcome the racial politics of the era. He seemed to be looking for an opportunity to revisit the *Mulatto* narrative when Jan Meyerowitz asked him for a libretto. Drawn by the music Meyerowitz had already begun to compose, Hughes made up his mind to transpose the play into a musical work; he was much more involved in the development of *The Barrier* than he was with *Mulatto*.[81] Overall, the opera received mixed reviews. When it opened on January 18, 1950 at Columbia University's Opera Workshop with ten performances, it was described as a "stunning success." The cast had two black leads, including Muriel Rahn (mother) and Mattiwilda Dobbs (sister), with Robert Goss as Robert and Paul Elmer as Colonel Norwood. Following the workshop performances, the opera seemed to be headed to Broadway. However, according to Sanders, critical hostility in Washington, DC, focusing more on the opera's story than the musical or literary merits, may have contributed to the show's eventual failure on the Great White Way. *The Barrier* opened on Broadway on November 12, 1950, closing two days later.

Hughes's return to commercial theatre took seven years with his next Broadway show, *Simply Heavenly*, a musical comedy loosely based on his popular "Simple" stories.[82] Gerald Bordman describes the play as "a light-hearted, affectionate look at a small group of Harlem characters."[83] The protagonist, Jesse B. Simple, is reminiscent of Bert A. Williams's Jonah Man:

> the man who, even if it rained soup, would be found with a fork in his hand and no spoon in sight, the man whose fighting relatives come to visit him and whose head is always dented by the furniture they throw at each other. There are endless variations of this idea, fortunately; but if you sift them, you will find the principle of human nature at the bottom of them all.[84]

Many of the characters resemble prevailing stereotypes from the minstrel tradition and early musical comedies. A closer look, though, reveals that Hughes consciously incorporates these types in order to comment on the conflating of "the folk" with "stereotypes."

The story focuses on Simple and his predicament: he is stuck in a love-less marriage, and although separated from his wife, he is unable to afford a divorce in order to marry the wholesome Joyce. His on-again-off-again relationship with the sensual Zarita threatens his plans to marry Joyce when the opportunity arises after a letter from his wife announces she has found a suitor who will pay for their divorce so that they can be rid of each other. Although Simple encounters various challenges throughout the story, he succeeds in marrying Joyce and securing an apartment, as part of the usual happy ending for musical comedies.

Reanimating characters from the minstrel tradition and early musical comedies proves to be risky business for Hughes; he walks a fine line between challenging and reinforcing stereotypes. While stock characters in comedies tend to be flat and the narratives less complicated, Hughes encountered significant problems with the simplicity of these aspects in his own play. Having learned from *Mulatto*, he anticipated these challenges by including "Character Notes" in the play. Under "General Note," Hughes explains, "the characters in 'Simply Heavenly' are, on the whole, ordinary, hard-working lower-income bracket Harlemites."[85] The characters include but are not limited to: Joyce, "a quiet girl more inclined toward club work than bars, toward culture rather than good-timing"; Boyd, "serious-minded, pleasant-looking, trying to be a writer"; Zarita, "a lively bar-stool girl wearing life like a loose garment, but she is *not* a prostitute"; Miss Mamie, "a hard-working domestic, using biting words to protect a soft heart and a need for love too often betrayed"; and Gitfiddle, "a folk artist going to seed, unable to compete with the juke box, TV, and the radio, having only his guitar and his undisciplined talents."[86] The notes for these characters, along with Simple, as discussed below, reveal Hughes's concern regarding portrayals in performance.

Hughes also incorporates relevant dialog further to protect the characters from being performed and perceived as stereotypes. As Melon, a jovial fruit vendor, flirts with Miss Mamie, she engages in verbal battle with a "Character" who accuses Mamie and Melon of being stereotypes. Mamie blatantly rejects the label and reprimands him:

> MAMIE: (*Turns on him furiously*) Mister, you better remove yourself from my presence before I stereo your type! I like watermelons, and I don't care who knows it. That's nothing to be ashamed of, like some other colored folks are. Why, I knowed a woman once was so ashamed of liking watermelons that she'd make the clerk wrap the melon up before she'd carry it out of the store. I ain't no pretender, myself, neither no passer ... —passing up chitterlings and pretending I don't like 'em when I do. I like watermelon and chitterlings both, and I don't care who knows it. Why, its getting so colored folks can't do nothing no more without some other Negro calling you a stereotype. Stereotype, hah! If you like a little gin, you're a stereotype. You got to drink Scotch. If you wear a red dress, you're a stereotype. You got to wear beige or chartreuse. Lord have mercy, honey, do-don't like no blackeyed peas and rice! Then you're a downhome Negro for true—which I is—and proud of it! (*MAMIE glares around as if daring somebody to dispute her. Nobody does*) I didn't come here to Harlem to get away from my people. I come here because there's more of 'em. I loves my race. I loves my people. Stereotype![87]

There are several significant elements that demonstrate the ways that Hughes confronts the potential stereotyping of his characters in this passage. Mamie contradicts the Mammy stereotype she supposedly represents.[88] Later in the play, her implied sexual relationship with Melon completes the process of reversing the mammy stereotype.[89] She defies it primarily through her outspoken nature and financial independence, which are on exhibit throughout the play. She stands her ground in her confrontation with "Character," telling him to remove himself from her presence "before I stereo your type!" With this statement, she establishes herself as the center, whereas Mammy is generally considered to be a marginal character. In addition, Mamie identifies stereotyping as a violent and destructive act. Hughes further reiterates the sentiment later in the play when Boyd explains to Character that the Harlemites in the bar are not stereotypes, just folks.[90] Although Hughes endeavored to establish this with the play's characters and dialog, other critical, missing elements limit the possibility of the show being read as he intended it.

Through these characters, Hughes aimed to celebrate the "dignified comedy of black life," which Williams also alludes to in "The Comic Side of Trouble" in regard to his inspiration and portrayals of the Jonah

Man characters.[91] In the "general notes," Hughes describes Simple as "a Chaplinesque character," suggesting a return to the "Em-Fuehrer" character from his political play. But he signifies on the Chaplinesque character with a touch of the "Jonah Man" when he further describes Simple as being "dark with a likable smile, ordinarily dressed, except for rather flamboyant summer sport shirts. Simple tries hard to succeed, but the chips seldom fall just right. Yet he bounces like a rubber ball. He may go down, but he always bounds back up."[92]

Simply Heavenly was controversial, in part because of the characterizations as well as the light-heartedness of the narrative at a time of increasing tension in regard to the Civil Rights struggle. According to Sanders, "Hughes felt neither the actors nor the director understood how to convey a 'dignified comedy of black life,' falling into farce rather than understanding the nature of the simplicity that defined his characters."[93] Simple is exactly the type of character Williams perfected in his lifetime and career. Arguably, Williams's style of acting may have conveyed the simplicity Hughes saw in his characters. Ironically, during the latter years of his career, Williams was in search of such material that would effectively utilize his skills, which were underused in the Ziegfeld Follies. One can only imagine what possibilities may have been realized had Hughes's playwriting and Williams's performance prowess converged on Broadway or in other venues.

The challenges of these early black Americans on Broadway expose the various factors that limited the progress of black theatrical production on the American stage, especially on Broadway from the late nineteenth to mid twentieth centuries. These factors include static and flat characterizations of blackness (African and black American); limited opportunities to expand repertoires beyond limited and limiting dramatic structures and characterizations of the musical comedy and melodrama; and overall limited access to sufficient material, resources, and venues, etc. With the emergence of more writers, the limitations of the black performer became even more apparent. Yet their collaborative efforts sparked hope, as in the case of Bert A. Williams and Alex Rogers, and later Langston Hughes and Rose McClendon. Still, the exceptional gifts of these actors and their collaborations with gifted writers exposed a glaring lack in regard to general output of black theatrical production, best exemplified in Hughes's own critique of the limitations of his Broadway production of *Simply Heavenly*. The show may be remembered as a controversial play haunted by the stereotypes of the past, but it also demonstrates the evolutionary and revolutionary strategies employed in order to complete George Walker's initial task of eradicating the "darky" image without losing the value (and values) of the culture. Conflicting reactions to the show, which opened two years before Hansberry's *A Raisin in the Sun*, suggest audiences were hungry for more complicated portrayals of black experience, in spite of the production's inability to convey the folk of Hughes's imagination.

My goal in this chapter has been to illuminate the contributions of Williams and Walker and Langston Hughes as examples of early black American experience on Broadway. Further exploration of the roles of black women during this time will reveal that black women appeared in and supported the work of these black pioneers on the Great White Way, even if they do not feature prominently in this chapter. The featured examples demonstrate the evolving consciousness regarding black representation on Broadway, particularly in the hands of black artists and the complexity of black characterizations and themes at the time. A closer look at recent contemporary black productions on Broadway, and the lack thereof, reveals that the change George Walker predicted and initiated is still in progress, for some of the same reasons black Americans faced in the past. These cases reflect emerging artistic processes of self-actualization and empowerment, with Broadway serving as the symbol of achievement with conflicting, paradoxical results. Broadway still carries the connotation of Mecca for many but not all, and not in all ways.

NOTES

1 Langston Hughes, Arnold Rampersad, and David Ernest Roessel, "Note on Commercial Theatre," in *Langston Hughes* (New York: Sterling, 2006), 34.

2 Woodie King and Ron Milner (eds.), *Black Drama Anthology* (New York: Signet, 1972), x.

3 Most often attributed to August Wilson, the statement is credited to Lloyd Richards in Dena Kleiman, "'Joe Turner,' The Spirit of Synergy," *The New York Times*, May 19, 1986, Section C, 11, col. 1.

4 Miles M. Jefferson, "The Negro on Broadway: 1944," *Phylon*, 6.1 (1945): 42–3.

5 George W. Walker, "The Real 'Coon' on the American Stage," *The Theatre Magazine* (August, 1906): reprinted in liner notes to Bert Williams, *The Early Years, 1901–1909*, audio recording (Champaign, IL: Archeophone Records, 2004), 16–19.

6 Bert A. Williams, "The Comic Side of Trouble," *The American Magazine* (January, 1918), reprinted in Bert Williams, *The Middle Years, 1910–1918*, audio recording (Champaign, IL: Archeophone Records, 2005), 11–19.

7 For more information see Alan W. C. Green, "'Jim Crow' to 'Zip Coon': The Northern Origins of Negro Minstrelsy," *The Massachusetts Review*, 11.2 (Spring, 1970): 385–97; Robert C. Toll, *Blacking Up: The Minstrel Show in Nineteenth-Century America* (New York: Oxford University Press, 1974), 51–7. See also Carl Wittke, *Tambo and Bones: A History of the American Minstrel Stage* (New York: Greenwood Press, 1968 [1930]), 135–57.

8 See David Krasner, *A Beautiful Pageant: African American Theatre, Drama, and Performance in the Harlem Renaissance, 1910–1927* (New York: Palgrave Macmillan, 2002); Camille F. Forbes, *Introducing Bert Williams: Burnt Cork, Broadway, and the Story of America's First Black Star* (New York: Basic Civitas, 2008); Gerald Bordman, *American Musical Theatre: A Chronicle* (New York: Oxford University Press, 1992); Hugh F. Rankin, *The Theater in Colonial America* (Chapel Hill: University of North Carolina Press, 1965); Bernard L. Peterson, Jr., *Profiles of African American Stage Performers and Theatre People, 1816–1960* (Westport, CT: Greenwood Press, 2001); and Henry T. Sampson, *The Ghost Walks: A Chronological History of Blacks in Show Business, 1865–1910* (Metuchen, NJ: The Scarecrow Press, 1988). For more information also see Lisa M. Anderson, *Mammies No More: The Changing Image of Black Women on Stage and Screen* (Lanham, MD: Rowman & Littlefield, 1997; Daphne A. Brooks, *Bodies in Dissent: Spectacular Performances of Race and Freedom, 1850–1910* (Durham, NC: Duke University Press, 2006; Errol Hill, *Shakespeare in Sable: A History of Black Shakespearean Actors* (Amherst: University of Massachusetts Press, 1984); John Bush Jones, *Our Musicals, Ourselves: A Social History of the American Musical Theatre* (Hanover: Brandeis University Press, 2003); and Jo A. Tanner, *Dusky Maidens: The Odyssey of the Early Black Dramatic Actress* (Westport, CT: Greenwood Press, 1992).

9 Camille F. Forbes, "Dancing with 'Racial Feet': Bert Williams and the Performance of Blackness," *Theatre Journal*, 56.4 (2004): 603–25 (604).

10 Charles Gilpin was the black American performer who played the title character when the show opened on Broadway. For more information see Krasner, *A Beautiful Pageant*, 263–4; and Eugene O'Neill, *The Emperor Jones* (Cincinnati: Stewart Kidd, 1921).

11 In James V. Hatch's *Lost Plays of the Harlem Renaissance, 1920–1940*, Langston Hughes's play is listed as *The Em-Fuehrer Jones*, dated 1920. However, several of the references in the play, including those to Joe Louis and Jesse Owens, suggest that the play was written later, perhaps sometime in the 1930s or 1940s instead. Langston Hughes, *The Em-Fuehrer Jones*, in *Lost Plays of the Harlem Renaissance, 1920–1940*, ed. James Vernon Hatch and Leo Hamalian (Detroit: Wayne State University Press, 1996), 358–61.

12 Doris E. Abramson, "The Great White Way: Critics and the First Black Playwrights on Broadway," *Educational Theatre Journal*, 28.1 (March, 1976): 45–55 (46).

13 Langston Hughes, *Mulatto: A Tragedy of the Deep South* (1935), in *Black Theatre USA: Plays by African Americans*, 2 vols., ed. James V. Hatch and Ted Shine (New York: Free Press, 1996), Vol. II: *The Recent Period, 1935–Today*, 4–23.

14 Langston Hughes, *The Barrier* (1950), in *The Collected Works of Langston Hughes*, ed. Arnold Rampersad, Dolan Hubbard, and Leslie Catherine Sanders, 18 vols., Vol. VI: *Gospel Plays, Operas, and Later Dramatic Works*, ed. and introd. Leslie Catherine Sanders (Columbia: University of Missouri Press, 2004), 67–101.

15 Langston Hughes, *Simply Heavenly: A Comedy* (1957), in *The Collected Works*, 179–245.

16 Mary C. Henderson, *Theater in America: 200 Years of Plays, Players and Productions* (New York: Harry Abrams, 1986).

17 Bordman, *American Musical Theatre*, 1.

18 Rankin, *The Theater in Colonial America*, 117.

19 Green, "'Jim Crow' to 'Zip Coon,'" 385–6.

20 *Ibid.*, 389–90.

21 Forbes, *Introducing Bert Williams*, 56.

22 Peterson, *Profiles of African American Stage Performers*, xv.

23 Hill, *Shakespeare in Sable*, 14.

24 Bernth Lindfors, *Ira Aldridge, the African Roscius* (Rochester, NY: University of Rochester Press, 2007), 1.

25 Hazel Waters, *Racism on the Victorian Stage: Representation of Slavery and the Black Character* (Cambridge: Cambridge University Press, 2007), 58.

26 Hatch and Shine, *Black Theatre USA: The Recent Period*, 3.

27 Walker, "The Real 'Coon,'" 17.

28 Williams, "The Comic Side of Trouble," 17.

29 It is worth noting that Walker and Williams made a significant impact on the professionalization of black Americans in the entertainment industry, although this aspect of their work is not within the scope of this study.

30 Walker, "The Real 'Coon,'" 17.

31 *Ibid.*

32 Forbes, *Introducing Bert Williams*, 33.

33 *Ibid.*

34 *Ibid.*, 41.

35 Thomas Canary, of Canary and Lederer, promised to book the duo in a piece called "The Passing Show," but instead sent a telegram inviting them to join the cast of *The Gold Bug*. See Williams, "The Comic Side of Trouble," 17.

36 The combination of comedy and dance demonstrated by the Williams and Walker team appealed to black and white audiences, as evidenced in the vaudeville shows and all black revues in which they performed. These include an engagement at Koster and Bial's Music Hall (1896), and Hyde's Comedians' touring show starring white blackface comedians McIntyre and Heath.

37 "The first move was to hire a flat in Fifty-third street [*sic*], furnish it, and throw our doors open to all colored men who possessed theatrical ability and ambition. The Williams and Walker flat soon became the headquarters of artistic young men of our race who were stage-struck" (Walker, "The Real 'Coon,'" 18.).

38 "My partner, Mr. Williams, is the first man that I know of our race to attempt to delineate a 'darky' in a perfectly natural way, and I think much of his success is due to this fact" (*ibid.*, 19).

39 *Washington Post*, October 11, 1898.

40 J. B., "Bert Williams," *Soil*, 1.1 (1916): 19–23 (19; my emphasis).

41 Williams, "The Comic Side of Trouble," 13.

42 Walker, "The Real 'Coon,'" 18.

43 The duo billed themselves as the "Tobasco Senegambians" when they toured London. "Senegambia" refers to the British colony in Africa, an area with a rich history and cultures. It would have been more familiar to British audiences at the time than their US billing as the "Two Real Coons." This is only one example

of their business savvy intersecting with attempts to offer more diverse representations of blackness extending beyond the American "darky."

44 Hatch and Shine, *Black Theatre USA*, Vol. 1: *The Early Period, 1847–1938*, 64.

45 The long run of the show allowed the duo to experiment with various comic
situations and further perfect their act (Peterson, *Profiles of African American
Stage Performers*, 250).

46 Hatch and Shine, *Black Theatre USA: The Early Period*, 64.

47 Forbes, *Introducing Bert Williams*, 56.

48 Jesse A. Shipp, Will Marion Cook, and Paul Laurence Dunbar, *In Dahomey:
A Negro Musical Comedy*, in Hatch and Shine, *Black Theatre USA: The Early
Period*, 63–85.

49 *Ibid.*, 65.

50 Bordman, *American Musical Theatre*, 190.

51 Prominent cast members include but are not limited to Charles Moore as Je-Je,
a Cabocceer; Bert A. Williams as Shylock Homestead; George Walker as his
partner Rareback Punkerton; Alex Rogers as George Reeder, proprietor of an
intelligence office; Jesse A. Shipp as Hustling Charley, promoter of Get-the-Coin
Syndicate; Abbie Mitchell as Pansy, daughter of Cecilia Lightfoot (played by
Mrs. Hattie McIntosh); and Aida Overton Walker as Rosetta Lightfoot, "a
troublesome young thing."

52 Walker, "The Real 'Coon,'" 18.

53 *Ibid.*, 19.

54 Shipp, Cook, and Dunbar, *In Dahomey*, 72.

55 *Ibid.*

56 Hatch and Shine, *Black Theatre USA: The Early Period*, 65.

57 *Ibid.*

58 Shipp, Cook, and Dunbar, *In Dahomey*, 82–3.

59 Hatch and Shine, *Black Theatre USA: The Early Period*, 65.

60 *Ibid.*, 83.

61 After the Broadway run of *In Dahomey*, the first full-length all-black musical,
the show toured the British provinces; the cast returned to New York City in
1904 as celebrities. The show reopened at the Grand Opera House. A simultaneous production toured the United States for forty weeks while a second company headed by Williams and Walker imitators was sent to England, attesting to
the popularity and commercial appeal of the production (Forbes, *Introducing
Bert Williams*, 126–7).

62 Bordman, *American Musical Theatre*, 218–19.

63 *Ibid.*, 219.

64 Walker passed away at the age of thirty-eight, succumbing to paresis, a condition that manifests itself in loss of memory, emotional tantrums, alteration of
voice, stuttering, and unsteadiness. Walker began experiencing various symp-
toms throughout the run of *Bandana Land*, which led to his wife Aida Overton
Walker taking on his role, with him appearing on stage only occasionally. His
last appearance took place on February 9, 1909, after which he returned to
Lawrence, Kansas to live with his mother, Alice Myers, before being confined to
a sanatorium. He passed away on January 6, 1911.

65 Williams collapsed on a Detroit stage eight days before he passed away on March
4, 1922. The memory of his legacy and interest in his innovation of characters

like "the Jonah Man" were revived in 1981 when Broadway performer Ben Vereen donned blackface, performing Williams's pantomime poker routine and spotlighting his most famous song, "Nobody," during President Reagan's inaugural festivities. Melvin Van Peebles's *Classified X* (1998) and Spike Lee's *Bamboozled* (2001) also pay homage to the great performer and his legacy.

66 Peterson, *Profiles of African American Stage Performers*, 129–30.
67 Harry J. Elam, Jr. and Michele Elam, "Blood Debt: Reparations in Langston Hughes' *Mulatto*," *Theatre Journal*, 61.1 (March, 2009): 87.
68 Hatch and Shine, *Black Theatre USA: The Early Period*, 266.
69 Hatch and Shine, *Black Theatre USA: The Recent Period*, 4. Also see Leslie Catherine Sanders, *The Development of Black Theater in America: From Shadows to Selves* (Baton Rouge: Louisiana State University Press, 1988).
70 Hatch and Shine, *Black Theatre USA: The Recent Period*, 4.
71 Hughes, *Mulatto*, 13.
72 Elam and Elam, "Blood Debt," 98.
73 *Ibid.*, 100–2.
74 Hughes, *Mulatto*, 15.
75 Hughes, *The Barrier*, 88.
76 Elam and Elam, "Blood Debt," 98.
77 Hatch and Shine, *Black Theatre USA: The Recent Period*, 5.
78 *Ibid.* After the paradoxical success of *Mulatto*, Hughes vowed never to have anything more to do with non-commercial theatre. According to Sanders, *Street Scene* (with music by Kurt Weill, book by Elmer Rice, and lyrics by Langston Hughes), along with *Porgy and Bess* (music George Gershwin, book DuBose Heyward, lyrics Ira Gershwin) anchors the development of American opera. *Street Scene* opened on Broadway after *Mulatto* and before *The Barrier*. The production represents the first time two prominent white artists invited an African American collaborator onto a play about whites. This reason, and the fact that it is Hughes's only truly lucrative venture in theatre, may explain why Hughes was so excited about doing *The Barrier* as an opera. For more information see Rampersad, Hubbard, and Sanders, *Collected Works of Langston Hughes*, Vol. vi, 567.
79 Abramson, "The Great White Way," 53.
80 Cora Lewis was McClendon's last role before her death. She became ill during the run of the show and was forced to withdraw from the cast. She died before the show closed. See Peterson, *Profiles of African American Stage Performers*, 176.
81 Rampersad, Hubbard, and Sanders, *Collected Works of Langston Hughes*, Vol. vi, 67.
82 The stories were initially published in the *Chicago Defender* and *New York Post* before Hughes collected the stories into five volumes. See Rampersad, Hubbard, and Sanders, *Collected Works of Langston Hughes*, Vol. vi, 179.
83 Bordman, *American Musical Theatre*, 605.
84 Williams, "The Comic Side of Trouble," 11.
85 Hughes, *Simply Heavenly*, 182.
86 *Ibid.*
87 *Ibid.*, 192.
88 Anderson, *Mammies No More*, 9–43.

89 Hughes, *Simply Heavenly*, 216–17.
90 *Ibid.*, 197.
91 Rampersad, Hubbard, and Sanders, *Collected Works of Langston Hughes*, Vol. VI, 179.
92 Hughes, *Simply Heavenly*, 182.
93 Rampersad, Hubbard, and Sanders, *Collected Works of Langston Hughes*, Vol. VI, 179.

4

SOYICA DIGGS COLBERT

Drama in the Harlem Renaissance

Drama in the Harlem Renaissance begins with Angelina Weld Grimké's *Rachel* (1916). As an expression of the impact of lynching on women and families, the play considers the implications of the ghastly practice in terms of black female reproductivity. At the end of the first act, the eponymous protagonist learns that her father and half brother were lynched. She questions her mother about the current state of black people in the South and declares:

> Then, everywhere, everywhere, throughout the South, there were hundreds of dark mothers who live in fear, terrible, suffocating fear, whose rest by night is broken, and whose joy by day in their babies on their hearts is three parts—pain. Oh, I know this is true—for this is the way I should feel, if I were little Jimmy's mother. How horrible! Why—it would be more merciful—to strangle the little things at birth. And so this nation—this white Christian nation—has deliberately set its curse upon the most beautiful—the most holy thing in life—motherhood! Why—it—makes—you doubt—God." [1]

Rachel's declaration comingles a belated response to learning that a lynch mob murdered her father and her desperate acknowledgement that there will be no redress, legal, social, or communal, for the traumatic experiences that her adopted son Jimmy suffers when taunted on his way home from school by a group of boys shouting racial slurs and throwing rocks. The melodramatic tone counterbalances the excessive violence used to police black people and calls attention to how blackness functions as a stigma in the first decades of the twentieth century. By the end of the play, based on her familial history of racially motivated violence, Rachel vows not to have children. While a radical stance, *Rachel* demonstrates a black female character's attempt to mediate the racial trauma and violence endemic to her world. This chapter offers an overview of significant writers of the Harlem Renaissance by closely reading their plays with the aim of spotlighting how their themes are consonant with New Negro and Harlem Renaissance ideologies.

Grimké's play establishes the ways the drama of the period intersects with the New Negro Aesthetic. In the principal anthology of the Harlem Renaissance, *The New Negro*, the editor Alain Locke outlines the social changes that inaugurate the New Negro. He explains, "A main change has been, of course, that shifting of the Negro population which has made the Negro problem no longer exclusively or even predominantly Southern ... the trend of migration has not only been toward the North and the Central Midwest, but city-ward and to the great centers of industry."[2] Set in the North, *Rachel* depicts northern migration as a response to the terror of the lynch mob; the play trades the imagery of urban cosmopolitism and the public space of Harlem for a consideration of the struggles for social justice within the domestic sphere. *Rachel* emphasizes the way the domestic sphere becomes the battleground upon which Harlem Renaissance playwrights will negotiate for value – in terms of "distinction or exchange" – that the culturally prolific practice of lynching denies.[3] Although subcategories abound (folk drama, propaganda plays, anti-lynching drama), attributing value to black folk unites the drama of the Harlem Renaissance. Although scholars often mark the beginning of this period with the return of African American troops to the United States at the end of World War I in 1919, and demarcate the end in 1934 with the Great Depression, I situate Grimké's play as a starting point.[4] I also note that while the Harlem Renaissance bears the name of a neighborhood in New York City, Washington, DC was the locale for drama.

In the age of Jim Crow, certain factors came together to enable a group of African Americans including Grimké, Georgia Douglas Johnson, Willis Richardson, Eulalie Spence, Zora Neale Hurston, Langston Hughes, Alice Dunbar-Nelson, May Miller, Mary P. Burrill, and Marita Bonner to cultivate a distinctive period of African American drama:

> Shortly after the production of *Rachel*, there followed a series of protest or "propaganda" plays authored by black women. The issue of lynching remained a dominant topic until the 1930s. This is understandable given the climate of America during the period. An estimated 3,589 blacks, including 76 women, were lynched between 1882 and 1927. According to historian John Hope Franklin, "In the very first year of the new century more than 100 negroes were lynched, and before the outbreak of World War I the number for the century had soared to more than 1,100."[5]

The vigilante form of ritualized torture, according to Lindon Barrett, secures "the fetishized boundary between racial blackness and whiteness" and "documents [a] relation between value and violence in a hyperbolic fashion."[6] Value distinguishes lives worth protecting from those deemed expendable; part of the Harlem Renaissance project was to add value to black life through cultural production. As Shane Vogel explains:

> The Harlem Renaissance sought on the whole to redefine the meaning of blackness and racial identity in American popular consciousness and to forcefully assert the role of African Americans in the shaping of American culture. The original architects of the Harlem Renaissance envisioned a movement that would counter images and representations of black inferiority with more "truthful" representations and evidence of serious black cultural accomplishment.[7]

In response to vigilante, legal, social, and cultural practices that sought to devalue blackness, African American playwrights articulated a set of cultural values – through practices and ways of being – that affirmed the worth of black lives. Playwrights depicted characters' struggles with social issues such as colorism, domestic abuse, and familial relationships to present the way cultural hierarchies inform black life, and to acknowledge the practices black people have cultivated to resist the denigration of black life.

Cultural sponsors of African American drama

The seemingly sudden emergence of a number of black playwrights in the first decades of the twentieth century did not occur in a vacuum but reflected the efforts of Alain Locke, Montgomery T. Gregory, W. E. B. Du Bois, and Georgia Douglas Johnson to cultivate Black theatre.[8] All three men graduated from Harvard University. Locke and Montgomery were Howard University Professors, and Du Bois was one of the founders of the National Association for the Advancement of Colored People (NAACP). Locke and Du Bois had distinctive opinions about the nature of the aesthetic work that each would cultivate. Often represented as Locke's investment in folk drama and Du Bois's penchant for propaganda plays, the men certainly held differing perspectives on the work drama could and should do. While folk plays seek to depict the experiences of black people, propaganda plays have a specific political purpose: to end the racial oppression of black people. The drama that emerges demonstrates the inherent value of black life through storytelling and political advocacy. It serves as a visual medium that countered problematic contemporary popular cultural images (evidenced in *The Emperor Jones*, *Green Pastures*, and *Porgy*) as well as those of the past.[9]

Drama in the Harlem Renaissance is not only haunted by the specter of lynching but also by that of minstrelsy. Working against stereotypes that white performers presented in nineteenth-century minstrel shows (such as the lazy plantation "darky") and black performers' presentations of ignorance in variety shows (such as malapropisms in Bert Williams's and George Walker's sly comedies), Locke's formulation of the New Negro created a tension with minstrelsy around the question of value. Locke argued, "The day of 'aunties,' 'uncles' and 'mammies' is equally gone. Uncle Tom and Sambo have passed on …The popular melodrama has about played itself out, and it is time to scrap the fictions, garret the bogeys and settle down to a realistic facing of facts."[10] More of a social movement than an idealized person, the New Negro stood for the cultural values emerging in response to the Great Migration and northern urbanization of over a million black people. While Locke acknowledges the ways that black people in the USA differed in terms of class, he also insists that cultural and social shifts in the early twentieth century differentiate Negroes as a collectivity from the stereotypical, popular cultural depictions of the late nineteenth century.

In an effort to mark this distinction, Locke and Gregory cultivated their student playwrights at Howard. Gregory, as a professor in the Department of Dramatic Arts, sought to offer the best training in the world to black theatre professionals; "It was through the Howard Players that many black women received their initial training in playwriting."[11] The playwrights, once trained, needed venues to share their work with the public. Du Bois and Charles S. Johnson provided such an opportunity. Du Bois, as editor of the NAACP's *Crisis* magazine, and Johnson, as editor of the National Urban League's *Opportunity* magazine, created literary contests that resulted in the publication of several one-act plays. These contests helped introduce the world to the playwriting of Spence, Bonner, Hurston, and Johnson, among others. In addition to establishing the *Crisis* literary contest, Du Bois played a key role in organizing the Krigwa Players, founded in 1925 by the *Crisis* magazine. The name of the company, originally Crigwa, is an acronym of the Crisis Guild of Writers and Artists. Well-known members of the group included visual artist Aaron Douglas, who painted scenery for the group, and playwrights Burrill, Richardson, Miller, and Johnson. The group encouraged writing, and provided training and production opportunities for original drama by, for, and about black people.

While the Howard trio provided institutional support for the growing modern Black theatre movement in the USA, Georgia Douglas Johnson offered more personal and intimate encouragement to writers, which proved to be equally important to the development of drama in the Harlem Renaissance. Born in Atlanta, Georgia, she graduated from Atlanta University's Normal School in 1893 and became a schoolteacher. After serving as an educator for almost a decade, she retired from teaching in 1902 and attended Oberlin Conservatory. After graduating from Oberlin, she returned to Atlanta and married Henry Lincoln Johnson, an attorney. In 1910, the couple moved to

Washington, DC with their two sons, Henry Lincoln, Jr. and Peter Douglas, where Henry, Sr. established a law firm.[12] Soon thereafter, President William H. Taft appointed him to a government position as the Recorder of Deeds, which placed the family securely in the ranks of Washington, DC's black middle class. From 1910 to 1925, Johnson spent most of her time caring for her family and home; she did, however, publish two books of poetry in those years. In 1925, her husband died, leaving her as the breadwinner for the family, but also providing the opportunity for her more fully to express her creativity. That year, Johnson founded a Saturday-night gathering of artists and scholars that would become known as the S Street Salon, marking the address of Johnson's home, 1461 S Street, NW.

Writers such as Grimké, Richardson, Hughes, Hurston, Locke, Bonner, Gregory, Du Bois, Jean Toomer, Jessie Redmon Fauset, Carter G. Woodson, James Weldon Johnson, Countee Cullen, and Anne Spencer would attend the S Street Salon gatherings. Hughes, Hurston, and Du Bois would go whenever they were in Washington, and Spencer would come up from Virginia on occasion, making Johnson's home a meeting ground for artists scattered along the East Coast. Her salon became a space where artists conceived of new work and received feedback on work in progress: "It is not unlikely that scenes from dramas by Johnson, Grimké, Richardson, Burrill, and others were read and critiqued by the playwrights as well as by other artists who were gathered in Johnson's home for the evening."[13]

As cultural curator and artist, Johnson left an indelible mark on the drama of the Harlem Renaissance. In 1926, the *Opportunity* magazine contest awarded Johnson an honorable mention for her play *Blue Blood*, and, in 1927, a first prize for her play *Plumes*. Her work serves as an example of Harlem Renaissance plays that function as propaganda, folk, and lynching drama. Her work intervened in popular cultural representations of black folk, as it depicted the consequences of black people being denied access to democratic privilege. Through her consideration of identity and black people's limited access to democracy, she engages with the two central, organizing themes of Harlem Renaissance drama. In Johnson's work, the two most striking examples of these themes are *Sunday Morning in the South* (1925) and *Blue Blood*.

A classic lynching drama, *Sunday Morning in the South* depicts a case of mistaken identity that results in the lynching of Tom, the wrong man. Situating the struggle in the South in clear opposition to depictions of the urban life distinguishing the New Negro aesthetic, many of the playwrights of the period emphasized the importance of southern culture as a source of inspiration, indicating the South as the ground of continued political struggle. Set on a Sunday morning, Sue Jones, her grandsons Tom and Bossie, and her friend Liza discuss the proliferation of lynchings in their community. Distressed, Tom decides that he will study the law in order to give potential victims and their families some protection from vigilante justice. Moments later, two police officers knock on the door with a recently raped white woman looking for her assailant; at the same time, singing from the church next door fills the house. Although the rape survivor does not make a positive identification, the police officers deem Tom close enough to her description and drag him out of the house. The white woman's unwillingness to identify Tom as her attacker demonstrates how, as Judith Stephens has observed, "Lynching plays represent a challenge to the social order of white male supremacy by revealing how the exploitation of black men and women and white women was interdependent and vital to such an order."[14] Moments later, before Sue has the chance to respond, white community members lynch Tom. As a professionally trained musician, Johnson uses music – the hymns streaming into the house from the neighboring church – to communicate the hypocrisy of a Christian community murdering one of its members and denying him due process of law. Although the characters assure Tom that his standing in the community – his social value – will protect him from falling victim to the lynch mob, the play concludes moments later that no black family is safe from mob violence in the South, even on a Sunday morning.

Less deliberately focused on African Americans' inability to access democratic privileges than *A Sunday Morning in the South*, Johnson's comedy *Blue Blood* questions the value attributed to whiteness as a category of identity. It also discusses how individual citizens' rights adhere in familial relationships. Set on May Bush and John Temple's wedding day, the bride's mother and the groom's mother squabble over the social value of their light-skinned children. Exasperated, Mrs. Bush reveals that May's father is a wealthy white banker and that May has blue blood running through her veins. Stunned, Mrs. Temple confesses that the same man raped her and fathered John. Determined to maintain their children's social status while protecting them from the taint of incest, the mothers conspire for May to run off with another suitor, Randolph Strong. Although the play ends with the new couple leaving to be married, the emotional and psychological toll that the mothers paid for their blue-blooded children is not lost on the viewer.

Social value and identity

While Johnson balanced her critique of hierarchies based on identity with challenges to the disenfranchisement of African Americans, most of the playwrights of the Harlem Renaissance either focused on questions of identity or mounted social protest in their work. Both endeavors sought to demonstrate the richness of black life and culture. In terms of questions of identity, class and racial background preoccupied writers attempting to contend with the vaunted status of the New Negro; they found inspiration from all facets of black life. Willis Richardson, deemed by some the father of Harlem Renaissance drama, also considers how the vicissitudes of life impact the precarious class position of many African Americans in the first decades of the twentieth century in *The Chip Woman's Fortune*.[15] As a teenager, Richardson attended Washington, DC's famous M Street High School, and studied with playwright Burrill. After graduating from High School, he took a job as a government clerk. His play, *The Chip Woman's Fortune*, was the first non-musical play written by an African American to be staged on Broadway. The play depicts a family struggling to pay their bills. The setting of the play suggests the trappings of the middle class, particularly the Victrola that stands by the door. We learn, however, that Silas Green, the father of the family, will lose his job if he does not finish paying for their Victrola. His boss considers Silas's history of not making payments on the Victrola a mark against his character and threatens to fire Silas if he does not pay off the record player. His wife Liza suffers from poor health and depends on the assistance of a friend, Aunt Nancy (the Chip Woman). Aunt Nancy lives with Silas and Liza rent-free – a housing arrangement Silas finds unsatisfactory when he learns that he may lose his job. He tells Liza that he will evict Aunt Nancy if she does not begin to pay rent. Nearly destitute, Aunt Nancy does have a small sum of money that she has saved for her son, Jim, who has recently been released from prison. Silas asks Aunt Nancy to give him the money she has saved, but she refuses. As workers come to take the Victrola away, a sure sign of Silas's professional fate, Jim arrives and gives Silas some of the money that Aunt Nancy saved. The play ends with Jim and Aunt Nancy leaving together. Richardson's drama calls attention to the power of charity as it debunks social hierarchies.

Demonstrating the way social circumstances determine individuals' value prior to Jim's arrival, Silas derides Aunt Nancy for saving money for a convict when she could have paid rent. Aunt Nancy defends her choice and admits that Jim made a poor decision. Nevertheless, she stands by her son and refuses to give Silas the money. In a much too obvious conclusion, the man that Silas disparages shows Silas how to exercise compassion in the same way that Aunt Nancy cared for Liza and helped to restore her health. Spence's *Undertow*, Hurston's *Color Struck*, and Hughes's *Mulatto* also call the relationship between markers of identity and social value into question, but they focus on the way colorism functions as a sign of status.

Undertow (1927), a domestic comedy, depicts a deadly love triangle. Spence, born in Nevis, West Indies, came to the USA in 1902 at the age of eight. She grew up in New York City, received a B.A. from New York University in 1937, and her M.A. from Columbia Teachers' College in 1939. While a student at Columbia, Spence studied playwriting, making her one of few playwrights in her circle to study the craft formally. Spence became a high school teacher of English, elocution, and dramatics. Joseph Papp, the founder of the Public Theater, was one of her students. A fastidious playwright, Spence worked to master her craft and collaborated with the Krigwa players, even though she disdained propaganda plays. She contended, "We go to the theatre for entertainment, not to have old fires and hates rekindled."[16] Her play *Undertow*, which focuses on a domestic squabble that explodes with an expression of unbridled rage, certainly meets the criterion of entertaining. Yet it also engages with social protocols of respectability that served a political function for many black people in the modern period.[17]

In *Undertow*, Hattie and Dan suffer through a marriage plagued by infidelity and resentment. At the beginning of their relationship, Dan had an affair with Clem, a light-skinned black woman. Although he remains faithful after the early indiscretion and provides for his family for twenty-five years, Hattie never recovers from the betrayal. Paying a daily penance, Dan returns home from work each day to face his wife's vitriolic, verbal attacks. Her verbal abuse not only destroys what could have been at the very least an amicable relationship, it also undermines Dan's relationship with their son Charley. After years of suffering in an unhappy marriage, Dan runs into Clem; he realizes that she is the woman he should have married. Unwilling to be the other woman again, Clem goes to Hattie and asks Hattie to grant Dan a divorce. Hattie, as vindictive as ever, tells Clem that she can have Dan, but that Hattie will not grant him a divorce. Clem pleads her case, explaining that she does not want to live with Dan out of wedlock because she would be ashamed to do so in front of her daughter. Hattie delights in Clem's predicament and her inability to achieve the status of middle-class respectability because of her choice to have a child with Dan as his mistress. Returning home shortly after Clem has begun to explain to Hattie why she needs Hattie to consent to the divorce, Dan becomes enraged with his wife's mocking of the woman he loves. When Hattie calls Clem a prostitute, it is the last verbal assault Dan will bear; he chokes her to quiet her fiery tongue. Upon releasing her, she falls and hits her head hard, which kills her. Dan's act of rage, a response to years of verbal abuse, quickly transfers him from one prison to another. While the play suggests Hattie's insecurities about her darker complexion make her miserable, it also calls into question how mandates for domestic respectability trap African Americans in insufferable binds.

Zora Neale Hurston's *Color Struck* (1925) also depicts a love triangle among a handsome man, John; his dark-skinned girlfriend, Emma; and a light-skinned woman, Effie. While *Undertow* features the domestic drama of the middle class, *Color Struck* depicts a working-class woman struggling with her inability to access a privileged position in the USA, either socially or economically. Throughout the first two-thirds of the play, on their way to and after arriving at a cakewalking (dancing) contest, Emma and John squabble. Although Emma and John are the two best cakewalkers at the contest, Emma refuses to dance with John; she feels betrayed when he pays Effie too much attention. John, frustrated with Emma's refusal to dance, decides to cakewalk with Effie instead, leaving Emma alone on stage, alienated from the action of the longest scene in the play. The value Emma attributes to Effie's complexion disables her from participating in the dancing, as it points to a set of social hierarchies that privilege whiteness and deride cultural practices steeped in southern black culture such as the cakewalk. Perhaps ubiquitously denigrated, cakewalking's association with minstrelsy draws it securely into a line of association Locke sought to sever.

Color Struck makes several references to the black minstrel show tradition, which often closed with a grand cakewalk. Hurston's choices to foreground the influences of minstrelsy comment on the way modern black culture attempts to gain value through a refusal of certain cultural histories. Hurston's play implicitly resists the turning away from rural southern cultural traditions that Locke's ideal of the New Negro requires; she questions both the devaluing of Emma based on her physical inability to approximate whiteness and the devaluing of black cultural forms that do not aspire to the aesthetic ideals of high Modernism. Hurston's use of the cakewalk does not, however, suggest some authentic form of black cultural expression. Cakewalking has a complex history filled with the influences of black and white practitioners.[18] It does, however, call attention to the struggle and compromise black people made in the late nineteenth and early twentieth centuries to express themselves on stage at the personal costs of such expression.

Discussing the social pressures on Negro writers to produce respectable forms of expression, Langston Hughes famously wrote in "The Negro Artist and the Racial Mountain":

> We younger Negro artists who create now intend to express our individual dark-skinned selves without fear or shame. If white people are pleased we are glad. If they are not, it doesn't matter. We know we are beautiful. And ugly

Figure 4.1 Carl Van Vechten, portrait of Zora Neale Hurston, 1938.

too. The tom-tom cries and the tom-tom laughs. If colored people are pleased we are glad. If they are not, their displeasure doesn't matter either. We build our temples for tomorrow, strong as we know how, and we stand on top of the mountain, free within ourselves.[19]

Naming the affective dimensions that threaten to police black artists' choices about the modes of their production, Hughes affirms that "without fear or shame" he plans to express himself. His willingness to embrace beauty and ugliness disrupts the function of value through binaries that are then placed in a hierarchy: black and white, beautiful and ugly, clean and dirty. Although most people do not fall completely within one binary or the other, one's approximate position to the favored category increases one's value. Hughes alternatively asserts that the cultural value attributed to his art will not stem from a system of worth that depends on dichotomies and hierarchies. Hughes and Hurston were kindred spirits in that sense. They both understood the rich history of black diasporic expression and saw it as a source of their work, even if it revealed what Toni Morrison calls the "funkiness" of life.[20]

Expressing America's long history of racial intermixing, Hughes's *Mulatto* (1927) depicts a mixed-race young man, Bert Norwood, whose only desire – a desire he is willing to kill for – is his white father, Colonel Tom's recognition. In terms of the play, Colonel Tom's recognition would both implode the social order of modern, southern gentility and instantiate the intimate intermingling of white and black people in the nineteenth century. Colonel Tom, therefore, must refuse Bert; in order to define a coherent home – a southern, white home – Bert may only occupy the positions of laborer and servant, *not son.*

In the literature of the Harlem Renaissance, the mixed-race character is often female and represented as tragic – the tragedy being that although she is chaste and well-mannered and, visibly speaking, appears to be white, she must remain a part of the Negro class. Or, conversely, although she appears to fit into white society, her racial status either causes her rejection or consistent feeling of being torn asunder. The mulatta figure possesses a different kind of threat to the racial hierarchy than that of the mulatto. At the rise of the play, Colonel Tom anticipates the return of his insubordinate son, Bert. Norwood angrily laments to his children's mother, Cora:

[COLONEL TOM]: Yes, I know what you're going to say. I don't give a damn about him! There's no nigger-child of mine, yours, ours—no darkie—going to disobey me … Another word from you and I won't send your (Sarcastically) pretty little half-white daughter anywhere, either. Schools for darkies! Huh! If you take that boy of yours for an example, they do 'em more harm than good. He's learned nothing in college but impudence, and he'll stay here on this place and work for me awhile before he gets back to any more schools. *(He starts across the room)*[21]

The ambiguity that colors the Colonel's categorization of his children ("no nigger-child of mine, yours, ours—no darkie—going to disobey me") reinforces the role of masquerade central to the genealogical backflips the Colonel must perform to render his children bastards. Hughes's choice of language draws attention to the purposeful denial necessary to maintain racial hierarchies – a denial further magnified by the physical similarities between Bert and his father, similarities a theatre audience would readily notice. Colonel Tom must deny the self-same reflection he sees when he looks in Bert's eyes in order to solidify his house – his standing as a plantation owner in Georgia. Bert's bravado and willingness to subvert authority draw attention to the way that gender and race intersect in depictions of the mulatto by Harlem Renaissance artists during the modern period. For the most part (save James Weldon Johnson's *The Autobiography of an Ex-Colored Man*), writers depict the mulatto as a mulatta. Her vulnerability to threats, sexual and otherwise, call her to negotiate mandates for respectability and status as a product of whiteness but not necessarily a danger to it; this makes her a fitting tragic figure. Therefore, although annoyed, Colonel Tom feels at ease taking the liberty to admire Sallie, his "pretty little half-white daughter," knowing that she does not have the power to disrupt his house: in marriage, she will eventually become incorporated into another man's family.

The true tragedy of Hughes's play is the familial relationship the Colonel sacrifices in order to maintain his privileged position. Cora remembers one day when Bert "went runnin' up to Colonel Tom out in de horse stables when de Colonel was showin' off his horses ... to fine white company from town ... He went runnin' up and grabbed a-holt de Colonel and yelled right in front o' de white folks' faces, 'O, papa, Cora say de dinner's ready papa!'"[22] William, Bert's older brother, adds, "and when de company were gone, he beat that boy unmercifull."[23]

Astonishingly, Tom beats Bert after the company leaves. His choice to wait indicates that he is trying to teach Bert a lesson and not, solely, that he is invested in keeping up appearances. Bert gives voice to what the Colonel only feels comfortable leaving unspoken. Bert's enunciation, "O, papa," threatens the Colonel's status as a father and as a white man. While the tension between fathers and sons that arises in response to their perception of each other's level of respect dogs many relationships, the added dynamic of race creates a dangerous combination. The play depicts the final deadly confrontation between Bert and his father as a racialized primal scene, rendering race as the terrain upon which the most intimate, challenging, and personal dynamics will be negotiated. After killing his father in a fit of anger, Bert shoots himself, spilling his blood to pay the toll for killing a white man.

Unequal access to democratic privilege

Hughes's play foregrounds the domestic nature of the dispute between Colonel Tom and Bert. But as the tangled history between Thomas Jefferson and Sally Hemings has shown, the questions raised in *Mulatto* have significance for how we understand the organization of the national body. When Colonel Tom denies Bert the status of son, he also reinforces Bert's subordinate social status in general; from being treated like a second-class citizen at the post office to having to enter through back doors, the protocols of the domestic sphere spill out into the public sphere. Therefore, questions of genealogy inevitably bear on notions of citizenship and individual access.

The imagery of Bert's blood spilling in the name of a certain historical order recalls the question Dunbar-Nelson raises in *Mine Eyes Have Seen* (1918) of whether African Americans should serve in the armed forces. Dunbar-Nelson was born in New Orleans and studied English literature at Cornell University. She married twice, first in 1898 to poet Paul Laurence Dunbar, and second in 1916 to Bobo Nelson, a journalist. After marrying Nelson, she moved to Wilmington, Delaware and became a schoolteacher. *Mine Eyes Have Seen* was first performed at her high school, and published in *The Crisis*.

Set in a "manufacturing city in the northern part of the United States," the play presents the competing allegiances of three siblings: Dan ("the cripple"), Chris ("the younger brother"), and Lucy ("the sister").[24] After losing their father to mob violence and their mother to "pneumonia and heartbreak," Lucy and Dan, who was "maimed for life in a factory," depend on Chris for financial support.[25] At the beginning of the play, the family learns that Chris has been drafted. Chris wonders, "Must I go and fight for the nation that let my father's murder go unpunished? That killed my mother – that took away any chances for making a man out of myself?"[26] While Chris questions sacrificing himself for a country that diminishes his value by denying him and his family equal protection under the law, Dan, although bitter, chastises Chris for his lack of patriotism, and recalls the rich history of black Americans in arms. The play ends with "The Battle Hymn of the Republic" streaming into the apartment from a band parading outside with no resolution to the debate. Chris is left "rigidly at attention" in the center of the stage, performing the posture of a soldier even as he resists the way Jim Crow and vigilante justice cheapen black life.[27]

May Miller's *Stragglers in the Dust* (1930) also considers the implications of military service for African American men, examining the government's treatment of them as second-class citizens. Set in a graveyard, the play presents white characters discussing the possibility of an African American being buried in the tomb of the unknown soldier. Although considered a folk dramatist, Miller's play raises questions about national belonging without being didactic. As a student of Locke and Gregory, Miller balances Locke's call for folk art and Du Bois's charge for politically inspired art. Miller's drama offers a happy meeting ground. As a youth, she attended Paul Laurence Dunbar High School in Washington, DC and studied with Grimké and Burrill. After graduating from High School, she went on to study at Howard, where her father taught. With her fine pedigree, Miller would go on to become "the most widely published black female playwright of this period."[28]

Miller's play calls attention to historical gaps, situating history as yet another important democratic privilege denied African Americans. Her teacher, Burrill, also used folk drama to communicate the unequal treatment of poor African Americans. Burrill's play *They Sit in Darkness* (1919), a play advocating for reproductive rights, depicts a mother of seven children, Malinda Jasper, who suffers from exhaustion. The oldest of her children, Lindy, has been accepted to Tuskegee and plans to attend, but also fears leaving her mother to care for her siblings with her father away at work all day. Although Miss Shaw, a nurse, orders Malinda to rest after the recent birth of her seventh child, Malinda immediately resumes her duties as a washerwoman. The play implies that Miss Shaw could offer Malinda some advice about contraception that she could actually use instead of suggestions to rest, which would leave her children to fend for themselves and deprive her family of the much needed added income her labor provides. Miss Shaw, bound by law, refuses to give Malinda the information she needs. As Miss Shaw leaves the house, she admonishes Malinda to rest and takes her to bed. Moments later, the nurse rushes out of the bedroom to inform Lindy that her mother has died. The play ends with the haunting suggestion that Lindy too will be sucked into the cycle of poverty propagated by denied access to information that would enable her to make informed decisions.

Locke and Du Bois saw the crippling effects of unequal access to information as a central roadblock to African Americans' enfranchisement. Marita Bonner's surrealist drama *The Purple Flower* (1928) also depicts knowledge as a fundamental component to obtaining freedom; the play suggests too that totalizing freedom requires monetary wealth and physical sacrifice.

Bonner was born in 1899 in Boston, Massachusetts, and attended Brookline High School. She matriculated to Radcliffe College in 1918 and studied creative writing. After graduating from Radcliffe in 1922, she moved to West Virginia to become a teacher, and then to Washington, DC. There, Bonner quickly joined the circle of the cultural makers, attending Johnson's S Street Salon and publishing work in the *Opportunity* and *Crisis* magazines. Her first play, *The Pot Maker*, is a folk play within a rural setting that reflects Johnson's influence. Her second play, *The Purple Flower*, challenges the conventions of Harlem Renaissance drama, offering an allegorical narrative instead of a realist one that depicts freedom as unattainable without blood sacrifice. While some of the other dramas, particularly lynching drama, showed the sacrificing of black men's blood, *The Purple Flower* calls for a revolutionary overthrow of the group called "Sundry White Devils."[29] The Us's, who vary in complexion from "white as the White Devils, as brown as the earth, as black as the center of a poppy," have toiled for years to gain some land in "Somewhere," but to no avail.[30] Their pursuits of land, education, and wealth have been fruitless. At their breaking point, different factions debate the best way to counter the hegemonic control of the White Devils. Old Man, a vocal member of the Us's, finally concludes, "The Us toiled to give dust for the body, books to guide the body, gold to clothe the body. Now they need blood to birth so the New Man can live."[31] The play returns to Locke's description of the dawning of a new era and the emergence of a New Negro. Bonner's play suggests, however, that the diplomacy Locke advocates for when he says, "this new phase of things is delicate; it will call for less charity but more justice; less help, but infinitely closer understanding," will not address disenfranchisement.[32] Disenfranchised populations may only garner understanding through physical resistance that will necessarily result in bloodshed.

In Locke's introduction to *The New Negro*, he depicts the rich pluralism of black people in the USA and describes that multiplicity as fundamentally American, as deeply woven into the national fabric. He argues that the lived reality of many Americans does not parallel the representation of complete segregation among the races. He contends, "The fiction is that the life of the races is separate, and increasingly so. The fact is that they have touched too closely at the unfavorable and too lightly at the favorable levels."[33] Bonner paints a similar picture: "The Us who work for the White Devils get pushed in the face – down off of Somewhere every night. They don't even sleep up there."[34] While Locke sees these cultural contact zones as signs of the interweaving of American culture, Bonner's play suggests these points of contact clarify the unwillingness of the White Devils to cede any social or monetary privileges to the Us's.

Bonner's play acts as a stunning counter-narrative to the calls for assimilation implicit in Locke's and Du Bois's politics. Her setting, a "stage ... divided horizontally into two sections, upper and lower, by a thin board," points to the stark social divisions Jim Crow produces.[35] *The Purple Flower* suggests that unless the points of contact result in some real material change for the Us's, then they are meaningless. Representing black people as only valuable as a source of labor but not meriting full compensation or equal treatment, *The Purple Flower* insists that their revaluation will occur through a revolutionary change to the social order. In its unconventional style, foreshadowing the stylistic innovation of Adrienne Kennedy and Suzan-Lori Parks, the play poses a challenge to calls for diplomacy.

Drama in the Harlem Renaissance serves to highlight the value of black folk, but does not do so by focusing on African Americans' similarities to white Americans (although some of the drama does depict commonalities). Instead, it emphasizes the rich history of cultural forms and ways of being in black culture, and the complex social relations black people face on a daily basis. Presenting the humanity of black people, the drama of the Harlem Renaissance participates in affirming the worth of black life and black culture.

NOTES

1 Angelina Weld Grimké, *Rachel*, in *Strange Fruit: Plays on Lynching by American Women*, ed. Kathy A. Perkins and Judith L. Stephens (Bloomington: Indiana University Press, 1998), 42.

2 Alain Locke (ed.), *The New Negro* (New York: Touchstone, 1992), 5.

3 Lindon Barrett, *Blackness and Value: Seeing Double* (Cambridge: Cambridge University Press, 1999), 12.

4 In *When Harlem Was in Vogue*, David Levering Lewis describes the Renaissance's bookends as "its authentic beginnings in 1919, with soldiers returning from the Great War, to its sputtering end in 1934, with the Great Depression" (David Levering Lewis, *When Harlem Was in Vogue* [New York: Penguin Books, 1997], xxviii). For a history of the Harlem Renaissance, also see Nathan Huggins, *Harlem Renaissance* (New York: Oxford University Press, 1971). For cultural examinations of the Renaissance see Houston Baker, *Modernism and the Harlem Renaissance* (Chicago: University of Chicago Press, 1987); George Hutchinson, *The Harlem Renaissance in Black and White* (Cambridge, MA: Belknap Press, 1995); David Krasner, *A Beautiful Pageant: African American Theatre, Drama, and Performance in the Harlem Renaissance, 1910–1927* (New York: Palgrave Macmillan, 2002); and Cheryl Wall, *Women of the Harlem Renaissance* (Bloomington: Indiana University Press, 1995).

5 Kathy A. Perkins, introduction to *Black Female Playwrights: An Anthology of Plays before 1950*, ed. Kathy A. Perkins (Bloomington: Indiana University Press, 1989), 9–10.

6 Barrett, *Blackness and Value*, 18.

7 Shane Vogel, *The Scene of the Harlem Cabaret: Race, Sexuality, Performance* (Chicago: University of Chicago Press, 2009).

8 I borrow the term "cultural sponsor" from Gloria T. Hull's description of Johnson. See Gloria T. Hull, *Color, Sex, and Poetry: Three Women Writers of the Harlem Renaissance* (Bloomington: Indiana University Press, 1987), 6.

9 *The Emperor Jones*, *Green Pastures*, and *Porgy* represent black life and culture as not worthy of fully realized characters. The structures of the dramatic works reduce the characters to primitive types that function to satisfy the gaze of white viewers.

10 Locke, *The New Negro*, 5.

11 Perkins, introduction to *Black Female Playwrights*, 7.

12 See Krasner, *A Beautiful Pageant*, 132–3.

13 Judith L. Stephens, introduction to Georgia Douglas Johnson, *The Plays of Georgia Douglas Johnson: From the New Negro Renaissance to the Civil Rights Movement*, ed. Judith L. Stephens (Urbana: University of Illinois Press, 2006), 15.

14 Judith L. Stephens, introduction to Perkins and Stephens, *Strange Fruit*, 7.

15 Koritha Mitchell challenges depictions of Richardson as the inaugurating figure of Harlem Renaissance drama, beginning her exploration of anti-lynching plays with a consideration of *Rachel*; Koritha Mitchell, "(Anti-)Lynching Plays: Angelina Weld Grimké, Alice Dunbar-Nelson, and the Evolution of African American Drama," in *Post-Bellum, Pre-Harlem: African American Literature and Culture, 1877–1919*, ed. Barbara McCaskill and Caroline Gebhard (New York: New York University Press, 2006), 210–30.

16 Quoted in James V. Hatch and Ted Shine (eds.), *Black Theatre USA: Plays by African Americans*, 2 vols. (New York: The Free Press, 1996), Vol. 1: *The Early Period, 1847–1938*, 198.

17 See Evelyn Brooks Higginbotham, "The Politics of Respectability," in *Righteous Discontent: The Women's Movement in the Black Baptist Church, 1880–1920* (Cambridge, MA: Harvard University Press, 1993), 185–230.

18 For more information on this complex history, see Eric J. Sundquist, *To Wake the Nations: Race in the Making of American Literature* (Cambridge, MA: Harvard University Press, 1998), Chapter 4; Krasner, *A Beautiful Pageant*, Chapter 6; and Daphne Brooks, *Bodies in Dissent: Spectacular Performances of Race and Freedom, 1850–1910* (Durham, NC: Duke University Press, 2006), Chapter 4.

19 Langston Hughes, "The Negro Artist and the Racial Mountain," in *Within the Circle: An Anthology of African American Literary Criticism from the Harlem Renaissance to the Present*, ed. Angelyn Mitchell (Durham, NC: Duke University Press, 1994), 59.

20 Toni Morrison, *The Bluest Eye* (New York, Plume, 1994), 83.

21 Langston Hughes, *Mulatto*, in *The Collected Works of Langston Hughes*, ed. Arnold Rampersad, Dolan Hubbard, and Leslie Catherine Sanders, 18 vols., Vol. v: *The Plays to 1942: Mulatto to The Sun Do Move*, ed. Leslie Catherine Sanders and Nancy Johnston (Columbia: University of Missouri Press, 2004), 20.

22 *Ibid.*, 29.

23 *Ibid.*, 30.

24 Alice Dunbar-Nelson, *Mine Eyes Have Seen*, in Hatch and Shine, *Black Theatre USA: The Early Period*, 170.
25 *Ibid.*, 171.
26 *Ibid.*
27 *Ibid.*, 174.
28 Perkins, *Black Female Playwrights*, 143.
29 Marita Bonner, *The Purple Flower*, in Perkins, *Black Female Playwrights*, 191.
30 *Ibid.*, 191, 193.
31 *Ibid.*, 198.
32 Locke, *The New Negro*, 10.
33 *Ibid.*, 9.
34 Bonner, *The Purple Flower*, 193.
35 *Ibid.*

5

JONATHAN SHANDELL

The Negro Little Theatre Movement

On September 17, 1821, a company of actors of African descent performed Shakespeare's *Richard III* for an audience of black spectators at New York City's African Grove pleasure garden. The production was the inaugural offering of the African Theatre, founded by a former merchant seaman named William Alexander Brown. For three years, the African Theatre performed at various venues in New York City. Brown and his troupe sparked the interest of many African American patrons, and aroused curiosity and some hostility among white New Yorkers, before the company quickly disbanded (for reasons that are unclear to historians). This troupe is now celebrated as "the first known black theatre company in North America," with William A. Brown recognized as "the true father of African American theatre."[1] The African Theatre introduced New York audiences to the first production of a black playwright's script (with William A. Brown's own *The Drama of King Shotaway*), and to the first African American actors renowned for dramatic acting: James Hewlett and Ira Aldridge.

The African Theatre was the first step in a more far-reaching movement of African American theatre artists and audiences away from mainstream professional activities, toward participation in new venues and situations that they could more readily identify as their own. Despite this important first step, the obstacles facing black theatre artists in America during the 1800s were formidable. White corporate impresarios ruthlessly controlled Broadway and the nation's major touring circuits. These producers mostly peddled products of proven profitability: melodramas, variety shows, and musical diversions. Within that commercialized landscape, the status of African Americans was marginal. Only falsified, demeaning roles existed for aspiring black actors; opportunities for African American playwrights, directors, and designers were all but unheard of in the professional American theatre. Meanwhile, the hardships facing black America – geographical dispersion, trenchant poverty, and socioeconomic disadvantages with respect to education, employment, housing, and political autonomy – made the goal of founding and maintaining theatre companies that could follow the precedent of the African Company an elusive one throughout most of the nineteenth century.

It is remarkable, then, that "By the mid-1920s nearly every major urban center had an African American theatre group. African American professionals and amateurs, especially in Harlem, Washington, DC, and Cleveland, formed theatres and presented plays, musicals, and staged readings."[2] James V. Hatch and Errol G. Hill report that "by 1925 ... more than three thousand amateur groups – schools, women's clubs, men's lodges, churches and settlement houses – had built raised playforms for stages and 'put on plays.'"[3] Historians have labeled this swell of activity in the early twentieth century as the "Negro Little Theatre Movement." From roughly the mid 1910s until the late 1930s, an assortment of independent, non-commercial African American theatre companies producing dramatic works grew throughout the United States. These companies took root in library auditoriums, churches, community centers, universities, and anywhere else a platform could be built and artists and audiences might gather. In a multitude of ways, with a highly varied repertory, these little theatre groups addressed vital needs of African American communities: authentic self-expression, political protest, intellectual and artistic development, and communal celebration and solidarity. This chapter will trace the history, ideology, and cultural impact of the Negro Little Theatre Movement, demonstrating the influence that its participant artists exerted in the development of African American theatre, an influence that continues to be seen into the twenty-first century.

The most immediate impetus for a Negro Little Theatre Movement came from within African American communities as black artists, critics, and audiences sought meaningful alternatives to the racist tendencies of American culture. False and demeaning portraits of black life pervaded the American theatre. The stage was filled with caricatures and stereotypes derived from minstrelsy, with sensationalized treatments of blacks as an exotic and primitive "other," and various other marginalized or undignified character types (criminals, lynching victims, servants, and so forth). Intellectual leaders of the 1910s and 1920s called on African American playwrights to compose new "Negro dramas" that might replace these popular worn-out clichés and offer a more enlightened perspective on black identity. In an essay in Alain Locke's seminal collection, *The New Negro*, Howard University professor T. Montgomery Gregory wrote, "The hope of Negro drama is the establishment of numerous small groups of Negro players throughout the country who shall simply and devotedly interpret the life that is familiar to them for the sheer joy of artistic expression."[4] Gregory and other Harlem

Renaissance leaders saw theatre as an ideal medium for advancing the wider objectives of the New Negro Movement: the fostering of African American self-expression, and the promotion of race consciousness and pride. There were serious disagreements among these thinkers as to *how* dramatists might use the stage most effectively. Still, calls to arms for black playwrights throughout the 1910s and 1920s sparked the founding of new venues that could bring the emerging dramas to life for African American audiences.

The Negro Little Theatre Movement also drew inspiration from the successes of other "little theatres" (or "art theatres," as they are sometimes labeled) across Europe and the United States. The impulse to create smaller and more autonomous companies that exist outside the demands and profit motives of the commercial stage recurs throughout modern theatre history. As Constance D'Arcy Mackay explains in her study of American little theatres:

> The very name Little Theatre is salted with significance. It at once calls to mind an intimate stage and auditorium where players and audience can be brought into close accord: a theatre where unusual non-commercial plays are given; a theatre where the repertory and subscription system prevails; where scenic experimentation is rife; where "How Much Can We Make?" is not the dominating factor. Little theatres are established from love of drama, not from love of gain.[5]

Throughout the late nineteenth and early twentieth century, little theatres sprouted up across Europe: upstarts like Paris's Théâtre Libre, London's Independent Theatre, Berlin's Freie Bühne, and Stockholm's Intima Teater. These companies rejected popular genres and commercial formulae, and helped ignite an explosion of Modern aesthetics. Artists across the Atlantic followed suit, initiating an American little theatre movement that revolutionized the art form throughout the nation. Groups like Boston's Toy Theatre, New York's Provincetown Players and Washington Square Players, and Chicago's Little Theatre separated themselves from the crass commercialism purveyed by Broadway and the nation's largest touring circuits, and took up the Modernist mantle of rebellion and experimentation for adventurous American audiences.

In many ways, the participants in the Negro Little Theatre Movement fashioned themselves after these European and American little theatres. Their spaces were intimate, makeshift, and modestly equipped. Their budgets were limited. Most importantly, their sense of rebellion against a commercial status quo and their disregard for traditional artistic formulae were palpable. Dublin's Abbey Theatre and the Moscow Art Theatre (both of which toured the United States in the early twentieth century) were particularly influential in demonstrating to American audiences and theatre artists how drama could be used to articulate complex visions of ethnic identity and cultural belonging. Stirred by the success of the Abbey and the vibrancy of many small Yiddish theatres on the Lower East Side of New York, Gregory imagined, in a 1921 editorial, "What the Irish players have done for the Irish people, what the Jewish players are doing for the Jewish race, the Negro should have the opportunity of doing for his race."[6]

During this same period, certain white American dramatists achieved notoriety for experimenting with more enlightened treatments of black characters within their drama. In 1917, Ridgley Torrence's triptych of one-acts entitled *Three Plays for a Negro Theatre* opened at the Garden Theatre in New York. This was the first dramatic appearance of an entirely African American cast on a Broadway stage. Susan Curtis identifies this production as "the first major confrontation of racialized assumptions about art and nationality in the twentieth-century American theater."[7] Eugene O'Neill's expressionist tragedy *The Emperor Jones*, which the Provincetown Players debuted in Greenwich Village and subsequently brought to Broadway in 1920, was even more influential. O'Neill's play dramatizes the rise and fall of Brutus Jones, a former Pullman porter and escaped prisoner who seizes the throne of a Caribbean island nation until the local natives' desire for revenge against his corruption and thievery drives Jones to suicide. Though some recent critics have found the play riddled with "the oldest and most loathsome white stereotypes of black character,"[8] in its era, *The Emperor Jones* represented to many the first American play to achieve wide commercial success with "a negro protagonist … in a dramatic action of universal human significance." Its star, Charles Gilpin, won a Drama League Award for his performance and garnered acclaim as a "Negro Genius."[9] Many African Americans saw the successes of *The Emperor Jones* and other white-authored "Negro dramas" of the early twentieth century as an encouraging trend. While some took exception to the appropriation of black identity and to certain depictions of African American life by white writers, these experiments encouraged African Americans toward new ventures in the theatre. The "Negro dramas" (short folk plays of rural lower-class black life) of North Carolina playwright Paul Green would become staples for the repertoire of many little Negro theatres.

The Negro Little Theatre Movement presents much variability, both in the plays selected for production and the artistic objectives pursued. Some companies (following the precedent set by the African Theatre's first production of Shakespeare) took the approach now termed "color blind" casting by mounting classical and mainstream commercial dramas with African American actors. Former dancer and theatrical pioneer Anita Bush founded one such theatre in Harlem in 1915 called the Anita Bush Stock Company, later renamed the Lafayette Players. Sister M. Francesca Thompson identifies this group as "the first major professional Black dramatic company in America."[10] The Lafayette Players produced melodramas and recent Broadway hits (using makeup to lighten the complexions of darker-skinned actors when necessary) for eleven years in Harlem, and briefly established branches in Chicago and Washington, DC. The company moved to Los Angeles in 1928 before disbanding in 1932 owing to hardships brought on by the Great Depression. Another ensemble working primarily in this vein was the Ethiopian Art Theatre of Chicago, created in 1922 when "a group of influential black and white Chicagoans recognized a desire within the black community to develop its cultural institutions further."[11] Raymond O'Neil, the white founding artistic director of the Cleveland Playhouse, led the venture. The Ethiopian Art Theatre became the first company to produce the work of an African American playwright on Broadway (Willis Richardson's one-act folk drama *The Chip Woman's Fortune*, performed during a 1923 visit to New York). This milestone aside, the ensemble mostly staged the work of white dramatists – such as Shakespeare, Molière, Oscar Wilde, and Hugo von Hofmannsthal – during its brief three-year history.

A "color blind" approach has historically produced (and often continues to engender) sharply divided reactions among artists and critics working to promote African American theatre. Some within the Negro Little Theatre Movement saw the insertion of black performers into traditionally white roles as a mark of progress. *Messenger* columnist Abram Harris responded to an Ethiopian Art Theatre classical double-bill by proclaiming "The great works of Shakespeare, Molière and others are not the indisputable heritage of the white man which constitute his forbidden territory of drama upon which none but Caucasians should trespass." Here was, Harris argued, an important refutation of an insidious "mental parallelism of white art for white folk and black art for black folk,"[12] and thus a crucial step toward equality of opportunity. Other commentators, however, saw dalliances into traditional drama as distractions from a higher calling for black theatres to develop new playwrights and dramatize African American experience. In 1924, critic Theophilus Lewis took issue with the Lafayette Players for their approach: "In a decade of almost continuous activity [the company] has neither found an embryo Piñero in its own ranks nor inspired a would-be Yeats to write a single sensible play; it has made no appreciable effort to bring the lush and colorful life of the black belts on the stage."[13] Years later, venerated actress Rose McClendon made a similar argument in a letter published in *The New York Times*. "What makes a Negro theatre," McClendon proclaimed, "is not so much the use of Negroes as the selection of plays that deal with Negroes, with Negro problems, with phases of Negro life, faithfully presented and accurately delineated. Any other approach is doomed to failure."[14] Disagreements about the legitimacy of color-blind casting for African American actors persist, as evidenced most visibly by the "Wilson–Brustein debates" of the late 1990s. In a 1996 speech (later published), playwright August Wilson decried the practice as "an aberrant idea [and] an assault" on the historical identity of African Americans; white director and critic Robert Brustein responded by denouncing Wilson's argument as divisive and retrogressive, tinged with the "language of self-segregation."[15]

While some theatre artists worked to insert black actors within popular and canonical dramas, much of the energy of the Little Negro Theatre Movement flowed elsewhere, toward the development and presentation of works by black playwrights that directly addressed the realities of African American life. Perhaps the most enduring and inspirational voice for that project was W. E. B. Du Bois – the scholar, essayist, and African American political leader who helped establish the National Association for the Advancement of Colored People (NAACP) in 1909. In 1926, Du Bois founded the Krigwa Players in the basement of New York's 135th Street Library as a venue for staging the prize-winning dramas from playwriting contests sponsored by *The Crisis* (NAACP's official magazine). The company only lasted for about three years, but its impact on the Negro Little Theatre Movement (and on all of African American theatre history) springs largely from the manifesto Du Bois published in *The Crisis* articulating the company's core ideals. The most famous passage of this essay declares "four fundamental principles" that "a real Negro theatre" must follow in assembling its repertoire:

> The plays of a real Negro theatre must be: 1: "About us." That is, they must have plots which reveal Negro life as it is. 2: "By us." That is, they must be written by Negro authors who understand from birth and continual association just what it means to be a Negro today. 3: "For us." That is, the theatre must cater primarily to Negro audiences and be supported and sustained by their entertainment and approval. 4: "Near us." The theatre must be in a Negro neighborhood near the mass of ordinary Negro people.

By repeatedly invoking "us" as the foundation for his new enterprise, Du Bois sought to emancipate black theatre artists from "the demands and ideals of the white group and their conception of [the Negro as] a minstrel, comedian, singer and lay figure of all sorts."[16] Such a project fit within the larger push toward self-expression and self-determination that burgeoned within African American communities of the 1920s. According to historian Ethel Pitts Walker, the Krigwa's philosophy represents a milestone in using the theatre toward "furthering the spirit of racial pride, giving support to the [black] nationalistic spirit of the Harlem Renaissance."[17]

In less than three years of existence, the Krigwa Players debuted new plays by Willis Richardson, Eulalie Spence, Georgia Douglas Johnson, Frank Wilson, and other African American dramatists. Its highest-profile success came with Spence's comedy *Fool's Errand*, which won second prize ($250) at the 1927 Samuel French Little Theatre Tournament. The honor also proved to be the theatre's downfall, as a dispute over the use of the prize money led quickly to resentment against Du Bois's leadership of Krigwa that fractured the company. Though this Harlem ensemble and its various offshoots in Washington, DC; Philadelphia; Cleveland; and other cities were short-lived, the Krigwa Players' legacy lived on. By converting the Harlem Library's basement into a small theatre, Du Bois and his colleagues created a venue that would house a succession of other little theatres for the nation's largest black community. Subsequent groups to occupy the Harlem Library Theatre included the Negro Experimental Players (1929); the Harlem Experimental Theatre (1929–33); the Harlem Players (1931); and the American Negro Theatre (1940–9).[18] More importantly, the Krigwa's philosophy of a theatre by, about, for, and near African American communities endures (thanks to Du Bois's foresight in writing and publishing a statement of vision) as an inspirational template for generations of theatre artists.

Even among those subscribing to a vision for African American theatre that centered on new plays, difficulties and contentious debates arose. Worthy scripts by black playwrights were scarce, and fledgling little theatres lacked the time and resources needed to nurture new playwrights. Moreover, as David Krasner points out, "The emergence of community-based African American theatres raised complex questions about the meaning of 'black drama.'"[19] *What kinds* of plays by black authors should a company stage? *How* should African American writers depict the lives and the culture of black people on stage? What sort of dramatic vision could make the most meaningful statement to African American audiences and the nation at large? Such questions consumed those who worked within and commented on the Negro Little Theatre Movement. Debates over the nature and purpose of theatrical expression, the efficacy of crafting direct political protest on stage, the relationship black drama should have toward mainstream "white" Euro-American theatrical traditions, and the implications of using Negro dialect on stage hovered over the activities of these little theatres.

A central fault line of critical difference pitted Du Bois against Locke in what has come to be known as the "art vs. propaganda" debate. Du Bois (whose outlook on theatre and drama fluctuated throughout his career as an essayist) declared in a 1926 speech, "All Art is propaganda and ever must be, despite the wailing of the purists ... I do not care a damn for any art that is not used for propaganda. But I do care when propaganda is confined to one side while the other is stripped and silent."[20] For Du Bois, "one side" (white America) had for decades circulated a racist "propaganda" of caricatures and falsifications that had undermined the drive for full equality and equal opportunity. The counterweight to such pernicious depictions of black identity would be another kind of propaganda, one driven by idealized notions of beauty, truth, and justice. As Samuel Hay explains, generations of African American theatre artists have translated Du Bois's call for "propaganda" into self-consciously political drama marked by "characters and situations that depicted the struggle of African Americans against racism [and] show people not only as they actually were but also as they wished to be."[21] In contrast, Locke advocated for a more apolitical and idiomatic approach, one that emphasized folk culture and more prosaic characters and situations. "Despite the present lure of the problem play," Locke wrote in response to Du Bois, "it ought to be apparent that the real future of Negro drama lies with the development of the folk play. Negro drama must grow in its own soil and cultivate its own intrinsic elements; only in this way can it become truly organic, and cease being a rootless derivative."[22]

Public discussion of these divergent models for black drama helped energize the Negro Little Theatre Movement, and continued to influence African American artists throughout the twentieth century. In Hay's view, "Locke and Du Bois drew up the ground plans for modern African American drama."[23] In a few notable instances, Negro little theatres worked directly from a Du Boisian blueprint for propagandist theatre. The Drama Committee of the NAACP was earliest and perhaps most influential in sparking divisions among intellectuals over the future of Black theatre. The committee – a group of black intellectual leaders that included both Du Bois and Locke – was convened in 1915, in response to D. W. Griffith's virulently racist silent film, *The Birth of a Nation*. Its task was to explore how artists might best use drama to advance the cause of racial justice. After much internal wrangling, Du Bois and his propagandist vision won out. The committee commissioned from teacher and writer Angelina Weld Grimké the protest play *Rachel*, described by the NAACP as "the first attempt to use the stage for race propaganda in order to enlighten the American people relative to the lamentable condition of ten millions of Colored citizens in the free republic."[24] As a result of the committee's bent toward political drama, Locke resigned in protest. *Rachel* – a tragedy that dramatizes the injustices of racism, and portrays the profound material and psychological effects of a brutal lynching on the lives of one victim's surviving wife, daughter, and grandson – was staged in Washington, DC in 1916 under the auspices of the NAACP. The

Drama Committee arranged for other stagings of *Rachel* in New York and Boston. The group folded soon after, but is now credited as an early catalyst of Negro little theatre activities.[25]

Another short-lived endeavor along propagandist lines was the Harlem Suitcase Theatre, founded in 1938 by Langston Hughes and Louise Thompson, a secretary of the Harlem chapter of the International Workers' Order (IWO). The name of this undertaking articulated its kinship with the ideals of the Little Theatre Movement; the group was committed to presenting low-budget productions that utilized few enough props to fit within a single suitcase. According to its constitution, the company's stated goal was "to fill a long-felt need in this community for a permanent repertory group presenting plays dealing with the lives, problems and hopes of the Negro people."[26] The Harlem Suitcase Theatre took up residency in the IWO's Community Center auditorium in the spring of 1938. In doing so, according to Hughes's biographer Arnold Rampersad, there was a "tacit confirmation that the Harlem Suitcase Theatre would be explicitly a radical theatre. Linked to the Communist Party, the IWO openly appealed to the masses 'to join the struggle against capitalism and for a system where all power belongs to the working class.'"[27] The Communist Party – with its message of working-class unity and interracial solidarity to combat economic injustice – had won many converts in Harlem during the Depression. Though not officially affiliated with the Party, the Harlem Suitcase Theatre reflected the neighborhood's growing affinity for leftist political ideals.

This new theatre created a sensation with its first production: Hughes's *Don't You Want to Be Free?* The drama chronicles African American history from the arrival of the first slaves in North America through the Great Depression, stitching together scenes of dialog, African American music, and familiar Hughes poems to protest America's long history of racial oppression and to call for a new age of solidarity. *Don't You Want to Be Free?* ran for two years in Harlem, with a special appearance in June of 1938 at the national conference for the New Theatre League (a confederation of workers' theatres). Despite ambitions toward permanence in the community and the success of its first offering, however, the Suitcase Theatre lost momentum and struggled to maintain itself. In June of 1939, Langston Hughes severed his affiliation with the group, and by the fall, the company had disbanded. As should now be evident from the examples discussed in this chapter, many participants of the Negro Little Theatre Movement experienced a similar life cycle: a birth from idealistic ambitions, an adolescent flurry of activity and enthusiasm, a maturation period marked by growing pains and organizational challenges, and a relatively rapid demise within a few years.

In contrast to the politicized stance associated with Du Bois, the group most immediately identified with an apolitical vision of "art" in the Negro theatre was one that Locke himself helped organize while serving as professor of philosophy at Howard University. On Howard's campus, Locke found a partner in Montgomery Gregory, who was appointed head of the Speech Department in 1919. Together, Gregory and Locke rechristened the Campus Dramatic Club (which dated back to 1909) as the Howard Players. They steered the group toward their shared vision of an African American theatre defined by an apolitical pursuit of "art." In a 1921 interview, Gregory contended, "the Negro has a wonderful opportunity through drama to win a better standing in the community. Not through the production of plays of propaganda; that would be a mistaken effort. I believe that we can win broader recognition of our rights and responsibilities as citizens by demonstrating our abilities as artists."[28] Though founded on the ethos of a "little theatre," the goal of the Howard Players was to "establish a National Negro Theatre where the Negro playwright, musician, actor, dancer, and artist in concert shall fashion a drama that shall merit the respect and win the admiration of the world."[29]

The Howard Players would make important strides in their early years toward realizing this vision, though suitable scripts by black playwrights proved difficult to find. Gregory addressed this deficiency in part by staging original works by Howard University's students and faculty. As an outgrowth of the nation's pre-eminent Negro college, the Howard Players' goals were both artistic and educational. The troupe "provided practical training and enabled students to gain real-world skills" much needed within emerging black theatre troupes.[30] The visibility and success of the Howard Players also contributed to the growth in dramatic activities at other Negro colleges. By the mid 1930s, there were enough training programs and university troupes in existence to form two distinct interstate associations of university troupes: the Negro Intercollegiate Dramatic Association (NIDA), and the Southern Association of Dramatic and Speech Arts (SADSA). These associations furthered the study and teaching of theatre at black colleges by mounting festivals and tournaments for member groups, facilitating the exchange of play scripts and expertise, and fostering intercollegiate dialog. Thanks to its far-reaching and multifaceted contributions to African American theatre and drama, Annemarie Bean concludes, "In spirit and in practice, the Howard Players may be the closest to a black national theatre inspired by the Harlem Renaissance."[31]

The ideological and tactical debates that gave shape to the Negro Little Theatre Movement lingered over the ensuing decades, as various African American playwrights and companies situated themselves artistically and politically. A palpable tension between the poles of "art" and "propaganda" resurfaced most noticeably in the 1960s and 1970s. During these decades, strident voices of outrage formed the Black Arts Movement, which sought a theatre dedicated solely to revolutionary politics. In counterpoint to Black Arts radicalism, more temperate and apolitical voices also emerged, in what Samuel Hay labels a "Black Experience" movement of theatre.[32] As important as the "art vs. propaganda" binary has been, it is worth remembering that reality often proves itself more complicated than ideology. Thus the repertoire of the Howard Players, despite Locke and Gregory's passionate commitment to African American "folk drama," included dramas by white European writers (Shakespeare and Lord Dunsany) as well as the "Negro plays" of O'Neill, Torrence, and Green. Similarly, the productions of the Krigwa Players (under Du Bois) constituted a mix of political and non-political dramas. When plays are few and resources meager, it takes more than a leader's vision or a well-articulated philosophy to bring a full season of theatre to life.

Thus the most important struggles and accomplishments of the Negro Little Theatre Movement were not over ideology, but in the more prosaic pursuit of survival, continuity, and stability. Amid so many short-lived initiatives that flared up and died out quickly, the most remarkable survivor of all has been (and continues to be, to the present day) the Karamu Theatre of Cleveland. This ensemble began as an adjunct of the Playhouse Settlement community center. Social workers Russell and Rowena Woodham Jelliffe founded the Playhouse Settlement in 1915 to serve the needs of the Western Reserve district, an area to which many black southern families flocked during the Great Migration. Theatre soon became an important part of the Jelliffes' work with the community. In the summer of 1921, an ensemble that called itself the Dumas Dramatic Club (named in honor of the father-and-son French authors Alexandre Dumas, who were of partial African ancestry) began staging evenings of one-act plays at various local school auditoriums. The Dumas Club's performances attracted neighborhood audiences as well as some wider notice throughout the city; audiences at this early phase of its history were predominantly white.

The company raised its profile in 1922, when Charles Gilpin came to Cleveland on tour with *The Emperor Jones* and attended a performance. An inspirational post-show address from this famous dramatic actor, and a $50 donation he made to the company, inspired the group to rename itself the Gilpin Players. According to Reuben Silver's exhaustive history, Gilpin's remarks also spurred the company to start thinking beyond what had been its "standard little theatre plays, the 'white' plays, with which it had begun its life," and to consider "the Negro play" as a part of its repertoire.[33] In the mid and late 1920s, the Gilpin Players staged white-authored "Negro dramas," and subsequently added the works of African American playwrights (Zora Neale Hurston, Langston Hughes, Countee Cullen, Arna Bontemps, and others) to its offerings. Meanwhile, growing popularity and larger audiences attracted by the Gilpin Players made the use of school theatres more challenging. In 1927, the Playhouse Settlement acquired and renovated an adjacent building as a permanent home for their players. They named the new venue "Karamu Theatre," using a Swahili word meaning "a joyful gathering place."[34]

The group thrived for twelve years in their new home, until fire destroyed their theatre in 1939. After several "dark years" and a brief residency at an interim space they called the "Studio Theatre," a new theatre opened in December, 1949. The Karamu Theatre remains active and vibrant at that location today: one of the nation's pre-eminent venues for African American theatre. Space does not allow for an adequate summary of this organization's long and varied history. Political and non-political plays, one-act dramas to full length works, scripts by black dramatists and white dramatists, with and without "Negro content" (as Silver terms it) all gained hearings with the Dumas/Gilpin/Karamu ensemble. The one constant has been its perseverance, and in that respect, the Karamu Theatre was exceptional among so many short-lived efforts at building an enduring home for African American theatre.

A full accounting of this movement in African American theatre history must also include the Federal Theatre Project (FTP) and its "Negro units." President Franklin D. Roosevelt's administration created the FTP as part of the Works Progress Administration (WPA) in 1935. As one part of that effort, director Hallie Flanagan established more than a dozen "Negro units" in Boston, New York, Chicago, Los Angeles, Seattle, and other cities across the country. These companies were charged with providing assistance to and creating work opportunities for unemployed black artists and entertainers. In many ways, the goals and accomplishments of the FTP's Negro units corresponded closely with those of other little Negro theatres. As historian Rena Fraden summarizes it:

> The FTP gave African American theatre professionals and amateurs new opportunities. Some for the first time gained technical training and joined theatre craft unions; writers wrote plays that departed from minstrel stereotypes; and directors chose Shaw and Shakespeare for Negro units, allowing actors a chance to play parts very different from the usual maid or field hand. By providing the opportunity for young actors to train and giving older actors roles to match their talents, the FTP helped foster an ongoing black theatre.[35]

These new outlets created for black playwrights, actors, and audiences during the four years of the FTP's existence came at a crucial historical moment – just as other Negro little theatres struggled with (and, in many cases, collapsed beneath) the economic realities of the Depression. The nationwide initiative, underwritten by federal money, allowed the African American theatre to survive and progress during the leanest years of the twentieth century.

Influential and vibrant though they were, the FTP's Negro units do not fit neatly under the label of "little" theatres. As parts of a massive governmental program, they were enmeshed within the bureaucracy of the WPA and beholden to its demands. In certain units, a little-theatre ethos of adventurous play selection, responsiveness to local audiences, and artistry over commercialism did prevail. But increasingly, the high hopes that the program might lay the foundation for "a national race theatre for Negroes" gave way to a different reality: "[t]he white bureaucracy of the FTP never could relinquish its almost complete control, down to what plays would be produced, for how long, and in which theatres."[36] A spirit of self-determination – so integral to the *idea* of the little theatre from its beginnings in nineteenth-century Europe, and in particular to the case of Negro theatres struggling against white American cultural hegemony – never definitively took hold for African Americans through the FTP (which was killed by an Act of Congress in June, 1939).

In evaluating the FTP (as with the preceding Negro little theatres of the early twentieth century), a wider historical understanding must supersede any concern for shorter-term struggles waged by those involved. Despite the hurdles encountered and the brevity of this program's lifespan, "The FTP's idealism continued to flow into the black theatres of the 1940s and 1950s,"[37] just as earlier currents of idealism had flowed from many other short-lived Negro little theatres into the work of the FTP. The direction, the force, and the progress of these currents – no matter the detours and obstacles that have impeded it over time – make up the remarkable legacy and enduring influence of the Negro Little Theatre Movement. Companies have mostly come and gone. The flow of their beliefs and ideals continues.

NOTES

1 Errol Hill and James Vernon Hatch, *A History of African American Theatre* (Cambridge; New York: Cambridge University Press, 2003), 24, 40. The African Theatre's manager/playwright William Alexander Brown had no relation to the playwright William Wells Brown (1814–84), whose 1856 play *Escape; or, A Leap to Freedom* became the first published play by an African American playwright.

2 David Krasner, *A Beautiful Pageant: African American Theatre, Drama, and Performance in the Harlem Renaissance, 1910–1927* (New York: Palgrave Macmillan, 2002), 207.

3 Hill and Hatch, *A History of African American Theatre*, 262.

4 Montgomery Gregory, "The Drama of Negro Life," in *The New Negro*, ed. Alain Locke (New York: Atheneum, 1923), 159–60.

5 Constance d'Arcy Mackay, *Little Theatre in the United States* (New York: Henry Holt, 1917), 1.

6 Montgomery Gregory, "For a Negro Theatre," *The New Republic*, 28.363 (November 16, 1921): 350.

7 Susan Curtis, *The First Black Actors on the Great White Way* (Columbia: University of Missouri Press, 1998), 13.

8 John R. Cooley, "*The Emperor Jones* and the Harlem Renaissance," *Studies in the Literary Imagination*, 7 (1974): 80.

9 "Negro Genius in Greenwich Village," *Theater* (January, 1921), Provincetown Players Scrapbook, New York Public Library for the Performing Arts, New York, microfilm.

10 Sister M. Francesca Thompson, O.S.F., "The Lafayette Players, 1917–1932," in *The Theatre of Black Americans*, ed. Errol Hill (New York: Applause, 1987), 211.

11 Addell Austin Anderson, "The Ethiopian Art Theatre," *Theatre Survey*, 33 (November, 1992): 132–3.

12 Abram L. Harris, "The Ethiopian Art Players and the Nordic Complex," *Messenger*, 5.7 (July, 1923): 775.

13 Theophilus Lewis, "Theatre," *Messenger*, 6.9 (September, 1924): 291.

14 Rose McClendon, "As to a New Negro Stage," *The New York Times*, June 30, 1935, X1.

15 August Wilson, "The Ground on which I Stand," *Callaloo*, 20.3 (1998): 498–9, available online at JSTOR, www.jstor.org/ (last accessed May 20, 2012); Robert Brustein, "Subsidized Separatism," *American Theatre*, 13.8 (October, 1996): 26, available online at EBSCOhost, http://search.ebscohost.com/ (last accessed January 1, 2012). On January 28, 1997, Wilson and Brustein held a public debate at the Town Hall in New York City, moderated by playwright and performer Anna Deveare Smith. At this event, the two continued to exchange arguments about "color-blind casting" and other issues related to race in the American theatre before a public audience of ticket buyers.

16 W. E. B. Du Bois, "Krigwa Little Negro Theatre: The Story of a Little Theatre Movement," *The Crisis*, 32 (July, 1926): 134.

17 Ethel Pitts Walker, "Krigwa, a Theatre by, for, and about Black People," *Theatre Journal*, 40.3 (1988): 348.

18 Bernard L. Peterson, *The African American Theatre Directory, 1816–1960: A Comprehensive Guide to Early Black Theatre Organizations, Companies, Theatres, and Performing Groups* (Westport, CT: Greenwood Press, 1997), 89.

19 Krasner, *A Beautiful Pageant*, 208.

20 W. E. B. Du Bois, "Criteria of Negro Art," in *The Seventh Son: The Thought and Writings of W. E. B. Du Bois*, ed. Julius Lester (New York: Random House, 1970), 319.

21 Samuel A. Hay, *African American Theatre: An Historical and Critical Analysis* (Cambridge; New York: Cambridge University Press, 1994), 3.

22 Alain Locke, "The Drama of Negro Life," *Theatre Arts Monthly*, 10 (1926): 89–90.

23 Hay, *African American Theatre*, 5.

24 Angelina Weld Grimké, quoted in Montgomery Gregory, "A Chronology of the Negro Theatre," in *Plays of Negro Life*, ed. Alain Locke (Westport, CT: Negro University Press, 1970 [1927]), 414.

25 Peterson, *The African-American Theatre Directory*, 142–3.

26 Constitution of the Harlem Suitcase Theatre, Langston Hughes Papers (Box 512, folder 12781), Beinecke Rare Books and Manuscript Library, Yale University, New Haven, CT.

27 Arnold Rampersad, *The Life of Langston Hughes*, 2 vols., Vol. 1 (New York: Oxford University Press, 1986), 354.

28 Montgomery Gregory, quoted in *Black Female Playwrights: An Anthology of Plays before 1950*, ed. Kathy A. Perkins (Bloomington: Indiana University Press, 1989), 7.

29 Howard Players company announcement, quoted in Gregory, "A Chronology of the Negro Theatre," 417.

30 Adrienne Macki, "Staging the 'Folk': A History of Harlem's Little Theatre Movement, 1920–1940," Ph.D. dissertation (Tufts University, 2008), 37. See pp. 35–49 of this work for a detailed analysis of the educational and artistic activities of the Howard Players.

31 Annemarie Bean, "Plays and Playwrights of the Harlem Renaissance," in *A Companion to Twentieth-Century American Drama*, ed. David Krasner (Malden, MA: Wiley–Blackwell, 2005), 95.

32 See Hay, *African American Theatre*, 1–134. Hay organizes his entire panoramic study of African American theatre around this central contrast between ideals of "art" and "propaganda."

33 Reuben Silver, "A History of the Karamu Theatre of Karamu House, 1915–1960," Ph.D. dissertation (Ohio State University, 1961), 112.

34 In 1941, the Playhouse Settlement would follow the lead of its theatre group by changing its name to "Karamu House." The names "Karamu House" and "Karamu Theatre" remain for these organizations today.

35 Rena Fraden, *Blueprints for a Black Federal Theatre, 1935–1939* (Cambridge; New York: Cambridge University Press, 1994), 4.

36 *Ibid.*, 7.

37 Hill and Hatch, *A History of African American Theatre*, 334.

6

ADRIENNE MACKI BRACONI

African American women dramatists, 1930–1960

Writing about the out-of-town premiere of her play *A Raisin in the Sun* in a letter to her mother, Lorraine Hansberry remarked:

> Mama, it is a play that tells the truth about people. Negroes and life and I think it will help a lot of people to understand how we are just as complicated as they are—and just as mixed up—but above all, that we have among our miserable and downtrodden ranks—people who are the very essence of human dignity. That is what, after all the laughter and tears, the play is supposed to say.[1]

Hansberry's emphasis on telling the truth and infusing her plays with comedy and pathos equally describes the works of Eulalie Spence and Alice Childress, whose plays blazed a trail for Hansberry with their investment in the overlapping effects of racism and class status within mid-twentieth-century black life. Accordingly, this chapter not only engages class, race, and gender issues; it serves a recuperative purpose that introduces the theatres of two seminal playwrights who inspired, or otherwise forged a path for Hansberry.

The interstices of the Great Depression, World War II, and the Civil Rights Movement shaped the careers of these three significant African American playwrights. All three nurtured their dramaturgy and activism in New York while working with the social and cultural leaders of their era, each achieved critical acclaim, and each saw her plays published and produced during her lifetime. Though it is challenging to categorize their work, as all three have resisted tidy structuralist groupings, their plays are at once about black life and culture, and about all humanity. Their plays often rely on social realism to provide searing portraits of the economic exigencies of their times, from the consumer practices of American society in a capitalist system to the commodification of black bodies harkening back to slavery. The dramas of Spence, Childress, and Hansberry reveal a compulsive desire for property rights, illuminating the effects of poverty, the plague of materialism, the struggle for fiscal power, and the politics of social class. Their works suggest how the lack of economic control can compromise and consume black culture. If the business of slavery (which historically marginalized and commercialized African Americans) and its aftermath inform the playwrights' dramaturgy as well as the content of their work, then their thematic concerns recall transatlantic commerce and how black bodies were exploited, traded as capital, viewed as property, and used to further colonial enterprises.

Eulalie Spence

Though Eulalie Spence (1894–1981) is not as well known as Lorraine Hansberry and Alice Childress, Spence helped to develop a theatre tradition that was more hospitable to black women, paving the way for Childress, Hansberry, and Ntozake Shange, among others. She was one of the most prolific black playwrights of the Harlem Renaissance as well as a teacher, performer, and director. Elizabeth Brown-Guillory describes Spence as a "daring and vociferous woman playwright who might one day be credited with initiating feminism in plays by black women."[2] Spence's pioneering efforts and focus on gender and class anticipate the sociopolitical plays of Childress and Hansberry. Similarly to her contemporaries Georgia Douglas Johnson, May Miller, Shirley Graham, Alice Dunbar-Nelson, and Thelma Duncan, Spence began playwriting in the 1920s. She dedicated her career to arts education and staging not-for-profit productions in the community of Harlem. Often overlooked because she wrote during the same period as other more prominent black playwrights and authors such as Langston Hughes and Zora Neale Hurston, Spence's theatrical contributions as a dramatist, actress, and director have earned her a rightful place in literary and dramaturgical history.

Like many West Indian immigrants, Spence's family initially resided in the ethnically diverse community of Harlem before moving to Brooklyn, where Spence attended Wadleigh High School and the Normal Department of New York Training School for Teachers. Spence studied at the National Ethiopian Art Theatre School in the early 1920s where her first production, *Being Forty*, was staged at the Lafayette Theatre in October, 1924. She earned her B.S. at New York University in 1937 and an M.A. in speech from Columbia University in 1939. Besides directing student plays, Spence taught elocution and English at the Eastern District High School in Brooklyn. She played a pivotal role in the lives of her students, including the young Joseph Papp, who would later become an acclaimed director and producer with the New York Shakespeare Festival. In turn, Papp (who described Spence as one of his greatest influences) was instrumental in the careers of Alice Childress and Ntozake Shange.[3]

Spence remained active in Harlem, and this vibrant community emerged as the backdrop in several of her plays through her representation of the urban black's struggle. In addition to writing thirteen scripts, Spence contributed to the Negro Little Theatre Movement, helping to establish the Dunbar Garden Players in the late 1920s. She was also a founding member of W. E. B. Du Bois's Krigwa Players in residence at the Harlem Branch of the New York Public Library. The Krigwa Players mounted several of Spence's dramas from 1926 to 1927.

Writing in a time when many of her contemporaries like Marita Bonner were creating plays to be read as literature, Spence was committed to presenting theatre in a public forum. She declared in her essay "A Criticism of the Negro Drama" that theatre must be *performed*: "to every art its form ... and to the play, the technique that belongs to it," speaking to theatre's unique ability to affect audiences.[4] At least seven of her plays were produced in her lifetime, whereas her female contemporaries may have had (at most) one or two of their dramas staged, if any at all. The D.C. branch of Krigwa Players performed *The Hunch* in 1927, and in the same year the Harlem division also presented *Her*, *Fool's Errand*, and *Foreign Mail*. Seven of Spence's plays were published, including *The Starter* (1927), *Foreign Mail* (1927), *The Hunch* (1927), *Fool's Errand* (1927), *Episode* (1928), *Help Wanted* (1929), and *Undertow* (1929). Spence achieved visibility nationally, not only through performance, but also through publication in such journals as *Opportunity* and *The Crisis*, two major black periodicals. *The Crisis*, the mouthpiece of the National Association for the Advancement of Colored People (NAACP), was "from its founding in 1909 to the 1930s, the most widely read publication in Negro America."[5] Spence also earned more recognition than any of her peers in the play competitions sponsored by *The Crisis* and *Opportunity*, receiving five awards. In addition, *Fool's Errand* won the Samuel French Prize for best new unpublished play at the national Little Theatre Tournament following its May, 1927 premiere at the Frolic Theatre in New York City.

In the 1920s, theatre became a site for African Americans to redefine their identity, especially since members of the black intelligentsia like Alain Locke hailed its potential to foster cultural identity and pride. Locke and W. E. B. Du Bois encouraged African American playwrights to eradicate derogatory images from the stage, expounding the need for a national black theatre. While Locke and Du Bois both agreed drama had the power to refute negative stereotypes, they employed different approaches. Accordingly, like many African American women playwrights of the Harlem Renaissance, Spence's plays illuminate a recurring controversy in black drama: whether theatre should employ art for propaganda or utilize art for its own sake.[6]

Spence resisted Du Bois's requests to write protest dramas because she maintained that propaganda plays did not appeal to black audiences. By focusing on the everyday life of African Americans and balancing audience demand with "appropriate" subject matter, Spence's plays illustrate Alain Locke and T. Montgomery Gregory's preference for folk art, with its emphasis on common folks, reflecting their struggles and joys as well. Such works often included references to African American religion, ritual, and spirituality, and representation of African American music, song, and dance.

Though Spence ostensibly advocated for theatre for theatre's sake, her preoccupation with class, gender, and race issues can be detected within her plays. With the exception of *Her, Undertow,* and *La Divina Pastora* (1929), Spence favored comedies in which racial concerns (initially) appear absent, though closer analysis reveals that her plays are more socially minded and complex than previously realized. This is due to the fact that Spence's work is double-voiced, conveying the intentions of her characters while at the same time refracting the playwright's objectives. Similarly, a double consciousness, the challenge of internalizing black and American identity but continually experiencing an irreparable divide (what W. E. B. Du Bois describes as "two unreconciled strivings; two warring ideals in one dark body"), emerges in Spence's plays.[7] Such dialogic discourse requires greater attention to discern what is at stake in Spence's comic critique.

Spence introduces a range of difficulties facing African Americans, such as materialism, domestic abuse, and depravity in *Hot Stuff* (1927). Her depiction of an organized crime ring in Harlem, rife with blackmail, racketeering, and prostitution, spoke to the absence of legitimate financial institutions in the African American community and the limited opportunities for African Americans to improve their economic condition. Fanny, a dishonest numbers runner (who pockets the winnings from one of her customers), promises sexual favors and cash to a peddler for a stylish fur wrap, a symbol of her desire for upward mobility. Fanny's negotiations cost her dearly: she is nearly killed by her jealous husband when he discovers her betrayal. Yet, Fanny clutches her possessions like a compulsive addict: "She places the wrap close to her face, stroking it with her cheek. She braces up suddenly. She slips the coat about her shoulders. She walks across the floor, painfully, and then as she reaches the mirror, a little sob breaks from her."[8] Though clearly hurt from the assault, Fanny twirls repeatedly to admire her purchase, and quips, "Some bargain!"[9] The stage business and her line serve as an understated reminder of the moral and material cost of the fur coat and her life's choices: a violent marriage, an exploited body, and a dangerous job in racketeering, pointing to the few paths open to her because of class, gender, and ethnicity.

Similarly, *The Starter* (1923), a comedy and one of Spence's most popular plays, also pulls on this thread regarding financial struggle, class, and the impact of limited employment opportunities. In a park in Harlem on a hot summer evening, Thomas Jefferson (T. J.) Kelly waits for his girlfriend, Georgia, to arrive. What follows explores their courtship, fraught with financial tensions and economic uncertainties. The play's narrative is driven by questions of money: Georgia insists on full disclosure of T. J.'s savings and earning potential before agreeing to marry him, while T. J. pursues Georgia with greater interest when he learns of her nest egg. Their spirited dialog about their jobs and financial situation speaks to a long history of the economic valuation of black bodies as well as the state of American industrial relations before the Great Depression.

The play's title takes its name from T. J.'s occupation: he is an elevator starter, one of the common professions available to African American men. Georgia is a garment worker commonly referred to as a "finisher," one of the few career paths open to black women at the time. Their union not only comically pairs their job titles, but also critiques the over-representation of African Americans in lower-paying service jobs. When Georgia describes her place of employment as a "dump," remarking that it is so "low down" that it brings African Americans, Jews, and Italians together, Spence evokes the challenges that some races faced while assimilating as well as the deplorable working conditions for garment workers in the United States.[10] As Ethel Carolyn Brooks writes, "gendered division of labor and gender gaps in pay" as well as "raced division of labor" were all too typical during this period.[11]

Spence's last attempt at playwriting, and only full-length play, *The Whipping* (1934) bears mention for its bold subject matter and reflection of the challenges Spence attempted to overcome in producing it. *The Whipping* dramatized (white) journalist Roy Flannagan's novel about a promiscuous, modern young woman, Marigold, whose arrival upsets her provincial town's status quo. The Klansmen set out to teach her a lesson, whipping her for her immorality, and try to run her out of town. To their chagrin, Marigold identifies the Klansmen and leverages her sudden celebrity in order to pursue a theatrical career.

Since Spence could not stand up against the Ku Klux Klan, the white character of Marigold serves as a projection for what many black women would have liked to do. Though Spence proclaimed that she was personally unfamiliar with the racial violence of the Klansmen, she was not unaware of their activities. And, though she claimed that "We go to the theatre for entertainment, not to have old fires and hates rekindled," her choice of subjects begs the question: why dramatize this story of the KKK?[12] While the narrative provides an inversion of the racist group, it also illuminates women's oppression by men – a recurrent theme in Spence's playwriting.

As Spence adapted the subversive plot for the stage, she contacted Flannagan and his publisher to secure the rights and convinced Audrey Wood from Century Play Company (Tennessee Williams's agent) to represent her. Spence eagerly anticipated the production's premiere at the Empress Theatre in Danbury, Connecticut with Queenie Smith in the title role, but, without explanation, the show was canceled days before its debut.[13] In what was a significant transaction, Spence sold the manuscript in November, 1933 to Paramount Films for $5,000 (which is worth more than $83,000 today). It was adapted and made into a film *Ready for Love*, directed by Marion Gering with Ida Lupino and Richard Arlen.[14] Then and now, there were few writers of color in Hollywood, and though Spence failed to see her play staged professionally, she made headway against the very real limitations that made it difficult for black women in theatre (and film) before Lorraine Hansberry.[15] As Margaret Wilkerson argues: "Women playwrights before 1950 were full partners in the theatre's protest against conditions for blacks … Not until mid-century however, would their voices reach beyond their communities in to the highly competitive world of professional theatre."[16] The economic uncertainties of Spence's era proved overwhelming and thwarted her career in the theatre. Spence seemed to have retreated from the public eye after *The Whipping*, and focused on teaching, directing, and mentoring in educational and community settings.

Alice Childress

Like Spence, Alice Childress migrated to Harlem and emerged as one of the most significant African American women in theatre in the mid-century. Born in 1916 in Charlestown, South Carolina, Childress moved to Harlem as a child and was raised by her grandmother.[17] Childress was mostly self-educated and only attended three years of high school (the same secondary school as Spence, Wadleigh High School) before she was forced to provide for herself when her mother and grandmother passed away.

Spence and Childress are considered "transitional" writers, whose works – with their focus on urban life and authentic, gritty representations of black experience – foreshadow Ntozake Shange's.[18] Spence's and Childress's contributions to black drama are largely unheralded because they tended to produce dramas reflecting the conventions of dramatic realism. Critics often overlook their subtle variations on the form, including such innovations as bold thematic content; assertive, complex female characters; and a focus on lower-class and middle-class blacks. Childress counted herself among those working-class blacks who populated her scripts; she held several jobs from domestic work to retail sales while raising a child as a single parent.[19]

Childress, like Spence, secured much of her early theatrical training in the little theatre circuit and was a founding member of the American Negro Theatre (ANT), one of the most prominent black theatre companies in the 1940s. Her apprenticeship with ANT required her to work in all facets of theatre, from administration to designing costumes and acting. Early in their careers, she worked with Ruby Dee, Ossie Davis, and Sidney Poitier. Childress proved herself first as an actress, moving to Broadway with the *Anna Lucasta* cast in 1944, and received a Tony nomination for her performance.

Feeling unfulfilled artistically and responding to the need for more black scripts, Childress began writing plays, penning a total of eighteen that were "written, produced, and published over a period of four decades," the only black playwright in America to do so.[20] Her earliest works include *Florence* (1949), an adaptation of Langston Hughes's *Just a Little Simple* (1950), and *Gold through the Trees* (1952). The last two were produced professionally and, according to Elizabeth Brown-Guillory, Childress was the first black woman playwright to earn this distinction.[21] Childress also achieved acclaim for her novels, such as *A Hero Ain't Nothing but a Sandwich* (1973).

Florence, which was produced by the Committee for the Negro in the Arts in September, 1950 and set in the waiting room of a train station, creates a liminal space symbolic of the racial divide in America and migratory patterns of African Americans seeking refuge in the North. The play's title takes its name from the absent character of Florence who, like Childress, is a single parent trying to make it in the theatre. Florence's mother, Mrs. Whitney, intends to travel to New York to persuade her daughter to give up the theatre and return home, but after meeting Mrs. Carter, a racist, unemployed white actress, Mrs. Whitney realizes she must encourage her daughter's dreams. The play urges African Americans to fight for their desires in the face of nearly insurmountable obstacles, and demonstrates the conditions that often make it difficult for blacks to succeed. Throughout the play, Mama tightly clutches her hard-earned savings, which she contemplates giving to Florence, even if it means not having money for rent. Mrs. Whitney's check (referenced repeatedly throughout the play) signifies dreams deferred. Anticipating Hansberry's *A Raisin in the Sun*, each member of the Whitney family has different ideas about how the money should be spent. The family's matriarch also struggles with whether or not she should fund Florence's dream. Mrs. Whitney decides to send the check to her daughter with encouragement to "keep trying" to be an actress rather than a maid.[22] The check signifies on a long history of the profits assigned to black bodies, from slave auctions to the disproportionately high number of African Americans employed in domestic labor and the lower-paying service sector. Mama illustrates the pragmatic need for money to support her daughter's goals and realizes that following one's dreams is a basic right that must be observed at all costs.

Childress continues her theme of blacks' disenfranchisement in the arts in *Trouble in Mind*, which debuted at the Greenwich Mews Theatre in New York in November, 1955. Wiletta Mayer, a seasoned performer, refuses to acquiesce to the condescending white director's vision of racial performance. As a group of actors rehearse a (fictional) anti-lynching drama, *Chaos in Belleville*, by a white author for an upcoming Broadway production, Wiletta finds herself alone in her efforts to change the problematic script, which implicitly endorses stereotyped roles; the rest of the cast acquiesces rather than band together to protest for what is right. Accordingly, the play illustrates Childress's concern with the power of money, which forces African Americans to make compromising choices, sacrificing their integrity for financial gain. In a case of art reflecting life, Childress faced such temptation when a Broadway producer bought the rights and demanded revision of the play's ending. Her refusal to supply the ending the producer desired kept the production off Broadway.[23]

Similarly, her refusal to revise the ending of *Wedding Band: A Love/Hate Story in Black and White* (first performed in 1966) limited the play's commercial success.[24] Described as her "most popular play," *Wedding Band* met with controversy because of its treatment of interracial love.[25] Set in 1918 in a small southern town, it concerns an interracial relationship torn apart by black and white racial intolerance. Julia, a black woman, must face the truth of her go-nowhere ten-year relationship with Herman, a poor, Polish baker. Miscegenation laws force the couple to keep their relationship a secret, but when Herman falls ill, their relationship is made public. Julia longs for connection and family, which becomes more evident in light of the economic factors contributing to the relationship's failure. Herman's hesitancy to move from the South is complicated by prejudice, economic self-interest, and family obligation, especially because his mother loaned him money to start his bakery. His livelihood becomes a means of escape and a source of conflict, particularly when his mother demands the return of her investment upon learning about Herman's relationship with Julia.

Accordingly, the interplay of racism and class consciousness characterizes much of the play's dramatic action – from the rancorous argument between Julia and Herman's mother to Julia's neighbors' failure to see that a relationship between a black woman and a white man may amount to more than exploitation.[26] Each character clings to an identity shaped by financial realities, including those characters on the brink of ruin as well as the more financially secure landlady. She states,

> I'm the first and only colored they let buy land 'round here ... When I pass by they can say ... "There she go, Fanny Johnson, representin' her race in-a approved manner" ... 'cause they don't have to worry 'bout my next move. I can't afford to mess that up on account-a you or any-a rest-a these hard-luck, better-off-dead, triflin' niggers.[27]

As Rosemary Curb persuasively writes, "Childress dramatizes the daily frustrations and minor crises that tempt the impoverished to despair and self-hatred. She demonstrates that maintaining personal dignity and hope for the future in the midst of destitution and social rejection can be heroic."[28]

The much anthologized *Wine in the Wilderness* (1969) also shows the struggles of poor black women and the trappings of material culture when Tommy loses her home and possessions in a race riot. Through her will to survive and spirituality, she perseveres and comes to appreciate her African heritage. Tommy argues that she represents the authentic African American woman worthy of esteem and recognition and demands that her likeness ought to be celebrated in a painting on black womanhood. She explains: "If my hair is straight, or if it's natural, or if I wear a wig, or take it off ... that's all right; because wigs ... shoes ... hats ... bags ... and even this *(She picks up the African throw she wore a few moments before ... fingers it)* They're just what ... what you call ... *access* ... *(Fishing for the word)*."[29] As Tommy struggles to find the word "accessories," what she says instead, "access," is quite fitting. "Access" evokes concerns with permission, freedom, and the ability to pass or enter without hindrance. Access suggests that an individual has agency, power, and the means to affect change. Tommy gives herself authority to be and do what she wants when she realizes that clothing is a marker of conspicuous consumption, facilitating movement from one class to another. Tommy's empowering transformation into an African queen as she removes her wig and mismatched clothing suggests how accessories not only signify wealth and status, but also work on multiple levels as tools or signs to convey identity or give one the right to speak. For Tommy (and for Childress) access is as much about the cultural trappings of class as well as divisions engendered by education and politics. Tommy's speech is a metaphor for the play's overarching concerns about hypocrisy and self-hatred.

Several of Childress's lesser-known plays equally illustrate her commitment to economic change, including *The World on a Hill* (1968), a one-act play involving a confrontation between a well-off white woman and a poor West Indian boy who resorts to thievery and robbery to survive. Childress offers a way to remediate financial inequity by dramatizing the youth's realization that he does not want to rob the woman; he simply wants an opportunity to go to school as an alternative to his dead-end path. Meanwhile *String* (1969), a reworking of Guy de Maupassant's nineteenth-century short story, "La ficelle," focuses on the effects of class prejudice. Childress shows the desperate actions of the play's most destitute character when he is accused of stealing a wallet. Similarly, *The African Garden* (1963), later revised and adapted to form *Gullah* (1984), demonstrates the dangerous consequences of materialism and capitalism, asking can one overcome capitalist corruption with faith and love?[30] Both plays follow the marital and moral decline of Pete and Evalina as they lose their home, identity, and culture. Like Childress's other plays, *The African Garden* features protagonists who struggle financially and face even greater losses when confronting challenging circumstances. Paradoxically, a sizable, unexpected inheritance from Pete's derelict brother leads the couple to become ethically and spiritually bankrupt. These two plays, *The African Garden* and *Gullah*, among the least realistic of Childress's dramas, also reflect her commitment to social and economic reform, characteristic of Hansberry's plays as well.

Lorraine Hansberry

Born in 1930 in Chicago, Lorraine Hansberry came to New York in 1950 for "an education of a different kind," joining a community of other socially minded activists and liberal progressives.[31] Unlike Childress, Hansberry's middle-class background enabled her to attend the University of Wisconsin at Madison for two years, where she took classes in drama, stage design, art, and literature. After a summer session at Roosevelt University, Hansberry moved to the Lower East Side of New York and took courses in photography and short story writing at the New School for Social Research in 1950.[32]

While working as a reviewer for progressive periodicals such as *Freedom* and *New Challenge*, Hansberry saw Childress's plays and was inspired to write for the theatre. At the time, Hansberry also maintained a slew of part-time clerical positions in addition to her journal work. In 1953, she married Robert Nemiroff; when her husband's financial circumstances changed, Hansberry gave up those jobs to concentrate exclusively on writing.

Undoubtedly most renowned for *A Raisin in the Sun* (1957), Hansberry surpassed Childress in terms of recognition and prestige when she became the first black woman playwright to see her work professionally staged on Broadway, blazing the path for Ntozake Shange, Suzan-Lori Parks, Lynn Nottage, Katori Hall, and Lydia Diamond.[33] Hansberry was the youngest American and first African American to receive the New York Drama Critics

Figure 6.1 Lorraine Hansberry, March 25, 1958.

Circle Award. *A Raisin in the Sun* was not only a critical success but a financial one as well, playing for 538 performances to mixed audiences. It has become "one of the most produced plays in the United States."[34] Though cut short by an untimely death to cancer at age thirty-four, Hansberry's impact has been profound. *Raisin*, which originally debuted on Broadway in March, 1959, was revived in 2004, earning a Tony Award for best revival, as well as best lead actress and featured actress for Phylicia Rashād and Audra McDonald respectively. Hansberry's play was adapted into a film in 1961, a musical in 1975 (which received a Tony Award), and two other made-for-television films in 1989 and in 2008. The 2008 television adaptation received an NAACP Image Award, and earned special recognition for Rashād (reprising her stage role) and actor/producer Sean Combs. This seminal play has also inspired new works such as Bruce Norris's Pulitzer-Prize-winning play *Clybourne Park* (2009), a fictional response to *Raisin* that imagines the home the Youngers purchase before they move in and fifty years later, when the neighborhood is in the midst of gentrification.[35]

In James Baldwin's introduction to Hansberry's autobiography, *To Be Young, Gifted, and Black*, Baldwin remarked, "I had never in my life seen so many black people in the theatre. And the reason for that was that never before, in the history of the American theatre, had so much of the truth of black people's lives been seen on stage."[36] This notion of representing the truth of black life as a call for change anticipated the dramaturgical concerns of Amiri Baraka and the playwrights of the Black Arts Movement. However, Baraka and the artists of the 1960s initially considered *Raisin* to be "conservative" and "passive" next to black militant dramas such as Baraka's *Dutchman* (1964) and James Baldwin's *Blues for Mr. Charlie* (1964). Baraka later admitted that "we missed the essence of the work – that Hansberry created a family on the cutting edge of the same class and ideological struggles as existed in the movement itself and among the people."[37]

Scholars such as David Krasner, Steven Carter, and Margaret Wilkerson agree that Hansberry's dramaturgy was pointedly informed by and responding to the sociopolitical exigencies of her milieu. She participated in protests and rallies, represented Paul Robeson at an international peace conference in Uruguay, and followed her father's lead in decrying racial injustice.[38] Indeed, Hansberry's activism informed all of her artistic endeavors. In a letter, she wrote, "I am sick of poverty, lynching, stupid wars and the universal maltreatment of my people and obsessed with a rather desperate desire for a new world."[39] Flanked by the 1954 *Brown* v. *Board of Education of Topeka, Kansas* Supreme Court decision, the 1964 Civil Rights Acts banning segregation in public accommodation and employment, and the 1965 Voting Rights Act legislation, the play "established a socially conscious African American theatre."[40] As Wilkerson states, it would be near impossible for Hansberry not to be affected by the world events surrounding her – namely "the beginning of the Cold War between the United States and Soviet super-powers, a rising demand by blacks for civil rights at home, and a growing intransigence and rebellion by colonized peoples throughout the world."[41]

Hansberry's frustration with poverty and institutional racism, as well as her desire for a new, liberated world, are paramount in *A Raisin in the Sun*. Accordingly, much of the Hansberry scholarship rightly notes the playwright's desire for economic change. Indeed, the preoccupation with money is a constant tension throughout the play, from Travis asking his mother for money, to Walter considering a bribe from Mr. Lindner to give up their new home in Clybourne Park. Ruth contemplates abortion largely because they are overcrowded and cannot afford to keep the baby. Ruth and Walter's marital strife is exacerbated by financial stress.

Wilkerson maintains that both Lena Younger and her son Walter "seem to be pursuing the American dream of upward mobility – property and money – when, in fact, Hansberry is using their aspirations as metaphors for the dream of freedom and the right to be regarded as not only a citizen but as a human being."[42] While Wilkerson makes a strong point, the play's dramatic conflict is nevertheless animated by the family's competing desires surrounding what to do with the $10,000 life insurance inheritance, so much so that the money serves as a vehicle propelling the play's action. Similarly, Mama's disappointment with her son's obsession with money leads her to inquire:

> MAMA: Son – how come you talk so much 'bout money?
> WALTER: *(With immense passion)* Because it is life, Mama!
> MAMA: *(Quietly)* Oh – *(Very quietly)* So now it's life. Money is life. Once upon a time freedom used to be life – now it's money. I guess the world really do change ...
> WALTER: No – it was always money, Mama. We just didn't know about it.[43]

This exchange reflects the playwright's recognition that liberation requires economic control and access (which mirrors Childress's concern in *Wine in the Wilderness*) as well as Hansberry's own discomfort with wealth. She further articulates this sentiment in *To Be Young, Gifted, and Black* when she describes herself as "antagonistic to the symbols of affluence."[44] As Hansberry explains, Walter is representative of an "almost maniacal lusting for 'acquisitions,'" which the play reconciles in the conclusion. Walter recognizes the importance of dignity and integrity, and rejects the offer from Mr. Linder and the Clybourne Park Association.[45]

Walter's desire to open a liquor store represents a capitalist imperative to own his own business and profit from Mama's investment, thus revising a history that denied him property rights. Yet, his choice of business is especially provocative, and speaks to a consumer convenience culture as well as to the disproportionately higher number of liquor stores per capita in largely African American neighborhoods as compared to white or racially integrated communities (such disparity became more obvious in the 1960s as neighborhoods became segregated). Several recent studies charge that commercial districts in black neighborhoods are more likely to have fewer supermarkets, and more fast food restaurants and carry-out liquor stores.[46]

If *Raisin* introduces the desire for economic control as a means to ensure freedom, then Hansberry's *Les Blancs* (which suggests the Mau Mau Revolution from 1952 to 1965 in Kenya), furthers this assertion. *Les Blancs*, produced posthumously in 1970 on Broadway, emerged as Hansberry's response to Jean Genet's absurdist play *The Blacks* (*Les nègres*). It combines social realism, ritual, and supernatural forces to form a particularly violent play about racial tensions in Africa as a metaphor for racial global violence and colonialism. Set in a mythical African village, the play focuses on the conflicted choices of an African intellectual, Tshembe Matoseh, who has returned home to bury his father and must decide whether or not to take his father's place as the resistance movement's leader or turn his back on his country and heritage. Scholar Philip Uko Effiong contends that Hansberry "advances the need for dialogue between the oppressed and the oppressor, yet she insists on action and commitment, supports the procurement of sovereignty at any cost, and visualizes the genesis of a new black world."[47]

As Hansberry's collaborator, literary executor, and former husband Robert Nemiroff notes in his introduction, *Les Blancs* addresses the problems of race, power, and colonialism "on a world scale," revealing the dynamics between the "capitalist West and the Third World."[48] By describing how white colonialists plundered Africa for her land, her labor, and precious minerals, Hansberry suggests that such conditions in Africa reflect a series of economic transactions motivated by power and greed. To Hansberry's point, Gatimu Maina's study, "The Paths of the Mau Mau Revolution: Victory and Glory Usurped," demonstrates that when Africans were slow to participate in the cash economy, the government imposed hut and poll taxes to incentivize Africans to work.[49]

Moreover, Hansberry's representation of colonialism is also reflected as a form of pervasive corruption, with economic imperialists infiltrating institutions and industry as well as individuals exploiting their own countrymen in pursuit of profit and upward mobility. For example, the church's role is indicted when Tshembe, referring to Abioseh's Roman Catholic vestments, accuses Abioseh of selling out. Tshembe locates their struggle in the "marketplace of Empire," where "the sale dear brother has been completed and you are wearing the receipts!"[50] Pointing to Abioseh's silver crucifix, Tshembe rails against his brother's hypocrisy: "I know the value of this silver, Abioseh! It is far more holy than you know. I have collapsed with fatigue with those who dug it out of our earth!"[51] As Hansberry makes obvious, African labor has extracted the land's great riches, contributing to a vicious cycle of oppression and economic decline.

Hansberry is unafraid to implicate capitalism's role in colonial oppression. She frames the play's discussion of colonialism in such terms when Charlie asks if the Reverend has "'capitalized,' so to speak, on the backwardness he found here."[52] Similarly, Tshembe's and Charlie's satirical conversation about Tshembe's career plans reveal capitalism's impact, indicating the way the marginalized often participate in their oppression:

TSHEMBE: It is my expectation to go into the textile business!
CHARLIE: Ah, a capitalist to the marrow.

TSHEMBE: Incipient, but to the marrow, yes. I think Reverend Nielsen and I shall get out a line of resort wear. Do you know any New York buyers, Mr. Morris?[53]

His new-found fascination with textiles is a metaphor for the superficial but well-intentioned tourist mentality of those who claim to want to help, but fail to invest in practical, long-term solutions. When Tshembe quips, "Mr. Morris, if you don't mind I have a business to build!," it reflects the way Africa has been abused and commercialized.[54] The conversation, though in jest, is a means for Tshembe to avoid discussing his reluctance to participate in the struggle, and critiques those who exploit the products of his country for personal gain. Dramaturgically, such discourse frames the larger forces at work in colonial oppression.

Likewise, *The Drinking Gourd*, Hansberry's unproduced 1959 screenplay about slavery and southern plantation masters, dramatizes two families at the beginning of the Civil War. It focuses on the economic system of slavery, its profitability, and the horrendous injustices it perpetuated. Kristin Matthews adds that the play "clearly identifies slavery as the foundation of America's economic system and oppression."[55] Plantation owner Hiram Sweet (who is near death) promises one of his oldest slaves, Rissa, that he will save her son (Hannibal) from the fields, but he is unable to do so when his eldest son, Everett, seizes control of the estate. Everett appoints a vicious overseer who blinds Hannibal for learning to read (a flagrant offense for slaves).

The teleplay exposes the truths of slavery, particularly its part in early transatlantic commerce, when an omniscient narrator in the guise of a Civil War soldier explains:

> some planters will tell you with pride that the cost of maintaining one of these human beings need not exceed seven dollars and fifty cents—a year. You see, among other things, there is no education to pay for ... There are of course no minimum work hours and no guaranteed minimum wages. No trade unions. And, above all, no wages at all.[56]

Similarly, Everett's attempts to persuade his father to increase production or face bankruptcy perpetuated this cycle of slave economy. Everett says, "You don't seem to understand, Papa, we don't have much choice. We have got to up our yield or go under."[57] Everett envisions a more productive and efficient model for the plantation that entails longer hours and harsher working conditions for the slaves. Like the colonialists in *Les Blancs*, Everett is not invested in the betterment of the land, but merely capitalizes on both it and the laborers by hiring an overseer to run the plantation with an iron fist. Hansberry makes clear that slavery continues because it is economically viable, derived in part by farmers like Zeb, the cruel overseer, who hopes to make enough money to buy more land and slaves of his own in order to participate fully in the exchange of slave-produced commodities.

The plays of Spence, Childress, and Hansberry encompass a diversity of themes and styles. Yet their work is unified by their spirit and commitment to self-actualized black characters fighting against oppression and consumption while struggling to maintain racial and gender subjectivity. Though beset with contradictions, these dramatists and their characters confront the paradoxes of their lives, responding to their circumstances in surprising ways. Often criticized for not being "radical" or political enough, their work has long been considered "conservative" in form and content, which belies their powerful critique of gender, race, and class. With honesty, humor, and anger, Spence, Childress, and Hansberry identify the need for economic power as an instrument for personal liberation.

NOTES

1 Lorraine Hansberry, *To Be Young, Gifted, and Black: Lorraine Hansberry in Her Own Words*, adapted by Robert Nemiroff (Englewood Cliffs: Prentice-Hall, 1969), 91.

2 Elizabeth Brown Guillory, *Their Place on the Stage: Black Women Playwrights in America* (New York: Praeger, 1990), 4.

3 Helen Epstein, *Joseph Papp: An American Life* (New York: Little, Brown, 1994), 44.

4 Eulalie Spence, "A Criticism of the Negro Drama," *Opportunity*, June 28, 1928, 180.

5 Henry D. Miller, *Theorizing Black Theatre: Art versus Protest in Critical Writings, 1898–1965* (Jefferson, NC: McFarland, 2011), 12.

6 The distinctions between folk art drama and protest drama are discussed in Samuel A. Hay, *African American Theatre* (Cambridge; New York: Cambridge University Press, 1994), Chapters 1 and 2; and David Krasner, *A Beautiful Pageant: African American Theatre, Drama, and Performance in the Harlem Renaissance, 1910–1927* (New York: Palgrave Macmillan, 2002), Chapters 1 and 10. Du Bois maintained that race drama must focus on the clash of race life while providing social analysis, and emphasized "defining and elucidating racial identity through facts, truth and history" (Krasner, *A Beautiful Pageant*, 224). Alain Locke maintained that the folk arts, infused with Afrocentric ideas and themes, offered playwrights and actors richer material for the betterment of African Americans. In "Art or Propaganda," Locke described the propaganda play as "one-sided and pre-judging," whereas he sought balanced, interesting, and detached descriptions of black life full of real people, springing from all walks of life. Besides well-developed characters, Locke encouraged clear plots with a beginning, middle, and end. See Alain Locke, "Art or Propaganda?" *Harlem*, 1 (November, 1928): 12–13.

7 W. E. B. Du Bois, *The Souls of Black Folk* (New York: Barnes & Noble, 2003 [1903]), 9.

8 Eulalie Spence, *Hot Stuff*, in Elizabeth Brown-Guillory (ed.), *Wines in the Wilderness: Plays by African American Women from the Harlem Renaissance to the Present* (New York: Praeger, 1990), 50.

9 *Ibid.*

10 Margaret B. Wilkerson, introduction to *9 Plays by Black Women*, ed. Margaret B. Wilkerson (New York: Penguin, 1986), 382.

11 Ethel Carolyn Brooks, *Unraveling the Garment Industry: Transnational Organizing and Women's Work* (Minneapolis: University of Minnesota Press, 2007), 59.

12 Spence, "A Criticism," 180.

13 Eulalie Spence, interview by Joshua Carter, audio recording (Recorded Sound Division, Schomburg Center for Research in Black Culture, 1973). Queenie Smith was a Broadway favorite in the 1920s, renowned for her soubrette roles in comedies, musicals, and films such as *Show Boat* (1936). According to a brief press release, the production, which was scheduled to open on July 17, 1933 as part of the New York Phoenix Theatre Company's summer season, had been canceled. *New York Times*, July 13, 1933, 17.

14 Spence, interview. The film, *Ready for Love*, dir. Marion Gering (Paramount, 1934) does not list Spence in the credits.

15 Gerald Horne, *Class Struggle in Hollywood* (Austin: University of Texas Press, 2001), 74, 77; Jorja Prover, *No One Knows Their Names: Screenwriters in Hollywood* (Bowling Green: Bowling Green State University Popular Press, 1994), 123.

16 Wilkerson, *9 Plays*, xviii–xix.

17 Sources provide differing dates for Childress's year of birth, noting October 12 in either 1916 or 1920 as her birth date. Elizabeth Brown-Guillory cites it as 1920 and La Vinia Delois Jennings cites it as 1916. I have chosen to go with 1916.

18 Christy Gavin (ed.), *African American Women Playwrights: A Research Guide* (New York: Garland, 1999), 18.

19 La Vinia Delois Jennings, *Alice Childress* (New York; London: Twayne; Prentice-Hall, 1995), 3.

20 Elizabeth Brown-Guillory, *Their Place on the Stage: Black Women Playwrights in America* (New York: Greenwood Press, 1988), 28.

21 Though Spence's *Fool's Errand* was produced at the Frolic Theatre, it was an amateur production held during a play competition with other little theatre, community theatre troupes, whereas Childress's productions featured professional, union actors. See Brown-Guillory, *Their Place*, 29.

22 Alice Childress, *Florence*, in Brown-Guillory, *Wines in the Wilderness*, 121.

23 The play had several endings. In an interview, Childress discusses how the producers at the Greenwich Mews wanted a "happy ending" where united black and white cast members all threaten to leave the show and successfully convince the director to change the play. Childress regretted making the change and later reinstated the play's original ending. See Jackson R. Bryer (ed.), *The Playwright's Art: Conversations with Contemporary American Dramatists* (New Brunswick: Rutgers University Press, 1995), 53.

24 Spence's former student Joseph Papp later produced and directed *Wedding Band* in 1972 at the New York Shakespeare Public Theatre and saw that it was televised on ABC.

25 Soyica Diggs, "Dialectical Dialogues: Performing Blackness in the Drama of Alice Childress," in *Contemporary African American Women Playwrights: A Casebook*, ed. Philip C. Kolin (London; New York: Routledge, 2007), 36.

26 Rosemary Curb, "An Unfashionable Tragedy of American Racism: Alice Childress's *Wedding Band*," *MELUS* 7.4 (1980): 57–68.

27 Alice Childress, *Wedding Band*, in Wilkerson, *9 Plays*, 105.

28 Curb, "An Unfashionable Tragedy," 61.

29 Alice Childress, *Wine in the Wilderness*, in Brown-Guillory, *Wines in the Wilderness*, 148 (my emphasis on "*access*").

30 *The African Garden* was copyrighted in 1963. However, most scholars refer to a 1971 version of the play that was published in *Black Scenes*, ed. Alice Childress (New York: Doubleday, 1971). The earlier text, now in the Alexander Street Press database, seems to have been reworked multiple times during the 1960s and 1970s.

31 Hansberry, *To Be Young*, 93.

32 Steven R. Carter, *Hansberry's Drama: Commitment and Complexity* (Urbana: University of Illinois Press, 1991), viii.

33 Though Spence's *Fool's Errand* was presented on a Broadway stage, it was not professionally produced with a paid cast and director or royalties for the playwright.

34 Margaret B. Wilkerson, "Political Radicalism and Artistic Innovation in the Works of Lorraine Hansberry," in *African American Performance and Theater History: A Critical Reader*, ed. Harry J. Elam and David Krasner (New York: Oxford University Press, 2001), 40.

35 See Rebecca Ann Rugg and Harvey Young (eds.), *Reimagining* A Raisin in the Sun: *Four New Plays* (Evanston, IL: Northwestern University Press, 2012).

36 James Baldwin, introduction to Hansberry, *To Be Young*, x.

37 Amiri Baraka, "A Critical Reevaluation: *A Raisin in the Sun*'s Enduring Passion," in Lorraine Hansberry, *A Raisin in the Sun and The Sign in Sidney Brustein's Window*, ed. Robert Nemiroff (New York: Vintage, 1995), 19.

38 Carl Hansberry, an active member of the NAACP and Urban League, fought back against segregated housing in Chicago and took his case to the Supreme Court.

39 Hansberry, *To Be Young*, 83

40 Krasner, *A Beautiful Pageant*, 22.

41 Wilkerson, "Political Radicalism," 45.

42 *Ibid.*, 40.

43 Hansberry, *A Raisin in the Sun*, 73.

44 Hansberry, *To Be Young*, 37.

45 Julius Lester, introduction to Lorraine Hansberry, *Les Blancs: The Collected Last Plays of Lorraine Hansberry*, ed. Robert Nemiroff (New York: Random House, 1972), 8.

46 See Roland Sturm, "Disparities in the Food Environment Surrounding US Middle and High Schools," *Public Health*, 122.7 (2008): 681–90; S. N. Zenk, A. J. Schulz, B. A. Israel, S. A. James, S. Bao, and M. L. Wilson, "Fruit and Vegetable Access Differs by Community Racial Composition and Socioeconomic Position in Detroit, Michigan," *Ethnicity & Disease*, 16.1 (2006): 275–80.

47 Philip Uko Effiong, "History, Myth, and Revolt in Lorraine Hansberry's *Les Blancs*," *African American Review*, 32.2 (1998): 273–83.

48 Robert Nemiroff, introduction to Hansberry, *Les Blancs*, 43.

49 Gatimu Maina, "The Paths of the Mau Mau Revolution: Victory and Glory Usurped," *Kasarinlan: Philippine Journal of Third World Studies*, 19.1 (2004): 92–112.

50 Hansberry, *Les Blancs*, 79–80.

51 *Ibid.*, 80.

52 *Ibid.*, 112.

53 *Ibid.*, 117–18.

54 *Ibid.*, 119.

55 Lorraine Hansberry, *The Drinking Gourd*, in *Les Blancs*, 573.

56 *Ibid.*, 227.

57 *Ibid.*, 248.

7

AIMEE ZYGMONSKI

Amiri Baraka and the Black Arts Movement

In a 1994 *Time* magazine cover piece on black creativity, noted scholar Henry Louis Gates, Jr. tracked the various "renaissances" of black art in the United States. Gates defined three movements of the twentieth century: the rise of literary figures at the turn of the century, including writer and activist W. E. B. Du Bois and poet Paul Laurence Dunbar; the fabled Harlem Renaissance of the 1920s; and then, almost as an afterthought, the Black Arts Movement, deeming it the "most short-lived of all" and, by the 1970s, "dead."[1] While his chronological history quantifies the small moment in time in which the Movement occurred, Gates fails to identify the impact of the Movement on today's artists. Black Arts was not so much a movement in time, but rather an overlapping of artistic expressions and political transformations during a heightened moment in America's history. The art and ideas shared and produced during Black Arts not only affected those involved at the time, but also those who came after. As Larry Neal wrote in a seminal essay on Black Arts, "If art is the harbinger of future possibilities, what does the future of Black America portend?"[2] In viewing the trajectory of Black theatre, it is clear the Movement's philosophies reverberate in the plays of artists such as Ntozake Shange, August Wilson, and Suzan-Lori Parks.

Since the Black Arts Movement spans a decade of artists and work, theatrical and poetic, visual and musical, this chapter examines the Black Arts Movement through one of its key players: Amiri Baraka, the Movement's undeclared founder, poet, and playwright. In-depth case studies of Baraka's 1964 play *Dutchman* and the short-lived Black Arts Repertory and School demonstrate the complex relationships between the political undergirding of the Movement and its artistic creations. While *Dutchman* came before the assassination of Malcolm X and Baraka's total disillusionment with black–white equality, the play foreshadows Baraka's growing rage spurred by the nascent Black Nationalist Movement. It is the play's precarious position and

Baraka's own transitional growth that makes the reading of *Dutchman* so important to understanding Black Arts.

The early 1960s were a time of great upheaval in the social fabric of American society. The period from 1964 to 1968 was an especially intense period for the Civil Rights Movement as well as the then emergent Black Power agenda. It is no coincidence, then, that the Black Arts Movement informed and inspired so many African American artists to participate in cultural production. As Baraka reflected in a 1994 essay, he wanted

> Black Art that was 1. Identifiably Afro American ... 2. We wanted it to be a *Mass* Art ... 3. We wanted an art that was revolutionary. We wanted a Malcolm Art, a by-any-means-necessary poetry. A Ballot or Bullet verse. We wanted ultimately, to create a poetry, a literature, a dance, a theatre, a painting, that would help bring revolution!"[3]

While the Black Arts Movement ultimately did not bring revolution to American culture, the artists changed the way in which radical literary movements affect communities, harnessing the power of political motivation through performance and art.

From Leroy to Leroi, Jones to Baraka

Amiri Baraka began his writing career ensconced in the Beat counter-culture of Greenwich Village. He was born Everett Leroy Jones in Newark, New Jersey in 1934, attended the prestigious Howard University for a time, and then joined the Air Force in 1954.[4] Although the branches of the military had been desegregated in 1948 after World War II, Baraka felt alienated by his military service and was later dishonorably discharged for writings that the military found to be "Communist-leaning." He moved to New York City's Greenwich Village and embraced the Beat poetry movement, starting his own press with his Jewish wife Hettie Cohen Jones, and befriending, as well as publishing works by, Allen Ginsberg, Jack Kerouac, and Frank O'Hara. After traveling to Cuba in 1960, Baraka became inspired by Castro's revolution and increasingly frustrated with the apolitical nature of the Beats. He began to distance himself from them. His 1963 *Blues People: Negro Music in White America* signals his interest in black culture and political expression in the arts. The book focused on the music and cultural history of African American blues and jazz, one of the first books published to pinpoint the important work of free jazz musicians in the late 1950s and early 1960s, such as John Coltrane, Ornette Coleman, and Sun Ra.

Interested in the non-realistic work of downtown playwrights such as Edward Albee, Baraka tried his hand at playwriting.[5] In 1964 *Dutchman* premiered, along with three of his other short plays the same year, including *The Slave*, *The Toilet*, and *The Baptism*. These four plays begin Jones's transformation from apolitical Beat poet to Black Nationalist. Baraka has told interviewers that he wrote *Dutchman* literally in one evening (ironically reminiscent of the story of Jack Kerouac writing *On the Road* on one continuous roll of paper in three weeks). The play's two main characters inhabit the car of a subway train in the "flying underbelly of the city … the subway heaped in modern myth."[6] On the surface, one could describe the plot simply as the meeting of two people – Clay, a young black man, and Lula, a slightly older white woman; however, as the encounter unfolds, the conversation begins to complicate quickly. Somehow, without having met him before, Lula knows quite a bit about Clay. Surprised at Lula's ability to size him up, Clay assumes that she knows a friend, but Lula's evasive and coy answers do not give her away. "I lie a lot. It helps me control the world," she tells him with a smile.[7] This veiled repartee continues between Clay and Lula, Clay trying to figure out what Lula's intention is, Lula delighting in being enigmatic and contradictory. Lula toys with Clay until she (presumably) achieves the proper reaction: a slap across the face from Clay. His monologue (now famous for its line about his "pumping black heart") follows, as does his death.

On the playbill with two other one-acts (Samuel Beckett's enigmatic *Play* was one of these), *Dutchman* struck critics with its urgency and obscenity, its rage and its lyricism. *New York Times* critic Howard Taubman seemed to not know what to make of it, calling it an "explosion of hatred rather than a play" and a "mélange of sardonic images and undisciplined filth," but praising the play as "one that bespeaks a promising, unsettling talent."[8] Famous Group Theatre director turned critic Harold Clurman wrote in *The Nation* that the premiere of *Dutchman* signaled "the emergence of an outstanding dramatist," while *Wall Street Journal* critic Richard Cooke believed it was "not a play for the 'nice' world."[9] Overall, though, the response was overwhelmingly positive, and *Dutchman* earned Off-Broadway's highest honor in 1964: an Obie for Best Play.

While plays written after *Dutchman* reflect a deeper connection to the tenets of the Black Arts Movement's underlying philosophy, they can be difficult to read since much of the play's message connects directly with stage images created for the original production, audience involvement, and music that cannot be contextualized in simple, written stage directions. *Dutchman* has since become the de facto example of the Black Arts Movement, even though the play was written in the year before Baraka and others coalesced their shared frustrations into a formal literary and cultural movement. The play's structure still follows a traditional European realistic model, offering greater accessibility to wider reading (and viewing) audiences. Yet, as the play unfolds, its realistic setting becomes more surreal, and the characters become subsumed into metaphoric allusions, multifaceted and layered with meaning. Both the play's dialog and themes reveal Baraka's struggle with his nascent Black Nationalist philosophy, and for this reason, *Dutchman* showcases the inner turmoil representative of the Black Arts Movement. The following close reading of the text demonstrates how Baraka constructs a dialectic between language and action, strength and weakness, and, ultimately, black and white.

Dutchman

The symbolic title of the play refers to the nautical legend of a ghost ship doomed to sail the seas without ever reaching port. To Baraka, the allusion of the *Flying Dutchman* spoke to him in many aspects of the play: "I didn't know if I wanted the train to be the Dutchman or the dude to be the Dutchman or the woman to be the Dutchman. So I just said, Fuck it, it's all Dutchman."[10] The symbolic piece of folklore pervades the play in ways that Baraka himself could not articulate at the time of its writing. Certainly, the rushing subway car that they ride sails Clay to his own personal doom (death) as Lula strolls down its aisles looking for a victim. Lula herself is a trapped figure stuck on this subway, destined to stalk each young black man that enters the train car, wondering if she can provoke – through verbal taunting – their anger.

Lula's insults invoke many historical stereotypes attributed to African Americans, as she accuses Clay of everything from African primitivism to Uncle Tom complacency. Her first question directed towards him, after asking if she can sit next to him, is "Weren't you staring at me through the window?"[11] As Clay seems confused, she continues to press him, insinuating that as a young black man he stared at her with sexual intent, as if all black men stereotypically and licentiously want white women. "You think I want to pick you up, get you to take me somewhere and screw me, huh?," she asks him, and proceeds to size him up, assuming where he's from (New Jersey), that he has a friend who pretends to speak with a British accent (Warren), and that he's trying to grow a beard. Confused, Clay presses to understand why she seems to know so much about him. She flatly retorts, "I told you I didn't know anything about *you* ... you're a well-known type."[12] She proceeds to label his grandfather a slave (he wasn't), and Clay an "escaped nigger," a "middle-class black bastard," and finally an "Uncle Thomas Woolly-Head" and "Uncle Tom Big Lip."[13] This last insult, referring to the title character in Harriet Beecher Stowe's 1851 novel *Uncle Tom's Cabin* who became an enduring stereotypical symbol of the black man catering to white needs before his own, pushes Clay over the edge.

Clay is not the only one who could be perceived through various stereotypes. Lula herself plays into notions of a loose woman, bohemian and sexy, looking for any willing sexual partner. Voraciously eating a bag of apples as the scene progresses, and swishing her long red hair as described by Baraka in the stage directions, Lula visually embodies the common image of Eve as Temptress. Through most of the play, Lula flirts with Clay verbally and physically, placing her hands on his body, placing his hands on her body. Her act is so over the top at times Clay asks her if she's not an actress. In the second half, Lula prompts Clay to help her complete the story of how their night could end: Clay walks her home to her apartment, they talk "endlessly" and then, according to Lula, they "screw." Clay almost suppresses a laugh with his retort, "We finally got there," the use of the word "finally" highlighting Lula's overt seduction.[14] However, reading Clay and Lula as mere incarnations of stereotypes, regardless of how the characters use stereotypes to define each other, is too simplistic. Lula's use of assumptions to describe – and at times define – Clay's existence mirrors the way in which Baraka sees white society using stereotypes to define African Americans. Clay makes the final joke on her as he retorts, "Plantations were big open whitewashed places like heaven, and everybody on 'em was grooved to be there. Just strummin' and hummin' all day."[15] Lula's emphatic answer of "yes" clearly shows that she does not understand that Clay is toying with her ignorance.

While Clay does see through Lula's manipulations, Lula's main goal in her goading focuses on pushing Clay toward some monumental action. Through their dialog, Baraka explores the dialectic between the primacy of language and the immediacy of action. While Clay relies upon his command of language, Lula needles him to see if he will act. Lula bursts into the subway car and into Clay's seat, immediately initiating her attack, accusing Clay of staring lustfully at her through the car window with the intent to provoke him. It is clear from the subtext of her dialog that she is not just trying to paint Clay as the hypersexualized, stereotypical black buck to the *audience*, but rather to paint him as the black buck to *himself*, so that he will react. The reaction Lula looks for is not apparent initially, but her constant barrage of insinuations, declamations, and insults presupposes that she does have an intended outcome. Does she ultimately want Clay to murder her to relieve her of this never-ending cycle (*à la Flying Dutchman*), or fall into her trap to fulfill the stereotype of violent, lust-crazed blackness? Whatever an audience may suppose Lula's initial intention to be, she charts her path methodically. She first lays claim to knowing his friends, and then picks apart the suit he wears, noting that "those narrow-shoulder clothes come from a tradition you ought to feel oppressed by." When Clay doesn't quickly take the bait, she more overtly attacks his blackness and class, telling him "I bet you never once thought you were a black nigger."[16] The stage directions note that Clay is shocked at the comment, but quickly rallies, presumably choosing to disregard Lula's insult. As this quick reversal does not elicit the reaction Lula hopes for, she becomes sullen, noting not a minute later "You are murderer, Clay, and you know it."[17] This accusation by Lula seeks to push Clay to action. But why murder? Does Lula assume that because Clay is black he fulfills the common stereotype of the black as criminal? Obviously, Clay is not clueless in his interactions with Lula. Rather, instead of jumping quickly to action, he sits back and plays defense, letting Lula spin her racist web, only jumping in occasionally to correct her inaccuracies.

Lula's final desperate attempt to incite Clay to do something involves a two-pronged attack – insulting him with black stereotypes and provoking him sexually. "Come on, Clay. Let's do the nasty. Rub bellies. Rub bellies," she keeps chanting, as Clay is "embarrassed."[18] This physicality, connected with her cries of "you middle-class black bastard," "you ain't no nigger, you're just a dirty white man," and various insults toward his parents finally push Clay into slapping Lula.[19] Lula's desire for action seems a veritable stand-in for Baraka's nascent political philosophies in his evolution as a cultural activist as she yells at him, "Clay, you got to break out. Don't sit there dying the way they want you to die. Get up."[20] With this directive, Lula may well be Baraka's Black Revolutionary voice and not just a stereotype of whiteness. As Andrzej Ceynowa writes,

> Even her execution of Clay is of a piece with Black revolutionary ideology. Having already achieved the level of consciousness at which a revolutionary could be born, and equipped with the knowledge and skills to lead his people, Clay renounces his social responsibility and retreats into individualism, allowing the growth of Black consciousness into revolutionary consciousness to take its own sweet, slow pace. In a word he betrays his revolutionary vocation and his people.[21]

Another trope running through *Dutchman* is Baraka's meditation on black masculinity, with Clay serving as an example of the emasculated black male. His first reactions to Lula's advances are sheepish at best, with innocent interjections like "Really?" and "Oh boy." Lula points out that he is trying to grow a beard and that instead of the facial hair making him more masculine, the patchy stubble calls attention to his boyish features. When Lula leads him through the proposed plan of walking back to her apartment, she declares that, once there, they will talk "endlessly … about your manhood, what do you think? What do you think we have been talking about this whole time?"[22] Her flippancy at Clay not understanding the obviousness of their conversation further highlights Lula's feminization of Clay through her dialog. The comparison with Uncle Tom serves to emphasize his severe emasculation.

The set-up of Clay by Lula not only stresses the ways in which white society has emasculated the black man, but also portrays how such emasculation leads to the death of the black man. Since the violence of the Middle Passage, literature has brimmed with examples of the inevitability-of-black-death trope, in texts by both white and black writers. The horrors of slavery and lynching, the stereotypical sacrifice of blacks for their masters or companions – many of these examples appear in fiction, short stories, and plays from the 1800s through today. Baraka is certainly not alone in exploring this complicated narrative. Other African American writers influenced by Baraka's generation have also taken up the mantle – think of Milkman in Toni Morrison's *Song of Solomon*, the last scene of August Wilson's *Fences*, and Suzan-Lori Parks's full-length meditation on black death, *The Death of the Last Black Man in the Whole Entire World*. Thus, the play could also be viewed as a dramatization of Baraka's fears – or quite possibly Baraka's cynicism – at the time. Whether or not Clay wishes to fight and take action, or quietly leave the train and be who he wants to be, it does not matter: Lula will kill him anyway, for he is a black man and thus expected to die.

Although Clay does not choose to act, Baraka does impart the character with an impassioned monologue detailing his simmering black rage (and indicating the change in Baraka's own assumptions as he moves from the apolitical Beat culture toward a leadership position in the Movement). Clay's monologue resembles Baraka's oft-quoted poem "Black Art," published five years later: "We want 'poems that kill.' / Assassin poems, Poems that shoot / Guns."[23] At first read, the poem merely advocates armed resistance, but symbolically, it addresses the overriding philosophy of Black Arts: creating art that incites social change, poetry that encourages revolution, aesthetics that reflect the community. What finally forces Clay to speak is not Lula's racist insults, but her line "You're afraid of white people. And your father was."[24] It is this accusation to which Clay responds, at first emotional and then moving toward eerily restrained rationalism. Clay's monologue is dramatic dialog that also "kills."

Clay initially counters Lula with anger, telling her that he could "murder [her] now" or "rip her lousy breasts off." He attacks her silly suggestion of rubbing bellies, noting that she as a white woman would have no conception of such a thing. He then expands his own frustration with that of many blacks, noting that Bessie Smith and Charlie Parker really say "Kiss my black ass" with their music, intoning the pain and violence underlying early blues and jazz. Although Clay admits that murder "would make us all sane," he concludes that he is "safe with his words" and that "my people … don't need any defense."[25] Clay's final decision to berate Lula and then get off the train could be interpreted as a giving-up, a man content with stasis, trapped in the endless continuum of white power. But it is also a swift dismissal. As a white woman, Lula will never understand what it means to be black, so it is pointless to carry on trying to explain it to her.

As he ends his tirade, Clay predicts that when whites agree to the eventual acceptance of African Americans as equals, "they'll murder you, and have very rational explanations."[26] Clay could be mocking the concept of "Uncle Tom" blacks who "become" white *or* see such infiltration as purposeful. This appeal to rationalism has usually been interpreted as Clay's inability to act. Through a different lens, though, one could read Clay's side-stepping as intentional and directed at the white audience watching the performance (as Baraka most likely knew what the racial makeup of his first audience would be). It is as if Clay is telling Lula (and the audience) it is not worth explaining any of this any more, because regardless of whether black Americans could eventually become "stand-up Western men, with eyes for clean hard useful lives, sober, pious and sane," the desire to rise up against the establishment cannot be whitened away and "they'll murder you."[27] Lula's swift reaction to knife Clay then is read not as her frustration with his lack of action, but rather with his ability to see through Lula's façade of equality through social change as opposed to black separatism.

Personally, Baraka himself faced such a knife to the gut with the assassination of Malcolm X. For him, the loss of such a figurehead for the African American community made Baraka's disillusionment with the downtown crowd of white artists, patrons, and critics complete. The year 1965 was a pivotal one for Baraka: he divorced his white wife, moved uptown to Harlem, and started the Black Arts Repertory and School. For Baraka, moving to Harlem was not only a geographic shift, but a symbolic one. In his *Autobiography*, he writes, "even more than the Harlem geography, the Black Arts Movement reflected that black people themselves had first moved to a political unity, despite their difference, that they were questioning the US and its white racist monopoly capitalism."[28] The Black Arts Repertory and School was an outlet, a meeting place, and a resource to do just that.

The Black Arts Repertory and School: a glorious failure

Baraka and his local contemporaries hatched the idea of the School in the spring of 1965 before Baraka moved to Harlem. Funded by donations, benefit music concerts, and receipts from Baraka's plays running at the downtown

St. Mark's Playhouse, the School was established in an old Harlem brownstone on West 130th Street. The School and its impact on the community best represent the Black Arts Movement's mission with regard to theatrical performance. At its core, the School was a community center and producing organization that furthered the Movement's philosophy through public arts, intending to become a cultural institution that championed black art aesthetics. Artists involved directly with the School and devotees of the growing Black Arts Movement envisioned that its programming would radicalize and revolutionize African American cultural assumptions by celebrating and enjoining the Harlem community and beyond.

Reflecting the Du Boisian ideals of theatre for, by, about, and near blacks, the School held lectures and classes, poetry readings and concerts, and toured up and down the streets of Harlem with theatre and spoken word. Noted theorist Harold Cruse taught classes, followers of the Nation of Islam held meetings, Sun Ra performed concerts; the School was more than just a "school," it was a veritable rallying cry for prioritizing black cultural production. To enhance the School's activities, as much of their early programming was on a volunteer or donation basis, Baraka discovered HARYOU (Harlem Youth Opportunities Unlimited), which had procured large grants from the Johnson administration's War on Poverty program called "Project Uplift." After securing HARYOU funds for the summer, the School sponsored and produced a variety of creative programming – outdoor art exhibitions that would move each night to a different spot in Harlem, live music in parks and playgrounds, poetry readings, and trucks with removable stages for plays. As Baraka remembered, "When we got our regular programs going, concerts, readings, plays in the downstairs auditorium we made by tearing down a couple of walls, black artists flowed through those doors. Some for single performances, some for longer relationships, some to absorb what it all was. We were trying to grow together."[29] Baraka and his colleagues appealed to audiences through a variety of means, constantly working to bring people to the School. For example, to draw audiences to a production entitled *Black Ice*, members of the production staged a mock chase through the streets of Harlem with a black man chasing a white man down the street. Interested in what was going on, spectators followed, and thus ended up watching the "real" production. As Jerry Watts writes, "the Repertory Theater was undoubtedly one of the key launching pads for the crystallization and emergence of the Black Arts Movement, as it encouraged traditional black intellectuals and artists to begin to question their intended audiences."[30]

In a time of such growth, many individuals associated with the School had varying visions of what it would and should be. Infighting between

those who wanted to run the School marred its cohesiveness, and differences of opinion on the direction of Black Nationalism and how it related
to the arts conflicted with the School's message. In *Autobiography*, Baraka
expressed his belief that one of the major instigators was interested in changing the mission of the School, and thus tried to protest and oppose many
of their major functions and directions for the future. Regardless of the political infighting, the School still had to be accountable for the federal money
received from HARYOU; proper steps were not taken to document its particular uses. Because of its (at times) volatile programming, complaints and
bad press warranted a visit from Sargent Shriver, known as the architect
of Johnson's "War on Poverty" campaign and director of the federal government's program that administered funds to local organizations such as
HARYOU. Baraka refused to let Shriver and his colleagues in the door.
Obviously, this did not bode well for future funding. The School promptly
lost its funding from the HARYOU program, and quickly descended into
financial insolvency. As Baraka admitted later, "we were too honest and too
naïve for our own good. We talked revolution because we meant it; we
hooked up programs of revolutionary and progressive black art because we
knew our people needed them, but we had not scienced out how these activities were to be sustained on an economic side."[31] Baraka does not disclose
that the School, while promoting black separatism, willingly received money
from a government supported by the white power structure.

Public street corner performances of *Dutchman* were one of the primary
reasons the School lost its public funding. When performed at the downtown Cherry Lane Theatre, it was an Obie-Award-winning Off-Broadway
production. When performed on the streets of Harlem, whites perceived it as
incendiary and obscene. Funding agencies held the viewpoint that no community center receiving government funds should produce such provocative
plays. White columnist Gertrude Wilson, who wrote the "White on White"
column for the black newspaper *New York Amsterdam News*, called Baraka
the "big man of bathroom literature ... a shock treatment for society, like
crawling through a sewer pipe." She criticized the aims of the School, arguing "what Jones proposes and encourages in Harlem's youth amounts to
a roadway to destruction."[32] However, the same day Wilson's column hit
newsstands in New York, the black newspaper *The Chicago Defender* wrote
an op-ed piece on the School, advocating that "Jones' Black Arts School
brought a ray of light into the Harlem Community ... hope for the rewards
of a future so long denied." The piece further made a call for donations,
stating, "We support you in whatever you undertake to help bring about
pride and dignity for little children of color!"[33] This paradox reflects the
stumbling blocks that the entire Movement faced. On one hand, artists were

calling for a revolution, encouraging the severing of ties between blacks and whites. Many African Americans supported this, but with conviction and inspiration, not necessarily dollars. Thus economically, artists still had to interact with whites – either by working with publishing houses or theatre producers, or, in the case of the School, federal funding organizations.

The same year the School created its vital programming, Baraka's controversial essay "The Revolutionary Theatre" was published in the Black Arts-motivated magazine *Black Dialogue*, after *The New York Times* had refused to print it (despite the fact they had originally commissioned it). While the essay has been accused of being unnecessarily inflammatory, as well as contradictory, it is a passionate example of the spirit of the Movement, its anger at the establishment, and the ideals of theatre affecting social change. As Baraka writes:

> The Revolutionary Theatre must Accuse and Attack anything that can be accused and attacked. It must Accuse and Attack because it is a theatre of Victims. It looks at the sky with the victims' eyes, and moves the victims to look at the strength in their minds and their bodies ... The Revolutionary Theatre, which is now peopled with victims, will soon begin to be peopled with new kinds of heroes ... not the weak Hamlets debating whether or not they are ready to die for what's on their minds, but men and women (and minds) digging out from under a thousand years of "high art" and weakfaced dalliance. We must make an art that will function as to call down the actual wrath of world spirit.[34]

Although Baraka advocates, in some ways, for an Artaudian Theatre of Cruelty, he does not encourage the introspection Artaud favored, rather demanding theatre that will activate audiences.[35] This was the spirit in which the Black Arts Repertory and School was founded, and reflected the ways in which Baraka and others believed that theatre could be at the forefront of the struggle for black liberation. In the middle of the funding crisis at the School, Baraka left the tumult of Harlem and moved to Newark to focus on his own writing and furthering the ideal of Black Arts throughout the country. This move to Newark was transformational for many reasons, not only for Baraka, but also for the Black Arts Movement. He began Spirit House, modeled on the School, but with smaller, more realistic and attainable goals. Baraka married a black woman, Sylvia Robinson (later to be called Amina Baraka), and continued to write poetry and short plays, his work increasing in its politicism and directive toward the philosophy of Black Arts. The School did not survive, but the focus on African American community arts did. As Mike Sell writes, "Whether BART/S really embodied Jones's theoretical principles or managed to escape the contradictions inherent in the idea of a 'Black avant-garde' is moot. Of greater significance is the fact that angry, honest art was being brought to working-class African Americans."[36] The School was an example, however fleeting, of the fact that arts programming directed by and for African Americans was critical and necessary.

After the close of the School, other black theatre companies began producing work in New York that had longer staying power than the highly volatile Black Arts School. Robert Macbeth started the New Lafayette Theatre in 1967, which supported black actors and artists for six years. Ed Bullins was its first playwright in residence, a relationship that fostered the creation of many of Bullins's plays alongside other emerging black playwrights, including Sonia Sanchez and Ron Milner. After moving from Detroit, Woodie King, Jr. started the New Federal Theatre (its name an homage to the 1930s government-sponsored Federal Theatre Project), and Ellen Stewart started La Mama, although the space catered (and still does) to mostly white European avant-garde ideals. Barbara Ann Teer, after working with the Negro Ensemble Company but frustrated by its lack of connection to the black community, moved to Harlem and started National Black Theatre, a company devoted to ritual theatre and the training of artists. The theatre began producing plays in the early 1970s, during the waning years of the Black Arts Movement. It is striking to note that all of these theatres still exist, institutions that far outlived the initial revolutionary and reactionary impetus for their creation. The Movement's contribution to theatre history may not be just the plays written and subsequently analyzed and anthologized, but rather the importance of black cultural institutions and the encouragement of new waves of black theatre artists.

But what really was Black Arts?

James Edward Smethurst writes, "Black arts poetics could be more accurately described as a series of debates linked to ideological and institutional conflict and conversation rather than a consistent practice."[37] Put another way, Black Arts aesthetics were an ever changing, ever evolving series of cultural productions, literary or dramatic, visual or aural, categorically connected by shared political philosophies. Thus, dramatic output of the artists may possess similar political tendencies, stylistic choices, or structural formats, and possibly all three. Smethurst characterizes the movement as "popular avant-garde," borrowing from the culturally conceived notion of literature, art, and music, among other cultural creations that reject the values and structure of the establishment in favor of work that is outside the norm. The avant-garde is ahead of its time, forward-moving, literally an "advance guard." Black Arts was not avant-garde in the way that Beckett, Genet, Ionesco, and their contemporaries were in post-World

War II Europe, creating total dismissal of literary structure and popular styles. Rather, the Movement embraced aspects of popular culture and conventional literary structure within their transformative work. For example, Baraka's *Dutchman* adopts a recognizable theatre structure – a linear tragic narrative consisting of the introduction of characters, the staging of a central conflict, and the death of the protagonist – in order to express the political philosophies of the artistic movement. Performance, particularly poetry readings but also theatrical stagings, was crucial to the development of the Movement, not only for its ability to reach many people at a given time, but also because of the personal connection forged between performers and audience. Performance "enabled Black artists to articulate a specifically African *American* ethos, an ethos anchored to the traditions, tones, and trickery of African American urban and rural neighborhoods."[38] Because many of the artists were poets, live poetry readings also spread the political messages of the Movement, borrowing techniques from theatrical performance.[39]

While it is difficult to pinpoint particular dates, the Movement spanned the years between the mid 1960s and early 1970s, and was very much a reaction to the politics of the time. To contextualize the historical moment, in artistic circles of the 1940s, socialist and Communist ideals were popular because of the leveling of class distinctions and the support of union and organized labor. However, with the advent of the red scare of McCarthyism in the 1950s and the build-up of the military industrial complex, conservatism in America reached new heights. The Civil Rights Movement coalesced into a strong social force in the 1960s with marches on Washington, bus boycotts, and lunch counter sit-ins. Internationally, African countries were in waves of colonialist revolt, with the liberation and independence of Ghana, Senegal, Ivory Coast, and Kenya, to name a few, at the end of the 1950s and early 1960s. Martin Luther King, Jr. advocated non-violence in the desire for equality. Yet it was Malcolm X, with his teachings from the Nation of Islam (NOI), and subsequent philosophies after his break with the NOI until his assassination in 1965, who became the Movement's unofficial spiritual leader. As Amiri Baraka reflected, "Malcolm X put words to the volcanic torrent of anger and frustration many of us felt with the civil rights movement."[40] Baraka and his fellow contemporaries favored a Black Nationalist philosophy of becoming independent from white-dominated society and developing sustainable black communities that would become self-reliant. Creating a cohesive community – of artists as well as audience/ residents – was a key goal of the Movement. Larry Neal wrote that the Movement was "radically opposed to any concept of the artist that alienates the artist from his/her community."[41] The establishment of and the focus on such community were reflected in the art that was created and the ways in which such art was dispersed among the people.

During these years, Baraka, Neal, playwright Ed Bullins, and others' activism and writing formulated a new black aesthetic. This black aesthetic was about overthrow and survival: not about existing peacefully alongside whites, but eschewing them altogether. As Neal writes, "the motive behind the Black aesthetic is the destruction of the white thing, the destruction of white ideas, and white ways of looking at the world."[42] Theatre and writing groups formed in cities across the country, from Philadelphia to Chicago to Los Angeles, forging community through artistic expression.[43] As Amy Abugo Ongiri explains, "The Black Arts Movement dreamed of creating an artistic tradition that not only celebrated the cultural impulses of the African American Community but also became a natural part of the constructing and maintaining of that community."[44] These artists saw themselves as cultural revolutionaries, intent on reorienting (and in many cases, destroying) current American cultural practices that were white-centered and middle- and upper-class-focused.

Historically, the Movement has traditionally been viewed as a northern urban movement, centering in the metro area of New York City. When assessing the artistic creation of all writers and artists associated with it, though, the Movement can be seen as much more widespread. Since the Harlem Renaissance, Harlem had long stood as a symbolic bastion of black culture. However, in practice, the region had lost much of its luster as other, vibrant black artistic communities – in Chicago and Detroit, among other places – developed between 1940 and 1965. Although adhering to the same general principles of the Movement, a responsibility to speak to and for the black experience, these new artistic communities did not share the same radical values as Baraka and Neal. The Movement in the South was an outgrowth of the Civil Rights activities, Martin Luther King's non-violent approach, and participants from the Student Nonviolent Coordinating Committee (SNCC). The Free Southern Theatre, a theatre group started in Mississippi and then centered in New Orleans, was community-based and did not see its ideals as exclusionary toward other races, although its aims were to create and tour theatre with black families and communities in mind.

The West Coast, particularly the Bay Area, was another hot bed for political formations, especially Oakland, the home base of the Black Panther Party. Neal cites that Black Arts was the "sister" of the Black Power Movement and shared many of the same tenets of Black Power, specifically to "speak to the spirit and cultural need of Black people."[45] Yet Black Arts and Black Power were not always synonymous or harmonious with each other, as seen later in the 1960s clashes between the artists and members of the Panthers.[46]

Playwright Ed Bullins, who for a time served as the Minister of Culture for the Panthers, West Coast poet and playwright Marvin X, and their fellow artists created Black House in San Francisco, a cultural and community center modeled on the Black Arts Repertory and School. Like the School, Black House lasted less than a year. Eldridge Cleaver, Minister of Information (and author of *Soul on Ice*), accused Bullins and his contemporaries of being "cultural nationalists" who were intent on "symbolic gesture" in their work, rather than the real political work of the Black Power Movement.[47] This ousting was yet another example of how the Black Arts Movement sought to create political change through cultural and artistic expression, whereas the Black Panthers and larger Black Power Movement attempted to foment political change and revolution by taking them to the streets.

The geographical spread of these movements and the varying attitudes with regard to investment in Black Nationalism were not the only limiting factors to the longevity of Black Arts. Like many avant-garde movements, the economics of creating art in a capitalist society became an issue for Movement members because of the struggle of reaching a community that did not have discretionary funds for events like theatre. While producing organizations did not want to charge high ticket prices, and thereby alienate the community that the theatre intended to reach, they needed income to sustain their activities. Ultimately, economic factors led to the closing of small theatrical ventures, making poetry (not novels or plays) the Black Arts Movement's primary means of artistic expression. Poetry was quick to read and inexpensive to publish. Even journals, magazines, and self-produced pamphlets were easier to fund than theatre rentals or gallery spaces. By the late 1960s, the publication – as opposed to performances – of plays was a primary means of reaching audiences. The year 1968 saw two important published projects for the Black Arts writers: a special issue of *Drama Review*, edited by Bullins; and Baraka and Neal's *Black Fire*, an anthology of essays, poetry, short fiction, and plays that typify the range of literature and theories expressed by key participants in the Movement. The publishing of *Black Fire* set off a wave of publications reflecting the work created during this time, with over thirty anthologies released between 1967 and 1973. These collections offered a variety of articulations of the new black aesthetic formulated by Black Arts artists, and provided longevity to the Movement when institutional projects dependent on staffing and funding could not.[48]

In 1968 Baraka abandoned his "slave name" for an African given name, Imamu Amiri Baraka (Bantuized Muslim, for spiritual leader, prince, blessed).[49] Not long after, he dropped the "Imamu" from his name: the "spiritual leader" of the Black Arts was beginning to move on. So too was the Movement. While the dispersion of Black Arts across the country made it more localized for the black communities it was trying to reach, this dispersion also diffused the message. By the early 1970s, fervent black arts were no longer categorized under the rubric of the "Movement" per se, instead becoming a part of mainstream cultural production.

One of the intents of the artistic output of the Black Arts Movement, outlined by Larry Neal, was to "raise the level of black struggle to a more intense expression … an art that would actually reflect black life and its history and legacy of resistance and struggle."[50] Baraka's poetry, essays, and plays spoke to this need, influencing other Black Arts artists to create, publish, and inspire. During the few years that Black Arts was technically a "Movement," journals, pamphlets, writers' groups, theatre companies, compositions, and visual art by African Americans flourished in a proliferation that had never been seen in the history of the country. Arguably, this cultural revolution changed the trajectory of black artists, and such reverberations are visible in the art that has followed. Indeed, August Wilson always credited Baraka as an inspiration. Likewise, Ntozake Shange writes in her 1978 book, *nappy edges*, "around 1966/abt the time I went to barnard I thot leroi jones (imamu baraka) was my primary jumping-off point. that I cd learn from him how to make language sing and penetrate one's soul."[51] *Dutchman*, and the issues Baraka wrestles with through its dialog, reflect the changes in Black theatre where playwrights began to express their rage at the injustices of American society. This is not to say that Baraka himself singlehandedly changed the face of Black theatre; rather, the Black Arts Movement and its engagement within the African American community affected the work written and produced in years to come.

NOTES

1 Henry Louis Gates, Jr., "Black Creativity: On the Cutting Edge," *Time*, October 10, 1994.

2 Larry Neal, "The Black Arts Movement," in *A Sourcebook of African-American Performance: Plays, People, Movements*, ed. Annemarie Bean (London; New York: Routledge, 1999), 67.

3 Amiri Baraka, "The Black Arts Movement," in *The LeRoi Jones/Amiri Baraka Reader*, ed. William J. Harris (New York: Thunder's Mouth Press, 2000), 502. Baraka references here two of Malcolm X's famous quotes, from speeches given in 1965 and 1964, respectively: the first, "We declare our right on this earth to be a man, to be a human being, to be respected as a human being, to be given the rights of a human being in this society, on this earth, in this day, which we intend to bring into existence *by any means necessary*." The second is from one of his most famous speeches, usually titled "The Ballot or the Bullet."

4 For clarity's sake (and to respect Baraka's current name change), I have chosen to refer to him as "Amiri Baraka" throughout this chapter, even if through most of the Movement's duration he was LeRoi Jones.

5　In fact, the plotline of Baraka's *Dutchman* has been compared to Albee's *Zoo Story*, although it seems most critics merely link the long monologues of Clay and Jerry and the inevitable knifing at the end of both plays.

6　LeRoi Jones, *Dutchman and The Slave: Two Plays* (New York: Morrow Quill, 1964), 3.

7　*Ibid.*, 9.

8　Howard Taubman, "The Theater: 'Dutchman,'" *New York Times*, March 25, 1964, 46.

9　Harold Clurman, *The Naked Image: Observations on the Modern Theatre* (New York: Macmillan, 1966), 90; Richard Cooke, "The Theater: Racial Shocker," *Wall Street Journal*, March 26, 1964, 14.

10　Amiri Baraka and Kalamu ya Salaam, "Amiri Baraka Analyzes How He Writes," *African American Review*, 37.2/3 (2003): 214.

11　Jones, *Dutchman*, 6.

12　*Ibid.*, 12.

13　*Ibid.*, 29, 31–3.

14　*Ibid.*, 26.

15　*Ibid.*, 30.

16　*Ibid.*, 18.

17　*Ibid.*, 21.

18　*Ibid.*, 30.

19　*Ibid.*, 31.

20　*Ibid.*

21　Andrzej Ceynowa, "The Dramatic Structure of *Dutchman*," *Black American Literature Forum*, 17.1 (1983): 18.

22　*Ibid.*, 25.

23　Baraka, *Baraka Reader*, 219.

24　Jones, *Dutchman*, 33.

25　*Ibid.*, 35–6.

26　*Ibid.*, 36.

27　*Ibid.*

28　Baraka, *Baraka Reader*, 369.

29　*Ibid.*, 370.

30　Jerry Gafio Watts, *Amiri Baraka: The Politics and Art of a Black Intellectual* (New York: New York University Press, 2001), 160. It is important to note that Watts's study of Baraka is not a biography, but a highly critical treatise on Baraka, his writing, and his politics.

31　*Ibid.*, 382.

32　Gertrude Wilson, "Theater of Despair," *New York Amsterdam News*, November 6, 1965, 17. Gertrude Wilson was actually a pseudonym used by Justine Tyrrell Priestley, who wrote the column in the black weekly for twelve years.

33　"Urge Support for Black Arts School," *Chicago Defender*, November 6, 1965, 26A.

34　Amiri Baraka, "The Revolutionary Theatre," *Black Dialogue*, July, 1965, available online at National Humanities Center, Toolbox Library, http://nationalhumanitiescenter.org/pds/maai3/protest/text12/barakatheatre.pdf (last accessed November 14, 2009).

35 Artaud advocated his theories in the 1938 book, *The Theatre and Its Double*, suggesting that western theatre was too text-centered, causing audience complacency. Thought and gesture, symbolism and meaning would offer audiences a new way of seeing themselves. For Artaud, cruelty is not in the sense of violence, but rather the stark vision of truth.

36 Mike Sell, "The Black Arts Movement: Performance, Neo-Orality, and the Destruction of the 'White Thing,'" in *African American Performance and Theater History: A Critical Reader*, ed. Harry J. Elam, Jr. and David Krasner (Oxford: Oxford University Press, 2001), 61.

37 James Edward Smethurst, *The Black Arts Movement: Literary Nationalism in the 1960s and 1970s* (Chapel Hill: University of North Carolina Press, 2005), 57.

38 Mike Sell, *Avant-Garde Performance and the Limits of Criticism: Approaching the Living Theatre, Happenings/Fluxus, and the Black Arts Movement* (Ann Arbor: University of Michigan Press, 2005), 17.

39 The Black Arts Movement's live poetry readings, and subsequent recordings of those readings, anticipate the popularity of the slam poetry explosion in the 1990s.

40 Baraka, *Baraka Reader*, 496.

41 Neal, "The Black Arts Movement," 55.

42 *Ibid.*, 56.

43 Muntu writing/reading group in Philadelphia, Third World Press (originating in Chicago), and the Watts Writers Workshop in Los Angeles's Watts community were all well-known and prolific writing collectives or publishing venues.

44 Amy Abugo Ongiri, *Spectacular Blackness: The Cultural Politics of the Black Power Movement and the Search for a Black Aesthetic* (Charlottesville: University of Virginia Press, 2010), 105.

45 Neal, "The Black Arts Movement," 55.

46 Black Panther cofounder Bobby Seale actually acted in one of Ed Bullins's plays in San Francisco before forming the party.

47 Smethurst, *The Black Arts Movement*, 283.

48 For more on the importance of *Black Fire* see Ongiri, *Spectacular Blackness*, 107–23.

49 Amiri Baraka, *The Autobiography of LeRoi Jones* (New York: Freundlich, 1984), 266. Baraka later dropped Imamu from his name when his politics shifted from black separatism to Third World Marxism, which is his current political and guiding philosophy.

50 Larry Neal, *Visions of a Liberated Future: Black Arts Movement Writings*, ed. Michael Schwartz (New York: Thunder's Mouth Press, 1989), ix–x.

51 Wilson always noted that his writing grew from his "4 B's" – the blues, artist Romare Bearden, Argentine writer Jorge Luis Borges, and Baraka; Ntozake Shange, quoted in Cheryl Clarke, *"After Mecca": Women Poets and the Black Arts Movement* (New Brunswick, NJ: Rutgers University Press, 2005), 96.

8

SAMUEL O'CONNELL

Fragmented musicals and 1970s soul aesthetic

Premiering as part of the 1971 Broadway season, Melvin Van Peebles's turbulent, strange, violent, authentic, funny, realistic, and pointedly exaggerated musical *Ain't Supposed to Die a Natural Death* debuted on Broadway with the expectation from critics that it would not run for more than two weeks. The same year that Marvin Gaye introduced a sense of political consciousness to the Motown sound with his landmark album *What's Going On?* also brought *Sweet Sweetback's BaadAsssss Song*, which revolutionized independent cinema – all but creating the blaxploitation genre in film. *Sweetback*'s multi-hyphenate writer-director-producer-composer-star, Melvin Van Peebles, stormed onto Broadway, that "Great White Way," with not one but two musicals depicting contemporary black life for white and black audiences: *Ain't Supposed to Die a Natural Death* and *Don't Play Us Cheap*. With these two shows, Van Peebles changed the look, sound, content, and audience that had typically come to define successful Broadway musicals, and by extension American musical theatre itself. With his vision of black life on "the Block" in *Ain't Supposed to Die*, Melvin Van Peebles brought the contemporary aesthetics of black creative expression to Broadway, and made it a success with the show ultimately running for 325 performances, earning a number of Tony Award nominations including Best Musical and Best Original Score. Despite Van Peebles's success with *Ain't Supposed to Die a Natural Death*, though, the aesthetic intervention into musical theatre was short-lived, as politically conscious musicals were gone from Broadway as early as 1975.

In this chapter, I use *Ain't Supposed to Die a Natural Death* to demonstrate the artistic and political potential of black music and black musicals, explaining the reasons for Van Peebles's singular and unrepeatable success on the Broadway stage. Coexisting with developments in Black theatre and Black Nationalism, and coming on the heels of Amiri Baraka's theatrical innovations of the 1960s and the Black Arts Movement, *Ain't Supposed to Die a Natural Death* was a revolutionary piece of musical theatre.

Unfortunately, the revolution was short-lived. Its aesthetic was co-opted and watered down into a successful, mainstream form that could appeal to white and black audiences. In the pages that follow, I open with an exploration of the many definitions of black musicals before suggesting a new definition that takes into account the role of black music, not just black casts or a black creative team. Following that, I discuss the development of Van Peebles's theatrical aesthetic, beginning with the influence of French political songs and continuing with his desire to capture the feel of the street, or "the Block," in 1970s Harlem, which culminated in the production of his politically engaged musical.

Defining the black musical

Allen Woll offers an overview of the black musical and its place and development under the auspices of that classic genre and commercial mainstay of the American theatre: the American musical. He writes:

> Black musical theatre, initially a separate and unequal stepchild of American musical theatre, has slowly been integrated into the musical comedy mainstream as it helped to Americanize and modernize the structure, music, and dance of musical theatre between 1898 and the 1920s, and ultimately in the 1960s and 1970s bring important political issues to an art form that had hitherto been dismissed as "escapist."[1]

Interesting to note here is the historical relegation of the black musical to the status of a stepchild, despite its importance in creating the very idea of American musical theatre from the turn of the twentieth century, as well as its integration into the category of musical comedy. That said, though, Woll's overview does not help us locate a definition of just what we critics and scholars mean when referring to the theatrical concept of the black musical. Perhaps this is because, as Woll himself points out, of an additional complication in defining the form: "*black musical* has defined a variety of theatrical presentations."[2] In attempting to define these theatrical presentations as black musicals, for instance, John Bush Jones seems to place the emphasis on the cast and/or characters of the musical, focusing his attention on "black-cast musicals on Broadway, whether written by blacks, whites, or mixed-race creative teams."[3] For Bush Jones, then, the emphasis is on a musical's narrative content, from which he concludes black musicals concern black protagonists and feature predominantly black casts. In addition to their dramaturgical emphasis on narratives about black characters, Bush Jones finds a commonality among black musicals throughout their history: "they all depicted African Americans' differences from whites – their indigenous music, dance, humor, and folkways."[4] While Bush Jones focuses his definition on the plot and character elements of these musicals, Elizabeth Wollman turns her attention to their perceived or even intended audience. Focusing on the history of the rock musical, Wollman's catalog looks at black musicals post-1965, thus dealing with those that specifically addressed their performances to predominantly black audiences, both on and off Broadway. Of the black musicals of the era, Wollman writes, "Interested in creating musicals that would specifically address black concerns, African American playwrights, performers, critics, and producers argued that black writers had to force themselves from the demands of white audiences, who had for too long dictated the ways that musicals by and about black people were written and performed."[5] The importance of the black musical for Wollman, then, is the audience; she continues, "In response to theater producers who argued that there was no black audience for the theater, black theater advocates insisted that the shows' creators were responsible for finding and cultivating a new generation of black theatre goers."[6] As a companion to Bush Jones's definition, we can see how Wollman adds a focus on black audiences to the mix of definitions for the black musical as a genre. But, between discussions of casts, stories, and audiences featuring black actors before black audiences, the idea of the black musical is still missing a crucial element: that of the music itself.

Offering his own stance on the difficulty in defining the genre, Woll writes, "at times the words connote an entirely Afro-American creation: blacks onstage and behind the scenes shaped the final work for black audiences. On other occasions (particularly in the context of the Broadway stage), black artists created these shows for white audiences."[7] Thus, among musical theatre scholars like Bush Jones, Wollman, and Woll, there is a broad spectrum within musical theatre scholarship of valid definitions for black musicals. From these definitions, we can see that the categories identifying a theatrical presentation as a "black musical" raise questions over a work's creation, including: authorship and musical composition; its production team, its cast, and its performance; and its audience, whether black or white. These categories of creation, production, and reception continue to remain indistinct in terms of defining the black musical as a genre or subgenre of American musical theatre. Perhaps this is a good thing, for as Harry Elam argues about the definition of black plays, "the definition of black play must be open and flexible, subject to changing times and contexts."[8] Given Elam's argument, the definition of what constitutes a black musical is and has been open and flexible within Woll's broadly defined categories of black presence in the art form. For my interest in looking at the musicals of the 1970s, though, each of these definitions and its determined focus miss what I consider to be a central element of a black musical: the music itself. Perhaps too obviously, black musicals contain black music, which is itself a category that defies easy categorization. But, it is the music, particularly of the musicals of the 1970s, that makes them uniquely able to speak to black audiences in the early part of the decade while crossing over musically and commercially to appeal to white and black audiences by 1975.

In his history of Black theatre in America, James Hatch identifies two great decades of the black musical: the 1900s and the 1920s. Appropriately, with a focus on the musical element of these musicals, he cites the ragtime of the 1900s and the jazz of the 1920s as integral features that lead to both their success and their blackness.[9] From a historical standpoint, I would argue that the third great decade in the history of the black musical would be the 1970s with Melvin Van Peebles's introduction of "soul" – the music of the African American ghettos of the era – to Broadway in his production of *Ain't Supposed to Die a Natural Death*. As one of the three great decades in which black music met Black theatre to create a resurgence of the black musical, the 1970s are uniquely situated politically, culturally, and socially within musical and theatre history.

In the 1970s, the black musical re-emerged (after the comparatively dormant 1960s musicals) as a potent force of musical theatre with successes on Broadway. John Bush Jones offers some ideas of where the black musical, a form that has been successful for over 100 years now, went during the 1960s, and why it may have returned to prominence in the 1970s. In his examination of the social history of the American musical, Bush Jones writes, "prior to the 1960s, every decade of the twentieth century had seen at least a few commercially successful black-cast musicals on Broadway."[10] Bush Jones continues, "But such entertainments virtually disappeared for the decade of the 1960s, only to return with renewed strength and vigor in the 1970s."[11] He offers several reasons for the disappearance of the black musical in the 1960s, namely that musicals focusing on "black singularity were out of sync with the times" of the Civil Rights Movement, during which the focus was on "a shared humanity."[12] Perhaps, though, it is because the commercially popular black music of the 1960s lacked an authenticity that pervaded the soul music of the 1970s.

Black music and the soul aesthetic

In discussing creative expression in Black theatre, Amiri Baraka notes:

> The use of music must be understood. Music goes more deeply into the spirit than the words; music is a living creature, a human intellectual and emotional

creation with a readily apparent spirituality that transcends the visible world of its creators. It goes out of the world as the colors of the world. The sounds carry whatever information rests in the frequencies and rhythms and harmonies of the world, some known to us, some unknown.[13]

Building on this idea, Paul Carter Harrison adds, "In black music, all the devices of song – metronomic cadence, melody, harmony, and rhythm – are devoted to the amplification of [Baraka's] 'frequencies' that reveal the 'unknown' yet recoverable qualities of the soul."[14] Adding to the conversation on black music, Paul Gilroy writes in *The Black Atlantic*, "examining the place of music in the black Atlantic world means surveying the self-understanding articulated by the musicians who have made it, the symbolic use to which their music is put by other black artists and writers, and the social relations which have produced and reproduced the unique expressive culture in which music comprises a central and even foundational element."[15] Working within these three writers' ideas on black music, we can see that there is an ineffable quality about black music that cuts across the music itself and its internal, purely musical elements; its composition and use; or its social qualities; and what Harrison identifies as its spiritual component: its ability to connect with one's soul. These elements are important when we talk about the black musicals of the 1970s and their incorporation of black music as an aesthetic, cultural, and political shift from the traditional Broadway score. But, Gilroy importantly asks, "What special analytic problems arise if a style, genre, or particular performance of music is identified as being expressive of the absolute essence of the group that produced it?"[16]

Though rhetorical, Gilroy's question gains particular relevance as he goes on to remind us that music is "a non-representational, non-conceptual form," thus creating a particular challenge when we begin to discuss a style, genre, or performance as "black music."[17] As he points out, "black music is so often the principal symbol of racial authenticity."[18] Relevant to Gilroy's point, particularly as this discussion concerns music in the theatre, are Harry Elam's comments about Black plays and Black theatre. Elam argues that we should continue to work to understand "what should constitute the relationship between black play and black politics, between black play and white play, between black play and the social and cultural lives of black people in America."[19] As it relates to black music, this interplay between play and politics, black play and white play, and the social and cultural lives of black people aligns with Michael Hanson's arguments about black music and what he defines as "aural blackness."[20] For Hanson, aural blackness identifies black music as a social practice that "registers racial differences in the modes of exchange that define its production, consumption, and social effect."[21] Further, and speaking to Gilroy's thoughts on racial authenticity, Hanson argues, "black music *speaks* blackness, as a shared abstract sense of collective experience, while also shaping how one can hear the multiplicity of black positions, diasporic layers, and historical traces of the local or the individual."[22] Thus, in using the arguments posed by both Elam and Hanson in a discussion of Gilroy's question, I suggest that important relationships between black music and black politics, white music, and the social and cultural lives of black people in America can be found and heard in the black music of the 1970s, particularly the genre of soul music.

Amiri Baraka has long asserted that a connection exists between black music and black politics, focusing his attention on jazz in most of its generic, stylistic, and performative manifestations in popular culture. In jazz, as a key genre of black music, he finds the musicians creating a revolution "against the Tin Pan Alley prison of American commercial mediocrity."[23] He hears these jazz musicians shouting through their various instruments, "Down with the popular song! Down with the regular chord changes! Down with the tempered scale!"[24] For Amiri Baraka, black music "bears witness to the nationalism which drove [his] understanding of what had to be done. That the Afro-American people must claim this music as our legacy and treasure and value the songs as the historic anthems of our lives and struggle."[25] For Russell Potter, "the deep down core of African-American music has been both a centre to which performers and audiences have continually returned, and a centrifuge that has sent its styles and attitudes outwards into the full spectrum of popular music around the world." He continues, "within black communities, there has been an ongoing need to name and claim a music whose strategic inward turn refused what was often seen as a 'sell-out' appeal to white listeners, a music that set up shop right in the neighborhood, via black (later 'urban contemporary') radio, charts, and retailers, and in the untallied traffic in dubbed tapes, deejay mixes, and bootlegs."[26] Thus, in order to understand the black musical, and particularly the black musicals of the 1970s, we need to be able to understand just what the black music of the 1970s was and how it was coded aesthetically, politically, and culturally for black, but also white, audiences.

Though there are many genres and styles that may be categorized as black music during the 1970s (such as funk, Motown, disco, rhythm and blues, etc.), I focus on soul music in relation to its effects on Broadway, the black musical, and American musical theatre. As one of the dominant musical styles of African American culture in the 1970s, soul occupies a unique position in its musicality, its social use including its production and consumption, and its underlying political messages related to the Black

Nationalist Movement. Additionally, soul occupies an important position on the continuum of black music that includes ragtime, jazz, rhythm and blues, soul, funk, and hip-hop. Its place on this continuum, and its eventual entrée into mainstream American popular music, position it well within the history of black music in consumerist American culture – particularly its eventual, and perhaps inevitable, mainstreaming and cooptation by white producers, musicians, and audiences. Finally, soul music has since come to define a particular time period, or era, of black life and creative expression: what Joanna Demers and Mark Anthony Neal define as the soul era, dating roughly from 1965 to 1980, or the long 1970s. The path of soul music during this era is mirrored in its use on the Broadway stage, as it transitioned from the vernacular music of "authentic" black musicals like *Ain't Supposed to Die a Natural Death* to the mainstreaming of funk and soul in the score of the wildly successful *The Wiz*, until Broadway audiences fell in love with the nostalgic Motown sound of *Dreamgirls*.

Writing on this era, Demers argues that the period between 1965 and 1980 is depicted as "a time in which African-American identity coalesced, and a new political consciousness was born."[27] Mark Anthony Neal adds that the soul era describes "the political, social, and cultural experiences of the African-American" during the "civil rights and Black Power movements,"[28] and in fact, "soul emerged as the next vivid and popular expression of an African-American modernity."[29] Neal continues, "as a 'modern' aesthetic, soul challenged the prevailing logic of white supremacy and segregation in ways that were discomforting and even grotesque to some, regardless of race or ethnicity."[30] As an acoustic representation of the modern sound of the African American experience in the 1970s, soul had certain musical qualities that differed from previous rhythm and blues music also tied to the Black Nationalist politics of the era. Detailing these, Russell Potter describes soul in relation to other genres of black music. According to Potter, as a style that took rhythm and blues to the next level, "soul was slower-burning yet hotter, more improvisational, more distinctly flavoured by the vocal characters of its performers, and more participatory."[31] In this description, we can intuit an inherent theatricality or performativity into the genre, partially through what Gilroy refers to as its antiphony, or call and response nature. Potter continues in his description, citing both soul's gospel-influenced vocal cues and rhythmic beats that were more supercharged than those of either rhythm and blues or rock 'n' roll (both of which are predominantly straight 4/4 meters, which Potter calls a basic "clap-along rhythm").[32] In soul, we also find an inherent, or inscribed, blackness in the musical and lyrical content of the genre. Beyond its blackness, though, it was a targeted sound, one that Demers refers to as a "ghetto sound" that "spoke specifically to the concerns of inner-city blacks, and delineated the separation between blacks and whites through music."[33] Beyond that, Demers notes that the music behind this "ghetto sound" used blues scales and jazz instrumentation, through which the musicians "code 'blackness' acoustically, choosing the ghetto as the centre of African-American identity."[34] Specifically, in terms of its musical genesis, soul was coming from black urban centers like Memphis's Stax Records; Philadelphia's Gamble and Huff; and, of course, Harlem, where "a new generation of politically conscious young street poets was emerging, improvising rhymes over conga beats and delivering a more militant kind of sermon."[35] These beats, according to Potter, have roots that "lay in the Black Arts movement and its devotion to Afrocentric jazz," once again coding blackness acoustically, existing well within Hanson's matrix of aural blackness. In addition to the musical qualities of soul, the lyrical content, too, coded blackness. Potter writes that there had always been a talking school of soul, but the "full range of black verbalism, the toasts, the dozens, or the 'hustler' rhymes ... had rarely made it onto recordings"[36] until the height of the soul era.

Reinventing the black musical

In many respects Melvin Van Peebles may be considered an outsider artist when it comes to music, and even more so musical theatre. As a classically *untrained* musician whose own singing voice has been described as "a frog on crack,"[37] Melvin Van Peebles first entered the music world with his 1968 album *Brer Soul*. Three years before Marvin Gaye's landmark, soulful album *What's Going On?*, Van Peebles's album introduced archetypal characters (The Drunk, etc.) from the inner city or ghetto. Having recently returned to the United States from France in the late 1960s, he was surprised by the music he heard written by black artists. Seeing the beginnings of "the black uprising in America" on the street corners of urban centers, like Harlem, he noted a marked disconnect between black music and black life. Interviewed in the liner notes to *Brer Soul*, Van Peebles recalled,

> I was surprised that none of the music I was hearing from black America was anything to do with what was going on politically. Songs at that time were just about parties and stupid shit. It wasn't what the French call chansom realiste [*sic*] – about what was really happening. There was Joan Baez and Bob Dylan but no black people doing it![38]

The music Van Peebles was hearing – "about parties and stupid shit" – was the commercially successful and culturally mainstreamed Motown sound. It represented a slice of black life in America that was palatable to white audience sensibilities, and thereby watered down the authenticity of a black sound for mainstream commercial success. Seeking to fill this gap and correct this oversight by doing it himself, Van Peebles recorded a record album.

Van Peebles never studied music. Inspired by the *chanson réaliste* style that he had experienced while living in France, Van Peebles's approach to writing *Brer Soul* was to create a hybrid form setting his 'street' poems to highly orchestrated modern jazz.[39] Additionally, "without a singing voice to speak of, he utilized the sprechgesang form of songwriting, where the lyrics were spoken over the music, a technique he'd adopted from plays he'd written in France."[40] Interestingly, Van Peebles's style included a French musical approach to subject matter, a German speak-singing style, and modern jazz music. As a result, his "fusion of funky jazz, soulful poetry, and political righteousness stamped its authenticity on black America in its day to the extent that Van Peebles adopted 'Brer Soul' as a nickname."[41] Whereas most genealogies of black popular music identify soul as an heir to rhythm and blues, Van Peebles's introduction of a European and jazz sensibility into an authentic representation of black cultural expression and the Harlem street reminds us of the question asked by Paul Gilroy of rap music: "Here we have to ask how a form which flaunts and glories in its own malleability as well as its transnational character becomes interpreted as some authentic African-American essence?"[42] In the case of the albums *Brer Soul* and its follow-up *Ain't Supposed to Die a Natural Death*, the answer comes in part from the fact that the characters and the lyrics of the songs were the familiar denizens of the Harlem street. The music itself may have been hybrid, transnational in origin based on Van Peebles's own life in Europe and his lack of formal musical training in a western or African diasporic sensibility. However, the scenes and the characters were specific representations of black life in Harlem in the late 1960s, holding a mirror to life that the Motown sound was not reflecting and would not delve into for another three years.

Though only moderately successful in its own right, at least commercially speaking, Van Peebles's work has had an amazing artistic legacy and influence in music, film, and theatre. Since the release of *Brer Soul*, Van Peebles's landmark album and spoken-word style have gone on to influence such spoken word artists as The Last Poets and the late Gil-Scott Heron, in turn providing a crucial cornerstone of the foundation for rap and hip-hop. Additionally, his "Brer Soul" persona and its connection to the black community presented *Sweet Sweetback's BaadAsssss Song* in 1971, kicking off what would become both independent cinema and blaxploitation cinema. Not surprisingly, *Sweetback* featured music and songs from *Ain't Supposed to Die a Natural Death*, most notably the repurposed "Come on Feet," which became the soundtrack to both Sweetback's escape and revolutionary return. Despite Van Peebles's legacy in music and film, it was his work in the theatre and his success in finding a black audience for Broadway that would revolutionize the black musical in the 1970s, changing the look and sound of Broadway.

As a work of musical theatre, *Ain't Supposed to Die a Natural Death* was based on the previously recorded and released albums of Melvin Van Peebles's spoken-word monologues. As such, it can be considered what Elizabeth Wollman refers to as a fragmented musical. In Wollman's words, fragmented musicals were particularly fashionable throughout the 1970s and "reflected both in form and in substance the fragmentation of American society as the 1960s drew to a close, the New Left and hippie cultures disintegrated, and the Vietnam War limped to its sad conclusion."[43] Of the era, Wollman contends that many of these musicals, including *Ain't Supposed to Die*, "reflected this cultural shift, from outward to inward; from hopeful to cynical."[44] In addition to representing a fragmented sense of American society on stage, these musicals also created splintered visions of musical theatre itself, breaking down the very musical and narrative structure of the integrated musical that had dominated the genre for decades. As such, fragmented musicals are non-traditional. They are, in Wollman's words, "more idea- or character-driven than they are plot-driven."[45] Continuing, Wollman writes, "In these musicals ... linear narrative is replaced by a more disjointed series of scenes and musical numbers, all of which contribute to the musical's main themes or the development of its characters."[46] Among the early successes of the fragmented musicals of the late 1960s and the 1970s, *Hair* became one of the hallmarks of the form. According to Raymond Knapp, "*Hair* marked a deliberate attempt to create a viable alternative to the musicals of the older generation, grounded in a documentary-like approach to life as it is naturally lived, and steeped in the emergent political issues, alternative life-style choices, iconoclastic manner of appearances – and, of course, the music – of the younger generation."[47] In *Hair*, Knapp finds all of the elements of the growing counter-culture: "Music, politics, appearance, and lifestyle were the central arenas of contention, to such an extent that all four were presumed to be in a fairly reliable alignment."[48] Continuing, Knapp argues that *Hair* may be considered a "redefinition of America, aspiring to establish an alternative mythology to displace those celebrated and elaborated on the American musical stage across the previous two-and-a-half decades."[49] Working between the musical histories of Wollman and Knapp, we can see how their discussions of the fragmented musical and the alternative mythologies enabled by a growing counter-culture run parallel to what Van Peebles was trying to do with his musical: combine music, politics, and lifestyle in a theatrical presentation that created an alternative vision of urban America in the 1970s. Central to his vision, then, is his understanding of the sound of "the street" or "the Block," as it had been represented through the characters and songs of the monologues on his albums that would now be performed in the theatre. Thus, it may be argued that *Ain't Supposed to Die a Natural Death* did for the black musical what *Hair* did for the rock musical: it instilled American musical theatre with a representation of life as it was lived in Harlem, complete with the emergent political issues facing black America, the lifestyle and appearances of a previously ignored demographic, and, crucially, the sound of black music.

Ain't Supposed to Die a Natural Death

With the houselights still on and the curtain up, revealing a set that is a "multi-level composite of all the urban black reservations,"[50] Melvin Van Peebles's musical *Ain't Supposed to Die a Natural Death* opens not with a traditional overture but with the "Star Spangled Banner" itself, which Van Peebles argues "in the firstplace [*sic*] poetic justicewise and symbolicwise its [*sic*] a natural."[51] Continuing, Van Peebles writes, "in the second place too the national anthem is perfect because it lays out to people where their heads are at nationwise, at least where they want other folks to think their heads are."[52] Importantly, the show's rendition of the national anthem, in contrast to the rest of the score, is "played straight, not jazzed up or solemned down, and the house lights stay up full so folks can make their statement and be seen and dig other people making theirs."[53] As the anthem comes to a close and the final notes remind the audience of the "home of the brave," the houselights dim and the band transitions straight into the show's first tune, from which point the music of *Ain't Supposed to Die a Natural Death* "does not stop."[54] Standing in stark contrast to the "straight" version of the "Star Spangled Banner," *Ain't Supposed to Die a Natural Death*'s score – and book – consists entirely of Van Peebles's own soul music and spoken-word monologues, including such numbers as "Come on Feet," "Lilly Done the Zampoughi Everytime I Pulled Her Coattail," and "The Dozens."

As a fragmented musical, there is little plot to speak of, and the characters are all stock types that were first introduced on Van Peebles's albums. What little structure there is in the musical David Finkle describes in *The Village Voice*: "Van Peebles makes Act One a day in the life and Act Two a day in the death."[55] Rather than focusing on a central narrative, Van Peebles creates a sense of life within the dramatic world of the musical: "that place black folks mean when they talk about the Block."[56] Thus, the stage is an abstracted representation of the Harlem streets of the early 1970s. As

described in the stage directions, "it is scarred and comic, dangerous and ten-
der, within things blending and shifting back and forth in an instant the way
they do in reality, there's a car carcass and there are light bulbs, lampposts,
signs, dark rooms, stoops, steps, corners, concrete, whiskey bars and prison
bars."[57] Among his characters, representations of "the populace of the slums
of Harlem," Van Peebles focuses on "the whore, the pimp, the corrupt black
policeman, the beggar, the militant rifleman, the bag lady, and the homosex-
ual queen, all of whom express their failings in Van Peebles' songs."[58] As a
theatrical presentation, then, *Ain't Supposed to Die a Natural Death* creates
a vision of black life in Harlem for Broadway audiences that is, in Allen
Woll's words, "a far cry from the cheery plantation life of *Purlie*."[59]

Over the course of the show, the musical's often-unnamed characters sing
directly to the audience – there is little dialog, and virtually no book – about
their day on the Block in Harlem. In the show's opening number, "Just Don't
Make No Sense," for instance, the audience meets "some cat [Sunshine] drag-
ging ass along in from stage left regretting every step he takes."[60] Describing
Sunshine's entrance, Van Peebles continues: "He sits on a stoop and rubs his
ankles, which is as close as he dares to get to the center of his pain. Lord
lord lord, he limps back up to his feet and looks back down the street … but
it's still empty … he shakes his head and tells it like it be."[61] At this point,
Sunshine begins singing the show's first number about the pain in his corns,
The Man's game, his inability to catch a bus as a black man – generally "laying out the black man's situation."[62] He sings:

> Frown – you hostile
> Smile – you a Tom
> Look tired you on junk
> Stumble – you drunk
> If I wash Im a pimp
> If I don't – Im a bum
> …
> All you folks think black folks is for is waiting
> Waiting for the Supreme Courts latest jive decision
> Waiting
> Waiting for the Man to pick who is qualified
> Waiting in the emergency ward to die
> Naw just don't make no sense the way these corns are hurting me[63]

As Sunshine finally boards a bus and either begins or ends his day on the
Block in the show's early morning hour, he finishes singing, "I don't get
me a seat the revolution is here / You step on these feet and the revolution is right now."[64] In the show's opening number, Van Peebles argues that
Sunshine "is rapping for every greasy-brown-bag-carrying brother and sister

round-tripping downtown and doing time on them lonely corners." In this introduction to the world of the musical, Sunshine touches on the themes of poverty, pain, and misery while also drawing connections between the seemingly disparate, though in actuality closely connected, stakes of a man's sore feet and revolution. Additionally, this song connects the musical's characters and the musical's audience, both assumed and actual. When Sunshine sings, "All you folks think black folks is for is waiting," the "you folks" in the line imagines or addresses a seemingly traditional, predominantly white Broadway audience. Telling it "like it be" over the musical score of Van Peebles's compositions, Sunshine's opening number appears to introduce an artistic representation of the real world of day-to-day life in Harlem to Broadway's white audiences.

As such, Sunshine's song both reveals truths about black life in Harlem to a white Broadway audience and establishes the tone of the show. The show's goal is to represent an authentic representation of the Block and its music while also introducing Broadway audiences to a new world, a world in which black men and women are subject to The Man's game, corrupt police officers, pimps, thugs, beggars, and drugs. As the show continues, then, each representative character from the Block gets their song to flesh out the portrait of the ghetto on Broadway. In "The Dozens," for instance, Van Peebles introduces "The Drunk," begging a little change to buy another drink from people standing in line to catch a movie. Singing about his situation to a crowd uninterested in his plight, Van Peebles writes, "a drunk is among the most dialobical motherfuckers one can confront in a street situation." This is because "the drunk makes us look at what it feels like to be without shame, without manners, without caring what or who anybody thinks we are. When most of us arrive at this sense we reject it because it brings us face to face with something ugly in ourselves."[65] Over the course of "The Dozens," then, the audience sees the drunk's situation and his pleas for any spare change, his abuse of the crowd that refuses him and mocks him in the process, and his eventual compliments and praise as soon as "somebody in line throws some change to him."[66] This monologue-song reveals the situation of both the drunk and those members of the cinema line, further depicting some vision of the totality of life on the Block. Additional songs like "Coolest Place in Town" and "Lily Done the Zampoughi Every Time I Pulled Her Coattail" give every character type their own voice to express themselves lyrically over the non-stop soul soundtrack. By focusing on characters either looking for a way out or holding on to a glimmer of hope, the Harlem of the 1970s comes into focus on the Broadway stage. In "Coolest Place in Town," the neighborhood Tomboy sings to a white police officer who thinks she's a suicide risk. She explains that she is in fact not a risk, despite outlining a number of reasons why she could be; rather, she's just on the rooftops because that's the coolest place in town on this hot, hot day. In "Lily," we meet an incarcerated man singing about one of his lost, last loves on the outside, detailing their sexual exploits. Both songs, as with many other numbers in the show, present an interesting balance of a day-to-day life that includes flashes of both happiness and relief, in the face of mountains of despair. All the while, the current of revolution, first introduced by Sunshine, rides under the songs' innovative music and the characters' lyrics and overall desperate situations.

The day-in-the-life portrait of the musical builds to the revolution-themed climax in the show's next-to-last number, "Come on Feet," and continues on into the closing number, "Put a Curse on You." The intro to "Come on Feet" involves a Junkie stealing a TV as police show up to investigate the scene. Seeing the action, one of the play's regular characters, Junebug, walks over to watch the scene only to run into the police standing with guns drawn. Since they "see sneakers-and-Afro," the police "call him over on G.P. [General Principle]."[67] The dilemma leaves Junebug facing the decision between cooperating or running, as he hesitates for a number of reasons outlined by Van Peebles: "If he isn't guilty why is he standing so far away? If he is innocent why does he look that way? Junebug knows there is no need trying to explain, he makes a break and the cops go after him."[68] At this point, the music kicks into high gear accompanying the chase scene unfolding on stage as Junebug dives under stairs and in and out of doorways, trying to escape the cops who are seeking to interrogate him without cause. The song begins with Junebug pleading with his feet, his legs, and his knees to do their thing and help him outrun the police. As he sings about escaping the police, though, the song becomes a hallucinatory vision of freedom and escape as "The Cop fires at the flashing form. Junebug's momentum swings him around the [light] pole, a wounded flag being lowered."[69] Having been shot by the cops, "a first drop of blood hits the ground before he does. He totters for a moment on the sidewalk, then he begins to run away, at least he thinks he does, but dying Junebug has to keep hanging on to the pole for support so he only turns in a hopeless circle."[70] As Junebug continues singing "Come on Feet" and pleading with his body to run faster, his death becomes the climax of the show, spawning the revolution of "the Block." Upon witnessing his death, all of the characters of the Block become enraged, and for the first time on any Broadway stage, "a niggerquake begins … WAR." The police officer grabs a gun, characters start rioting, and all-out chaos ensues until the omnipresent vision of "The Man steps in."[71] At this point, things change dramatically for the citizens of Harlem: "Suddenly blinding lights flash on, cutting everything short ... The light is harsh and horrifying, and the Block can be seen as a prison. High above the Block, the Man himself operates the main searchlight, he sweeps it back and forth across the camp grounds. The folks stagger around blinded and cowering."[72] Upon their attempt at revolution, the citizens of Harlem are stuck like puppets controlled by the symbolic presence of The-Man-as-puppet-master positioned high above the stage. Free from The Man's control, though, is the bag lady, an omnipresent figure on stage, dismissed throughout the show as a crazy woman, always present but rarely acknowledged by the other characters or the audience. Free from The Man's control as a result of her connections to the African Diaspora, she begins to invoke the spiritual power of black music that Baraka, Harrison, Gilroy, and others have pointed to:

> She lets out a wail from the bottom of her soul ... the first sound anyone has heard her utter. She spins downstage, swinging her scavenger sack ... she rests the bag on the ground and freezes, a humped ancient figure ... Finally, her head raises [sic] ... her eyes burn with grief and hate, a single drum, slow and deep, begins ... Her voice comes from somewhere most people have never been.[73]

At this point she sings, "Put a Curse on You," directly addressing the audience, cursing them with all of the plight and misery facing the urban black poor of America in 1971. The show then ends with her marching toward the audience, menacing and cursing them until the music stops. The audience is left with the final image onstage of an angry and revolutionary population of Harlem confronting them in a Broadway theatre.

Running on Broadway at the same time that the National Sun Theatre was creating a Black Nationalist theatre movement in Harlem, Van Peebles's work raises questions about the roles and functions of black musicals on Broadway. This question dominated much of the critical reception of the show, and most notably and controversially that of *New York Times* theatre critic Clive Barnes. He addressed his initial review to his presumably white readership upon finding that the show represented a world completely unknown, unfamiliar, and unimaginable to him. On Barnes's reception of the musical, its director Gilbert Moses posits, "It seems to me that the tendency is to relegate the variety of black theatrical expression to the garbage heap of 'black theatre.' I begin to mistrust [Clive Barnes's] ability to understand anything I do."[74] Here, Moses explicitly raises the issue of race in reception to Van Peebles's musical. Trying to interpret the show beyond that of a black musical and instead as a musical, full stop, Moses responds to Barnes and critics like him by repositioning the show not as a black musical but as a piece of musical theatre. He argues:

The ideas involved in *Ain't* I've seen in white lower-class neighborhoods. The point is to get past the character to the representation of humanity. The rag-lady is a woman you can see in any neighborhood be it Polish, Italian, or black. He [Barnes] just relegates it to the black community. If you had the Mad Woman of Chaillot or a group of white actors doing a street scene, he would have seen the humanity. But in black people, they don't see it. That's what the paragraph smacked of. "These are black people. There is nothing we can get out of this."[75]

Expanding his criticism to theatre critics more broadly, Moses adds, "Too many critics talk about black theatre as if it has nothing to do with their lives; they look at the black theatre movement without thinking that it has anything to do with theatre; that there are no innovations, etc."[76] But, in the case of *Ain't Supposed to Die a Natural Death*, Van Peebles's work and Moses's direction included statements about black life as it really was for both black and white audiences. Van Peebles created an innovative piece of musical theatre in which the spoken-word songs of his soul music created a new sound on Broadway, one that would influence the musicals of the 1970s by bringing an authentic black sound to the traditionally white form.

Coda: 1975 and the feel-good black musical

As the 1970s moved forward, the black musical made its transition along the similar path of black music cited by Russell Potter. Whereas Van Peebles created an authentic black musical, the subsequent black musicals of the 1970s offered a more watered-down approach for mainstream audiences. Having seen the ways in which Van Peebles's work split audiences along race lines, producers sought to retain his musical innovations while focusing on less politically and culturally controversial content. According to John Bush Jones, this new breed of black musical began in 1975: "with few exceptions these musicals abandoned protest in favor of pride in black heritage, culture, and music regardless of their creators' color."[77] Bush Jones continues, "this new breed of revue and book musicals took a sharp turn toward feel-good entertainment and an equally sharp one away from the strong statements of social significance."[78] The most successful of these new black musicals was *The Wiz*, an all-black adaptation of *The Wizard of Oz*, featuring a predominantly funk and soul score including such crowd-pleasing numbers as "Ease on Down the Road" and "Home." For Bush Jones, shows like *The Wiz* were notable as much for what they excluded as what they included: "Instead of addressing issues like racism, segregation, and discrimination as did the early '70s black musicals, the new black shows stressed black culture, black history, and black heritage, especially musical heritage."[79] Interestingly, and perhaps not surprisingly, Allen Woll observes that this shift was largely driven by the market and audience interest; he points out, "clearly, musicals that attracted blacks but refused to alienate whites were most likely to be profitable."[80] Turning his attention to *The Wiz*, he thus points out:

> Some might argue that *The Wiz* ignored contemporary black life, but it still drew on Afro-American culture in its music, choreography, design, and libretto. This seemed to be the lesson of *The Wiz*. Instead of addressing solely the difficulties of black life in America, a new musical might draw on positive aspects of black culture and history for inspiration and style.[81]

If the lesson of *The Wiz*, then, was how to make a commercially successful black musical by incorporating a watered-down version of black music for white and black audiences, it is not surprising to see, as the 1970s transitioned into the 1980s, creators and producers of black musicals conceive a show like *Dreamgirls*. As a fictionalized version of the story of Motown, *Dreamgirls* featured an extremely popular score full of nostalgic songs composed and performed in the successful Motown style of the 1960s and 1970s. As such, the creators of *Dreamgirls* made an extraordinarily popular, Tony-Award-winning musical that appealed to white and black audiences. Interestingly though, *Dreamgirls* built its score precisely on the songs Melvin Van Peebles found so devoid of political content or any actual representation of black life.

NOTES

1 Allen L. Woll, *Black Musical Theatre: From* Coontown *to* Dreamgirls (Baton Rouge: Lousiana State University Press, 1989), 278.
2 *Ibid.*, xiii (original emphasis).
3 John Bush Jones, *Our Musicals, Ourselves: A Social History of American Musical Theatre* (Waltham, MA: Brandeis University Press, 2003), 203.
4 *Ibid.*, 203–4.
5 Elizabeth Wollman, *The Theatre Will Rock: A History of the Rock Musical, from* Hair *to* Hedwig (Ann Arbor: University of Michigan Press, 2006), 111.
6 *Ibid.*
7 *Ibid.*, xiii.
8 Harry J. Elam, "Editorial Comment," *Theatre Journal*, 57.4 (December, 2005): 4.
9 James Vernon Hatch, "A White Folks Guide to 200 Years of Black & White Drama," *TDR*, 16.4 (December, 1972): 18.
10 Bush Jones, *Our Musicals, Ourselves*, 203.
11 *Ibid.*
12 *Ibid.*, 204.
13 Amiri Baraka, "Bopera Theory," in *Black Theatre: Ritual Performance in the African Diaspora*, ed. Paul Carter Harrison, Victor Leo Walker II, and Gus Edwards (Philadelphia: Temple University Press, 2002), 378.

14 Paul Carter Harrison, "Form and Transformation: Immanence of the Soul in the Performance Modes of Black Church and Black Music," in Harrison, Walker, and Edwards, *Black Theatre*, 321.

15 Paul Gilroy, *The Black Atlantic: Modernity and Double Consciousness* (Cambridge, MA: Harvard University Press, 1993), 74–5.

16 *Ibid.*, 75.

17 *Ibid.*, 76.

18 *Ibid.*, 34.

19 Elam, "Editorial Comment," 3.

20 Michael Hanson, "Suppose James Brown Read Fanon: The Black Arts Movement, Cultural Nationalism, and the Failure of Popular Music Praxis," *Popular Music*, 27.3 (2008): 343.

21 *Ibid.*

22 *Ibid.*

23 LeRoi Jones [Amiri Baraka], *Black Music*, Akashi Classics Renegade Reprint Series (New York: Akashi Books, 2010), 13.

24 *Ibid.*

25 *Ibid.*

26 Russell A. Potter, "Soul into Hip-Hop," in *The Cambridge Companion to Pop and Rock*, ed. Simon Frith, Will Straw, and John Street (Cambridge: Cambridge University Press, 2001), 143.

27 Joanna Demers, "Sampling the 1970s in Hip-Hop," *Popular Music*, 22.1 (January, 2002): 42.

28 Mark Anthony Neal, *Soul Babies: Black Popular Culture and the Post-Soul Aesthetic* (London; New York: Routledge, 2002), 3.

29 *Ibid.*

30 *Ibid.*, 4.

31 Potter, "Soul into Hip-Hop," 144.

32 *Ibid.*

33 Demers, "Sampling the 1970s," 45.

34 *Ibid.*

35 Potter, "Soul into Hip-Hop," 150.

36 *Ibid.*

37 *How to Eat Your Watermelon in Front of White People (and Enjoy It)*, DVD, dir. Joe Angio (New York: Breakfast at Noho LLC, 2008 [2005]).

38 Melvin Van Peebles, liner notes to Melvin Van Peebles, *Brer Soul*, compact disc (Los Angeles: RPM Records, 2010).

39 *Ibid.*

40 *Ibid.*

41 *Ibid.*

42 Gilroy, *The Black Atlantic*, 33–4.

43 Wollman, *The Theatre Will Rock*, 73.

44 *Ibid.*, 74.

45 *Ibid.*

46 *Ibid.*

47 Raymond Knapp, *The American Musical and the Formation of National Identity* (Princeton: Princeton University Press, 2005), 154.

48 *Ibid.*

49 *Ibid.*
50 Melvin Van Peebles, *Ain't Supposed to Die a Natural Death* (Toronto; New York; London: Bantam, 1973), 3. The opening stage picture of the houselights on and the curtain up interestingly recalls Thornton Wilder's instructions for *Our Town*, creating an interesting day-in-the-life connection between Grover's Corner and Harlem's streets.
51 *Ibid.*, 1.
52 *Ibid.*, 2.
53 *Ibid.*, 3.
54 Wollman, *The Theatre Will Rock*, 113.
55 David Finkle, "Classical Theatre of Harlem Revives the Acid Groove of Van Peebles's '70s Musical Ghetto Blasting," *The Village Voice*, October 6–12, 2004.
56 Van Peebles, *Ain't Supposed to Die*, 4.
57 *Ibid.*, 3–4.
58 Woll, *Black Musical Theatre*, 258.
59 *Ibid.*
60 Van Peebles, *Ain't Supposed to Die*, 5.
61 *Ibid.*, 5–6.
62 *Ibid.*, 8.
63 *Ibid.*, 8–9.
64 *Ibid.*, 10.
65 *Ibid.*, 61.
66 *Ibid.*, 64.
67 *Ibid.*, 142.
68 *Ibid.*
69 *Ibid.*, 142–3.
70 *Ibid.*, 143.
71 *Ibid.*, 150.
72 *Ibid.*, 150–1.
73 *Ibid.*, 152.
74 Bill Eddy, Gilbert Moses, Joseph Chaikin, Harold Clurman, and Wilford Leach, "4 Directors on Criticism," *TDR*, 18.3 (September, 1974): 24–33.
75 *Ibid.*, 26.
76 *Ibid.*, 27.
77 Bush Jones, *Our Musicals, Ourselves*, 224.
78 *Ibid.*
79 *Ibid.*
80 Woll, *Black Musical Theatre*, 265–6.
81 *Ibid.*, 266.

9

FAEDRA CHATARD CARPENTER

Spectacles of whiteness from Adrienne Kennedy to Suzan-Lori Parks

Transracial performances, on and off the formal stage, can be undoubtedly traced to the early 1600s when blacks, whites, and Native Americans first began to observe and visibly transcribe their critical impressions of each other. To date, many of the scholarly treatments that address transracial performance have focused on white-bodied impersonations of minoritized people, theatrical forms that are generally recognized in relation to blackface minstrelsy.[1] While there has been significant attention paid to representations of blackface in the past two decades (and, subsequently, theatrical portrayals of redface, yellowface, brownface, etc.), far less attention has been paid to dramatic iterations of *whiteness* in African American performance. There are, of course, some notable exceptions to this observation.

Scholars such as Dale Cockrell and Peter Reed have documented how whiteface performance in North America can be traced to the early nineteenth century in the Jonkonnu (or John Canoe) rituals of enslaved African Americans. These performances, with roots in West African and Caribbean traditions, were spectacular communal expressions in which elaborately costumed performers often wore "European clothing" and donned whiteface masks that were "clearly intended to represent Caucasian skin tones."[2] Likewise, theatre historians such as David Krasner, Errol G. Hill, James V. Hatch, and Nadine George-Graves have offered revelatory descriptions of black-authored, embodied whiteface performances on American stages.[3] In addition, Joseph Roach and Marvin McAllister have furthered the examination of whiteface by theorizing on "whiteface minstrelsy," thereby considering the ways in which embodied enactments of white-identified privileges and behaviors expand our understanding of African American performance and cultural expression.[4]

While my larger research project entails a visual and thematic exploration of whiteness in contemporary African American performance, this brief chapter contributes to the burgeoning discourse of transracial theatrical strategies by exploring specific *spectacles of whiteness* in the work of four African American playwrights. In so doing, it explores the ways in which these theatrical moments deconstruct notions of white supremacy, privilege, and purity while simultaneously complicating perceptions of blackness. Moreover, by examining dramaturgical expressions of whiteness, I hope to expand the ways in which theatre scholars, practitioners, and artists critically identify, assess, and utilize "whiteface" as a performance practice. To this end, my consideration of whiteface in contemporary African American performance extends beyond the "whitening up" of one's corporeal features by also reflecting upon other performance tactics used to signify embodied whiteness. Each of the plays I address stages visible signs of whiteness in discrete ways, from whiteface (as described in Adrienne Kennedy's *Funnyhouse of a Negro*, Douglas Turner Ward's *Day of Absence*, and Suzan-Lori Parks's *Topdog/Underdog*) to what I consider "non-traditional whiteface" (as enacted by the white doll in Lydia Diamond's stage adaptation of Toni Morrison's novel *The Bluest Eye*, or the costuming bits of Abraham Lincoln as described in Suzan-Lori Parks's *The America Play*). While the embodied cues of whiteness differ considerably from play to play, each piece reminds us of the power of theatrical spectacle to translate meaning, as well as the way staged performances reflect both our theoretical ruminations and lived realities.

In addressing both the theories and experiences that have inspired the works in question, I choose to examine these pieces through the lens of critical whiteness studies. It should go without saying, however, that critical whiteness studies has simply given a name to a long-lived practice. As scholars often attest, black folks have been closely analyzing white folks for quite some time.[5] Nevertheless, with the naming of "critical whiteness" as a formal field of study (in tandem with the relatively recent surge of academic treatments on the subject), certain conceptual touchstones and motifs have emerged, offering scholars a number of tropes to reference, substantiate, modify, and/or contest. Among the more persistent tropes of whiteness that have developed in this still-burgeoning dialog are the following: the (anti-)normativity of whiteness, the (de)privileging nature of whiteness, the (im)purity of whiteness, the (in)visibility of whiteness, the interdependence of whiteness and blackness, whiteness as a social construct, and whiteness as paradoxical. While these tropes are fruitful areas for debate across the humanities and social sciences, the ocularcentric dialog surrounding whiteness proves to be particularly prolific when applied to theatrical performances – cultural products that hold the promise of merging the spectacular powers of both literary *and* visual texts.

Funnyhouse of a Negro

When considering racialized spectacles on the American stage, perhaps no African American-authored text of the 1960s offers a more striking representation of whiteness than Adrienne Kennedy's *Funnyhouse of a Negro*. Although her play won critical attention and an Obie Award, many black critics of *Funnyhouse of a Negro* failed to recognize the ways in which Kennedy's play followed the tenets of America's burgeoning Black Nationalism. Afrocentric critiques of Kennedy's play targeted the depiction of its protagonist's psychological exile from her African American identity. Kennedy's protagonist, Sarah – a victim of societal racism and her own self-hatred – finds refuge through the creation of her alter egos: the Duchess of Hapsburg, Queen Victoria Regina, Jesus, and Patrice Lumumba.[6] This complex of character(s) simultaneously represents the protagonist's splintered psyche as well as suggests the unavoidable disparities that exist within any self-defined community.

The dramatic portrayal of black self-hatred and communal disunity in *Funnyhouse of a Negro* was met with understandable resistance by the social activists, artists, and citizens fervently trying to substantiate the 1960s' mantras of "Black Power" and "black is beautiful." However, Kennedy's work was far more aligned with the professed goals of the Black Arts Movement than often credited. As Lotta M. Löfgren illustrates in her intertextual reading of LeRoi Jones's [Amiri Baraka's] *Dutchman* and Kennedy's *The Owl Answers*, Kennedy's dramaturgy actualizes many of the tenets famously articulated in Jones's "The Revolutionary Theatre" and Larry Neal's "The Black Arts Movement."[7] During the Black Arts Movement, both LeRoi Jones and Larry Neal assertively critiqued notions of white cultural and spiritual superiority, with Neal famously asserting, "The motive behind the Black aesthetic is the destruction of the white thing, the destruction of white ideas, and white ways of looking at the world."[8] While the *protagonist* of *Funnyhouse of a Negro* clearly denigrates her blackness and idolizes whiteness, the play itself is rich with references that counter this sentiment. Throughout *Funnyhouse of a Negro*, Kennedy pointedly deconstructs and disempowers "the white thing" by staging both haunting and perverse images of whiteness.

One of the most visceral and immediate methods Kennedy uses to interrogate perceptions of whiteness in *Funnyhouse of a Negro* is the play's use of whiteface, a theatrical strategy clearly articulated within Kennedy's stage directions.[9] In describing the characters of Queen Victoria and the Duchess of Hapsburg, Kennedy writes:

> BOTH WOMEN *are dressed in royal gowns of white, a white similar to the white of the Curtain, the material of cheap satin. Their headpieces are white*

and of a net that falls over their faces. From beneath both their headpieces springs a headful of wild kinky hair. Although in this scene we do not see their faces, I will describe them now. They look exactly alike and will wear masks or be made up to appear a whitish yellow. It is an alabaster face, the skin drawn tightly over the high cheekbones, great dark eyes that seem gouged out of the head, a high forehead, a full red mouth and a head of frizzy hair. If the characters do not wear a mask then the face must be highly powdered and possess a hard expressionless quality and a stillness as in the face of death.[10]

As described, Kennedy's portrayals of Queen Victoria and the Duchess of Hapsburg fully animate a number of tropes employed in critical whiteness studies: whiteness is not only presented as a constructed identity, but it is made hyper-visible, strange, and even terrifying. Yet the playwright also deliberately notes that Victoria and the duchess "look exactly alike," thereby suggesting that whiteness, as a process and system of power, works in recurring and habitual ways.

Kennedy also offers potential producers two ways to connote the whiteness of these characters: through the masking properties of makeup or through the use of tangible masks. In both instances, the characters' highly visible "wild kinky hair" becomes highlighted rather than visually suppressed. By offering audiences a persistent reminder of the real body beneath the mask, Kennedy reminds us of the inescapably integrated (and miscegenated) reality of blacks and whites. These masking techniques bring attention to their own construction, thereby also emphasizing the fabricated nature of our racial identities.[11] To this end, Deborah Thompson observes the Signifyin(g) strategy of Kennedy's whiteface: that is, the way in which Kennedy's whiteface *references* blackface minstrelsy by adopting its use of transracial mimicry while simultaneously *revising* its meanings through enactments of white, rather than black, representation: "Adrienne Kennedy's *Funnyhouse of a Negro*, 'Signifyin(g) upon' racism's master trope of minstrelsy, asks fundamental social, philosophical, and ontological questions about what 'race' 'is,' how it comes to be reified, and how the impossible absolutes of 'black' and 'white' come to be internalized and even naturalized onto our skins and into our bodies."[12] Conveying the impossibility of racial absolutes, Kennedy posits her whiteface as resistant to strict delineations. Rather than actually being white in hue, her whiteface is envisioned as a "whitish yellow" or "alabaster." In painting her whiteface in such a matter, Kennedy not only illustrates the fact that pure whiteness is a mythic notion (for both black and white bodies), but she also stages Richard Dyer's assertion that "We need to recognise white [is] a colour too."[13]

Moreover, Kennedy does not simply stage generic references to white people; her parodic dramatizations are focused upon iconic, Eurocentric figures. Thus, Kennedy's garish spectacles animate several tropes of whiteness, the chosen subjects of her whiteface offering compelling considerations. As referenced earlier, Queen Victoria and the Duchess of Hapsburg are loaded images when it comes to symbols of power. In the words of Jacqueline Wood, these characters "merge as loci of power informed by contemporary global experiences of patriarchal imperialism and racism. They are dominant white figures, superimposed upon blackness, symbolizing the political imposition of European power ..."[14] While the queen and duchess serve as symbols of colonialism and white domination, it should be noted too that Kennedy's chosen characterizations are also commenting on the specific, personal narratives of these historic figures and, in doing so, further dismantle idealized perceptions of whiteness.

In the case of Queen Victoria, Kennedy's dramaturgical strategy is emboldened by the ways the queen exemplifies the height of Britain's colonial rule, while simultaneously representing the tenuous life of a royal figure.[15] A significant character in the annals of British history, Victoria represents the politically astute and influential historical period known as "The Victorian Age." Yet Victoria was also a woman who suffered from familial distress and bouts of debilitating depression during her reign. Relying heavily on the counsel of her prime ministers, Queen Victoria may have ensured the continuation of the monarchy despite its diminishing power; however, the fact remains that she was a symbolic, rather than political, leader. Thus, Queen Victoria's life symbolizes yet another form of masking: a mask of power that obscured the virtual impotence of a constitutional monarchy.

Similarly, the Duchess of Hapsburg may represent the prestige and power associated with nobility, but her personal history echoes the precarious mental condition of Kennedy's protagonist. Carlota, Duchess of Hapsburg was first cousin to Queen Victoria. In 1864, Napoleon III appointed Carlota and her husband, the Austrian Archduke Maximilian, to the Mexican throne, leaving them penniless and powerless against Mexican revolutionaries.[16] Although the Duchess of Hapsburg began to display signs of mental illness, she traveled to Europe to request aid from Napoleon III and Pope Pius IX, and eventually descended into full-blown schizophrenia.[17] While her husband was eventually tried for treason and executed by a Mexican military tribunal, Carlota was diagnosed as incurably insane and spent her remaining years banished to her family's castle.[18] Carlota's tragic story was dramatized in the 1939 motion picture *Juarez*, a film that so intrigued Adrienne Kennedy that she created the Duchess of Hapsburg character for *Funnyhouse of a Negro*.

Thus, rather than simply championing characters from the British monarchy, we can read Kennedy's dramatization of Victoria and the duchess as further evidence of the playwright's revisionist strategies. These royal representatives in *Funnyhouse of a Negro* symbolize British power, but they also symbolize the arbitrary and precarious nature of social status – befitting characters with which to question the assumed authority and idealized status of whiteness.

Just as Kennedy uses the queen and duchess to de-romanticize idealized perceptions of whiteness, so does her inclusion of "a hunchback, yellow-skinned" Jesus. Described further as a "dwarf, dressed in white rags and sandals,"[19] Kennedy's Jesus rebukes modern representations of a white, beautified Jesus, while also challenging notions regarding Christianity's inviolability. The misshapen and racially ambiguous Jesus violates the insistence on binary constructs such as good–evil, white–black, normal–abnormal. In addition, Jesus' embodiment – an amalgamation of various dichotomies – also speaks to the precarious and problematic role Christianity has played in the lives of enslaved and colonized people; he symbolizes Christianity as a comfort and liberation as well as a source of persecution and oppression. Subsequently, Kennedy's physical depiction of Jesus, with its anti-hegemonic hints of discord and resistance, signifies the potential for both racial and religious transgression.

While Kennedy's use of whiteface is visibly articulated through her unconventional representations of Queen Victoria, the Duchess of Hapsburg, and Jesus, masks are used throughout the play to interrogate and destabilize traditional notions of whiteness. Even the various material possessions collected by Kennedy's protagonist can be seen as an attempt at masking evidence of her blackness. Desperate to acquire privileges associated with whiteness, Sarah adorns her small New York apartment with miscellany – photographs of castles and plaster statues – with hopes of obscuring the ways in which she lives her black/white existence. The play's continual parade of whiteface, embellished spaces, and ornate objects creates a visual interplay that reveals how *racial* identities (like costumes, set pieces, and props) can be embraced or discarded by their proprietors.[20] Correspondingly, the whiteface countenances of Jesus, Queen Victoria, and the Duchess of Hapsburg – visceral evidence of the imprisoning nature of racial signatures – open the possibility for the play's audience to recognize how real physical cues represent, and misrepresent, *cultural* identities.

Day of Absence

Like the theatrical whiteface in *Funnyhouse of a Negro*, the whiteface in Douglas Turner Ward's *Day of Absence* is specified with great detail. Ward writes that the play "is conceived for performance by a Negro cast, a reverse minstrel show done in white-face. Logically, it might also be performed by whites – at their own risk. If any producer is faced with choosing between opposite hues, the author strongly suggests: "Go 'long wit' the blacks – besides all else, they need the work more."[21] The dramatic effect of Ward's white-face is heightened by the play's simple storyline: a small, southern township awakens to discover that all their "Negro" citizens are missing. Shock and confusion soon lead to anxiety and chaos as the white townspeople recognize how essential black folks are to their day-to-day lives. Thus, the white folks in question – the characters that lament and strategize over the disappearance of the town's Negroes – are portrayed by African American actors in whiteface makeup. There are two exceptions to Ward's whiteface specifications: the character of Rastus, the sole Negro revealed at the end of the play, and the white Announcer described as a "Huntley-Brinkely-Murrow-Savereid-Cronkite-Reasoner-type."[22] Another notable specification of the play's color-conscious scheme is Ward's specification that *Day of Absence* "is a red-white-and-blue play – meaning the entire production should be designed around the basic color scheme of our patriotic trinity."[23]

While the latter set directions could be read as a pointed affront to American patriotism (particularly considering the parodic pulse of the play), it was Ward's use of whiteface that was met with notable disdain by several theatre critics. Martin Gottfried of *Women's Wear Daily*, one of those unimpressed with the usage, wrote: "The theatrical thematic affect of a Negro in white face is enormous and could only be conceived by a royal artist like Genet. Ward's borrowing of it was presumptuous and his application of it to a play whose attitude basically is peevish, makes it obscene. *Day of Absence* is an elaborate pout."[24] Curiously, Adrienne Kennedy's *Funnyhouse of a Negro* – a play that preceded the debut of *Day of Absence* by a year – escaped such a scathing comparison. Perhaps Gottfried's conjuring of *The Blacks* was due to a number of factors: Jean Genet's critically acclaimed play not only featured black actors in whiteface, but it had only been four years since Genet's play had had its own American premiere at the very same theatrical venue. Even more strikingly, Douglas Turner Ward eventually replaced Roscoe Lee Brown in that premiere production. Thus, the relatively recent witnessing of *The Blacks* may have left *Day of Absence* particularly ripe for critical comparisons. However, as Terence T. Tucker asserts, Gottfried's bias in mentioning Genet "privileges Western inspiration, instead of the horrific legacy of blackface minstrelsy as the genesis for Ward's play."[25] Recognizing the political and artistic climate of the time, it is clear that Ward's theatrical strategy of whiteface intentionally countered the historic practice of blackface minstrelsy. Moreover, like most whiteface performances, *Day of Absence* provided a layered critique of society's institutionalized ideas of whiteness.

Figure 9.1 Carlton Molette, *Day of Absence*.

The content and character storyline of Ward's play offer multiple riffs on whiteness.[26] As concisely detailed by Brandi Wilkins Catanese, Ward's play offers a biting "meta-critique of American racial politics" by illustrating that whites are dependent upon blacks within the most private and public spheres of their lives, that blacks are equal contributors to the success and structure of American society, that intimacy between racialized groups is a reality, and that racial purity is a socially constructed fallacy. By embodying whiteness through black bodies and challenging the concept of "real" white bodies, Ward's play powerfully destabilizes traditional notions of whiteness while exposing the intrinsic relationship between whites and blacks – a relationship that can be neither visualized nor imagined without conceptualizing the other.[27]

However, in considering these layers of critique and observation, it becomes apparent that the styling of Ward's spectacle of whiteface powerfully reinforces the play's messages and meaning. Similarly to the whiteface in *Funnyhouse of a Negro*, the whiteface Ward describes for his actors does not fall within a spectrum of color that could be identified as flesh-toned.[28] Instead, the makeup is a bright white and decidedly "unnatural," simulating a whiteness that is so unreal it highlights the illusory nature and impossible truth of pure whiteness through its very presence.

As evidenced by a number of key productions, Ward originally envisioned the white makeup to be drawn *within* the outline of each actor's face, as if portraying ill-fitting masks. Fashioned in this way, the brown tones of the actors' faces, ears, neck, arms, hands, and legs were blatantly exposed – pointedly reminding audience members of the black bodies under the makeup. Once again, the styling of the whiteface makeup reveals a powerful relationship between the play's form and content by reinforcing a thematic rumination on the constructed nature of our racialized identities. Moreover, the whiteface makeup effectively animates how blacks are, literally and figuratively, "behind it all": despite the position of authority given to whites, the play argues, it is black folk that are responsible for the day-to-day success of civic life.

The extreme, opaque whiteface used in *Day of Absence* also conjures imaginings of the "Optic White" scene famously described in Ralph Ellison's *Invisible Man* (1952). In Ellison's classic novel, Kimbro (the supervisor at the Liberty Paint Company) schools the unnamed protagonist on the company's premier product, "Optic White" – "the purest white that can be found." In describing Optic White as a color that is "as white as George Washington's Sunday-go-to-meetin' wig and as sound as the all-mighty dollar," [29] Ellison's fictive scene (like the patriotic colors imbued in *Day of Absence*), mockingly marries the notions of whiteness with American patriotism. Most

Figure 9.2 Carlton Molette, *Day of Absence.*

significantly, however, the Optic White scene also suggests how the myth of ultra-whiteness is ultimately dependent on the presence of blackness. In Ellison's novel, the protagonist learns that the creation of Optic White paint requires ten drops of "dead black" in each bucket, thereby revealing that the popular paint is not really "pure" at all. In writing about this Liberty Paint

Scene, Harryette Mullen offers an analysis that also resonates when applied to Ward's creative intentions in *Day of Absence*:

> The American myth may rely for its potency on the interdependent myths of white purity and white superiority, but the invisible ones whose cultural and genetic contributions to the formation of American identity are covered up by Liberty White, those who function as machines inside the machine, know that no pure product of America, including the linguistic, cultural, and genetic heritage of its people, has emerged without being influenced by over three hundred years of multiracial collaboration and conflict.[30]

Also of note, the characters in *Day of Absence* are described as exceedingly "doll-like," exemplified by Ward's description of Mary, the play's utterly incompetent young mother.[31] Writing that Mary could well be portrayed with a "Kewpie-doll face, ruby-red lips painted to valentine-pursing, moon-shaped rouge circles implanted on each cheek" and a "blond wig of fat-flowing ringlets," Ward clearly articulates the desired design of his whiteface characterizations. Again, the artifice inherent in such costuming reveals Ward's intention to disclose the fallacies of whiteness. Unlike the ways in which some early blackface performances attempted to construct and perpetuate racist representations of blacks *as* authentic, Ward's whiteface is a transparent strategy that simultaneously highlights the inauthentic nature of both blackface and whiteface performances.

Ward's description of Mary offers readers another striking and curiously overlooked intertextual invocation of *Invisible Man* in relation to Ellison's "kewpie character." When describing his protagonist's sighting of the forlorn, white dancer in the Battle Royal scene, Ellison writes:

> The hair was yellow like that of a circus kewpie doll, the face heavily powdered and rouged, as though to form an abstract mask, the eyes hollow and smeared a cool blue, the color of a baboon's butt ... I wanted at one and the same time to run from the room, to sink through the floor, or go to her and cover her from my eyes and the eyes of the others with my body; to feel the soft thighs, to caress her and destroy her, to love her and murder her, to hide from her, and yet to stroke where below the small American flag tattooed upon her belly her thighs formed a capital V.[32]

Upon seeing the clownish visage of the curiously patriotic, kewpie-styled dancer, Ellison captures his protagonist's entangled feelings of desire and disgust. Ellison's kewpie character personifies a seductive, inaccessible, and tormented nation. Similarly, the doll-like characters in *Day of Absence* may initially strike audience members as innocuous and ineffectual in appearance, but – draped in the red, white, and blue colors of the American flag – their eventual expressions of resentment and antagonism ultimately betray the truths that lie underneath their dollish exteriors. Like the kewpie dancer in Ellison's passage, the white characters in *Day of Absence* animate America's complicated racial relations by dramatizing dueling feelings of desire and disgust, love and hate.[33]

The Bluest Eye

There is a similar spirit of conflicting emotions that help to propel the drama inherent in Toni Morrison's novel, *The Bluest Eye*. Within the novel, an emotionally ravaged girl, Pecola, yearns for the love and acceptance she mistakenly believes will be granted to her only if she acquires blue eyes. Like Sarah in Kennedy's *Funnyhouse of a Negro*, Pecola's tragic story revolves around her destructive idealization of whiteness. While the stage play (like Morrison's novel) wrestles with notions of black and white in a number of complex ways, it is the live presentation of playwright Lydia Diamond's stage production that offers one of the most direct, and prolific, spectacles of embodied whiteness in contemporary African American theatre.

In the 2006 stage adaptation of *The Bluest Eye*, Diamond recreates the scene in which Frieda, Claudia, and Pecola encounter Mrs. Breedlove's young, white charge. Diamond's stage directions effectively describe the little girl as Morrison penned her: "The little GIRL wears [a] pink sundress and pink fluffy bunny bedroom slippers." However, the playwright also offers – through the character of Claudia – an impression of the young white girl that is not found in Morrison's novel: "If her hair wasn't long and straight and blonde and her eyes blue instead of green, I might have mistaken her for Shirley Temple."[34]

As established earlier in both the novel and the play, the iconic figure of Shirley Temple becomes shorthand for unearned white privilege and mediated perceptions of whiteness, a whiteness not only brimming with youth and femininity, but fueled by consumer culture. The particularities of Shirley Temple – as both a real person and as the representative of Hollywood fantasy – are as irrelevant in the social fabric of the play as they were to the media machines in real life. What is essential (and essentialized) in the eyes of Pecola is the way Temple symbolizes an indisputable mythic whiteness. Temple's manufactured image is co-opted to represent the ideal model of American youth culture: its promise, purity, and innocence. This is made particularly clear by the stage play's acknowledgement of the obvious *difference* between the described visage of the young white girl and the famed child actress she supposedly resembles. While Mrs. Breedlove's charge may be blonde, she does not have Temple's signature ringlet curls; moreover, we are told her eyes are green while Temple's eyes were blue. One can presume that Diamond's pointed allusion to Shirley Temple is not only included as a dramaturgical strategy (it creates a through-line by reinforcing the play's earlier reference to the iconic actress), but it also suggests the market value of hegemonic whiteness. A reader/viewer may deduce that Claudia's reference to the girl is not prompted by any resemblance to Shirley Temple, but rather that her costuming of youthful, white femininity adequately satisfies the requisites needed to gain Temple's status: she's white, therefore she's right.

Diamond further interrogates the social construction of whiteness by indicating that a live actor should not portray the white girl in the play. Rather, the character should be represented "by a white, life-sized doll, manipulated by the actress who plays MAUREEN PEAL, wearing an identical outfit."[35] This dramaturgical strategy not only harkens back to Ward's *Day of Absence*, but also alludes to a number of instances in African American performance wherein whiteness has been theatricalized on the stage using dolls or dollish images.[36] In representing the white girl in this manner, the doll – in tandem with the matching outfit worn by the actor – moves beyond the suggestion of white*face* to become a full-body mask. While Claudia recognizes that she cannot "commit a systematic dismembering"[37] of real little white girls in the same way she dismembers her Christmas doll, the whiteface scene in the stage adaptation of Morrison's novel play offers yet another way to imagine the possibility of black authority over whiteness. While the reliance of a black body to effect the doll's movement dramatizes the fact that white people have profited from the labor of black bodies, this fully embodied whiteface also intimates that black people are often the unacknowledged (and unrewarded) "puppet masters" of white civic life – a suggestion also posed in *Day of Absence*.

Strikingly, the actor's handling of the white doll offers the visual representation of black manipulators as *producers*, even co-conspirators, in the creation of mythic whiteness.[38] Accordingly, this spectacle of whiteness implicates Maureen Peal as both a victim and a perpetrator of failed mimicry and intraracial prejudice. In the particular world of *The Bluest Eye*, Maureen Peal – the fair-skinned and well-to-do classmate of Pecola – is both privileged and penalized by her socio-economic status and lighter skin. She receives the undue attention of her peers and teachers, and is, in turn, handicapped by her unearned privilege, unable to make substantive connections within her community. Without the emotional and psychological satisfaction of healthy relationships, Pecola, like the doll, is a pretty package devoid of true substance.

Of course, Diamond also suggests that the white girl may be represented through the use of a stationary doll with the white girl's lines delivered as a voiceover.[39] In this scenario, the doll's inanimate nature is further emphasized. Staged this way, the scene answers the frustrated queries voiced by Claudia earlier in the play when she disdainfully reflects on the receipt of her "annual blonde, blue-eyed Christmas doll": "What made people look at them and say 'Awwww,' but not see me at all? Why was I invisible next to little white girls in pleated skirts and white knee-highs?"[40] Although the answer to this painful query is never directly articulated in the novel, Diamond uses the visual mode of the play to manifest a response: there is nothing inherently special about little white girls, other than the social capital placed on their whiteness. Accordingly, the doll's countenance underscores the absurdity of the pedestal on which Mrs. Breedlove places the white girl. Moreover, the voiceover works to reveal the same set of contradictory impressions yielded by the characters of the queen and duchess in *Funnyhouse*: while relaying the impression of an omnipresent and all-powerful force, she is also fundamentally powerless.

The America Play and Topdog/Underdog

The issue of representation, especially when it comes to those who are deemed as powerful versus those who are considered powerless, is also a central motif in the works of playwright Suzan-Lori Parks. While this thematic refrain can be found throughout Parks's oeuvre, it is especially pronounced in *The America Play* and *Topdog/Underdog*, plays in which the audacious spectacle of ordinary black men taking on the likeness of Abraham Lincoln serves as an ever-notable topic of discussion. Scholars frequently cite the re-enactments of President Lincoln in both plays as evidence of Parks's commentary on the construction of identity. Often framed in terms of race (the ways in which racial identification is inordinately and erroneously dependent on visual markers), this theatrical strategy of masking suggests the construction of American identity (especially in terms of how our nationalistic and patriotic narratives are produced and disseminated), as well as the perpetuation of mythos pertaining to Abraham Lincoln.

Similar to the way that Adrienne Kennedy uses the images of the queen and duchess to destabilize iconic images of white power and authority, Suzan-Lori Parks uses Abraham Lincoln as a masking device that helps to unveil truths about the fabrication of our layered, most sanctified narratives. Reminiscent of the two-ness evidenced in Kennedy's play, the iconographic figure of Lincoln-the-president is a symbol of both national strength and national discord. President Lincoln is also a rich subject for Parks's dramaturgy owing to the vexing way his legacy has been used within the discourse of America's race relations. As Verna Foster reminds us, Lincoln's role within African American history is replete with paradoxes: "The historical reception of Abraham Lincoln among African Americans has long been problematic. He has been both revered as the Great Emancipator and in the last half century or so criticized as a white supremacist."[41]

In *The America Play*, the first of Parks's works to incorporate an impersonator of President Lincoln, the character of the Foundling Father reports that the Lesser Known physically mirrors the Great Man in many ways: they are both tall and thin, with notably long legs and large hands and feet.[42] Most significant, however, is that the Lesser Known had been told "from birth practically"[43] that he "bore a strong resemblance to Abraham Lincoln"[44] – a comparison that persisted throughout the Lesser Man's life.[45] Repeatedly informed that he resembled the slain president, the Lesser Known accepts this observation as fact, thereby suggesting how our identities are invariably sanctioned and circumscribed through the eyes of others as well as through the repetition of performative acts.[46]

In addressing the ways in which the Lesser Known-as-Lincoln speaks specifically to the construction of racialized identity, the Foundling Father's ruminations on the Lesser Known's beards are particularly telling, especially in terms of how whiteness is construed in relation to privilege and possession:

> The Lesser Known had several beards which he carried around in a box. The beards were his although he himself had not grown them on his face but since he'd secretly bought the hairs from his barber and arranged their beard shapes and since the procurement and upkeep of his beards took so much work he figured that the beards were completely his. Were as authentic as he was, so to speak.[47]

While the Lesser Known is fully cognizant of the fact that he did not grow his beards naturally, the fact that he paid for their creation and invested in their upkeep prompts him to rationalize that "the beards were completely his." Thus, Parks's dramaturgy reinforces the idea that racial categories are not natural; rather, they – like the Lesser Known's beards – are created, appropriated, shaped, and cultivated until they are *naturalized*. However, this acknowledgement also prompts us to consider the possibilities and limitations in laying claim to a racial identity adopted by an individual versus one that is socially sanctioned. Does *The America Play* suggest the dawning of a new era in which people may effectively claim or reject a racialized identity for themselves?

In thinking about this query, and recognizing how the beards are not only signatures of Lincoln but signatures of *whiteness*, it is useful to consider Cheryl Harris's groundbreaking treatise "Whiteness as Property." In Harris's essay, the legal scholar cites how whiteness is "deployed as identity, status, and property, sometimes singularly, sometimes in tandem."[48] The fact that whiteness can be deployed as identity and status is made readily apparent in Parks's drama; however, the more complicated assertion that whiteness can be deemed as property is also evidenced in *The America Play*. In the most obvious sense, the Lincoln garb worn by the Lesser Known is tangible material that has been paid for, claimed, and kept. Thus, the costume is understood as property because it is owned by the Lesser Known man, and, accordingly, is something to which he can "attach value and have a right." As Harris explains, however, property rights are usually attributed to things that are fully alienable – material that can be sold or transferred from person to person. Since whiteness is generally understood as that which is *in*-alienable, that which cannot be sold or transferred, it does not neatly fall into our traditional ideas of "property." However, rather than problematizing our understanding of whiteness, this discrepancy actually helps to illuminate the slippery qualities of whiteness, prompting Harris to conclude that it is the inalienable nature of whiteness that "may be more indicative of its perceived enhanced value rather than its disqualification as property."[49] In dramatizing this slippage, Parks's play highlights the strategic inconsistencies of white representation, demonstrating how "the paradoxes and instabilities of whiteness also constitute its flexibility and productivity, in short, its representational power."[50]

The America Play wrestles with the paradoxes of whiteness in another moment when the Foundling Father speaks about his yellow beard, a costuming detail that is at once confounding and revealing. Of his blond beard, he states: "This is my fancy beard. Yellow. Mr. Lincolns hair was dark so I dont wear it much. If you deviate too much they wont get their pleasure. Thats my experience. Some inconsistencies are perpetuatable because theyre good for business. But not the yellow beard. Its just my fancy."[51] As discordant as the image of a blond Lincoln may be in terms of factual history, it is a reference that specifically underscores the ways in which we visually perceive whiteness. In the same way blue eyes are used in *The Bluest Eye* as short-hand for idealized whiteness, blond hair is habitually referenced as an exclusive trait of white identity, despite the fact that both blue eyes and blond hair are, indeed, physical traits shared by other racialized groups. At one point, the Foundling Father asks the audience to "pretend for a moment that our beloved Mr. Lincoln was a blonde [*sic*]."[52] Just as images of Jesus Christ have been refashioned as blond, we are asked to accept a refashioned image of Abraham Lincoln; a rewriting of historical accounts demonstrates how notions of whiteness are often centralized within American folklore. Moreover, Parks's suggestion that the Foundling Father imposes a deviation from the truth owing to his own sense of subjective "fancy" exposes the ways in which America's history has been written according to the whim and fancy of "founding fathers."

Of course, it must be noted that in the world of the play it is a black man that prompts these imaginings of whiteness, a fact that once again alludes to how we are all implicated in perpetuating racial projects, from the innocuous to the pernicious. This same complex perspective on the creation of racial tropes persists in Suzan-Lori Parks's other Lincoln Play – her 2002 Pulitzer-Prize-winning drama *Topdog/Underdog*. Within this Cain and Abel story, Parks features yet another character that dons the garb associated with the mythos of Abraham Lincoln. In *Topdog/Underdog*, however, the spectacle of whiteness is far more pronounced, in that the aptly named character Lincoln not only wears the famous top hat, frock coat, and (dark) beard associated with the sixteenth president of the United States; he also wears whiteface makeup to make his performative transformation complete.

Although Lincoln-the-character's whiteface makeup in *Topdog/Underdog* is highly theatrical and reactivates the way whiteface strategies have traditionally been used, the *removing* of Lincoln's makeup is actually one of the most provocative moments in the play.[53] By having Lincoln remove his makeup on stage (with cold cream, no less), Parks's play makes an unusual shift from highlighting the construction of race to emphasizing the *decon*struction of racial identity. Furthermore, this stripping of whiteness with whiteness acts as a visual cue for the anecdote that follows: it is during the removal of his whiteface that Lincoln shares the story of how he hustles a "little rich kid" into paying him ten dollars for President Lincoln's autograph. Since the boy only has a $20 bill, Lincoln tells him that he will take the $20 and "Honest Abe" will give him his change when he sees him on the bus the next day. Blinded by Lincoln's portrayal of Honest Abe, the young boy is stripped of his money: he will never get his $10 back. While audiences are right to condemn Lincoln's unscrupulous actions, it is equally problematic for anyone to assume that a celebrated configuration (whether an iconic figure or whiteness itself) is worthy of our unmitigated idealization. It was, after all, not merely Lincoln's clothing, but his apparent whiteness that placed him in a position of acceptance and authority. One is led to believe that this exchange (or even the initial request that precipitated it) would not have occurred without the special effect of whiteness working on Lincoln's behalf.[54]

Despite the vast differences between the plays addressed in this chapter, each playwright takes advantage of American audiences' ocularcentricity in order to challenge and subvert persistent assumptions regarding racial difference. While there are a number of dramaturgical strategies at their disposal, a common current throughout these selected texts is the use of the power of spectacle to defamiliarize whiteness and confront assumptions regarding white invisibility and power. Through marking and remarking on whiteness in various ways, *Funnyhouse of a Negro, Day of Absence, The Bluest Eye, The America Play*, and *Topdog/Underdog* actively resist the presentation of whiteness as ideal or even normative, encouraging us to recognize whiteness for what it is – a social, political, and economic construct. Furthermore, in exposing the fabricated nature of whiteness, these plays invariably destabilize the notion of blackness as well, thereby prompting us to interrogate the *intra*racial and *intra*cultural dynamics within contemporary African American discourse. In so doing, these enactments of whiteness do much more than simply invert racial representations and/or reify revised racial hierarchies. As revisionist tactics, these spectacles of whiteness complicate how we perceive Others as well as how we perceive ourselves.

NOTES

1 Among the book-length treatments of blackface minstrelsy are Eric Lott, *Love and Theft: Blackface Minstrelsy and the American Working Class* (New York: Oxford University Press, 1993); Annemarie Bean, James V. Hatch, Brooks McNamara, and Mel Watkins (eds.), *Inside the Minstrel Mask: Readings in Nineteenth-Century Blackface Minstrelsy* (Hanover, NH; London: Wesleyan University Press, 1996); Dale Cockrell, *Demons of Disorder: Early Blackface Minstrels and Their World* (New York: Cambridge University Press, 1997); and W. T. Lhamon, Jr., *Raising Cain: Blackface Performance from Jim Crow to Hip Hop* (Cambridge, MA: Harvard University Press, 1998).

2 See Cockrell, *Demons of Disorder*, 39. For a detailed exploration of Jonkonnu costuming and performance, see Peter Reed, "'There Was No Resisting John Canoe': Circum-Atlantic Transracial Performance," *Theatre History Studies*, 27 (2007): 65–85.

3 See David Krasner, *Resistance, Parody, and Double Consciousness in African American Theatre, 1895–1910* (New York: St. Martin's Press, 1997); Nadine George-Graves, *The Royalty of Negro Vaudeville: The Whitman Sisters and the Negotiation of Race, Gender and Class in African American Theater, 1900–1940* (New York: St. Martin's Press, 2000); and Errol Hill and James Vernon Hatch (eds.), *A History of African American Theatre* (Cambridge; New York: Cambridge University Press, 2003).

4 See Marvin Edward McAllister, *White People Do Not Know How to Behave at Entertainments Designed for Ladies & Gentlemen of Colour: William Brown's African & American Theater* (Chapel Hill: University of North Carolina Press, 2003); and Joseph Roach, *Cities of the Dead: Circum-Atlantic Performance*

(New York: Columbia University Press, 1996). In addition, Marvin McAllister's recently published book *Whiting Up: Whiteface Minstrels and Stage Europeans in African American Performance* (Chapel Hill: University of North Carolina Press, 2011) makes a fundamental contribution to the discourse of transracial performance.

5   David R. Roediger (ed. and introd.), *Black on White: Black Writers on What It Means to Be White* (New York: Schocken Books, 1998); and Ruth Frankenberg, "Introduction: Local Whitenesses, Localizing Whiteness," in *Displacing Whiteness: Essays in Social and Cultural Criticism* (Durham, NC: Duke University Press, 1997), 1–34.

6   Harry J. Elam, Jr. writes of this tactic in his discussion of August Wilson's play, *King Hedley*: "At times people suffering from various forms of psychosis imagine themselves to be kings, queens, or figures of royal standing, power, and privilege in order to combat their fragmented sense of self." Whether August Wilson was consciously paying homage to Kennedy in his crafting of *King Hedley* is uncertain, but the parallel is noteworthy. See Harry J. Elam, Jr., "August Wilson, Doubling, Madness and Modern African American Drama," *Modern Drama*, 43:4 (2000): 618.

7   Lotta M. Löfgren, "Clay and Clara: Baraka's *Dutchman*, Kennedy's *The Owl Answers*, and the Black Arts Movement," *Modern Drama*, 46 (Fall, 2003): 424–49; LeRoi Jones, "The Revolutionary Theatre," in *Home: Social Essays* (New York: William Morrow & Co., 1966), 210–11; and Larry Neal, "The Black Arts Movement," *Drama Review*, 12 (Summer, 1968): 29–39.

8   Neal, "The Black Arts Movement."

9   In utilizing the term "whiteface," I am referring to the temporary manipulation of skin color, hair, and/or facial features through the use of makeup or masking with the intent of suggesting an embodiment of racial whiteness.

10   Adrienne Kennedy, *Funnyhouse of a Negro* (New York: Samuel French, 1969), 5–6.

11   The character of Sarah verifies this notion when she informs the audience that Queen Victoria asks *her* (Sarah) to tell Victoria of whiteness, thus reinforcing the notion that such an identity is not innate, but constructed and defined (1) in relation to blackness, and (2) in accordance to power dynamics; Kennedy, *Funnyhouse*, 14.

12   Deborah Thompson, "Reversing Blackface Minstrelsy, Improvising Racial Identity: Adrienne Kennedy's *Funnyhouse of a Negro*," *Post Identity*, 1.1 (Fall, 1997): 14. For more on the rhetorical and literary strategy of Signifyin(g) see Henry Louis Gates, Jr., *The Signifying Monkey: A Theory of African-American Literary Criticism* (Oxford; New York: Oxford University Press, 1988).

13   Richard Dyer, *White* (New York: Routledge, 1997), 11.

14   For a more detailed discussion of *Funnyhouse* as a Bakhtinian reversal and parody of blackface minstrelsy, see Jacqueline Wood, "Weight of the Mask: Parody and the Heritage of Minstrelsy in Adrienne Kennedy's *Funnyhouse of a Negro*," *Journal of Dramatic Theory and Criticism*, 17.2 (Spring, 2003): 17.

15   See "Victoria,", in *Collier's Encyclopedia: With Bibliography and Index*, 24 vols. (New York; Toronto: Macmillian, 1990), Vol. XXIII, 121–2.

16 This reading of the events spawned by Napolean III is informed by Richard O'Connor, *The Cactus Throne: The Tragedy of Maximilian and Carlotta* (New York: Putnam, 1971).

17 *Ibid.*, 264–5.

18 Strikingly, Carlota's banishment, as described by biographer Richard O'Connor, is reminiscent of the maddening, museum-like milieu of Adrienne Kennedy's protagonist, Sarah. Of Carlotta's family castle, O'Connor writes:

> There Carlotta was incarcerated at the age of twenty-six in a setting that might have been chosen by Edgar Allan Poe for one of his hapless heroines, surrounded by sculptured knights, ancestral portraits of titled thugs, regiments of armor, acres of canvas and tapestry depicting scenes of conquest, walls bracketed with halberds, swords, battle axes, arquebuses and other souvenirs of a bloody past … Ultimately Carlotta, too, became a museum piece.
>
> (*Ibid.*, 276).

19 Kennedy, *Funnyhouse of a Negro*, 9.

20 For another discussion of the play's varied use of masks, particularly the African-influenced masks specified in the play, see Thompson, "Reversing Blackface Minstrelsy," 13–38.

21 Douglas Turner Ward, *Happy Ending and Day of Absence: Two Plays* (New York: Dramatists Play Service, 1966), 29.

22 *Ibid.*, 45.

23 *Ibid.*, 29.

24 James Vernon Hatch and Ted Shine, "Introduction: *Day of Absence*," in *Black Theatre USA: Plays by African Americans*, 2 vols. (New York: The Free Press, 1996), Vol. 1: *The Recent Period, 1935–Today*, 264–5.

25 Terence T. Tucker, "Furiously Funny: Comic Rage in Late Twentieth Century African-American Literature," Ph.D. dissertation (University of Kentucky, 2006). To this end, Douglas Turner Ward also forthrightly stated that his use of white-face in *Day of Absence* was his "revenge on them [white people] for Black-facing us." See Daniel Banks, "Unperforming the Minstrel Mask: Black-Face and the Technology of Representation," Ph.D. dissertation (New York University, 2005), 244.

26 I use "riffs" in deference to Ward's own reference to the dramaturgical structure of his play. In an interview with Daniel Banks, Ward explained: "It played on riffs – what the White critics didn't understand was the riffs. Duke [Ellington] could take an idea and then play all kinds of riffs around it, but still the singular through line." Banks, "Unperforming the Minstrel Mask," 254–5.

27 Brandi Wilkins Catanese, "Teaching *A Day of Absence* 'at [your] own risk,'" *Theatre Topics*, 19.1 (March, 2009): 31.

28 My reading of the makeup design in *Day of Absence* is based on Ward's stage directions, detailed photographs of the original production, and my viewing of the 1967 PBL televised version of the play, as well as photographs of the Signature Theatre Company's 2009 staged reading directed by the playwright.

29 Ralph Ellison, *Invisible Man* (New York: Vintage Press: 1980), 201–2.

30 Harryette Mullen, "Optic White: Blackness and the Production of Whiteness," *Diacritics*, 24.2/3 (Summer/Fall, 1994): 74.

31 The significance of making the whitefaced characters in *Day of Absence* highly stylized and "doll-like" was not lost on theatre scholar, playwright, and director

Carlton Molette when he directed the play at Florida A & M University in 1967 and the University of Michigan in 1976. Confronted with the fact that modern advances in costuming had made synthetic wigs "so natural looking that they would give an unwanted aspect of reality to the stage production," Molette opted to have all the whitefaced characters (men and women) wear yarn wigs, thereby giving the entire ensemble a striking "rag-doll" aspect. See Bettie Seeman, "Yarn Wigs: Design, Construction, and Styling," *Theatre Crafts*, May/June, 1976, 19–21.

32 Ellison, *Invisible Man*, 19.

33 With these seemingly dueling contradictions, Ellison also conceivably creates a blueprint for Lula in LeRoi Jones's *Dutchman*: a personification of a seductive, taunting, inaccessible, volatile, even murderous, America.

34 Lydia Diamond, *The Bluest Eye* (Woodstock, IL: Dramatic Publishing, 2006), 60.

35 *Ibid.*

36 One of the most striking, analogous uses of a white doll was in George C. Wolfe's 1996 *Bring in 'da Noise, Bring in 'da Funk*. Among the episodes in Wolfe's award-winning music-and-dance extravaganza is the memorable "Uncle Huck-a-Buck" and "Lil' Dahlin" scene, in which a life-sized doll (reminiscent of Shirley Temple) is attached to Savion Glover, granting the illusion of animation to the mute, lifeless doll.

37 Diamond, *The Bluest Eye*, 27.

38 This reading is inspired by the observations of Susan Willis, who writes, "Claudia's intractable hostility towards Shirley Temple originates in her realization that in our society, she, like all racial 'others,' participates in dominant culture as a consumer, but not as a producer." See "I Want the Black One: Is There a Place for Afro-American Culture in Commodity Culture?," *New Formations*, 10 (Spring, 1990): 77.

39 Diamond, *The Bluest Eye*, 60.

40 *Ibid.*, 27.

41 Verna Foster, "Suzan-Lori Parks's Staging of the Lincoln Myth in *The America Play* and *Topdog/Underdog*," *Journal of American Drama and Theatre*, 17.3 (Fall, 2005): 31.

42 Suzan-Lori Parks, *The America Play and Other Works* (New York: Theatre Communications Group, 1995), 159.

43 *Ibid.*, 169.

44 *Ibid.*, 159.

45 *Ibid.*, 163.

46 Haike Frank, "The Instability of Meaning in Suzan-Lori Parks's *The America Play*," *American Drama*, 11.2 (2002): 11; and Mary Brewer, *Staging Whiteness* (Middleton, CT: Wesleyan University Press, 2005), 166.

47 Parks, *The America Play*, 159–60.

48 Cheryl Harris, "Whiteness as Property," *Harvard Law Review*, 1061 (June, 1993): 104.

49 *Ibid.*, 110.

50 Dyer, *White*, 39–40.

51 Parks, *The America Play*, 163.

52 *Ibid.*, 168.

53 Suzan-Lori Parks, *Top Dog/Underdog* (New York: Theatre Communications Group, 2001), 11.
54 The privilege of whiteness, dramatized in this scene, is reminiscent of Eddie Murphy's *Saturday Night Live* sketch, "White like Me," in which Murphy – dressed as a white man – is granted a number of ridiculous privileges such as free merchandise from stores and a no-strings loan from a local bank.

10

NADINE GEORGE-GRAVES

African American performance and community engagement

I would probably have died if it hadn't been for that almost sacred
tradition of solidarity among slaves.

Tituba

Wholeness is no trifling matter.

Toni Cade Bambara, *The Salt Eaters*

In American theatre we have several ways of thinking about theatre and
community, and most of them are negative. "Community theatre" is disparaged as amateur kitsch, though it may be important for non-professionals.
Some performance subgenres actively disengage community – for example,
an "art-for-art's-sake" ideology, purporting art does not exist for the audience's sake. We also have the business of theatre that attends to community
cum subscribers, raising debates about art, economics, and the financing of
aesthetics. Many community outreach programs have come to create "community" as a euphemism for "ghetto," and focus on bringing culture to the
underprivileged (unfortunately, sometimes condescendingly). In the midst of
these uses we often lose sight of the meaning of community in the performing arts that functions to create solidarity and emotional connections among
people. At the core of African American performance history, I submit, is
the phenomenological desire for and commitment to a sense of shared community. The ebbs and flows of the personal relationships between any given
artist or group of artists devoted to work by, for, about, or near people of
African descent, and the inspiration and commitment to those people, com-
prise the fodder and tradition of African American performance.

What is of interest here is the ways in which, particularly in the performing arts, African American artists forge these relationships (practically, financially, theoretically, and ideologically) with larger African American social
missions. This chapter argues for the significance of community engagement by examining the intersections between African American performance, activism, and civic service, focusing on several important examples

in which artists make concerted efforts to use theatre and dance to activate particular communities. Though the concept of community itself is troubled, common strategies for bringing about solidarity, empowerment, and social change through performance are identified and scrutinized. In particular, I will show how an Africanist ethos derived from African Diaspora traditions becomes an important methodological guide used by many African American performing artists to create a sense of shared community against overtly oppressive and subtly hegemonic forces.

When Audre Lorde wrote that poetry was not a luxury, she called our attention to the revelatory distillation of experience through language that is not sterile word play. Similarly, performance is not a luxury in terms of African American theatre – and not just for economic reasons. Historically, performance has been a way to speak truth to power when other forms of communication were denied. It has been a way to model a more perfect union. It has been a mechanism for creating cohesion and social change. And no matter the style, no matter the ideological debate, this has been the case. African American theatre history is full of endeavors that operate/d under these principles. And many African American theatre artists have negotiated their responsibility to other African Americans: those who came before, those with whom we live, and those to come. For example, and perhaps most significantly, performance has been used to create allies in battling stereotypes and changing people's minds about who African Americans are and what they are capable of becoming. Narratively and aesthetically, we uphold the script of courage, fortitude, and triumph over adversity as the legacy of slavery looms large over black aesthetics – not necessarily as always something to move beyond. Like the polyrhythms of West African music, the interconnections between African American identities, African American theatre, and African American communities are complex and consequential, but historically, they have not been luxuries.

On the contrary, these projects are more often filled with difficulties. African American artists working by, for, about, and near African American communities have generally struggled financially. For example, Barbara Ann Teer of the National Black Theatre claimed: "The way grants are going in this country, social action, social change, all that is no longer *in vogue* … nobody is going to address social, cultural or economic change. We must begin to develop our own entrepreneurial skills."[1] Practical struggles and kinship-building are part and parcel of African American theatre. Despite the many restraints, Ossie Davis estimated that most African American artists in TV and the film industry worked in community theatres.[2] Also, one of the common traits of the approximately 50 black theatres to survive into this millennium from the 139 counted in 1973 was being rooted in surrounding communities: acting as community centers, offering classes, and serving the needs of the people.

Elsewhere I have written on the civic engagement of the contemporary dance theatre company Urban Bush Women.[3] What could not be a part of that investigation was a discussion of the ways in which those projects operate vis-à-vis a legacy of African American female modalities of performance in public service in the second half of the twentieth century. In this chapter, I want to acknowledge and examine that continuum through the work of Barbara Ann Teer and Ntozake Shange in order to argue that Urban Bush Women (via artistic director Jawole Willa Jo Zollar) builds on a tradition advancing the performative reclamation of the black body and voice through Africanist practices, leading directly to social engagement. Operating as cultural workers as well as artists, these women utilize common techniques and strategies for bringing about solidarity and healing. Ultimately, I show that Teer, Shange, and Zollar create performative discourses with audiences specifically by accessing "blackness" in their artistic and unity-building endeavors. The African Diaspora becomes not a site of dispersion but rather a means to congregate. It is an experiential foundation for creating societies committed to redressive justice, camaraderie, social interrogation, and change.

No doubt there are many people, movements, and aesthetics that one could examine here. Space limitations prevent full examination of all of these endeavors, but focusing on a few is useful. Teer, Shange, and Zollar are by no means the only women of color who are doing or have done these kinds of projects, though they make for a compelling triumvirate. Too, there are African American male artists, and indeed artists of all stripes and sizes, who engage or have engaged in similar efforts. W. E. B. Du Bois's scholarly writings and creative pageants, John O'Neal and the Free Southern Theater, the Jamaican theatre collective Sistren, and Augusto Boal's global Theater of the Oppressed are but a few notable examples. However, investigating these three women will help us access the potential of performance in the enactment of power in a particularly significant way.

Several influential factors set the stage for Teer, Shange, and Zollar. First, all three women spent their formative years surrounded by other African Americans in predominantly black environments. The influence of African American neighborhoods on major movements in arts and letters has been well rehearsed and I won't repeat those discussions here. Rather, it is important to recognize that whether seen as havens or ghettos, enclaves that are predominantly black are invaluable for producing this type of creativity. Whether enforced or intentional, these neighborhoods have produced the blues, gospel, jazz, the Harlem Renaissance, soul, hip-hop, rap, rock 'n' roll, stepping, and many other cultural movements. For artists like Teer, Shange, and Zollar, being surrounded by these aesthetics shaped their own imaginations, and we can trace their later engagements directly to the values instilled in them in their early years in these settings.

Next, we can look to a larger tradition of African American women actively trying to better conditions for people. Though this has occurred most prominently as part of the mission of black churches and civic organizations in the United States, the performing arts have also played a significant role in activism. Indeed, often these efforts converge. Teer's, Shange's, and Zollar's activities in this vein are also a direct outgrowth of black women in Civil Rights and Black Power advocacy. During these and subsequent movements, organizations like the Student Nonviolent Coordinating Committee (SNCC), the Black Panthers, and smaller organizations like Sisters Working Encouraging Empowering Together (SWEET) relied heavily on black women connecting neighbors around common goals. And often this took on spiritual dimensions. According to Rosetta E. Ross, "Black women's civil rights activism is their female enactment of Black religious values that reflected an internal concern for the Black community's survival and flourishing and a related external concern to address society's formal and conventional sources of inequality."[4] These women were trained to organize and educate community leaders to move toward grassroots self-empowerment. This training continues through the performing arts.

Also significant is the concept of community as diaspora. Out of the transatlantic slave trade route, West Africa has come to be seen as a homeland diasporically linking African Americans to other blacks. And community is at the heart of many important diaspora theories and aesthetics. The African proverb "I am because we are" is a meaningful guide to this philosophy. In this ideology, individual identity is linked to the group, and the health of one necessarily affects the health of the other. We might contrast this with the western philosophy "I think therefore I am," in which others are not necessary for identity, and existence depends only on cognition, not community. The mind and body are separated, and the intangible mind produces the tangible body. According to the Ubuntu proverb, however, body and mind are connected and exist only in terms of their relation to other bodies and minds. The only existence of importance is existence in community. Likewise the concept of Ubuntu expresses the meaning of the full human being in the context of community.[5] Archbishop Desmond Tutu offers the following definition: "A person with Ubuntu is open and available to others, affirming of others, does not feel threatened that others are able and good, for he or she has a proper self-assurance that comes from knowing that he

or she belongs in a greater whole and is diminished when others are humili-
ated or diminished, when others are tortured or oppressed."[6]

At the 2008 Ubuntu Women Institute's first South Sudan Project, he further explained:

> One of the sayings in our country is Ubuntu – the essence of being human.
> Ubuntu speaks particularly about the fact that you can't exist as a human
> being in isolation. It speaks about our interconnectedness. You can't be human
> all by yourself, and when you have this quality – Ubuntu – you are known for
> your generosity.
>
> We think of ourselves far too frequently as just individuals, separated from
> one another, whereas you are connected and what you do affects the whole
> world. When you do well, it spreads out; it is for the whole of humanity.[7]

Also, an ethos of care and commitment must be identified as influential to
African American performance and community engagement. In the early
1980s, Alice Walker identified Womanism as a guiding ideology, claiming
that Womanists are black feminists or feminists of color who are "outra-
geous, audacious, courageous or willful"; who seek political empowerment;
who affirm women's strength; who appreciate the cultural production of all
women of color; and who are universally "committed to the survival and
wholeness of entire people, male *and* female."[8] Like Ubuntu, Womanism
impacts this work by helping to create an attitude in these artists that moves
them toward expressing the meaning of the full human being in the context
of others. In other words, attending to the complexities of individual and
collective healing are part and parcel of one another.

In 1976, Wole Soyinka published an influential text for African Americans
that nicely lays out the stakes for the artistry of these three women. In *Myth,
Literature and the African World*, he articulates the African self-apprehended
world in myth and literature in resistance to hegemonic forces that would
distort or exploit Africanist positions. At the core of the text is a discussion
of the profound stakes of performance, namely the maintenance of cos-
mic totality. As African Americans (re)forged deeper Diasporic connections
with their African heritage through negritude or Afrocentricity, African
self-apprehension became the stakes for some African American artists. In
other words, though romanticized in many arenas, the function of some
(not all) performance (like poetry for Lorde) reaches to the levels of ritual,
justice, and morality – all essential elements for the maintenance of society.
Soyinka defines the ritualist model of performance as the site "where all
action and all personae reach deeply through reserves of the collective memory of human rites of passage – ordeal, survival, social and individual purga-
tion – into an end result which is the moral code of society."[9] The degree to

which African Americans maintain a relationship with these beliefs has varied over time, and they will no doubt continue to occupy multiple influences on African American identities. For our purposes, it is important to recognize this as part of the roots of African American performance and community engagement. Artists like Teer, Shange, and Zollar attempt to move performance (back) to the point of ritual, "a cleansing, binding, communal, re-creative force"[10] to effect real individual and social change. Performance is not the end in itself but the means to an end. The failure of this process, the severance of essence from self, of people from the cosmos, this discontinuity is the very definition of tragedy. Though we may think these African American artists are operating on relatively small scales, understood in these terms, the stakes cannot be underestimated.

I don't think it is coincidental that Zollar, Teer, and Shange use similar strategies for bringing about public advocacy and healing. Specifically, I want to identify five key elements common to the art of these women. (It is important to note that many of the tenets of this aesthetic are also found in those of the African-Diaspora-based cultural and spiritual celebration Kwanza.)

(1) *The use of Africanist values and aesthetics.* The African Diaspora provides the matrix out of which much of this aesthetic is based. These artists look to practices rooted in African societies to create their aesthetic and social practices. Whether articulated as Afrocentrism, blood memory, or neo-Africanisms, the process is an active willing to the fore of black traditions either alongside or instead of Eurocentric or Asian traditions.

(2) *The development of techniques alternative to mainstream performing arts initiatives.* Africanist values have led all three to develop what some might call non-traditional ways of working, but what we may ultimately recognize as the *most* traditional ways of working. They resist the contemporary American segregation of aesthetic genre and interweave movement, text, and music. They emphasize cooperation among a collective, and their processes are communal with boundaries and roles blurred.

(3) *The promotion of self-knowledge in terms of education and affirmation.* These artists also recognize that the re-education of African Americans about themselves is vital to aesthetic work. This will lead in turn to a reaffirmation of self and community, a recognition of the true nature of the hegemonic forces that devastate certain communities, and ultimately a new radical subjectivity. It is important to differentiate this from political aesthetics that are on the attack – art created by the oppressed for the oppressor to show the oppressor the evil of his/her ways. Rather, these processes focus on the oppressed. The mantra is "look to yourself." Change must happen in the individual in relation to her/his community

through positive energy before change can happen in the larger society. This is not to say that the ideology rejects fighting for one's rights and beliefs. Nor is it a denial of oppression – on the contrary. But first and foremost one must be firmly grounded in oneself. This is also a strategic move, as one might argue that changing oneself can diffuse much of the traumatic effect of oppression.

(4) *The embrace of spirituality.* That positive energy might be articulated as a spiritual relationship with divinity, either as a god from an organized religion or a recognition of the divine in oneself. At any rate, the individual cannot operate alone in the production of healing, transformation, and empowerment; all three artists are open about the role of spirituality in their projects.

(5) *The endeavor to affect transformation, empowerment, and liberation.* These performances are not thought pieces but attempts to see into motion the impetus for changing reality for the better.

But how do we theorize healing? How do we discuss transformation? How do we analyze empowerment? In many ways it is a leap of faith, though anecdotal feedback is certainly often given. In the aggregate we can point to the enormous support these women have been able to garner as evidence that these aesthetics speak to many. But we can also discuss intention in terms of transformation, empowerment, and liberation. Teer saw the performer as liberator. She wanted her audiences to have the same kind of transformative experience that many have in Pentecostal churches. Shange sees language as a liberator and the key to healing: "Language will allow us to function more competently and more wholly in a holistic sense as human beings once we take hold of it and make it say what we want to say."[11] Zollar and Urban Bush Women are moving the company more toward direct community-based political activism and social healing (voting rallies, literacy programs in local YWCAs and YMCAs, etc.).

In the following detailed discussion of each of these three artists, we should keep in mind the context from which these aesthetics emanate, and the implications and stakes for their continuance. As I lay out the particulars, we should recognize the ways in which these elements form a significant tradition in African American performance.

Teer

A number of years ago I lectured on Barbara Ann Teer and the National Black Theatre as part of a class on African American theatre. I had an African American student who dismissed what he considered a limited, isolationist vision that allowed black art to remain "other" and exclusive to black people's experiences. By chance, Teer was visiting campus as part of a congregation of artists of the Civil Rights era. (This was only a few months before her death in 2008.) I required my students to attend some of the events, and we discussed the two days at the next class. In those few days, this student had made a complete 180 on the importance of Teer's mission, and beamed when he spoke of the hug and encouragement that Teer had given him as a young director. This student told me that after meeting Teer,

> I was deeply moved and inspired by her call for self-empowerment, appreciation of the singular passion of one's artistry and call for encouraging all artists, not only black ones, to find their own voice, song, dance, expression. Her words became inclusive not exclusive and her vision rang with a new power of true community building that was deeper than culture or race.[12]

Growing up in the all-black neighborhood of East St. Louis, Illinois, surrounded by her family and many black community leaders, was an important source of Barbara Ann Teer's passion. She was an acclaimed professional actress and junior high school teacher. She later worked with the Group Theatre Workshop (the foundation for the Negro Ensemble Company). In the late 1960s (after garnering impressive credentials on Broadway and in film), Teer began formulating an aesthetic that emphasized ritual over entertainment and sought to counter the effects of urban racism on black men and women. She recognized a crisis with death (social, psychic, and physical) and destruction all around her in the Harlem of the late 1960s and early 1970s, and used performance to do battle. This observation, coupled with her exasperation at the lack of meaningful roles available to her as a professional actress, led Teer to throw her energies into addressing social ills through new techniques in performance. The Stanislavski, Strasberg, and Meisner techniques that Teer was studying downtown were irrelevant to the young people in Harlem. When she decided to devote her energies to this population, she had to experiment with new forms. According to Barbara Lewis, "Mired in chaos without a liberating myth to call its own, but on the point of transforming itself, the community was ripe for change."[13] Her mission was to teach African Americans about their culture, and also to respect themselves and to come together in solidarity. She saw the need to eradicate victim mentality from African Americans by putting them into a "heroic, liberated, victorious culture."[14] She and the members of her company visited churches, bars, revival meetings, and the Apollo Theater to discover ways to relate to audiences. In addition to producing performances, she spearheaded full-time pre-school and after-school activities, family productions, workshops, and lectures. She negotiated not only the artistic but also the

economic challenges by establishing the first revenue-generating Black theatre arts complex in the country.[15] Before Teer's death, Elizabeth McMillan
wrote, "By establishing the NBT [National Black Theatre: the Sun People's
Theater of 125th Street], she has not only brought a high level of artistic
performances and lectures to Harlem, but Dr. Teer is also in the process of
transforming a community, revitalizing its citizens and creating a new cultural paradigm for future generations."[16]

Teer felt the need to create an entire system and school for the development of her aesthetic that are ostensibly about the reduction of individual ego
(although we can recognize Teer's personality as a driving force) through the
arts. Artists in her theatre are committed to contributing to neighborhood
initiatives and operating as ensembles. Students attend church, performances, and social events together. National Black Theatre's audiences are
expected to participate fully in the events, usually by contributing personal
stories. During intermission at these huge community events, the audience
members engage with the performers in dialog. The goals for the National
Black Theatre have been articulated as creating and perpetuating a black art
standard, eliminating the competitive aspect of most commercial theatre,
re-educating audiences, restoring spirituality and a cultural tradition, creating an alternative system of values to the western concept, and creating a
black theory of acting and liberation.

Teer resisted western canonical Aristotelian-based theatre. She joined
other African American artists like Paul Carter Harrison, Robert Macbeth,
and the members of the New Lafayette Theatre in privileging the theatrical
event as ritual over the text-based play. She saw Africa as a motherland, and
she used Yoruba-based rituals (involving African music, song, and dance)
as the direct medium for her work. The Gelede performances of the Yoruba
that greatly influenced Teer paid homage to women's power for the benefit
of the entire society. In Gelede performance, as well as many other African
rituals, the line between audience and performer blurs; Teer advocated the
blurring of these lines in NBT performances. She also emphasized the connections between Africans and African Americans and ritualized practices in
order to evoke meaning. For example, in workshops students actively tried
to discover/rediscover African retentions in the ways they dance. In doing
so, the stakes for routine or secular movements are raised to the point of
ritual and spiritual. In fact, Soyinka singled out Teer's theatre as an important example of the drama (or ritual) of the gods to travel aesthetically and
passionately across the Atlantic.

Though she was committed to disenfranchised African American communities, Teer emphasized that her aesthetic was not militant and did
not "hate" white people, even while it resisted oppression from a white

hegemony. Focusing on anger and hate puts energy outside the self, she thought; it feeds the oppressive forces. Teer believed that negative energy would destroy black hope, and positive energy needed to be directed inwardly. Lundeana Thomas identifies this as the "autogenesis of dignity, confidence, and esteem."[17] Teer attempted to help those in her community rewrite the dictates of their lives by using performance in which anything is possible as a rehearsal for daily life. The individual, with the help of the collective, is able to dismiss oppressive images of her/himself, and through ritual conceive of an empowered self-image. There is no distanced/unaffected observer, as is possible in mainstream American theatre – all present are a part of the ritual.

In order to reach this level of awareness, NBT students focus on decolonizing their minds by recognizing the beauty of African American skin, hair, facial features, etc. Also, these students interrogate the dualness of African American identity – African Americans living in a white-dominated world through the practice of "code switching." Du Bois referred to it as "double consciousness," and Dunbar composed "We Wear the Masks" to describe it. For Teer, one must choose between an African and an American identity, and that choice could only be made with sufficient education and encouragement: "In performance, Teer wanted her students to begin unmasking the feelings and the faces they had disguised in coping with the white world."[18] She developed practices in the hope that these acts of unmasking would lead to a less mediated black identity. No longer would African Americans have to alter the ways in which they performed their identities depending on the racial makeup of others in the room.

Lastly, Teer's concept of "soul," consisting of a combination of Yoruba and Black Pentecostal spirituality, is vital to the National Black Theatre. The ecstatic reach for the sublime to heal and nurture black communities fuels this revolutionary spirit. It is, according to Teer, God-Conscious Art, not self-conscious art. These ritualistic revivals allow for ecstatic dancing, glossolalia, sacred dance, spiritual possession, call and response liturgy, heightened spiritual poetry, and communal trance. According to Thomas, "the single feature common among Yoruba tradition, Pentecostal worship and NBT performances is communion, or the absorption of the self into a larger community through the suppression of reason and the stimulation of deeper centers of awareness and attention."[19] For Teer, racism goes to the soul of people, and so NBT's mission is to work on soul people. As such, the theatre offers classes in evolutionary movement and dance, meditation, spiritual release, numerology, astrology, liberation theory and practice, and ideology – all with the aim of healing traumatized and oppressed African American communities and individuals.

Shange

I first saw *for colored girls who have considered suicide / when the rainbow is enuf* in college. Hekah, a new theatre company for women of color at Yale, produced it. The sense of purpose and solidarity during the production was palpable, and I immediately joined the company. During a recent conversation, I asked the founding artistic director why she formed the company and why she chose *for colored girls* as the first production. She told me that at that time in her life she was coming to terms with her identity as a light-skinned African American woman at this institution of higher education. She was searching for herself and needed to understand who she was in the company of other women of color.

Years later I saw a production of *for colored girls* at Steppenwolf in Chicago. I had been a subscription holder for a number of years and I had never had the kind of spectator experience at Steppenwolf or any other mainstream theatre as that evening. There were mostly black women in the audience. One brought her baby, and when the baby cried no one minded. At any given moment someone was standing up to testify. Audience members spoke back to the performers and the performers spoke directly to audience members. This was a performance event for "us" – to affirm "our" experiences and to assure each one of us that we are not alone in negotiating race and gender in America. This was over twenty years after the play was first written, and it still clearly spoke to audiences.

Ntozake Shange's original name is Paulette Linda Williams. She was born in Trenton, New Jersey to Paul T. Williams, a surgeon, and Eloise Williams, a psychiatric social worker and educator. Though she had a more affluent childhood than Barbara Ann Teer and was raised with all of the advantages available to the black middle class, her early years were also filled with strong black role models. Her childhood was filled with music, literature, and art. Dizzy Gillespie, Miles Davis, W. E. B. Du Bois, Chuck Berry, and other prominent African Americans were among the frequent guests at her parents' home. On Sunday afternoons, her family held variety shows with the different artists. She then attended Barnard College and graduated with honors in 1970.

Even though her childhood appears quite privileged she felt as though she was "living a lie." She explains that she was living in a world that defied reality as most people, black and white, knew it. Even with all this opportunity and confidence, she felt that she was at a disadvantage as a woman when the careers she chose for herself, like war correspondent and jazz musician, were dismissed as "no good for a woman." She chose to become a writer because "there was nothing left." Shange attempted suicide several times – once because of the frustration and hurt she felt by her separation from her first husband, another after an attempted rape, and again after an abortion. She drank Drano, she took alcohol and valium, and she drove her Volvo into the Pacific. She has described them not as desperate acts but as attempts to take control. She then began to focus her energies on the limitations society imposes on black women.

In 1971, while earning a Master's degree, she reaffirmed her self-determined identity and took on her African name, which means "she who comes with her own things" and she "who walks like a lion." Writing dramatic poetry became a means of expressing her dissatisfaction with the role of black women in society. She and a group of friends, including various musicians and the choreographer/dancer Paula Moss, would create improvisational pieces comprising poetry, music, and dance. They would perform in bars in San Francisco and New York. Moss and Shange moved to New York City and presented *for colored girls* at the Soho jazz loft. In November, 1975, Oz Scott and the producer Woodie King assisted them, and the show ran successfully off-Broadway at the New Federal Theatre. The following June, Joseph Papp became the show's producer at the New York Shakespeare Festival. *for colored girls* earned Shange an Obie Award.

The choreopoem form of *for colored girls* is an aesthetic that combines movement, dance, acting, poetry, song, and prose based in the African and African American traditions of storytelling, music, rhythm, and movement. Shange was particularly inspired by the choreography of Pearl Primus, who incorporated West African dance, blues, and spiritual motifs in her dances (especially images of strength); Mercedes Baptista, who taught Afro-Brazilian dance; Dianne McIntyre and her Harlem company, Sounds in Motion; and Katherine Dunham, who created Haitian-inspired dances, which are now American classics. Sandra L. Richards has identified Shange's African influences, and links Shange with Femi Osofisan through their use of Yoruba religious practices as a paradigm for dramatic structure. She argues, "through a creative deployment of the principles of Sixteen Cowrie and Ifá divination, Ntozake Shange and Femi Osofisan construct dramaturgies that empower audiences, challenging them to impose an interpretive hegemony that can extend from the symbolic to the sociopolitical order."[20]

Shange developed the choreopoem when typical play structures failed to meet her needs. All of the elements of the choreopoem combine to elicit an emotional and political response, tackling not only the complexities of race relations but also intraracial gender relations. Shange negotiates other complexities, recognizing simultaneously that feminism has influenced many men to challenge our misogynist traditions at the same time that there continue to be persistent devastating reports of violence against women in both violent and political crimes. She has appealed to both men and women to move toward a non-sexist, equal, and safe society (though she has been accused of being irresponsible to the image of black masculinity).

In order to effect change, Shange developed a new relationship to language. She engaged the western–African binary by choosing to reject one of the cornerstones of western hegemony – standard English. Her alternative uses of language privilege an African matrix. She manipulated the King's English as a way of taking control. According to Shange, "literature, if it does nothing else, should stimulate one's imagination to know that there is more – maybe not more 'out there,' but more inside of us that we can use for our own survival."[21] She has also claimed that she wants to engage the reader in a type of struggle. "The spellings reflect language as I hear it … The structure is connected to the music I hear beneath the words." Her goal is to "attack deform n maim the language that I was taught to hate myself in. I have to take it apart to the bones." We can see this as a direct attack on not only the Eurocentric standards of language and drama but a Eurocentric ethos as well. She has also said, "I have spent my life undoing language until it works for me. We must not only repossess language, we must deslaverize it."[22] This repossession of language creates a particular rhythm for her writing, and that rhythm leads to movement.[23]

Like Teer, Shange attempted to steer away from the negativity of hate through the focus on self or self-determining identity – the idea that black women have the power to claim their own individual identities and the realities of their experiences, instead of accepting the labels that have been imposed on them by white men, black men, white women, etc. The choreopoem "Somebody Almost Walked Off with All of My Stuff" neatly articulates the importance of radical subjectivity as the lady in green talks about almost losing herself (stuff) to a man. The performers in *for colored girls* develop the piece through ensemble improvisation and personalize the roles. There are no character names and the names of their cities change based on the performer. At the beginning of the play, each woman is on the outskirts of a city – outside. Spatially and psychologically, these women exist on borders and frontiers, beginning to discover a sense of self as they come together.

Black male critics and scholars (most viciously Robert Staples) have criticized Shange at length, claiming that the representation of black men is too negative and depicted as necessarily at odds with the representation and affirmation of black women. She has even been accused of "lynching" the black male. In her defense, she told a reporter,

> Half of what we discussed in *For Colored Girls* about the dissipation of the family, rape, wife-battering and all that sort of thing, the US Census Bureau already had ... We could have gone to the Library of Congress and read the Census reports and the crime statistics every month and we would know that more black women are raped than anyone else. We should know at this point that they think 48 percent of our households are headed by single females ... My job as an artist is to say what I see."[24]

Perhaps the dissatisfaction for some can be explained by virtue of the fact that the play was not written for black men.

Rather, *for colored girls* is intended to lead to a transformation for "colored girls" that incorporates both the self-determined identity and the divine. The next-to-last line is "i found God in myself & i loved her / i loved her fiercely." All the ladies repeat the lines to themselves until it becomes a song of joy. They sing to each other, then to the audience. In my experience of reading, teaching, and witnessing *for colored girls*, by the end of the play, a bond often forms between the performers and the audience/reader. Though it is difficult to talk about spirit in concrete terms, the show clearly attempts to function as ritual; the choreopoem is distinct in the way that it combines text with movement as ritual – a ritual that brings about healing. One of the ladies says, "We dance to keep from cryin / We gotta dance to keep from dyin." Dance is crucial to the rite of passage as a means for exorcising pain. The children's song "Little Sally Walker" tells colored girls to rise and wipe the tears away, then dance. Another lady says, "You hurt me more than I could ever dance outta into oblivion isn't far enuf to get outta this." The body is a site of knowledge and remembering. The body is the site of rape, abortion, and abuse, and the ladies must dance the pain out in the company of others to know, accept, and love their bodies. They dance and chant together in order to be liberated and to access the healing ritual of being touched lovingly – a laying-on of hands. This happens within, because of, and for the benefit of, the larger society.

Zollar

In the 2006/7 school year, I helped bring Urban Bush Women to the University of California, San Diego for a residency project called "Place Matters" (a process originally developed by the company to help artists and activists rebuilding New Orleans after the hurricanes) that included workshops on campus and around town. A relatively new campus (45 years old at the time of the residency), UC San Diego has about 25,000 undergrads and 5,000 grads. Before the economic fallout, UC San Diego grew at an enormous rate, and had been mandated to grow more. Despite this prosperity (or perhaps because of it), students often felt isolated in the goal-based science school that many felt didn't attend to campus life and social cohesion. Few felt that UC San Diego as a place mattered, and they did not have an identity qua UC San Diego student. A 2005 study of student satisfaction confirmed what many had been feeling: that the sprawling La Jolla campus was soulless and did not foster a sense of belonging or pride in the large student body population. Place Matters brought together about seventy UC San Diego students, faculty, and administrators to engage creatively in discussions about UC San Diego as a community. Students (mainly non-dancers) took classes around art activism, and created their own projects like a Happening on a campus shuttle bus in which unwitting travelers witnessed several riders standing up reciting spoken-word poetry about connecting to each other. The residency culminated in a performance about the students' relationships to their university. The project aimed at fostering a process of creativity and community engagement, using art to make a difference. Reliant on a faith in embodied knowledge, the participants championed the intellectual as well as creative missions. Students did research projects on the university and transformed that research into movement, storytelling, poetry, visual art, and music. According to Gabriele Wienhausen, a biochemist and provost of UC San Diego's Sixth College, who led one of the class sections and performed with the students, "When I'm forced to express my standing in the community in a movement, something happens inside my brain that never happens when I think about this intellectually. There is a power of imagining and a power of understanding … What the students came up with is that place has a history. Place has a soul. Place is determined by the people who are there, they shape it. Space is empty, it's waiting for meaning. We really do want to transform UC San Diego from a space to a place."[25]

Even though the issues tackled by this project were not centered on race per se, Urban Bush Women was able to foster this kind of project because of the vision and mission of artistic director Jawole Willa Jo Zollar. And like Teer and Shange, her aesthetic brings a sensibility rooted in an Africanist ethos of art and community. Zollar also cites growing up in a black neighborhood as formative to her artistry. She studied Afro-Caribbean Dunham technique, which advocates moving from an emotional impetus, resulting in an individual style. She did variety floorshows with other children in black social clubs. Later, she developed a deep commitment to black liberation and other social movements of the 1960s when working with her first company, Black Exodus. She was also influenced by Amiri Baraka; Larry Neal; the Civil Rights, Black Power, and Black Arts movements; and second-wave feminism.

In graduate school she was involved in many communities that influenced her, including women's support groups, the Black Theatre Guild, the dance department, and the local Yoruba population. She also read Artaud and decided that she wanted dance-theatre to have an impact. She studied Peter Brook as well as the Free Southern Theater. She studied Haitian dance, Cuban dance, Brazilian dance, Congolese dance, and "what we thought was African." She then moved to New York in 1980 and (like Shange) studied with Dianne McIntyre at Sounds in Motion, where she collaborated with live jazz music and developed a jazz-like dance improvisational aesthetic that valued many different body types. In 1984, she founded Urban Bush Women with six other women.

Zollar's choreography is rooted in the dances of the African Diaspora, particularly West African, Caribbean, and African American. Though she also blends ballet, modern, and eastern ways of moving, African Diaspora movement styles form the foundation for the choreography. Much of the movement is weighty, grounded, and heavy. The energy goes down into the earth so that the dancer may build from that secure foundation in order to leap up, spin fast, and toss limbs through the air with seeming abandon but precise control. The choreography often requires the dancers to maintain the "aesthetic of the cool," which is an African Diaspora performance trope that calls for discipline and control during even the most chaotic moments. This may also be understood as a social metaphor for a way to conduct oneself during trying times: "cool" results in expressions that are in command while bodies or emotions move frenetically.

Zollar developed an approach to choreography that de-emphasized the compartmentalization of styles. Rather than rejecting non-African ways of moving, Zollar incorporates them. Even though sometimes required to let go of formal training, Urban Bush Women dancers tend to be very well trained in West African dance, ballet, modern, Capoeira, Feldenkrais, Yoga, Qigong, acting, vocalization, and many other techniques. Zollar eclectically combines these styles to produce her aesthetic. This repertory of styles serves as another social metaphor. By integrating seemingly disparate techniques, Urban Bush Women's choreography moves all the techniques in new directions. They operate together, and the whole is more than the sum of its parts.

The company's efforts on and off stage all attempt to build up individuals and communities. This is perhaps most evident in the company's many community projects – classes, workshops, community sings, summer dance institutes, and community engagement projects. They have taken on women's issues, urban planning, racism, HIV/AIDS, voting rights, body image, beauty standards, gentrification, and disenfranchised neighborhoods, among other social concerns. Rejecting the term "outreach," Urban Bush Women creates processes for collaborating with individuals and communities to assess resources, skills, and strengths. Personal stories become group dances. Through a dialogic process, ideas, experiences, and information are shared in order to foster collective learning. In its community engagement projects, for example, the company attempts to foster an environment for a hosting community to bring about change. In all of these efforts, the company utilizes embodied learning techniques.

Recently, Zollar and the company members have decided to identify their core values. At the heart of them is the validation of individuals in terms of experiences, perspectives, relationships, etc. to form an epistemic base. Significantly, there is a corporeal foundation for this individualism. Specifically, Zollar has choreographed on many different body types, ages, and complexions, which perhaps stems from her own experiences dancing with a body type not considered by many as ideal for concert dance. This attitude about the body and individuality translates directly into the choreography and the message the dances convey to the audiences. Also, a philosophy about the way in which individuals connect with other individuals is affirmed in the dancer's working relationship as well as in the content of the choreography.

Attention to spirit is part and parcel of Zollar's mission. Siddha Yoga and Swami Muktananda guide Zollar in bringing spirituality to her daily life. Also, the call and response of the black church, the rises and falls, physically drive her choreography. Zollar is interested in getting at and freeing a spiritual essence, and many of the pieces affirm, question, and challenge many dimensions of spirituality (including the Godhead, faith, transformation, suffering, possession, and miracles, among others). Above all, these pieces participate in the dialog about the role of spirituality in the lives of all people, but black women in particular, by building on the long traditions of ritual dance in African and African American cultural and spiritual life. At one point, Zollar explained to me the stakes as she saw them:

> I think the world is in crisis. Not just women. And maybe we always exist in crisis. I don't know. We just know more now. We know what's going on in a remote village in a small country in Africa and we didn't use to know that. I think our biggest crisis in the United States is a crisis in values, and I don't mean that in any moralistic way, but a crisis of intellectual thought and values. I don't think that we have leadership that values intellectual thought. Once we start going towards a very simple solution to things it makes it easier for us to do abominable things.[26]

Zollar and Urban Bush Women refuse to condone simplicity in all respects. By remaining committed to community in addition to the stage, they offer a model to other activist artists. They have created ways to preserve aesthetic standards while involving diverse audiences. They promote strong leaders who are sustained by a supportive broader base of community artists/activists. Ultimately, they demonstrate (like Teer and Shange) that African Diaspora performance can lead to social activism and healing: "The arts can provide people with a vision. When you have a vision, you have hope ... for an empowered way of being in the world."[27]

NOTES

1 Errol Hill and James Vernon Hatch, *A History of African American Theatre* (Cambridge; New York: Cambridge University Press, 2003), 459.

2 *Ibid.*

3 See Nadine George-Graves, *Urban Bush Women: Twenty Years of African American Dance Theater, Community Engagement, and Working It Out* (Madison: University of Wisconsin Press, 2010).

4 Rosetta E. Ross, *Witnessing & Testifying: Black Women, Religion, and Civil Rights* (Minneapolis: Fortress Press, 2003), xiii.

5 Linda W. Thomas, "Christinah Nku: A Woman at the Center of Healing Her Nation," in *Embracing the Spirit: Womanist Perspectives on Hope, Salvation and Transformation*, ed. Emilie M. Townes (Maryknoll, NY: Orbis, 2001), 54.

6 Desmond Tutu, *No Future without Forgiveness* (New York: Image, 1999), 31.

7 "Ubuntu Women Institute USA (UWIU) with SSIWEL as its First South Sudan Project," www.ssiwel.org (last accessed July 8, 2011).

8 Alice Walker, *In Search of Our Mothers' Gardens: Womanist Prose* (New York: Harcourt Brace, 1984), xi.

9 Wole Soyinka, *Myth, Literature and the African World* (Cambridge: Cambridge University Press, 1976), 9.

10 *Ibid.*, 4.

11 Neal A. Lester, "At the Heart of Shange's Feminism," *Black American Literature Forum*, 24.4 (1990): 727.

12 Personal email interview, April 21, 2011.

13 Barbara Lewis, "Ritual Reformations: Barbara Ann Teer and the National Black Theatre of Harlem," in *A Sourcebook of African-American Performance: Plays, People, Movements*, ed. Annemarie Bean (London; New York: Routledge, 1999), 69.

14 Barbara Lewis, personal interview with Barbara Ann Teer, New York, August 22, 1997.

15 Unfortunately, after her death, the fate of the building is in peril owing to arrangements with financial partners.

16 Elizabeth McMillan, "Queen of Harlem," *Mosaec*, October, 1999, www.mosaec.com/mosaec/theaterdance/td_teer.htm (last accessed November 15, 2011).

17 Lundeana Marie Thomas, *Barbara Ann Teer and the National Black Theatre: Transformational Forces in Harlem* (New York: Garland, 1997), 37.

18 *Ibid.*, 80.

19 *Ibid.*, 62.

20 Sandra L. Richards, "Under the 'Trickster's' Sign: Toward a Reading of Ntozake Shange and Femi Osofisan," in *Critical Theory and Performance*, ed. Janelle Reinelt and Joseph Roach (Ann Arbor: University of Michigan, 1992), 65.

21 Lester, "At the Heart of Shange's Feminism," 729.

22 Rebecca Carroll, "Back at You: Ntozake Shange (Interview)," *Mother Jones*, 20.1 (1995): 69.

23 Most productions use African drumming to underscore the language and movement.

24 Connie Lauerman, interview with Ntozake Shange, *Chicago Tribune*, October 21, 1982.

25 Janice Steinberg, "'Place': Building a Community at UCSD," *The San Diego Union-Tribune*, February 18, 2007.

26 Personal interview, 2004.

27 Steinberg, "Place."

11

SANDRA G. SHANNON

Women playwrights who cross cultural borders

At the height of summer, 2011 and during the waning months of the same year, two high-profile events featuring women of color caught the world's attention by breaking through gender barriers that have long histories in the United States and in other parts of the world. Media organizations sat up and took note while critics marveled at the fortuitous timing: three African American female playwrights' individual works ran concurrently on Broadway, a feat that many still regard as extremely unusual, especially given conservative trends of the Great White Way along gender and color lines. The good fortunes of playwrights Katori Hall, Lydia Diamond, and Suzan-Lori Parks began anew a conversation not just about the historically few African American plays on Broadway, but, more particularly, about the infrequent productions of works by contemporary African American *female* playwrights. Director Kenny Leon told *The New York Times*, "I can't remember the last time there were three women playwrights on Broadway during the same season, let alone three African-American women."[1]

I evoke this recent scenario involving triumphant women of color to demonstrate that African American female playwrights, like these exemplary sisters, continue to be active agents of change on behalf of women – both in the United States and outside its borders – and they are doing so with an expert command of their craft and of the world stage. While some might see the coincidental convergence of Hall's *The Mountaintop*, Diamond's *Stick Fly*, and Parks's adaptation of *Porgy and Bess* upon Broadway as cause for celebration, skeptics might well discount all of the hoopla and label their good fortune as merely happenstance. Pessimism aside, however, might one conclude that Broadway's recent bumper crop of black female works signals the imminence of more frequent productions? Could the intersection of their work at this historical moment also herald a long overdue recognition that today's African American female playwright has indeed found her voice and is able to leverage it in a mighty way that would have a more universal impact?

This chapter will analyze the extent to which the external gaze of African American women playwrights beyond America's borders has impacted their writing, their global sensibility, and their geopolitics. Their increased focus upon cross-cultural issues and the passionate activism they bring to expose inhumane treatment suffered by people of color within and outside the United States cast them as a fierce new breed: "sista playwrights." To be sure, they are heirs of Lorraine Hansberry's legacy, but they are also mavericks who, according to Philip Kolin, "have radically departed from her realistic techniques and boldly interrogated and amplified her protests against racism and classicism."[2] The recent cause célèbre surrounding the confluence of works by three gifted African American female playwrights on Broadway stages provides occasion to investigate the continuum of both early and contemporary African American female playwrights similarly engaged in crossing cultural borders in their work. Able to take full advantage of mechanizations and increased mobility that are available to them now, this new crop of cultural workers' material reflects the inevitable shift toward more global awareness of cultures other than their own.

Their continually evolving aesthetics are in sync with equally evolving circumstances in the lives of today's women, both nationally and abroad. This continually evolving aesthetic is helped along significantly by an increase in global awareness among today's African American women in particular. Well travelled and well educated, politically and technologically savvy, wise to the ways of the media, and skilled at telling stories, these women look beyond cultural borders to promote an aesthetic that pays less attention to differences and more toward common concerns among women of all nationalities.

Lynn Nottage

Pulitzer-Prize-winning playwright Lynn Nottage is at the forefront of today's more global female artistic activism – one that involves extending her dramatic landscape across cultural and, more specifically, transatlantic issues and concerns. For Nottage, the ability to focus her creative gaze beyond American shores has much to do with the circumstances of her childhood and, ultimately, her place of employment for four years. Born to parents whom she regarded as "old-time New Yorkers,"[3] Lynn Nottage moved, at the age of four in 1968, to the racially mixed Gowanus section of Brooklyn where she played street games with the children of Latino and Irish immigrants. The 2010 MacArthur "Genius" fellowship recipient recalled spending her childhood in the midst of Native American and black families who found temporary housing in a nearby boarding house. "Gay politicians"

Figure 11.1 Lucas Jackson, portrait of Lynn Nottage, 2009.

and "a sprinkling of hippies" added even more flavor to this urban land-scape. This endearing – albeit confining – Brooklyn enclave was the extent of Nottage's world up until she enrolled in Harlem's High School of Music and Art, and became increasingly anxious about what she was missing out-side the borders of her neighborhood. She attended Brown University and, without interruption, she went on to receive her M.F.A. in playwriting at the Yale School of Drama.

Lynn Nottage's destiny as a storyteller on the world stage began in earn-est when, following her graduation from Yale, she found employment at the national human rights defense organization, Amnesty International. Her writing career took a four-year hiatus, which ended once this reluctant stu-dent determined that school was keeping her from what really mattered in her life. She explained to Alexis Greene:

> When I graduated from Yale, because I believed I hadn't had any life experi-ence, I was hungry to do something different. I was also feeling as though theater was decadent and not relevant to this culture that I was living in, and I got a job working at Amnesty International as a public relations person. Then after four years of doing that, I thought, "You know, theater *is* relevant. And I have to find a way of making it so."[4]

The more Nottage found out about the extent of human rights violations against women – both domestic and global – the more she came to realize that she could not effect the kind of lasting change that was needed, nei-ther in academia nor the private sector. Moreover, she doubted the sincerity of Amnesty International's position on stopping the ethnic killings between Rwanda's Hutus, Tutsis, and other warring groups. Disheartened about its slow response or non-response to such crimes, Nottage eventually returned to writing plays that she hoped would have better impact. As she recalled, time spent at this organization in the early 1990s informed her thinking about atrocities against women throughout the world and taught her that "shining a focused light on an injustice can actually lead to tangible change."[5]

Lynn Nottage's penchant for reaching beyond cultural borders seems par-tially driven by her uninhibited quest to "try just about anything to make the theatrical experience full and rewarding."[6] In her efforts to expose human rights violations and call attention to the plight of silent or silenced women, she admits to becoming "addicted to excursions and research ... because for me that's part of the joy of writing the play."[7] The results of Nottage's on-the-job exposure, her passion for research, and her willingness to travel to places unknown have shown up in plays variously set in the Guyana rain forest (*Por' Knockers*, 1995); in the French court of Louis XIV (*Las meninas*, 1989); and in the African Congo (*Ruined*, 2008). Her focus upon women's rights on both national and global scales has earned her a reputation as a women's rights ambassador, unrestricted by cultural borders.

Two of Nottage's growing list of plays extend her dramatic landscape significantly beyond the United States: *Las meninas* and *Ruined*. Her 2009 Pulitzer-Prize-winning play *Ruined* is the culmination of several trips to Africa where she not only interviewed refugee women and girls from Sudan and the Democratic Republic of the Congo, but also lived among them, gained their trust, and convinced them to share their stories. The play draws attention to the continuing, horrific rapes of these Congolese women, yet Nottage turns her playwriting skills toward making these women's sufferings not just *their* issue but *our* issue. By erasing cultural borders between similarly victimized sisters living across the Atlantic Ocean in Africa, she draws attention to African American women's shared history of capitalist-driven rape.

Nottage took great care once she had crossed over into the lawless cultural zones of Central Africa not to mix fact and fiction or to betray the fragile trust she had gained from an already demoralized community of women: "They told me their stories," she reminded herself, "they didn't give me their stories – and they are scared."[8] Each of the scenes in *Ruined* takes place in an out-of-the-way bar and brothel in the midst of a heavily wooded Congolese jungle. The soldiers, involved in an over-ten-year conflict over gold, copper, diamonds, and tin, shift their aggression onto the bodies of women and young girls they come upon there. This sort of makeshift oasis is run by the feisty matron, Mama Nadi, who walks a fine line with bullish soldiers on the prowl for liquor and sexual pleasures from her "girls."

During the rough-and-tumble, sometimes graphic sexual scenes that take place within Mama Nadi's place, Nottage choreographs a series of worrisome ironies that show the extent of the women's suffering, and force us to look behind the veil of our own willful and convenient cultural ignorance. What emerges gnaws at our sense of a common humanity: (1) these women – including Mama Nadi – have concluded that it is better to offer up their bodies for sale within this somewhat controlled setting than to risk being raped, maimed, and/or murdered in the surrounding bush; (2) Mama Nadi (who later reveals that she, too, has been "ruined") turns a profit by perpetuating the objectification and abuse of women; and (3) large-scale rape and female mutilation are not likely to prompt external intervention: viewed from outside the culture, these crimes are dismissed as collateral damage or the expected consequence of wars. In *Ruined*, Nottage manages to advance each of these unfortunate realities of female existence in a culture of "the other" in hopes of piercing through these cultural divides to reveal the suffering of fellow human beings, pressing for their relief. She shares a major lesson learned while on one of several trips to the Continent: "There are real ideals to be taken from African culture. You do discover in Africa that there is more American in you than you thought existed."[9]

Prior to the national and international spotlight occasioned by the success of *Ruined*, Nottage casts her gaze upon the French court of Louis XIV, demonstrating a predisposition for painstaking research and attention to women's issues on a global scale. In *Las meninas*, Nottage reaches across the Atlantic in search of dramatic material and thrusts together an unlikely cast of characters. In the process, she elicits a degree of sympathy for the demeaned queen as well as for her African lover, whose race assures that, during the play's seventeenth-century French setting, he is held in no higher regard than a pet or a toy. As such, *Las meninas* highlights several of the recurring themes in her work: voices rescued from history, discovery of silencing between the lines, and black women defining themselves.

Las meninas shows Lynn Nottage's skill at humanizing otherwise objectified and demoralized characters, eliciting concern and compelling audiences to listen to stories that others would prefer to forget and deem insignificant. The play, which takes its title from the famous Velázquez painting, dramatizes a romantic relationship between two outcasts: Queen Marie-Therese, the unhappy wife of King Louis XIV of France, and his consolation gift to her: Nabo, an African dwarf. As mutual confidants, they develop a close bond that ultimately yields a child between them. Furious, the King kills Nabo and banishes the child to a convent. The queen goes insane at the news of her double loss. Hence, *Las meninas* is framed as a story within a story, told in retrospect by the offspring of the tabooed relationship. Banished to a convent to avoid shaming her stepfather's reign, Louise, now an adult, insists upon bringing her mother's story to light. "I'm not demented," she tells her audience, "as the Mother Superior might have you believe, and no you won't go blind if you listen ... Now quiet, sweet sisters, and I will tell you again. *(Smiles gloriously)* This is the true story of the seduction of Marie-Therese ... the Queen of France."[10] Both *Ruined* and *Las meninas* evidence the unqualified depth and breadth of Nottage's concern for the dignity and humanity of oppressed people, particularly women and people of color, regardless of their culture or their stations in life. Comments shared with interviewer Alexis Greene reveal Lynn Nottage's membership among a growing number of African American female playwrights responsible for the constantly evolving aesthetic. "There are many different people who are inside of me," she admits, and then elaborates:

> Can a writer cross cultural boundaries? I certainly hope I am permitted to source the different aspects of myself. And those aspects may come across as

a white male or an Asian woman or a Latina. When I'm writing these people, I don't censor myself. And I think that all writers should be permitted to take that journey ... I think that there's something valuable in seeing how another culture perceives things, even if you disagree with the point of view ... Am I not to write about the experience of African-Americans who come from the Caribbean? Am I not to write an African character? Am I not to write a biracial character? Because these are not experiences that are indigenous to my imagination?[11]

Lynn Nottage owes much of her creative verve to the rewards of extensive travel, research, access to technology, and formal education; however, the emphasis upon transatlantic issues and global concerns of oppressed peoples did not start with her work. Shirley Graham Du Bois, Alice Childress, Lorraine Hansberry, and Adrienne Kennedy, for example, demonstrated global citizenship from multiple perspectives: as Africans, as Americans, as women, and as women of color. Will Harris rightly referred to the tension in their identities in terms not quite captured in Du Bois's double consciousness: a "dual liberation motif": "While dramatizing the plight of their race, as a means of both raising a black racial consciousness and appealing to a possible white audience, early black women playwrights also formulated dramatic strategies which enabled them to stage substantive, independent African American female presences, and thus propose their sexual equality."[12] Not coincidentally, these women either directly or indirectly benefited from an affiliation with the Pan-Africanist teachings of W. E. B. Du Bois – Graham as his wife, Childress and Hansberry as students in his class on African culture and History at the Jefferson School for Social Sciences in New York, and Kennedy through absorbing her father's many references to Du Bois's articles on the Negro Cause in *The Crisis*. This popular publishing venue, under Du Bois's editorship, opened its pages to a host of African American female talent. Du Bois's influence emboldened the social activism in these women and offered a space for them to write on behalf of the rights of women and to expand the scope of their social consciousness. Quite often this newly awakened social consciousness was manifested in a campaign to sustain ties with Africa, becoming a popular theme in plays such as Shirley Graham Du Bois's famous opera *Tom Tom* (1932), Alice Childress's *Gold through the Trees* (1952), Lorraine Hansberry's *A Raisin in the Sun* (1959) and *Les blancs* (1994), and Adrienne Kennedy's *Funnyhouse of a Negro* (1964). In writing plays that argued the cultural relevance of Africa among African Americans of their generation, each of them was compelled to expand their worldview beyond the United States' borders and to inspire, through their dramas, an emotional affinity with the sufferings of people from cultures other than their own.

While there is significant precedent for African American female play-wrights who have adopted what W. E. B. Du Bois termed "broad sympathy," or "knowledge of the world that was and is, and of the relation of men to it,"[13] what is new is an increase among the ranks of media-savvy, educated, well-connected, and well-traveled women who are able to maneuver with relative ease through patriarchal or racially hostile arenas that could easily impede the work of less vocal and engaged women. With African American female powerhouses, such as First Lady Michelle Obama and media mogul Oprah Winfrey, as possible models of strength and success, these women exude agency and comfort with their own identities. Coeditor Roberta Uno, who, along with Kathy Perkins, compiled *Contemporary Plays by Women of Color*, shares this optimism in her comments about the array of multicultural works within the collection. She commends the list of female contributors to the volume for "their keen minds and generous, fighting spirits ... creating not only a cultural continuum, but a sense that our isolation can no longer be enforced once we know about each other's work and struggles."[14]

Similar sentiments spring from editor and scholar, Margaret Wilkerson, who underscores in her introduction to her groundbreaking collection, *Nine Plays by Black Women*, the global sensibility of an early group of black female playwrights writing between 1950 and 1985: "Black women are a prism through which the searing rays of race, class and sex are first focused, and then refracted. The creative among us transform these rays into a spectrum of brilliant colors, a rainbow which illuminates the experience of all humankind."[15]

Alice Childress

Alice Childress was as much of a social activist as she was a writer. In many ways, like Lorraine Hansberry, she adopted a global perspective that was the result of her strategic professional relationships coupled with an enduring passion for asserting women's values, beauty, and strengths. Once a student at the noted Jefferson School of Social Science, she later went on to become a teacher herself, and in this capacity met Shirley Graham Du Bois, who eventually became a trusted friend and staunch supporter of her work. As noted by Kathy Perkins, the two women collaborated on activist causes, "working together in the CNA, the journal *Masses and Mainstream*, and Sojourners for Truth and Justice – a 1950s radical black women's civil rights group."[16] Most of Childress's nearly twenty plays feature strong-willed and independent female characters.

Like Hansberry, Childress came under the influence of Shirley Graham Du Bois's husband, W. E. B. Du Bois, who expanded her worldview, especially on Africa, and inspired her to use her plays to lessen the cultural divide between the *African* and the *African American*. In a 1989 interview with Kathy Perkins, Childress recalled her enthusiasm about enrolling in one of Du Bois's classes taught at the Jefferson School: "I went and took a course on Africa [with Du Bois] ... He was teaching on Africa and they said he was taking only twelve people and I flew!"[17]

Alice Childress's *Gold through the Trees* (1952) reflects, on several levels, Du Bois's Pan-Africanist influence and his wife's own work in this arena. In particular, this play, which adopts aspects of the fugitive slave narrative tradition, evokes the presence of Africa as a source of strength and pride, and as a reminder of its healing and redemptive powers. *Gold through the Trees* takes its figurative title from the joyful words uttered by the character of Harriet Tubman upon reaching freedom in the north: "The sun come like gold through the trees!"[18] The play's prologue chronicles, via the recollections of a grieving though resolute African queen, the devastation of her village carried out at the hands of slave captors. Plundering slavers destroy their villages and take their disgraced and disrobed king as hostage, along with many other skilled and valuable village laborers and artisans. Slave traders rob the village of the teacher, the runner, the wise, and the herdsman, leaving behind a bereft queen to rule over the infirm, the elderly, the women, and the children. But it is the women of the village who rebound and organize to avenge the kidnapped men of their village by going into battle:

BURNEY: We are not afraid to die, brother John. The other side of the grave holds no terror for us.
OLA: We weigh and consider carefully because we know what you expect of us. It is our job to go out and spread the word of resistance among the women and ask them to join us. You want us to ask the mothers and sisters to join up strong. Isn't this so?[19]

Childress's strategy in *Gold through the Trees* hinges upon one's ability to see meaning in the various juxtapositions that she sets up in the play's beginning, middle, and end. The play, whose acts and scenes bear telling subheadings, opens in the aftermath of a slave raid that devastates an African village. The action then shifts to three women (one of whom is Underground Railroad conductor Harriet Tubman) who have taken jobs as laundry women to raise funds to help fugitive slaves. In both instances, it is the heroic actions of the women that prove to be the salvation of their people.

Ultimately, it is the looming presence of Africa that provides women with their needed fortitude. Africa makes its presence known early in the play in the form of a female warrior-narrator who provides historical context for the slave trade that demoralized great African kings and held them as captors. A grieving queen is comforted by an Old Woman, or Africa personified, who offers her wise counsel: "Dry your eyes. We must lift the wounded and bind them. We must find food. We must live. Rise up! Take strength ... you are now king and queen."[20] Women occupy unmistakable roles in Childress's *Gold through the Trees* as forceful agents of change, the keepers of tradition, and culture bearers. From the Sumerian narrator – garbed in headdress, ribbons, beads, leaves, and flowers – to hotel washerwomen, Tubman and her laundry-washing colaborers proudly claim kinship with Africa and stand their ground in the face of tyranny. Hands blistered, terrified of being discovered, and deprived of sleep, the washerwomen persevere. Hence, the play spotlights the strength and solidarity of women in the face of the atrocities of slavery that diminish their men but embolden their determination to survive and thrive.

Perkins rightfully speculates that Childress's *Gold through the Trees* bears the unmistakable imprint of Shirley Graham Du Bois's musical *Tom Tom*. She observes, "[both] pieces trace the journey of Africans to America and employ a range of musical styles."[21] As in *Gold*, *Tom Tom* is based upon a cyclical narrative that begins in an African setting, moves to a location in America, and finally closes back on African soil. Early in the play, Graham depicts natives engaged in primitive rituals of sacrifice to their gods, only to be interrupted by slavers. The second part of the narrative shifts to a mass meeting in Harlem. Although Marcus Garvey's name is not invoked, he and his Back to Africa Movement are clearly the subject of this combative gathering. The beating of the tom tom drums punctuates the play and becomes an unmistakable symbol of Africa, noisily asserting its relevance as the debate over assimilation versus cultural preservation ensues. Tempers flare, words exchange, and the Voodoo Man succumbs to a wound to his chest from someone in the crowd. In the final scene of *Tom Tom*, a young boy steps forth to lead the charge to return to Africa.

Lorraine Hansberry

In the early 1950s, Lorraine Hansberry was embroiled in a campaign to lessen the huge cultural gulf that separated the *African* and the *African-American*. Following the lead of her uncle, African scholar William Leo Hansberry, and heavily influenced by Pan-Africanist pioneer W. E. B. Du Bois, she developed a profound interest in Africa, reading widely in the area of African Studies and making it the center of her growing social activism. Her education in world affairs was additionally enriched by affiliations with organizations that focused upon global politics. According to the online journal *Social Justice Movements*,

While attending the University of Wisconsin, Lorraine joined the Young Progressives of America and the Labor Youth League. These were organizations that fought for world peace and racial equality ... While taking a class at the Jefferson School, she was introduced to Paul Robeson. For her course, instructed by Du Bois, Hansberry wrote a paper entitled "The Belgian Congo: A Preliminary Report on Its Land, Its History, and Its People," demonstrating her expanding interest in global issues of justice and equality ... Regularly in contact with Robeson and Du Bois, Hansberry used the opportunity to expand her understanding of race, politics, and culture.[22]

With such firm grounding in African culture and politics, it seems inevitable that these two topics would merge in Hansberry's writing, leading to what art historian Robert Ferris Thompson would later theorize as a "flash of the spirit": images, rituals, verbal exchanges, gestures, etc. that suggest the presence of Africa and its abiding influence. Her plays, such as *A Raisin in the Sun* and *Les blancs*, bore the imprint of her Afrocentric consciousness on multiple levels. In *Raisin*, flashes of the spirit come in the persons of Asagai, Beneatha's African suitor; Beneatha, the hopelessly misguided romantic; and Walter Lee, her cynical brother. In its portrayal of each, the play challenges American audiences to see past differences of culture, color, and continent to discover a shared humanity. As her husband and editor, Robert Nemiroff, recalls in the "Critical Background" written for the posthumously published *Collected Last Plays*, Hansberry had already established her artistic agenda well in advance of *A Raisin in the Sun*'s Broadway debut. In what he describes as "her first formal address as a writer," she asserts that "the ultimate destiny and aspirations of the African peoples and twenty million American Negroes are inextricably and magnificently bound up together forever."[23]

Hansberry's *Les blancs* crystallizes ideas broached in *Raisin* about breaking the cultural divide between Africans and African Americans, but on a much more expansive scale. Although the play, set in a mission compound in Africa, is anti-colonialist at its core, it also strategically draws parallels to the black experience in America under an oppressive white power structure. The play becomes a dialectical exercise in the advantages of reaching across the cultural divide through dialog rather than armed conflict. While war remains ever an option for resolving differences in the play, Hansberry insists that "men must talk; they must establish a dialogue whose purpose is neither procrastination nor ego fulfillment but clarity, and whose culminating point is action: to find the means, in an age of revolution, to reduce the cost in human sacrifice and make the transition as swift and painless as possible."[24] Tshembe Matoseh, a young African man, returns home from his comfortable life in Europe to bury his father amid tensions between native

Africans and European missionaries. Tshembe wages a philosophical battle over whether he should join in to overthrow the European rule that has oppressed his homeland, but ultimately decides that it is his responsibility to defend his people and fight for their freedom. His decision is clearly a painful one, complicated by tangled relationships caused by his confusion over cultural borders and the clashing of the African and European within himself.

Hansberry's border-crossing agenda in *A Raisin in the Sun* and *Les blancs* was for the sake of creating solidarity among Africans and African Americans in their fight against racial oppression in 1960s America and in war-torn parts of Africa. As a woman and as a gifted playwright, she saw her role as a mediator, using the power of her words and the magic of the stage to tackle huge questions about culture and race on a global scale. In this sense both works may be read as allegories of social protest with emphases upon empathy, communication, and love for humanity. The words of scholar Margaret Wilkerson in her introduction to the playwright's *Collected Last Plays* provide some sense of Hansberry's belief in the power of theatre to de-emphasize differences and cross-cultural borders:

> In play after play, she sensed the mood of her times and anticipated the future – the importance that African politics and styles would assume, the regeneration of commitment among American intellectuals, the seductiveness of mercenary values for black Americans, the equality of men and women, and the proliferation of liberation struggles throughout the world. The theater was a working laboratory for this brilliant woman whose sighted eyes and feeling heart caused her to reach out to a world at once cruel and beautiful.[25]

Adrienne Kennedy

Adrienne Kennedy's interest in foreign landscapes crystallized in 1960 during what she refers to in her confessional *People who Led to My Plays* as "a miraculous voyage aboard the *Queen Elizabeth* to England, France, Spain and West Africa."[26] The itinerary shared with husband James and young son Joe also included eight months in Rome. With each new port of call visited, Kennedy gathered and stored images that would later emerge in her signature mental rant, *Funnyhouse of a Negro*. The personas of Queen Elizabeth I, the duchess of Hapsburg, Shakespeare, Chaucer, Patrice Lumumba, Anne Boleyn, the king of France, and Chopin make cameo appearances in *Funnyhouse* and in several of her other works.

Among the many eclectic images that populate Kennedy's *Funnyhouse*, that of West African black nationalist Patrice Lumumba, the first legally elected prime minister of the Democratic Republic of the Congo, is most

pronounced. Graphic images of his 1961 assassination held special meaning for Kennedy; as it turned out, she was actually in West Africa at the time
of his brutal execution by a Belgian firing squad. Emblematic of the trauma
of his murder, his brain-shattered, bloody image becomes deeply embedded
in Kennedy's psyche, ultimately manifesting as a constant reminder to protagonist Sarah that she must not deny her ties to African culture. As Philip
Kolin points out in *Understanding Adrienne Kennedy*, "Lumumba occupies
one of the most paradoxical roles in Sarah's nightmare world … compelling
Sarah to admit her African roots and to forget any pretenses or pretext of
being white royalty … Lumumba's blackness cannot be doubted – racially,
politically, sexually."[27] The art that Kennedy makes of this tragic circum-
stance reflects the extent of her own profound affinity with her African
ancestors' fight for sovereignty, as well as her profound disgust at learning
that the man some saw then as "the hope of Africa" had fallen victim to
an international conspiracy to gain control of the Congo's strategic raw
materials:

> Just when I had discovered the place of my ancestors, just when I had discov-
> ered this African hero, he had been murdered. Ghana was in mourning. There
> had been a deep kinship between Nkrumah and Lumumba. A few people we
> met had heard Lumumba speak. Even though I had known of him so briefly,
> I felt I had been struck a blow. He became a character in my play … a man
> with a shattered head.[28]

The cadre of African American female playwrights who wrote prior to
1959 and who contributed in some way to the now well-wrought traditions established by Lorraine Hansberry and Alice Childress also knew the
importance of theatre as a vehicle for social change and as a path toward
women's agency. Like Hansberry and Childress, many were educated, talented, and politically engaged women, but their stories were also reflective of and, to some degree, inhibited by prevailing conventions and social
norms. Plays written prior to Hansberry's *Raisin in the Sun* and *Les blancs*,
and before Childress's *Gold through the Trees* (such as Georgia Douglas
Johnson's anti-lynching drama *Sunday Morning in the South*, Mary Burrill's
Aftermath, or Shirley Graham Du Bois's *I Gotta Home* – cut from similar fabric), are set in insulated, familiar spaces within the home or within
the surrounding neighborhood. Margaret Wilkerson notes that many were
"produced largely within the fold – in churches, lodges, and social halls of
the sympathetic few,"[29] while Kathy Perkins observes that the action often
unfolded "in a domestic setting – the kitchen, dining room, or living room,
and the play usually opened with a woman sewing, cooking, cleaning, or
praying – rarely outside or far from the house."[30] This tradition also saw

landscapes transformed out of church congregations or local neighborhoods and familiar establishments.

African American female playwrights have announced their arrival in the twenty-first century in ways that reflect the benefits of the current age of technology. Their unprecedented mobility, their intellect, and their sophisticated knowledge of world affairs have become key weapons in the battle for political and social change. Lynn Nottage, as both woman and playwright, typifies this proactive new breed of African American female playwrights. Her 2009 Pulitzer-Prize-winning *Ruined*, which sparked a national dialog and jumpstarted a campaign for intervention on a global scale to stop the rape, murder, and physical abuse against Congolese women, makes no apologies for its undeniable political agenda of using art for change. She is well positioned to press the aesthetics of the discipline into even greater arenas, and to take "radical" and bold measures that simultaneously build upon and set her apart from her literary foremothers. Nottage inspires our international consciousness and takes audiences beyond cultural borders that are often avoided to find a common humanity in the sufferings of other people of color. With a string of high-profile and critically acclaimed works that skip about the globe, she continues to erase differences and to knock down borders. As fellow playwright Pearl Cleage most fittingly asserts about her "sistas" in the field, "there are other eyes besides the ones we're used to looking through ... there are other ways to see the world and talk about it and walk through it and become one with the parts of it that feel as familiar as your own right hand."[31] And, as Randy Gener observes of Lynn Nottage, "Few American dramatists aspire to such a panoramic view of the world or manage it so engagingly."[32]

NOTES

1 Charles Isherwood, "Playwrights Bring Uncommon Bond to Broadway," *The New York Times*, September 15, 2011.

2 Philip C. Kolin (ed.), *Contemporary African American Women Playwrights: A Casebook* (New York: Routledge, 2007), 1.

3 Alexis Greene (ed.), *Women who Write Plays: Interviews with American Dramatists* (Hanover, NH: Smith and Kraus, 2001), 337.

4 *Ibid.*, 342.

5 "100 Years of Honoring Women: Lynn Nottage," *Enough Time*, March 7, 2011.

6 Randy Gener, "Conjurer of Worlds," *American Theatre*, October, 2005, 23.

7 *Ibid.*

8 *Ibid.*

9 *Ibid.*

10 Lynn Nottage, *Las meninas*, in *Crumbs from the Table of Joy and Other Plays* (New York: Theatre Communications Group, 2004), 251–2.

11 Greene, *Women who Write Plays*, 358–9.
12 Will Harris, "Early Black Women Playwrights and the Dual Liberation Motif," *African American Review*, 8.2 (Summer, 1994): 205–21.
13 W. E. B. Du Bois, "The Talented Tenth," in Booker T. Washington, W. E. B. Du Bois, C. W. Chesnutt *et al.*, *The Negro Problem: A Series of Articles by Representative American Negroes of Today* (New York: J. Pott, 1903), 33–75.
14 Kathy Perkins and Roberta Uno (eds.), *Contemporary Plays by Women of Color: An Anthology* (New York: Routledge, 1996), 8.
15 Margaret Wilkerson (ed. and introd.), *Nine Plays by Black Women* (New York: New American Library, 1986).
16 Alice Childress, *Selected Plays*, ed. Kathy Perkins (Evanston, IL: Northwestern University Press, 2011), xvi.
17 *Ibid.*
18 Alice Childress, *Gold through the Trees*, in *ibid.*, 34.
19 *Ibid.*, 45.
20 *Ibid.*, 29.
21 *Ibid.*, xvi.
22 "Hansberry as a Social Activist," *Social Justice Movements*, http://socialjustice. ccnmtl.columbia.edu/index.php/Hansberry_as_a_Social_Activist (last accessed November 15, 2011).
23 Lorraine Hansberry, *The Collected Last Plays: Les blancs, The Drinking Gourd, What Use Are Flowers?*, ed. Robert Nemiroff (New York: New American Library, 1983), 31.
24 *Ibid.*, 33.
25 *Ibid.*, 21.
26 Adrienne Kennedy, *People who Led to My Plays* (New York: Theatre Communications Group, 1987), 111.
27 Philip Kolin, *Understanding Adrienne Kennedy* (Columbia: University of South Carolina Press, 2005), 44–5.
28 *Ibid.*, 119.
29 Wilkerson, *Nine Plays*, xv.
30 Kathy Perkins (ed.), *Black Female Playwrights: An Anthology of Plays before 1950* (Bloomington: Indiana University Press, 1989), 2.
31 Pearl Cleage, "Becoming Women of Color in the Theatre," in Perkins and Uno, *Contemporary Plays*, 2.
32 Gener, "Conjurer of Worlds," 24.

12

SANDRA L. RICHARDS

African Diaspora drama

In an anthology of criticism about African American theatre, an essay about African Diaspora drama may initially seem out of place because many of the authors and plays that can be grouped under this heading originate from and concern life outside the United States. Yet the inclusion is appropriate, for self-identification as black has always exceeded the nation-state. While the Jamaican born, Harlem Renaissance poet Claude McKay lamented that his "long-suffering race ... denied a human place" both in the "Christian West" and on the African Continent had, in fact, "no home on earth," "enslaved" people of African descent have sought to identify and create a home: that is, a material and psychic space where their worth is acknowledged.[1] "Diaspora" has functioned as a concept that has allowed them to posit a space of nurturance in the world. Indeed, as I will demonstrate, many African American playwrights, theorists, and audiences have not only posited emotional and political links with non-US black populations but have also looked outside these geographical confines for aesthetic concepts to guide their construction of theatre.

Despite a dehumanization that has persisted since the sixteenth-century establishment of the transatlantic slave trade, ideas concerning African or black solidarity have assumed many forms over historical time. Beginning with a review of ways in which the African Diaspora has been conceptualized, I propose several different categories of African Diaspora drama. The first two build upon the pioneering scholarship of W. E. B. Du Bois and Melville Herskovits, while the others reflect my own practices, developed over years of study and teaching. My objective is to identify ways in which similarity and difference – the paradoxical poles around which diaspora is enacted – have been articulated. I concentrate on written texts because up until relatively recently, these dramas circulated more easily than performers or videotape, and YouTube was non-existent. Though the African Diaspora is multilingual, this chapter concentrates on texts readily available in English.

African Diaspora discourses

Conceptualization of the African Diaspora has shifted over time. Etymologically derived from Greek, the word *diaspora* originally meant a scattering of seeds and did not carry negative connotations of forced exile.[2] But over time, the biblical example of the Jewish exile became dominant, and the term took on connotations of traumatic expulsion and subsequent alienation from the new environment in which those expelled attempted to recreate home. The African Diaspora was thus understood as communities of African peoples who had been forced from the Continent and resettled in the Americas as the result of the transatlantic slave trade. Largely forgotten were diasporic communities created by trade throughout the Mediterranean, and the Arab slave trade eastward to the Indian Ocean.[3] Given the accelerated movement of peoples across the globe since the second half of the twentieth century, the term *diaspora* has become popular with academics, journalists, and everyday people attributing a variety of meanings to the word.

In this chapter, I combine elements of the scholarship of Kim D. Butler,[4] Brent Hayes Edwards,[5] Stuart Hall,[6] and Kobena Mercer[7] in order to arrive at a definition. I retain the four traits that Butler argues characterize diaspora communities. They are: dispersal of a population from a homeland to at least two other locations; some relationship to an actual or imagined homeland; existence as a group over at least two generations (thereby distinguishing diasporic groups from those that find themselves in temporary exile); and self-consciousness of itself as part of an ethnonational group that not only binds it to a homeland but also to other dispersed communities. To these characteristics, the factor of marginalization should be added; that is, racial denigration and the denial of equal opportunities prompt these new arrivals and their descendants to express deep ambivalence about their new residence and nostalgia about the homeland. And though implicit in Butler's list, the dynamic of performance should be stressed, for in both its formal and pedestrian or daily manifestations, performance is a central mode through which any community experiences, develops, and asserts a distinctive identity.

Stuart Hall notes that identity is necessarily always an incomplete production that we have learned to think about in two opposing yet linked ways, namely as an ontological "true self" and as a dynamic becoming. As humans, we transmit intergenerationally stories and practices that change over time but that we regard as bestowing an essential and stable cultural distinctiveness upon a group defined as "ours." Pushed to the margins of recognition are those people and customs that are defined as exceptional to "our" norm. We alter traditions over time in response to specific conditions, yet we tell ourselves stories of unchanging stability. This dynamic interplay of perceived continuity and change obtains, certainly, for people of African descent, whose confrontations with racial violence have strengthened the impetus to name and champion a normative, in-group identity. Similarities in the African Diaspora experience in the Americas were substantive, with long-ranging impact: depending upon where and when they were off-loaded in the Americas, African ethnics discovered that they had brought with them a range of shared or closely related values and practices.[8] And, as Tiffany Patterson and Robin D. G. Kelley note of that transatlantic trade, "global processes ... incorporated black people through empire building. They were never uniform or fixed, but did create systems that were at times tightly coordinated across oceans and national boundaries."[9] But the economic, linguistic, social, and political regimes, to which the enslaved and their descendants have been subjected and thereby challenged to (re)fashion identities, have also differed throughout the Americas. *Diaspora* thus becomes a name for unity over difference, but because identity is lived as both a being and a becoming, what enables this recognition of similarity, Hall argues, is an articulation, similar to the link between a truck's cab and trailer. Just as a truck driver might drop off one trailer of goods and acquire another, this connection amongst Africa-descended people has the potential to result in a unity that is "not necessary, determined, absolute and essential for all times."[10] Hence, as Edwards has argued, we should think of diaspora as a conceptual prop or prosthetic that enables unity.

Embedded in this discussion is the element of hybridity, for while the dispersed population remembers (or reimagines) an ancestral home, it must also accommodate itself to local conditions. Observations by Kobena Mercer are particularly germane, for he recognizes that African Diasporans in their daily lives have pursued a dialogic tactic of selectively appropriating and refashioning dominant cultures to serve their own purposes. He says:

> Across a whole range of cultural forms there is a powerfully *syncretic* dynamic which critically appropriates elements from the master-codes of the dominant culture and *creolizes* them, disarticulating the given signs and rearticulating their symbolic meaning otherwise. The subversive force of this hybridizing tendency is most apparent at the level of language itself where creoles, patois, and Black English decenter, destabilize, and carnivalize the linguistic domination ...[11]

In summary, diaspora, as I am conceptualizing it in this chapter, is an analytic and a practice that entails a number of seemingly contradictory moves held in productive tension, namely: (a) a "backward" glance and affective affiliation with the site of collective origin; (b) alienation from, varying degrees of accommodation to, and critical appropriation or creolization of, norms of the host nation, which is ambivalent about the presence of diasporans within its borders; (c) subjective experience of identity as both rooted or fixed in a distinctive history, and routed or continually (re)articulated in relation to intersections of local, regional, national, and global particularities;[12] (d) recognition of affinity with other ethnonational communities displaced from the original homeland, accomplished by privileging similarity and unity over difference; and (e) identification and nurturance of a home in the world.

Finally, I should address my choice of the word *African* rather than *black* in relation to diaspora. I do so not to emphasize the Continent as a privileged site of origins, but as a way of reminding myself and others to include Continental Africans in our discussions.[13] In so doing, I depart from an Afrocentricism of the 1960s and 1970s that viewed Africa as the glorious prehistory to a morally bankrupt West. Remembering Africa will hopefully prompt us not only to study diasporic communities around the Indian Ocean and/or prior to Atlantic slavery, but also to engage contemporary diasporas-in-the-making on the African Continent itself.

Let us turn now to applications of the concept to drama. Because the term *African Diaspora* came into usage only with the establishment of black or African American Studies departments in the 1960s and 1970s and requires knowledge of multiple cultural traditions, relatively few academics analyze its meaning vis-à-vis drama. Most often, they apply Du Bois's formulation of black American drama and rely upon Herskovits's identification of African cultural retentions, both of which I will discuss momentarily.[14] I have followed suit, but, building upon current scholarship in globalization and post-colonial and cultural studies, I also propose several other categories of African Diaspora drama. We will see that they all raise the central question of what is at stake in invoking diaspora: what commonalities of experience are diaspora people recognizing in each other? What experiences of difference are they ignoring in order to produce unity, and for what purposes is this unity being mobilized?

African Diaspora drama as written by us

Early in the twentieth century Du Bois sought to counter the grinning Sambo that prevailed on the stage and permeated almost all facets of American life by defining black drama as those plays "About us ... By us ... For us [and] Near us."[15] He believed that, stigmatized by the blackface darky construction, African American authors would use their intimate knowledge of black life to create accurate representations; their primary audience would be fellow blacks whose experiences equipped them to evaluate the plays fairly, and the productions would occur in black communities, that at the time were legally segregated. Though elements of his definition lost their salience as African Americans successfully struggled to secure their civil rights, the issue of authorship – "By us" – has remained essential to definitions of black drama and, by extension, black literature. Indeed, for most contemporary scholars this position still obtains.[16]

Though a Pan-Africanist all his adult life, Du Bois did not routinely discuss drama after his involvement with the Krigwa Players during the Harlem Renaissance of the 1920s. But inspired by his scholarship and activism as well as by decolonization struggles, some analysts and practitioners extended Du Bois's pronouncements beyond national boundaries. From this perspective, Amiri Baraka's *Dutchman* and *The Slave*[17] or Djanet Sears's *The Adventures of a Black Girl in Search of God*[18] are Diaspora plays simply because they were written by a member of the African Diaspora in the United States and Canada, respectively. But this easy method of organizing by descent is not necessarily the most useful, for while it enables a focus on historical similarities, it may also ignore varying class, gender, political, or national investments that call into question possibilities for enacting diasporic unity. Melville Herskovits's identification of African cultural retentions provides one way of bringing further specificity to a group of black-authored texts.

African Diaspora drama as cultural retentions

Within a few short years of Du Bois's definition of black American drama, scholars like the anthropologist Melville Herskovits began to counter hegemonic rationalizations that black people in the Americas were cultureless people in need of civilization by identifying African cultural retentions that they continued to practice and that in some instances had been adopted into the mainstream. Although Herskovits's language of survivalisms may convey an impression of passivity on the part of cultural agents,[19] the labor and ingenuity required to reproduce traditions are significant, for traditions persist only to the extent that people value their relevance, have opportune conditions, and commit to maintaining them in circumstances that are also shifting over time. Plays under this rubric fall along a continuum ranging from those where African-inflected practices are present but remain unmarked; to others where those practices are integral to the plot but can also be rationalized within a western frame of reference; to another, closely related subset where retentions and neo-Africanisms shape dramatic structure.[20]

Some of the "folk plays" of the 1920s Harlem Renaissance offer examples of a literal reference that has largely escaped critical notice. Though Alain Locke recognized the importance of African culture for western – and specifically African American – art, he and the cofounder of the Howard Players, Montgomery Gregory, theorized folk plays as simple, entertaining representations of a southern way of life. Evidence of Diaspora culture went unnoticed, given what Herskovits identified years later in *The Myth of the Negro Past* (1941) as the operation of an acculturative "principle of disregard for outer form while retaining inner values, of Africans everywhere."[21] May Miller's 1929 one-act *Riding the Goat* is illustrative.[22] In her play a young, educated couple, ready to take up the responsibilities of Du Bois's Talented Tenth, resist participating in what they regard as the retrograde practice of the annual lodge parade that includes full-body masking of the grand marshal, which is in fact suggestive of many West African festival customs. Though the granny figure aligns with other stereotypes of elderly women deeply fearful of social change found in plays of this era, her devotion to the lodge as a site in which black men and women could find social dignity and enact community through ritualistic performance demonstrates an important aspect of Diaspora identity formation: New World blacks often appropriated European traditions like freemasonry[23] in accordance with an underlying, antecedent cultural logic, but did so in a manner that left those antecedents hidden in plain view.[24] Furthermore, their choices were subject to debate within and outside black communities. Ant Hetty's desire for a sumptuous, dignified burial conducted by the lodge may appear to its sophisticated 1920s audiences as comical or superstitious, if it remains unconnected to a larger belief system concerning the interpenetration of the material and spiritual realms.

This last observation raises the question of cultural literacy, or what may in this instance be equated with "diaspora literacy."[25] That is, all theatre demands that its audiences be able to recognize connections between the semiotic codes of a given production and the offstage world that that production is presumed to represent. But as the late performance critic VèVè Clark argued, diaspora literacy necessitates knowledge of multiple, dominant, as well as subaltern, cultures; given the marginalization of African Diaspora communities and acculturative tactics of creolized disguise, this interpretive strategy must be cultivated through "a knowledge of historical, social, cultural, and political development generated by *lived* and textual experience."[26]

Also within this Herskovitsian category are plays whose retentions have structural impact that defy the well-made play trajectory that has dominated much of western playwriting since the nineteenth century. Yet, though they offer alternative dramatic trajectories, some retentions are more easily rationalized within western frameworks than others. For example, Dennis Scott's *Echo in the Bone*,[27] set in 1930s Jamaica; Sistren Theatre Collective's *QPH*,[28] which takes place in Jamaica some fifty years later; and August Wilson's *Joe Turner's Come and Gone*,[29] located in a 1911 Pittsburgh boarding house, all feature ritual practitioners and believers who navigate between the material and spiritual realms, conceptualized as a seamless whole. All three plays contain characters receptive to the conflation of past and present in which the dead make their presence known to the living. But *Echo* and *QPH* announce their retentions at the outset, for the Scott play begins with preparations for a nine-nights (funeral wake) as observed by Pocomania believers,[30] and *QPH* opens on a set of three coffins arranged in a cross formation and a table-like altar whose rum, okra stew, and Bible signal a hybrid Christianity. Various props and performative practices are then layered onto this initial canvas. Because both plays dramatize the lives of people who have died, the appearance of these dead persons can be understood through the technique of the flashback or analepsis that interrupts a present narration to provide a prior narrative of causation. But a more complex reading is also available to the diaspora-literate: through the enactment of ritual, performers have literally raised the dead, merged past with present, producing a syncopated, discrepant temporality that challenges how both performers and spectators/readers locate themselves in the present and imagine possible futures: "Experiences of unsettlement, loss, and recurring terror produce discrepant temporalities – broken histories that trouble the linear, progressivist narratives of nation-states and global modernization."[31]

But in still other plays, the creolized appropriation of religious belief is finally resistant to western explanations. The coeval existence of the material and the spiritual is initially masked, rendering its inevitable, full irruption puzzling because the playwright seemingly has not adequately prepared her/his audience. Here, I am thinking of dramas that are stylistically quite different from each other, namely Ntozake Shange's *for colored girls*[32] and August Wilson's *The Piano Lesson*.[33] In pioneering the choreopoem as a performance genre, Shange eschews the linear trajectory that most American drama had pursued through the 1970s. Furthermore, she concentrates on the experiences of young black women at a time when they were just beginning to be viewed as worthy of artistic attention. But she makes her unusual choice of genre and subject matter recognizable to those early audiences by locating her concerns in the realm of secular experiences: high school graduation night, Afro-Cuban dances in Spanish Harlem, date rape, and abortion. Occasionally, this evocation of the familiar, enhanced by popular music, is punctuated by an expression of the power of music or poetry to transport one beyond social definition. References to Yoruba-inflected religious practices are hidden in plain view, as in the "one" poem in which a tantalizing woman entices young men into her bed only to dismiss them later in order to pursue her own creativity. The choice of colors associated with the woman and her actions suggests that she is related to the god or *orisa* named *Yemanja*, said to be the artistic principle itself.[34] Similarly, the concluding section yokes the secular and the divine. The "laying on of hands" occurs after the shocking infanticide committed by beau willie brown. In language mixing sexuality and various healing modalities – secular as well as Christian – with trance, these disparaged women find God in themselves. This moment aims at being simultaneously representational of African women's Diaspora histories of loss and resilience, and performative in seeking to effect a cure onstage and in the audience. Whether it succeeds is contingent upon multiple factors beyond the playwright's control. A younger generation of performance artists like ahdri zhina mandiela[35] and Trey Anthony[36] of Canada, or Sharon Bridgforth,[37] Kamilah Forbes and the Hip Hop Junction Theatre,[38] and Universes of the United States have refashioned Shange's innovations so that the transcendent bursts into performance in the guise of Diaspora history, lesbian sexuality, dub poetry and rap, or hip-hop battles between artistry and commercialism.

In Wilson's plays the operation of the spiritual, with its potential for transformative impact on the audience, seems surprising because his semiotic cues at the outset are dense and disguised within an aura of realism. *The Piano Lesson* appears initially as a fairly straightforward case of clashing sibling desires concerning the disposition of a family piano, with talk about unsettled ghosts being dismissed as "nonsense." Only relatively late in the play, after multiple stories (and blues songs) about ghosts, railroad adventures, and Jim Crow life in the South, that function to reanimate the past, does the audience itself experience what has been under debate. Spirits, understood as marginalized social issues,[39] make their presence manifest to all, challenging the descendant community – onstage and off – fully to acknowledge the past in its attempts to craft a more viable present and future.

African Diaspora drama as a resistance to colonial governance

Rather than arguing for cultural continuities, some playwrights have opted to launch overt, political and sociocultural attacks on the proclaimed superiority of western culture. I propose that the theme of resistance to colonial governance offers a productive way of identifying a subset of black-authored texts. Under this rubric, I group plays like Amiri Baraka's (aka LeRoi Jones) *Dutchman* and *The Slave*, set in urban United States;

Derek Walcott's *Dream on Monkey Mountain*,[40] set in Jamaica; Aimé
Césaire's *A Tempest [Une Tempête]*,[41] set on a Caribbean island much like
his native Martinique; Abdias do Nascimento's *Sortilege (Black Mystery)*,[42]
placed in Brazil; Kobena Seyki's *The Blinkards*,[43] located in the colonial
Gold Coast of present-day Ghana; or Adrienne Kennedy's *Funnyhouse of a
Negro* and *The Owl Answers*,[44] set in a tortured psyche. Though differentiated in terms of geographical locale, class, and gender, they were written
in the period of the mid 1960s to the late 1970s,[45] at a time when various
African colonies were achieving independence; war in Vietnam was escalating and provoking anti-establishment, sociopolitical upheavals were taking
place in France (the former colonial power) as well as in the United States;
and Frantz Fanon's 1961 *Les damnés de la terre*[46] (translated into English
as *The Wretched of the Earth* in 1963) provided progressives with a compelling argument for the legitimacy of violence waged in response to the
physical and psychic violence that colonialism institutes in order to fulfill
its objectives of domination. A comparative analysis allows one to begin to
understand race as a construction of colonial governmentality.[47] The inclusion of women playwrights and protagonists helps to foreground questions
of gender that went unmarked at the time of their initial productions – and
would, in fact, have provoked divisiveness had they been acknowledged.[48]
Furthermore, the inclusion of US American texts forces consideration of
the United States as a colonial power vis-à-vis some of its citizens. Let us
examine these claims through a brief analysis of the Césaire, Baraka, and
Kennedy plays.

Though written some five years after the Baraka and Kennedy plays,
Aimé Césaire's text is intellectually precedent in that he directly addresses
the oppressive weight of western civilization through his rewriting of
Shakespeare's *The Tempest*. Césaire retains the basic plot line of Prospero
and daughter Miranda, exiled on an unnamed, Caribbean-like island, served
by the spritely Ariel and the more earthly Caliban, and interacting with
Prospero's rivals, whom he has caused to become shipwrecked. But against
Shakespeare's assertion of a totalizing discourse – the respected "Bard of
Avon" terms his play *The Tempest* – Césaire posits a particular instance of
a colonial pattern in which Prospero, constructed as an Enlightenment figure pursuing both science and its alter ego, magic, seeks to bring everything
under his control. Caliban, whose name is an anagram for the Spanish word
for *cannibal*, not only remembers a language and culture prior to Prospero's
appearance on the island, but also utters words that Prospero does not
know (most significantly, *Uhuru*, which is a Kiswahili word meaning freedom), and insists on the right to rename himself as X, thereby "refus[ing]
to be interpellated as the linguistic subject of the master narrative."[49] In

using these terms, Caliban signals his imagined, diasporic affiliations with the African American Nation of Islam leader Malcolm X, as well as with Kenyan independence struggles.

More importantly, Césaire introduces two other substantive changes: stating that the performance is to have the ambience of a psychodrama (and thus a therapeutic objective for an engaged, invested audience), he instructs the performers to choose their masks/roles at the outset. Later, he brings onto the stage a disruptive character named Eshu, who is not simply the so-called "trickster" figure of Yoruba lore but also a metonym for the paradoxical principle of the constancy of change and, consequently, interpretive undecidability. These two changes have the effect of dramatizing the fabricated quality and performativity of race, rather than its assumed naturalness within the body, and of insisting upon an "excess" lying beyond all human explanatory systems. Though by the play's conclusion an aging, weakened Prospero remains on the island as Caliban's adversary, the play both looks forward to the dismantling of colonial empires and offers an implicit caution against subsequent regimes aiming to substitute their own totalizing discourses.

Written and premiered in New York in 1964 when Amiri Baraka was known as LeRoi Jones, *Dutchman* and *The Slave* function as companion pieces tracing the trajectory of the Black Power and Black Arts movements in the United States. For the sake of space, I will limit my comments to *Dutchman*, in which a young black man riding a New York City train is enticed into sharing an interracial fantasy with Lula, a slightly older, white hipster. Promising sexual trysts and freedom from a racialized history that he has chosen to forget, Lula gradually intensifies her attacks on Clay's carefully composed, middle-class façade until this young would-be poet can no longer contain his anger. He explodes, rejecting western culture as epitomized by the white woman. Crucially, he also argues that unbeknownst to whites who have always reveled in the "vitality" of black culture, black people have used arts – like blues music – as a coded form of rebellion. But having revealed an opposing worldview, Clay does not act on his knowledge. Instead he opts to "be safe with my words,"[50] whereupon Lula seizes the opportunity to kill him and prepares to hunt another young rebel. This symbolically allusive play operates on multiple levels simultaneously: it announces the onset of black militancy in northern urban environments in the United States, dramatizes the alleged appeal that whiteness holds for blacks – heterosexual men in particular – and yet cautions black spectators about the deadly consequences of failure to resist a political system that insists upon second-class status for its non-white citizens. From a Diaspora perspective, *Dutchman* links struggles within the United States to other anti-colonial struggles being waged internationally. Its representation of anti-colonialism as a black man's confrontation with a white female resonates most directly with Derek Walcott's *Dream on Monkey Mountain* – which premiered in 1967, some five years after the island nation of Trinidad-Tobago achieved its independence from Britain – and with Abdias do Nascimento's *Sortilegio* (*Sortilege – a Black Mystery*), which premiered in 1957 as an "attempt to ransom the dignity of the black man and his culture" by denouncing Brazil's myth of being a racial democracy.[51]

Like Aimé Césaire and Amiri Baraka, Adrienne Kennedy also confronts the impact of western culture on a non-white subject in plays like *Funnyhouse of a Negro* and *The Owl Answers*. But while the former couch rebellion in cultural/political registers, Kennedy deftly dramatizes the sexual economy of racism or colonial governance that constructs blacks as hypersexual and culturally deficient; promises seeming social acceptance to those blacks knowledgeable of dominant culture; and yet preserves the power of white heterosexual, elite men to exercise control over everyone designated unlike them. *The Owl Answers*, which is also set on a New York subway train, revolves around a woman who is attempting to see her father but is prevented from gaining access by a shifting, nightmarish group of characters that include Shakespeare, Chaucer, and William the Conqueror. In this stylistically abstract play that proceeds through the accelerated accretion of repeating images, Kennedy's characters take on and shed multiple, interrelated identities that leave traces of each other. The protagonist is She who is Clara Passmore; her name paradoxically signals clarity and her intermediate, discursively non-existent racial status – between black and white, and between the absolute purity of the white woman and the excessive sexuality of non-biracial, black men and women.[52] She who is becomes at various points the Virgin Mary – who retains her high status as the mother of Jesus – but shifts into the Bastard character when she exercises her sexuality outside marriage, and transforms yet again into the Owl, a pre-Christian symbol of women's wisdom and power independent of men. Similarly, the Goddam Father locked in London's Tower of London, whom She who is trying to see, sometimes is the "Richest White Man in the Town" who seduced his black cook (who is Clara's biological mother and said to be a whore) and at other times functions as the black Reverend Passmore, who demands religious and familial subservience from his wife and adoptive daughter. Repeatedly denigrated by a chorus that proclaims that a Negro has no place in the western cultural lineage, She who is offers multiple narratives to the Negro Man, whom she has picked up on the subway, concerning her attempted union with her father. Fantasizing like her adoptive mother that her sexual movement toward the Negro Man constitutes the Christian

God's loving acceptance of her black/mulatta body, She who is achieves an apotheosis whereby she transmogrifies into the Owl. As such, She attains various, contradictory meanings revolving around wisdom associated with the Greek goddess Athena, harlotry, infidelity to Christian beliefs, death, and sterility.[53] In that She's last words are the Owl's hooting call of "whooo," Kennedy powerfully evokes the agonizing, phantasmagoric journey of the black intellectual woman's "search for meaning in a white culture that supplies her with no ancestral or sacred roots."[54] Such is the psychic damage that western colonialism has instituted, and these African Diaspora dramatists vigorously resist.

Dramatizing the return

In that the desire for return to a hospitable, nurturing environment is central to many definitions of diaspora, a number of plays enact that theme, hence our next category. Generally such dramas deploy the following trajectory. A contemporary descendant of slaves journeys to an African location. That this site may or may not have been involved in the transatlantic trade is almost irrelevant, for the "Africa" that is sought is more psychic than actual. Overwhelmed by the sights, sounds, smells, tastes, and mis-recognitions, she nonetheless perceives similarities between herself and the people who generously extend welcome. She has found "home," a point of origin and orientation that cancels out racist ascriptions. Like a long lost, but not forgotten, child, she has *returned* home and can then return, self-assured, self-possessed, and properly equipped for struggle in that other home in the Americas or Europe. Not surprisingly, this trope is taken up more by playwrights outside the continent, dramatists like US Americans Oni Faida Lampley in *The Dark Kalamazoo*[55] and Carlyle Brown in *The Fula from America: An African Journey,*[56] or Canadian Djanet Sears in *Afrika Solo.*[57]

Ama Ata Aidoo in *Dilemma of a Ghost,*[58] and Tess Onwueme in *The Missing Face,*[59] are among the Continental African playwrights tackling this trope,[60] but they do not necessarily subscribe to the trajectory of successful return. Aidoo leaves her "returnee" on the African Continent in an ambiguous relationship to Ghanaian in-laws with whom she can barely communicate. Onwueme constructs a contradictory text: on the one hand, she devotes much space to a spectacular picture of a family that, after initial difficulties, is able to reunite its Continental and diasporic members. But this family includes a Nigerian African American teenager, unimpressed by stories of an heroic Africa because they cannot teach him how to survive in the urban jungles of the United States. Though allotted much less dramatic space and perhaps overshadowed in performance by the theatrics of dance and praise recitation celebrating tradition and family unity, this teenager, nonetheless, significantly marks the potential irrelevance of diaspora.[61]

In contrast, some playwrights like Winsome Pinnock of Great Britain route the return not to the African Continent but to the Caribbean. In Pinnock's *Talking in Tongues*,[62] Leela resolves the psychic alienation she experiences in England through her contact with Sugar, a Jamaican resort worker, who acerbically comments on the emotional mammy-work or nurturing that all tourists expect of her. She says:

> I don't understand you people at all. Mikie right. He say you all sick, say unno come out here because you broken people ... What you want from me? ...You tell me what you looking for. Unno tourist think you belong here. But you come out and you don't know where to put yourself: one minute you talking sisterhood, the next minute you treating us like dirt. You just the same as all the others tourists them.[63]

Similarly, the husband in Mustapha Matura's *Meetings*[64] looks to the rural, Trinidadian peasantry as a site of authenticity that will counter the sterile materialism of his middle-class life and encourage resistance against development schemes advanced by the global North. Familiar foods from his childhood, now cooked by a young maid down from the hills, become the mechanism of a psychic return.

Comparing these plays of return, we can easily identify the reification of place, class, and gender operative in diasporic desire. Perhaps requiring us to exercise more compassion in our critiques is confrontation with the motivations directing such gestures: what conditions and wounds in the "other home" propel diaspora subjects to imagine these zones of purity and welcome, divorced from contemporary history? With what scars are people grappling in these imagined sites of origin? What are their strengths; what are diasporan strengths? How are these conditions similar and yet different? How might home – both in its present location and elsewhere – be imagined, not as the place of unchanging, family coherence, but as the ground of love and struggle, dynamic, open to difference, and responsive to the challenges of history in the present?

Multiple and overlapping diasporas

Consideration of dramas by playwrights like Pinnock and Matura also spotlights the existence of multiple and/or overlapping diasporas. Bearing in mind that the affective, cultural boundaries of diaspora are porous and shifting because these displaced people and their descendants must devise contingent modes of accommodation with their new environment that is itself dynamic, we might think of multiple diasporas in at least two distinct ways. One revolves around African Caribbeans who migrate to other Caribbean islands, North America, Britain, or elsewhere, eventually constituting a second, more temporally immediate diaspora. For example, Simone Schwarz-Bart addresses the isolating poverty of a farm laborer in Martinique who yearns for his wife back home in Haiti in *Ton beau capitaine*[65] (translated into English as *Your Beautiful Captain*). Black British plays like Kwame Kwei-Armah's *Elmina's Kitchen*[66] and Winsome Pinnock's *Leave Taking*,[67] or African-Canadian dramas like Maxine Bailey and Sharon M. Lewis's *Sistahs*[68] and US African American Lynn Nottage's *Intimate Apparel*,[69] all feature Caribbean characters, descendants of the historical African Diaspora, who have settled in the global North, which welcomes their labor but is hostile to their presence. Lest we think of multiple diasporas only in terms of migration from one destination to another, plays such as Pinnock's *A Hero's Welcome*[70] and *Mules*[71] offer a significant correction, because they dramatize longing for the colonial metropole among those who remain at home in the Caribbean, and a shuttling back and forth between so-called periphery and center. For many of the characters in this category, home as a site of stability and nurturance is non-existent; episodic movement, alienation, and desire for elsewhere shape their subjectivity.[72]

As in the case of the Du Boisian category discussed earlier, these works are foremost grounded in particular national realities: in some instances, playwrights choose to dramatize migrants' deep ambivalence about their location(s), while at other times, they see their work as part of a struggle to establish economic and political clout in the host nation. In making the critical intervention of grouping these plays together, we are once again engaging questions of what factors enable – or disable – recognition of similarities and shared fates amongst different national and transnational communities. Additionally, we are probing the meanings blackness or Africanness obtains – or sheds – as people and ideas circulate, dialog with each other, and confront local conditions.

A second example of multiple diasporas concerns what some, like historian Earl Lewis, have termed "overlapping diasporas" or instances, where people from one racial diaspora come into contact with members of another racial diaspora.[73] Again, the Caribbean offers examples, given the history of Indian and Chinese migration following the full emancipation of Africans in British colonies in the mid 1840s. But the term "overlapping" is problematic because it retains an assumption of bounded communities and does not gesture toward the power- or status-differentials operative in these encounters. Scripts by M. Nourbese Philip or Mustapha Matura, for example, capture some of that complexity. Born in Tobago, living and working in Canada since the 1970s first as a lawyer and then as a poet, novelist, and essayist,[74] Philip has written *Coups and Calypsos*,[75] a play that raises issues about douglarization through the prism of a failing marriage.

> "Douglarization" refers to racial mixing in a reproductive context in Trinidad and Tobago, where Indian and African populations are concentrated in almost equal numbers. The children of such unions are called "dougla," which is simply the extant Hindi variety for the word "two," but various negative connotations have evolved over time including the stigma of bastardization. "Douglarization" itself is a singularly nuanced term depending on which group uses it.[76]

Set against the backdrop of intermittent news of the 1990 coup, the couple's painful exposure of the racism each has experienced both on the islands and in England, where they have been schooled, becomes commentary on the larger challenges of fashioning social cohesion in the context of a racialized history, as it is lived both nationally and transnationally.

Matura, himself a *dougla* from Trinidad and long-time resident in England,[77] dramatizes in *Play Mas* interactions between Afro- and Indo-Trinidadians in the two decades prior to Philip's play. The two-act play revolves around preparations for Carnival in the pre-and post-independence periods. The ethnic hatred fostered by British imperial, divide-and-conquer labor policies is on full display in Act I, while in the post-colonial world of Act II, the reversal of roles celebrated in carnival has become a sinister reality. The once lowly Afro-Trinidadian shop employee has now become the chief of police determined to contain a Black Power rebellion by enticing his former Indo-Trinidadian boss to spy on the rebels with promises to route through his business large orders of military uniforms purchased with US American aid. Heady visions of independence in a just, multicultural society, animated by the national motto "All 'o we is one" and the assumed liberatory potential of carnival, have devolved into a world where everyone – a greedy black elite, complicit Indian business community, and even so-called Black Power advocates – is willing to "play mas" or be coopted by whoever has more material resources.[78] The drama critiques post-independence governance, but going beyond the text and the stage, one might ask whether these ethnic histories, repeatedly mobilized for political gain by self-serving groups, can be re-envisioned for the benefit of the majority.

African Diaspora drama as circulation

Another category of diaspora plays revolves around the circulation of an idea or text. One such idea is that of "Haiti" as the exemplar of resistance to racial slavery and dehumanization. Here we might group together such plays as Langston Hughes's *Emperor of Haiti* (aka *Troubled Island*),[79] C. L. R. James's *The Black Jacobins*,[80] Aimé Césaire's *The Tragedy of King Christophe*,[81] Edouard Glissant's *Monsieur Toussaint*,[82] Maryse Condé's *In the Time of the Revolution*,[83] and Derek Walcott's *The Haitian Trilogy*.[84] If we are not assuming, like Du Bois, that African Diaspora drama must necessarily be written by "us" black folk, then Eugene O'Neill's *The Emperor Jones*[85] or John Houseman and Orson Welles's 1936 *Black Macbeth* might be included as other examples of how that successful slave revolt fired imaginations concerning the possibilities of black governance. In examining the circulation of the idea of Haiti, we would focus necessarily on critical appropriation and reception: that is, on how different audiences of writers, directors, designers, performers, and spectators interpret, and how these various local understandings dialog with each other. Such study would raise questions like: how has "Haiti" been gendered? For which diaspora populations is it a symbol?[86] Does its non-resonance in other African Diaspora sites signal a limit of the concept?

The diversity of political positions espoused by this group of playwrights raises other questions concerning the saliency of diaspora as an organizing concept. We will want to consider what specific mode(s) of affiliation has/ have attracted a particular writer to the idea of Haiti. For example, factoring into comparative analysis the biographies of writers such as C. L. R. James or Aimé Césaire would lead to the question: what is the relationship of diaspora studies to internationalism as practiced by black people? Patterson and Kelley's advice is: "Our point here is that black internationalism does not always come out of Africa, nor is it necessarily engaged with pan-Africanism or other kinds of black-isms. Indeed, sometimes it lives through or is integrally tied to other kinds of international movements – socialism, communism, feminism, surrealism, religions such as Islam, and so on."[87]

Furthermore, while particular conditions in a given diaspora venue may point to a black globality or embeddedness in processes that are not exclusively black,[88] a text's circulation to another diaspora site may prompt a different reading of its appeal. Consider productions of Wole Soyinka's *The Beatification of Area Boy*[89] that occurred in locations as diverse as Leeds, England; Brooklyn New York; Sydney, Australia; and Kingston, Jamaica between 1995 and 1997/8. Given limited space, I will comment on only two locations, namely Leeds and Kingston.[90] Originally scheduled to premiere in Nigeria, this play about governmental and elite corruption eventually opened in Leeds after Soyinka was forced to flee because of military dictator Sani Abacha's order for his imprisonment. At the time of its premiere, the Nigerian government had issued a death sentence against playwright-activist

Ken Saro-Wiwa and his Ogoni Nine colleagues, and during the run of the play, all were executed. Critic James Gibbs has written that for English audiences, these performances assumed the character of eavesdropping on an intense debate amongst Diaspora Nigerians deeply concerned about political events in their home nation. Some two years later in Kingston, where many neighborhoods were terrorized by armed gangs of young people, artistic director Sheila Graham and her production team chose the play for its perceived critique of the impact of state-sponsored violence on youth.[91] Working with Soyinka, Graham's The Company Ltd. developed a Theatre for Development project with teens whose hunger for art, Soyinka has written, reminded him of the heady beginnings of his Orisun Theatre during the early years of Nigerian independence.[92] Perhaps Jamaican performers, designers, and audiences discovered in this play moments of felt, ancestral connection to the African Continent, but it is plausible to suspect that *Area Boy*'s appeal stemmed more from a consciousness of their shared status with Nigerians as residents of post-/ neo-colonial states whose fate is determined by the global North and complicit national elites.

(Re)thinking home queerly/quarely

As I have been arguing throughout, diaspora is an analytic and practice whereby systematically despised, marginalized communities recognize each other and imagine a nurturing home for themselves. The award-winning trilogy *The Brother/Sister Plays*,[93] written by African American Tarell Alvin McCraney, offers an invitation to (re-)examine the heteronormative assumptions underlying diaspora. Although diaspora signals a conceptual affiliation beyond the nation-state, it shares with nationalism a devotion to heterosexuality, the family, and home as sites where good citizens are produced. As we saw with Kennedy's female protagonist, woman's purity and reproduction guarantee the boundaries of the nation, differentiating it from those aliens beyond its borders and from those marginalized within its geography. "Within the familial and domestic space of the nation as imagined community, non-heteronormative sexuality is either criminalized, or disavowed and elided; it is seen both as a threat to national integrity and as perpetually outside the boundaries of nation, home, and family."[94]

Further, given its backward orientation to a point of cherished origin, diaspora longings can unleash images of an Eden-like plenitude and return to the mother's loving embrace.[95] "Queer" or same-sex desire disrupts this trajectory, for it remembers home as a space of painful contradiction and exclusion. Thus, an acknowledgement of queers in diaspora raises in a different register fundamental questions concerning the constitution of human affiliation, of unity within difference. Furthermore, the term *queer* points beyond the binarisms of fixed sexual identity, as in heterosexual/homosexual or gay/lesbian.[96] Yet in everyday as well as academic practice, it pays insufficient attention to race. Performance studies scholar E. Patrick Johnson proposes instead the neologism *quare*, derived from linguistic practices and familial experiences of growing up black in the Jim Crow South. From this perspective, he theorizes that a quare studies "must not deploy a totalizing and/or homogeneous formulation of identity, but rather a contingent, fragile coalition in the struggle against common oppressive forms."[97]

Although McCraney's trilogy revolves around three generations of a family living in the fictional city of San Pere near the Louisiana Bayou, *The Brothers Size* is most appropriate for this discussion because it repeats some characteristics of African Diaspora drama with a critical difference.[98] The play centers on Ogun Size, who owns an auto repair shop; his brother Oshoosi, who has just been released from the penitentiary; and Oshoosi's prison-buddy, Elegba. Ogun continually urges his younger brother to find a job, while Oshoosi and Elegba seem more interested in enjoying their freedom. The latter two steal a car, but Ogun opts to confront the police so that Oshoosi can flee, as Ogun tells him, without stopping until he is free. As their very names indicate, these characters are intimately related to the Yoruba and Fon gods of West Africa who accompanied their enslaved worshippers to the Americas. Like their divine namesakes, Ogun works with iron and can expertly repair cars, Oshoosi possesses a kind of warrior spirit and is searching for his unique mission in life, while Elegba navigates the liminal spaces between the living and the dead – by working at a funeral home – and between conscious and subconscious desire – by feeding Oshoosi's dreams.[99] According to Yoruba cosmology, Elegba – also known as the so-called trickster god Eshu – presides over the operation of fate by providing the individual with choices. Thus in McCraney's play, though it is Elegba who introduces the idea of stealing a car, it is Oshoosi who warms to the suggestion and acts, thereby setting in motion the sequence of events that result in his flight and possible discovery of his purpose in life. Dramatized are various implications of the term *brother*: is a brother simply a biological sibling? Or, can it be a man who has shared one's burden in times of extreme distress? How may a man express deep affection for his brother, particularly if that brother is a lover rather than a relative? To what extent is one responsible for his brother?

What is most innovative about this McCraney play is its sensitive exploration of black men's interiority in the context of a United States that imagines them primarily as strong, hypersexual bodies without minds or regard for social propriety. Assuming same-sex desire as generative, McCraney instead projects a range of emotions amongst his black male characters, thereby enlarging the boundaries of who constitutes family, community, race, and nation. Though much of the critical response to date has understandably focused on the trilogy's seemingly novel allusions to Yoruba cosmology, his use of this resource is quite old, harkening back to Herskovits's concept of Diaspora as retentions of African culture. We should note, however, the dynamic, contemporary quality of these so-called retentions, for, as McCraney has explained in interviews, not only was his grandfather a Baptist minister who dramatically acted out his sermons, but many of his neighbors in the Miami housing project, where he grew up, were immigrants from the Caribbean who loved telling stories rooted in syncretized, African-inflected religions, like *vodoun* from Haiti and *santería* or *lucumi* from Cuba.[100] In this instance, the homeland to which McCraney himself, his neighbors, and his characters are oriented is not the "Mother Africa" of imagined, pristine origins, but "Africa" in both its historical and ongoing, dialogic relationships to Europe, the Americas, and the rest of the world.[101]

Conclusion

This chapter has attempted to cover a lot of analytic and geographic ground by proposing various ways in which we may define African Diaspora drama. Poet Claude McKay, with whose vision the chapter began, despaired that black people had been rendered inhuman and homeless in the world. We have seen that peoples of African descent have deployed Diaspora as one analytic and practice whereby a collective family and home were re-established. In recognizing similarities amongst various, far-flung communities, they necessarily opted to ignore differences. This examination of drama has sought to identify the bases upon which unity was proclaimed.

Moving from the largest organizational category of African Diaspora drama as simply those plays written "by us" who are of African descent, I have proposed several other modalities of recognition: the presence of African "survivalisms" as content or structure; resistance to colonial governance; "return" to the site of an imagined authenticating origin; multiple and/or overlapping sites of origin and affiliation; circulation amongst various diaspora communities with concomitant shifts in the meanings attached to black- or African-ness; and quareness, with its subversive challenge to the heteronormativity of most definitions of diaspora. In arguing that we understand African Diaspora drama as a range of articulations, I have asserted that we are challenged not only to identify similarity but, equally importantly, to reflect upon how we may be instituting exclusion. At stake in all these articulations are fundamental questions: how do we recognize the humanity of (an) other and build community? How do we as spectators, readers, and/or practitioners use the space of drama and theatre to imagine, rehearse, and share hopes for a better world in which people can be at home?

NOTES

1 Claude McKay, *Harlem Shadows: The Poems of Claude McKay*, introd. Max Eastman (New York: Harcourt Brace, 1922).

2 Jana Evans Braziel and Anita Mannur cite the Greek origins, while Giles Mohan and A. B. Zack Williams assert that the Greeks originally conceived of the word in terms of production diffusion. See Jana Evans Braziel and Anita Mannur, *Theorizing Diaspora: A Reader*, Keyworks in Cultural Studies 6 (Malden, MA: Blackwell, 2003); and Giles Mohan and A. B. Zack, "Globalisation from Below: Conceptualising the Role of the African Diasporas in African Development," *Review of African Political Economy*, 29.92 (2002): 211–36.

3 See Edward A. Alpers, "Recollecting Africa: Diasporic Memory in the Indian Ocean," *African Studies Review*, 43.1 (2000): 83–99; Joseph E. Harris (ed.), *Global Dimensions of the African Diaspora*, 2nd edn. (Washington, DC: Howard University Press, 1993); Colin A. Palmer, "Defining and Studying the Modern African Diaspora," *Journal of Negro History*, 85.1–2 (2000): 27–32; and Paul Tiyambe Zeleza, "Rewriting the African Diaspora: Beyond the Black Atlantic," *African Affairs*, 104.414 (2005): 35–68.

4 See Kim D. Butler, "Defining Diaspora, Refining a Discourse," *Diaspora*, 10.2 (2001): 189–219.

5 See Brent Hayes Edwards, *The Practice of Diaspora: Literature, Translation, and the Rise of Black Internationalism* (Cambridge, MA: Harvard University Press, 2003).

6 See Stuart Hall, "Cultural Identity and Diaspora," in *Identity: Community, Culture, Difference*, ed. Jonathan Rutherford (London: Lawrence & Wishart, 1990), 223–37.

7 See Kobena Mercer, "Diaspora Culture and the Dialogic Imagination: The Aesthetics of Black Independent Film in Britain" (1988), in Braziel and Mannur, *Theorizing Diaspora*, 247–60.

8 Michael A. Gomez, *Exchanging Our Country Marks: The Transformation of African Identities in the Colonial and Antebellum South* (Chapel Hill: University of North Carolina Press, 1998).

9 Tiffany Ruby Patterson and Robin D. G. Kelley, "Unfinished Migrations: Reflections on the African Diaspora and the Making of the Modern World," *African Studies Review*, 43.1 (2000): 11–45.

10 Lawrence Grossberg (ed.), "On Postmodernism and Articulation, an Interview with Stuart Hall," *Journal of Communication Inquiry*, 10 (1986): 45–60.

11 Mercer, "Diaspora Culture," 255.

12 In deploying the contrast between *rooted* and *routed*, I am citing Paul Gilroy. See Paul Gilroy, *The Black Atlantic: Modernity and Double Consciousness* (Cambridge, MA: Harvard University Press, 1993).

13 Indeed, Ivy Wilson and Ayo Coly, in introducing a journal issue devoted to diaspora topics, note the "gradual recession of Africa in diasporic discourse." See Ivy G. Wilson and Ayo A. Coly, "Black is the Color of the Cosmos; or, *Callaloo* and the Cultures of the Diaspora Now," *Callaloo*, 30.2 (2007): 415–19 (417).

14 Paul Carter Harrison and Carlton and Barbara Molette are erudite examples of this tradition. See Sandra L. Richards, "'Function at the Junction?': African Diaspora Studies and Theater Studies," in *The African Diaspora and the Disciplines*, ed. Tejumola Olaniyan and James H. Sweet (Bloomington: Indiana University Press, 2010).

15 Note that though the essentialism of this declaration has been disavowed, there may be good economic reason for retaining Du Bois's formulation. White playwrights, directors, designers, and theatres have enjoyed considerable success in representing black experiences – think of the recent example of Tony Kushner's *Caroline, or Change* on Broadway – and they continue to benefit from a legacy of greater resources being allocated for their efforts. See W. E. B. Du Bois, "Krigwa Players Little Negro Theatre," *The Crisis*, 32 (July, 1926): 134–6.

16 A notable exception to this assertion is Kenneth Warren's book in which he contends that African American literature is an historical designation that no longer obtains today because of the final dismantling of Jim Crow discrimination; according to Warren, though African Americans continue to write, they no longer create African American literature. See Kenneth Warren, *What Was African American Literature?* (Cambridge, MA: Harvard University Press, 2011).

17 See LeRoi Jones [Imamu Amiri Baraka], *Dutchman and The Slave: Two Plays* (New York: Morrow Quill, 1964).

18 See Djanet Sears, *The Adventures of a Black Girl in Search of God* (Toronto: Playwrights Canada Press, 2003).

19 Note the critical observation of J. Lorand Matory, that many aspects of African Diaspora culture that we term "survivals" are, rather, the product of active dialog, travel, and interactions between African and diaspora communities. See J. Lorand Matory, "Surpassing 'Survival': On the Urbanity of 'Traditional Religion' in the Afro-Atlantic World," *The Black Scholar: Journal of Black Studies and Research*, 30.3–4 (2000): 36–43; and Melville Herskovits, *The Myth of the Negro Past* (New York: Harper, 1941).

20 James V. Hatch coined the term "neo-Africanisms" to designate "deliberate and conscious attempts by Black Americans to use African themes and materials" in distinction from Africanisms "as familiar to Americans as yams in the grocery store, and because they are common as the earth ... less visible and therefore unacknowledged." See James Vernon Hatch, "Some African Influences on the Afro-American Theatre," in *The Theater of Black Americans: A Collection of Critical Essays*, 2 vols. (Englewood Cliffs, NJ: Prentice-Hall, 1980), Vol. 1, 13.

21 Herskovits, *The Myth of the Negro Past*, 298.

22 See May Miller, *Riding the Goat* (Alexandria, VA: Alexander Street Press, 2004).

23 Corey D. B. Walker, *A Noble Fight: African American Freemasonry and the Struggle for Democracy in America* (Urbana: University of Illinois Press, 2008).

24 The phrase "hidden in plain view" refers to the reputed use of quilts to guide runaways to freedom on the underground railroad. See Jacqueline Tobin and Raymond G. Dobard, *Hidden in Plain View: The Secret Story of Quilts and the Underground Railroad* (New York: Doubleday, 1999).

25 VèVè A. Clark, "Developing Diaspora Literacy and *Marasa* Consciousness," *Theatre Survey*, 50 (2009): 9–18.

26 *Ibid.*, 42 (original emphasis).

27 See Dennis C. Scott, *An Echo in the Bone* (Alexandria, VA: Alexander Street Press, 2002).

28 See Sistren Theatre Collective, *QPH*, in *Postcolonial Plays: An Anthology*, ed. Helen Gilbert (London: Routledge, 2011), 157–79.

29 See August Wilson, *Joe Turner's Come and Gone*, 1st edn., The August Wilson Century Cycle (St. Paul, MN: Theatre Communications Group: 2007).

30 Renu Juneja, "Recalling the Dead in Dennis Scott's *An Echo in the Bone*," *Ariel: A Review of International English Literature*, 23.1 (1992): 97–114.

31 James Clifford, *Routes: Travel and Translation in the Late Twentieth Century* (Cambridge, MA: Harvard University Press, 1970), 263.

32 See Ntozake Shange, *for colored girls who have considered suicide / when the rainbow is enuf* (New York: Scribner Poetry, 1997).

33 See August Wilson, *The Piano Lesson* (New York: Dutton, 1990).

34 Maya Deren, *Divine Horseman: The Living Gods of Haiti* (New Paltz, NY: McPherson, 1983).

35 See ahdri zhina mandiela, *Speshal Rikwes* (Toronto: Sister Vision, 1985).

36 See Trey Anthony, *'Da Kink in My Hair* (Toronto: Playwrights Canada Press, 2005).

37 See Sharon Bridgforth, *Love Conjure/Blues*, 1st edn. (Washington, DC: RedBone Press, 2004).

38 See Kamilah Forbes and Hip Hop Junction Theatre, "Rhyme Deferred," in *The Fire This Time: African American Plays for the 21st Century*, ed. Harry J. Elam and Robert Alexander (New York: Theatre Communications Group, 2004).

39 Avery F. Gordon, *Ghostly Matters: Haunting and the Sociological Imagination* (Minneapolis: University of Minnesota Press, 1997).

40 See Derek Walcott, *Dream on Monkey Mountain and Other Plays* (New York: Farrar, Straus, and Giroux, 1970).

41 See Aimé Césaire, *A Tempest [Une Tempête]: Based on Shakespeare's* The Tempest, *Adaptation for a Black Theatre* (London: Oberon, 2000).

42 See Abdias do Nascimento, *Sortilege (Black Mystery)*, *Callaloo*, 18.4 (Fall, 1995): 821–62.

43 See Kobina Sekyi, *The Blinkards*, African Writers Series 136 (London: Heinemann, 1974).

44 See Adrienne Kennedy, *Adrienne Kennedy in One Act* (Minneapolis: University of Minnesota Press, 1988).

45 *The Blinkards* is an exception in that it was written in 1915. *Dream on Monkey Mountain* premiered in 1967; *Une Tempête* premiered in 1969 and was translated into English as *A Tempest* in 1985; *Sortilegio* premiered in Brazil in 1978 and was translated into English around the same year; *Funnyhouse of a Negro* and *The Owl Answers* premiered in 1964 and 1965 respectively.

46 See Franz Fanon, *The Wretched of the Earth* [*Les damnés de la terre*], trans. Richard Philcox (New York: Grove Press, 2004).

47 H. Barnor Hesse, "Forgotten like a Bad Dream: Atlantic Slavery and the Ethics of Postcolonial Memory," in *Relocating Colonialism*, ed. David Theo Goldberg and Ato Quayson (Oxford, Blackwell, 2002).

48 One need think only of the critical firestorm that the premiere of Shange's feminist *for colored girls* provoked, or feminist critiques of Fanon. See Erskine Peter, "Some Tragic Propensities of Ourselves: The Occasion of Ntozake Shange's *for colored girls who have considered suicide / when the rainbow is enuf*," *The Journal of Ethnic Studies*, 6 (1978): 79–85; and T. Denean Sharpley-Whiting, *Fanon: Conflicts and Feminisms* (Lanham, MD: Rowman & Littlefield, 1998).

49 Helen Gilbert and Joanne Tompkins, *Post-Colonial Drama: Theory, Practice, Politics* (London: Routledge, 1996), 32.

50 Jones, *Dutchman*, 35.

51 Nascimento, *Sortilege*, 823.

52 Jeanie Forte, "Kennedy's Body Politic: The Mulatta, Menses, and the Medusa," in *Intersecting Boundaries: The Theatre of Adrienne Kennedy*, ed. Paul K. Bryant-Jackson and Lois More Overbeck (Minneapolis: University of Minnesota Press, 1992), 157–69.

53 Robert L. Tener, "Theatre of Identity: Adrienne Kennedy's Portrait of the Black Woman," *Studies in Black Literature*, 6.2 (Summer, 1975): 3.

54 *Ibid.*

55 See Oni Faida Lampley, *The Dark Kalamazoo*, in Elam and Alexander, *The Fire This Time*, 143–69.

56 See Carlyle Brown, *The Fula from America: An African Journey* (Alexandria, VA: Alexander Street Press, 2004).

57 See Djanet Sears, *Afrika Solo* (Toronto: Sister Vision, 1990).

58 See Ama Ata Aidoo, *The Dilemma of a Ghost* (Accra: Longmans, 1965).

59 See Osonye Tess Onwueme, *The Missing Face* (Alexandria, VA: Alexander Street Press, 2002).

60 Note that Onwueme is a long-time resident of the United States; in that she travels back and forth between her natal home in Nigeria and Michigan, she may wish to describe herself as both a Continental African and a diasporan.

61 See Sandra L. Richards, "Dramatizing the Diaspora's Return: Tess Onwueme's *The Missing Face* and Ama Ata Aidoo's *The Dilemma of a Ghost*," in *The Legacy of Efua Sutherland: Pan-African Cultural Activism*, ed. Anne V. Adams and Esi Sutherland-Addy (Banbury: Ayebia Clarke, 2007), 113–21.

62 See Winsome Pinnock, *Talking in Tongues*, in *Black Plays Three*, ed. Yvonne Brewster (London: Methuen Drama, 1995).

63 Richards, "Dramatising the Diaspora's Return," 223.

64 See Mustapha Matura, *Play Mas; Independence; and Meetings: Three Plays*, Methuen New Theatrescript 7 (London: Methuen, 1982).

65 See Simone Schwarz-Bart, *Ton beau capitaine*, in *Plays by Women: An International Anthology*, ed. Catherine Temerson and Françoise Kourilsky (New York: Ubu Repertory Theatre, 1988).

66 See Kwame Kwei-Armah, *Elmina's Kitchen* (London: Methuen, 2003).

67 See Winsome Pinnock, *Leave Taking*, in *First Run: New Plays by New Writers*, ed. Kate Harwood (London: Nick Hern, 1989), 139–89.

68 See Maxine Bailey and Sharon M. Lewis, *Sistahs*, in *Testifyin': Contemporary African Canadian Drama*, ed. Djanet Sears (Toronto: Playwrights Canada Press, 2000).

69 See Lynn Nottage, *Intimate Apparel* (New York: Dramatists Play Service, 2005).

70 See Winsome Pinnock, *A Hero's Welcome*, in *Six Plays by Black and Asian Women Writers*, ed. Kadija George (London: Aurora Metro Press, London Arts Board, 1993), 21–55.

71 See Winsome Pinnock, *Mules* (London: Faber, 1996).

72 Carole Boyce Davies, *Black Women, Writing and Identity: Migrations of the Subject* (London: Routledge, 1994).

73 See Earl Lewis, "To Turn as on a Pivot: Writing African Americans into a History of Overlapping Diasporas," *American Historical Review*, 100.3 (1995): 765–87.

74 "Biography of M. NourbeSe Philip," www.nourbese.com/biography.htm (last accessed February 17, 2012).

75 See Marlene Nourbese Philip, *Coups and Calypsos: A Play* (Toronto: Mercury Press, 2001).

76 Ramabai Espinet, "Introduction to *Coups and Calypsos*," in Sears, *Testifyin'*, 81.

77 "Mustapha Matura," www.mustaphamatura.com/biography.php (last accessed February 17, 2012).

78 Raimund Schaffner, "Carnival, Cultural Identity, and Mustapha Matura's *Play Mas*," *New Theatre Quarterly*, 18.2 (2000): 186–95.

79 See Langston Hughes, *Emperor of Haiti*, ed. Leslie Catherine Sanders and Nancy Johnston (Cambridge: ProQuest, 2005).

80 See C. L. R. James, *The Black Jacobins: Toussaint L'Ouverture and the San Domingo Revolution*, 2nd edn. (New York: Vintage Books, 1989).

81 See Aimé Césaire, *The Tragedy of King Christophe* [*La tragédie du roi Christophe*]: *A Play*, trans. Ralph Manheim (New York: Grove Press, 1970).

82 See Edouard Glissant, *Monsieur Toussaint: A Play*, trans. J. Michael Dash with the author (Boulder, CO: Lynne Rienner Publishers, 2005).

83 See Maryse Condé, *In the Time of the Revolution* (Alexandria, VA: Alexander Street Press, 2003).

84 See Derek Walcott, *The Haitian Trilogy*, 1st edn. (New York: Farrar, Straus, and Giroux, 2002).

85 See Eugene O'Neill, *The Emperor Jones* (Cambridge: ProQuest, 2005).

86 Cilas Kemedjio asks a related question: "The Caribbean holds a memory of Africa, but what place does the Caribbean occupy in the imaginary of African peoples?" See Cilas Kemedjio, "Glissant's Africas: From Departmentalization to the Poetics of Relation," *Research in African Literatures*, 32.4 (2006): 92–116 (112).

87 Patterson and Kelley, "Unfinished Migrations."

88 *Ibid.*, 24–8.

89 See Wole Soyinka, *The Beatification of Area Boy: A Lagosian Kaleidoscope* (London: Methuen Drama, 1995).

90 For an extended discussion of the circulation of *Area Boy*, see Richards, "'Function at the Junction?'"

91 Awam Amkpa, *It's All about Downtown*, video recording (Amherst, MA: Five Colleges Incorporated/Mt. Holyoke College, 1997).

92 See Wole Soyinka, "Foreword: A Letter from Kingston," in *Theater Matters: Performance and Culture on the World Stage*, ed. Richard Boon and Jane Plastow (Cambridge: Cambridge University Press, 1998), xi–xviii; and "From Ghetto to Garrison: A Chronic Case of Orisunitis," *Research in African Literatures*, 30.4 (Winter, 1999): 6–23.

93 The trilogy consists of *In the Red and Brown Water*, workshopped and produced first in 2006; *The Brothers Size*, produced first in 2007; and *Marcus; or, The Secret of Sweet*, also premiered in 2007. The entire trilogy was first produced in 2008–9 by the McCarter Theatre Center. See Tarell Alvin McCraney, *The Brother/Sister Plays*, 1st edn. (New York: Theatre Communications Group, 2010).

94 Gayatri Gopinath, "Nostalgia, Desire, Diaspora," in Evans and Mannur, *Theorizing Diaspora*, 263.

95 Hall, "Cultural Identity."

96 E. Patrick Johnson, "'Quare' Studies; or, (Almost) Everything I Know about Queer Studies I Learned from My Grandmother," in *Black Queer Studies: A Critical Anthology*, ed. E. Patrick Johnson and Mae G. Henderson (Durham, NC: Duke University Press, 2005), 128.

97 *Ibid.*, 136.

98 Here I am riffing on the practice of repetition with a critical difference that scholars like Henry Louis Gates, Jr. and playwrights like Suzan-Lori Parks identify as one of the key features of black cultural production. See Henry Louis Gates, Jr., *The Signifying Monkey: A Theory of Afro-American Literary Criticism* (Oxford; New York: Oxford University Press, 1988).

99 The names have variant spellings, depending on different New World languages: spelled Oshoosi in McCraney's play, this god's name can also be spelled Oxossi (in the Brazilian religion of *candomblé*) or Ochosi (in Cuban *santería*). Similarly, Elegba, who functions as the divine messenger of the most powerful god Oludumare, has several spellings: to the Fon of West Africa he is Legba; to the Yoruba of West Africa he is Esu, Elegba, and Elegbara; to *candomblé* devotees he is Exu; and to *lucumi* or *Santería* followers he is Eshu Eleggua.

100 Christine Dolen, "Dreams of a Bright Moon," *American Theatre*, 25.3 (March, 2008): 54–5.

101 "Collaboration and Connection: Director Tina Landau and Playwright Tarell Alvin McCraney Discuss *The Brother/Sister Plays* with Steppenwolf Artistic Director Martha Lavey," Steppenwolf theatre program, January 21–May 23, 2010, 22–6.

13

HARRY J. ELAM, JR.

Black theatre in the age of Obama

10 years after writing the essay "equation for black people on stage" I'm standing at the same crossroads asking the same questions. No sweat. Sometimes you can walk a hundred miles and end up in the same spot. The world ain't round for nothing right? What is a black play? The definition is housed in the reality of two things that occurred recently and almost simultaneously: 26 August 05, playwright scholar poet king August Wilson announces he is dying of cancer, and hurricane Katrina devastated the Gulf Coast. It feels like judgment day. What I'm talking about today is the same and different. I was tidy then. And now Im tidier. Tidier today like a tidal wave.

What is a black play?
A black play is angry.
A black play is fierce.
A black play is double voiced but rarely confused.
A black play got style.
A black play is of the people by the people and for the people.
A black play is smooth but not slick, heavy but not thick, can't be tamed,
often does not comb its hair, wipes its mouth with the back of its black hand
or with a linen napkin whichever is more readily available.
A black play is late.
A black play is RIGHT ON and RIGHT ON TIME.
A black play is deep.
A black play is armed / to the teeth.
A black play bows to god then rows the boat ashore.
A black play makes do if it got to / fights / screams / sings / dreams / WORKS
IT / talks in code and tells it like it is ALL UP IN YA FACE.
A black play gives you five.
A black play is robust and alive.
A black play is in the house and looking *good*, too.
A black play is *bad* motherfucker.
A black play does not exist.
Every play is a black play.
SAY WHAT?[1]

In this extended epigraph from her essay, "New black math," Pulitzer-Prize-winning playwright Suzan-Lori Parks foregrounds the issues I examine in this chapter: how should we understand what constitutes a Black play and Black theatre in the twenty-first century? At the outset of her remarks in 2005, Parks returns to questions she had addressed some ten years earlier. Today, in the age of Obama – the period following the election of the first black president of the United States, Barack Obama – the matter of how we should define or categorize Black theatre still has critical, cultural, and political relevance. In fact, these are questions that have been reborn and revisited again and again with answers that are always contextual, politically charged, and historically specific. Parks goes on to proclaim simply that "A black play IZ." Here she underscores the fixed state of black theatre as an institution and practice, and even as a subject of academic study. For black theatre scholars, students, spectators, and practitioners, surely black theatre "is." However, if Black theatre history has taught us anything, it is that this constant is constantly reconstructed: Black theatre therefore is not simply a being but a doing; it is a thing done. Thus, Parks's "New Black Math," appropriating rhetorical strategies from Ralph Ellison's famous prologue to *Invisible Man*, assures us that while Black theatre "is," Black theatre, just as assuredly, ain't. Indeed, this is a profound and productive contradiction.

How do we define Black theatre, and what are the ethics of it? Throughout Black theatre history, as well as in the new millennium, these have been complex questions. In 1926, W. E. B. Du Bois now famously called for Black theatre to be "About us ... By us ... For us [and] Near us."[2] The notion of "About us" in Du Bois's four fundamental principles for Negro theatre foregrounds the necessity of having plays that document black experiences. Yet, after writing the classic, groundbreaking play of the African American theatrical canon, *A Raisin in the Sun* (1959), African American playwright Lorraine Hansberry chose to focus her next play, *The Sign in Sidney Brustein's Window* (1964), not around Alvin, the solitary black character in the drama, but rather on the central Jewish figure in the play, Sidney Brustein, and his crisis of consciousness. Du Bois's call for Black theatre to be "For us" becomes further complicated in the contemporary period by the achievements of the late August Wilson. On the one hand, with a Broadway theatre in his name dedicated in 2005, August Wilson seems to represent as the fulfillment of Du Bois's manifesto: black art of the highest quality. Wilson stands as not only the most significant African American playwright, but the most important American playwright of the late twentieth century. Yet, notably, Wilson's plays premiered principally in regional theatres, not in theatres situated within black urban enclaves. In fact, Wilson was the most produced American playwright of the 1990s as well as of the first decade of the twenty-first century. This means that audiences coming to see his work were not singularly, or even overwhelmingly, black. Even then, with the example of the two most prominent African American playwrights, Hansberry and Wilson, the definition of what constitutes Black theatre must be repeatedly reassessed, potentially reconstituted, and recognized as dependent on the social and cultural context of the work as well as the artistic agency and agendas of theatre practitioners.

Accordingly, in the age of Obama, in a time that some have argued is post-soul, or post-black, or even post-racial, the concepts and practices of how we understand Black theatre have been continually contested and even redrawn, with borders challenged and potentially rearticulated. A new cadre of black playwrights has emerged, each writer with very different responses to how they situate themselves and their work as black artists. These playwrights' new self-assessments have occurred at the same time as the debuts of an unprecedented number of plays about race written by non-black playwrights. Not since the 1920s and the work of Ridgely Torrence, DuBose Heyward, Paul Green, and Eugene O'Neill have white playwrights or non-black playwrights felt as authorized to investigate black experiences. *Race*, by white Jewish playwright David Mamet, came to Broadway in 2009. Also in 2009, the critically acclaimed avant-garde play, *The Shipment*, written and directed by Korean American playwright Young Jean Kim, appeared off Broadway. Then, in 2010, the controversial Broadway musical *The Scottsboro Boys* – with music by John Kander and Fred Ebb, book by David Thompson, directed and choreographed by Susan Stroman, all white artists – received twelve Tony Award nominations. The late fall of 2010 brought the white playwright John Guare's epic tale, *Free Man of Color*, to Lincoln Center, featuring the talented black actors Mos Def and Jeffrey Wright, and noted black director George C. Wolfe. Du Bois's call for Black theatre in part responded to the romantic racialism of the 1920s that witnessed the exploitation of black representation by white authors. O'Neill's *Emperor Jones* (1920) and *All God's Chillun* (1924), Marc Connelly's *Green Pastures* (1920), Paul Green's *Abraham's Bosom* (1927), and DuBose Heyward's *Porgy* (1927) all to varying degrees portray blacks as primitives, as noble and flawed savages. Problematic for Du Bois was not only how these playwrights depicted blackness, but also that the mechanisms of social power in America and the implicit hierarchies of race licensed such cultural production. If the social context of black life and the inequitable system of racial privilege enabled such portrayals of race then, what of now and this particular resurgence of the creation of black images by non-black playwrights? What does the current moment and its reformed politics of race, in which we have elected a black United States president, tell us about the evolving meanings of blackness and who controls these meanings?

Certainly the politics of race during and after the election of Barack Obama have impacted the definitions of, and access to, African American theatre. Opinion polls of young voters, aged eighteen to thirty-five, who overwhelmingly voted for Obama, reveal that they perceive race quite differently from earlier generations of United States citizens. Moreover, in his campaign and subsequent election, Obama has ushered in a new age of black politics that has deliberately looked back to, and has moved beyond, earlier paradigms of race-based political patronage. As a presidential candidate, Obama did not pitch his campaign primarily at purportedly African American issues such as social justice and civil rights. Rather, he effectively reached across racial divides and appealed to what he perceived as the common concerns of all Americans. His own family history as the son of a white mother from Kansas and a black African immigrant from Kenya complicates the matters of race. Even as Obama identifies as black and checked the black box on his 2010 census, his heritage has allowed others to construct different narratives; he was black but different; he was mixed race and not black, or, for those in the extreme, not even American.

Correspondingly, in the age of Obama, emerging black artists have sought to find new labels for their work and have attempted to push beyond previous definitions of black art. These young artists, as Mary Schmidt Campbell notes, "found the label 'black art' imprisoning culturally and esthetically. They expressed the need to participate more expansively in a world that, in their eyes, had grown more connected, geographically mobile, culturally fluid, and porous."[3] The idea that the social environment encourages increased creative freedom has propelled black artists to desire more capacious or alternative understandings of their aesthetics. Art curator Thelma Golden, in the catalogue for the 2001 "Freestyle" exhibition, has christened this new moment in artistic production "post-black." According to Golden, the post-black is "characterized by artists who were adamant about not being labeled solely as 'black' artists, though their work was steeped, in fact deeply interested, in redefining complex notions of blackness."[4] The post-black does not connote a move beyond blackness nor imply that race no longer matters. Rather, the post-black involves expanding and interrogating what blackness means. Golden maintains that "post-black" is "the new black."[5] The dynamism of the post-black emerges in this rich racial paradox. Liberated from past racial exigencies, post-black artists can push beyond previous racial borders and explore new racial meanings. Golden continues, "[post-black artists'] work, in all its various forms, speaks to an

258

individual freedom that is the result of this transitional moment in the quest
to define ongoing changes in African-American art and ultimately to ongoing
redefinition of blackness in contemporary culture."[6] This "new black," then,
reflects the changing political climate in which race signifies differently. The
post-black represents a new black that is simultaneously free from, and yet
connected to, the legacies of the black past.

Suzan-Lori Parks's 2005 essay, "An Equation for Black People Onstage,"
functions as a manifesto for how this new black artistic movement might be
realized in Black theatre:

> There are many ways of defining Blackness and there are many ways of pre-
> senting Blackness onstage. The Klan does not have to be outside the door for
> black people to have lives worthy of dramatic literature ... And what happens
> when we choose a concern other than race to focus on? What kind of drama
> do we get? Let's do the math: ... BLACK PEOPLE + x = NEW DRAMATIC
> CONFLICT (NEW TERRITORY).[7]

As evidenced by the quote above, Parks calls for Black theatre to move
beyond portraying blackness in relation to whiteness. She calculates a different value for black cultural production – unlike the dogmatism of Amiri
Baraka's 1965 manifesto "The Revolutionary Theatre," which proclaims
that the utility of black art depends on its viability as a weapon in the struggle for black liberation.[8] Rather, Parks proposes that post-black playwrights
must construct a Black theatre that celebrates and advocates the diversity of
black experiences. The social climate in which America has elected a black
president has proven conducive to such artistic creation. At the same time,
it is this new black art that is helping to define blackness in the age of
Obama.

Obama comes to the theatre

In fact, a watershed moment in the development of Black theatre in America
occurred in June, 2009 when Barack Obama and his wife Michelle went to see
white director Bartlett Sher's production of August Wilson's *Joe Turner's Come
and Gone* at Lincoln Center. *Joe Turner* had originally appeared on Broadway
in 1988 under the direction of famed black director Lloyd Richards, and won
that year's New York Drama Critics Circle Award for best play. Keith Herbert
and Matthew Chase proclaimed in *New York Newsday*, "The nation's first
black president was in town for a date night with his wife Saturday night that
included a play about the sons and daughters of newly freed slaves."[9] Set in the
progressive era of 1911, as blacks began the great migration from the South to
the North, *Joe Turner* is the most metaphysical and non-realistic play within

Wilson's cycle of twentieth-century plays, and, accordingly, is a challenge for any director. It is the author's favorite play, as well as one that scholars have repeatedly examined and re-examined with its assertion of the African presence in America, with its articulations of the power of the spirit, its representation of ritual observances and spiritual rebirth. Thus on one hand, the fact that the president of the United States and the First Lady went on a date night to a production of *Joe Turner* brought increased publicity and public awareness to this revival and to its celebrated African American playwright, August Wilson. After all, this was still the honeymoon period for America's first black president and the early height of his international popularity. Obama's attendance functioned then as an official affirmation of the value and vibrancy of Wilson's drama, and of Black theatre more generally.

At the same time, even as Obama's date night at *Joe Turner* provided sanction for the Lincoln Center revival, it also pointed to the complex nature of blackness, as well as the layered signification and often problematic ramifications of this production for Black theatre. The play, the playwright, and the president represent an illuminating triad: Obama, the son of an African and white American attending a play by the son of a white German baker and an African American that attempts to foreground the Africanness still resonant in African American life. Both Wilson and Obama, even with their mixed heritage, proudly identify as black. In so doing, they testify to blackness not as a fixed entity but as a product of social construction and lived experience. Yet, the fact that a white director mounted this particular production of *Joe Turner* raises important issues about the cultural transmission of blackness and the production of Black theatre. Notably, in the late 1980s, Wilson refused to let his Pulitzer-Prize-winning play *Fences* (1986) become a Hollywood film without a black director. He outlines his rationale for this decision in an essay entitled, "I Want a Black Director." "No wonder I had been greeted with incredulous looks when I suggested a black director for *Fences*. I sat in the office of Paramount Pictures suggesting that someone who was affected by an undesirable condition, who was a violator of public regulations, who was sullen, unqualified, and marked by a malignant influence, direct the film."[10] Wilson's ironic comments reflect his sense of the pejorative values attached to black people in Hollywood. He desires a black director who would have cultural familiarity with, and sensitivity to, the material, but who would also help to revise the unequal politics of representation in American film and media.[11] As Michael Awkward writes,

> Of preeminent importance to the playwright, I believe is whether, given the preeminence of caucacentric discourse and actions in our nation, Afro-Americans can afford to allow patterns of expressive cultural distribution to continue

wherein blacks remain pawns to the whims and racialist will of white entrepreneurial forces interested primarily in economic bottom lines rather than in
working to destroy the still-evident barriers to social, economic and cultural
power for a large portion of the black population.[12]

Awkward maintains that Wilson's demand for a black director serves as an
act of resistance against the dominant racial hierarchy that limits black social
and cultural agency. Yet some have argued that with the changing percep-
tions of race evident in the age of Obama, such political stands as those of
Wilson are no longer necessary. In the years since Wilson's death in 2005,
the number of white directors staging black plays has steadily increased.
In fact, Wilson's white assistant directed Wilson's own final one-man show,
How I Learned What I Learned, performed in 2004 at the Seattle Repertory
Theatre. Still, the selection of Sher to mount the highly visible 2009 New
York revival of *Joe Turner* caused considerable unrest in Black theatre circles.
Marion McClinton, who had directed New York productions of later Wilson
works such as *Jitney* in 2000 and *King Hedley II* in 2001, called the decision
"straight up institutional racism."[13] McClinton's reaction points to the continuing system of white control over cultural production that determines the
access to directing opportunities for him and other black directors.

Bartlett Sher, in accepting the assignment of directing *Joe Turner*, consciously sought to respond to the existing racial climate as well as to the
racial politics at play in his selection. Discussing the play with *The New
York Times*, Sher – the 2008 Tony Award and Drama Desk Award winner for the Broadway revival of Rodgers and Hammerstein's *South Pacific* –
asserts the relevance of Wilson's classic, set in 1911, to the United States
in 2009: "Every show I do has to speak to the times."[14] In fact, within this
same interview, Sher relates his decision to direct *Joe Turner* to the election
of Barack Obama. Journalist Mike Glitz writes, "The finale [of *Joe Turner*]
is bloody and wrenching but somehow hopeful, with the characters stepping out of the darkness of slavery into an unknown future filled with danger but at least the possibility of something better. After eight years of [US
President George W.] Bush, that's where Sher sees America: shaking off a
terrible period and facing East."[15] Notably, this comment moves the question of meaning within *Joe Turner* from the cultural specificity of African
American experiences to an overall concern for the United States emerging
from the reputed failures of the Bush regime and into the age of Obama.

One of the enduring qualities of Wilson's twentieth-century cycle has
been his ability to find cross-cultural commonality by exploring the specific details of his black characters at very particular historical moments.
Throughout his all too brief career, Wilson fiercely clung to the aspiration

to celebrate and explore artistically the cultural particularity of African American experiences. This desire drove his early demand for a black director for the film version of *Fences*, as well as his proclamations for Black theatre made in his now famous 1996 speech to the Theatre Communications Group. In this talk, entitled "The Ground on which I Stand," Wilson relates his own toils within the American theatre to the historic struggles of African Americans for freedom and equality: "I have come here today to make a testimony, to talk about the ground on which I stand and all the many grounds on which I and my ancestors have toiled, and the ground of theatre on which my fellow artists and I have labored to bring forth its fruits, its daring and its sometimes liberating and healing truths."[16] Reimagining then the paradigms of cultural nationalism, Wilson links the ground of the American theatre with the ancestral ground of African American labor. It is this distinctive past, the efforts of his black forebears, that inform his dramaturgy.

And yet Sher, in directing *Joe Turner*, lacked the specificity of cultural experiences and cultural knowledge that Wilson championed. In order to compensate, Sher depended on the cultural knowledge of his black cast. He notes, "I've learned more from this cast than any group that I've ever worked with."[17] LaTanya Richardson Jackson, who played Bertha, remarks in an interview, "And from the start he was so collaborative. He would say, 'I know this,' and we would say, 'Yeah, but you don't know this ...' As directors go, he was an amazing listener."[18] Sher sought the cast's assistance with moments such as the powerful spiritual Juba Dance, steeped in African American tradition and African retentions, that ends Act 1. Yet, is such dramaturgical advice enough? If listening functions as recompense for intimate cultural awareness, what then is potentially lost in this dramatic equation?

Interestingly, the New York critical establishment raved about Sher's interpretation of Wilson's play. The play went on to be nominated for six Tony Awards, including Best Director, and to win two. In a long, glowing review, Ben Brantley writes in *The New York Times*,

> Yet the revival of August Wilson's "Joe Turner's Come and Gone," a drama of indisputable greatness, feels positively airborne. Much of Bartlett Sher's splendid production, which opened Thursday night at the Belasco Theatre, moves with the engaging ease of lively, casual conversation ... It would be a shame if this production doesn't find a wide and enthusiastic audience. It's an (almost) unconditional pleasure to watch.[19]

Certainly, reviews such as this, coupled with the publicity that surrounded the Obamas' date night, helped the play to find "wide and enthusiastic audiences." Joe Dziemianowicz adds in the *New York Daily News*: "Bartlett Sher seamlessly integrates realistic elements and the metaphoric, including the evocative set – fanciful floating windows with a so-real-you'd-pick-it vegetable garden. Sher has staged scenes that are dizzyingly powerful or beautiful (or both) – an ecstatic dance, a furious fit and a shimmering conclusion. But it's the compelling characters, superbly realized, that keep you rapt for 2 1/2 hours."[20] Both Dziemianowicz and Brantley in their reviews emphasize the collective appeal of Sher's production and of Wilson's text. They effusively place *Joe Turner* among the great works within the American dramatic canon. Brantley opines, "And, yes, in both soliloquies you hear Mr. Wilson's America lifting its voice in song." What does such strong praise portend for Wilson, and Black theatre more generally? To be sure, Wilson's work belongs amongst the celebrated works of American theatre history. Yet, such exalted status should not be at the expense of his dramas' cultural particularity. Accordingly, Wilson, in "The Ground on which I Stand," does not call for a separate Black theatre, but asserts "We are not separatists ... We are artists who seek to develop our talents and give expression to our personalities. We bring advantage to the common ground that is American theatre."[21] The advantage to which Wilson refers comes to black artists not in spite of their black experiences and black specificity, but rather because of it. Such claims do not attempt to essentialize Black theatre and black artists. Rather, for Wilson, such assertions respond to the cultural particularity of the dominant culture that has delimited and devalued black cultural production.

Evident with the selection of Bartlett Sher to direct *Joe Turner* and the subsequent production are particularly racialized politics of representation. On one hand, one could imagine celebrating the *Joe Turner* revival marked by the Obamas' attendance as a triumph for Black theatre, opening it up to wider interpretation by an award-winning, critically acclaimed director, rather than limiting the possibility of directing Wilson only to blacks. Mike Glitz in his interview with Sher strikes a note seemingly for democracy and anti-discrimination in defending Sher's right to direct Wilson's work. "Aren't the plays just too good? Wouldn't any director bridle at NOT being allowed to tackle one of America's greatest playwrights?" "Exactly," Sher says. Yet, present in Glitz's comment is a veiled white paternalism: Wilson is "too good" to be left just to the hands of black directors. Moreover, he ignores the fact that in the American theatre, it is not so much a matter of who would want to direct, but who has access and agency to mount a production. Sher did ask and receive permission to direct the play from Wilson's widow, Costanza Romero. As executor of the Wilson estate, Romero believes her responsibility is to keep Wilson's work in the public eye. "My work is to get these stories out there ... and to help ensure that audiences walk out of the plays with a deeper understanding for these American stories and for the ways our cultures intertwine."[22] Yet even more than Romero's consent, what enabled Sher to direct the revival was the fact that André Bishop, the producer of the Lincoln Center Theater, selected Sher, a resident director at Lincoln Center. The white-controlled theatrical hierarchy that Wilson had railed against some fifteen years earlier was very much still in place. The Lincoln Center power structure determined how, when, and by whom *Joe Turner* would be reproduced.

And yet, the dynamics of race within the United States in 2011 have evolved. A black president was only a dream just ten years previous. Echoing such sentiment, Sher, in rationalizing his decision to direct the play, tells Mike Glitz that while he respects Wilson's earlier position on a black director, "times [have] changed."[23] The idea he expresses is that because race is no longer of the same consequence, whites should have more license to direct black work. Costanza Romero voices similar sentiment in explaining her decision to grant Sher permission: "It's the quality of the work that matters now."[24] A cadre of new black playwrights who have emerged in the current age of Obama, such as Terrell McCraney, Eisa Davis, Lynn Nottage, and Marcus Gardley, have also had major productions of their work produced by white directors. And yet, if the paths of these new playwrights and the choice of Sher to direct *Joe Turner* truly represent the fact that the racialized politics of representation in the United States have changed and white directors could, and should, now produce the plays of black playwrights, then logically, the converse should be equally true. Black directors should have more opportunities to stage the works of non-black playwrights. Invariably, however, the only time that white theatre producers have called on black directors is to mount the one black show in their season, often one of the plays of August Wilson. Kenny Leon, who directed the Broadway productions of Wilson's *Gem of the Ocean* and *Radio Golf* as well as the 2006 revival of Lorraine Hansberry's *A Raisin in the Sun*, laments that Broadway lacks "a level playing field." According to Leon, "I have to work with my agent to remind people that, yes, I direct comedies, I do musicals, I do plays about all races of people just like other directors do."[25] Leon's comments reflect an unequal distribution of power that is still operative within the American theatre. My point here is not to suggest that white directors should never direct Black theatre, just as I would not deny black, Asian, and Latino directors the opportunity to stage Henrik Ibsen or William Shakespeare. Rather, my aim is to draw attention to the politics of representation and to consider how, within this equation, race in 2011 American theatre still matters.

A return to blackface

The evidence of this racialized politics is palpably clear in the 2010 Off-Broadway production of the musical *The Scottsboro Boys*, the recipient of twelve Tony nominations. With book by David Thompson, music by the late Fredrick Ebb, lyrics by John Kander, and direction by Susan Stroman, but featuring an overwhelmingly black cast (just one white actor) with subject matter taken directly from the history of African American struggles against oppression, *The Scottsboro Boys* troubles the question of what constitutes a black play. The play is based on the infamous trials of nine young African American men falsely accused of raping two white women aboard the box car of a train in Alabama, 1931. Back in 2002, while researching significant American trials, the production team came across the case of the Scottsboro Boys and determined to tell the story. In neo-Brechtian style, their musical unfolds as a minstrel show with the one white actor playing the master of ceremonies incorporating not only song and dance, but blackface. The specter of Black actors in blackface recalls an earlier painful history of Black theatre and black performance at the turn of the century in which the only way that blacks could appear on the Broadway or Vaudeville stage was to apply burnt cork make up and appear as the darky the white audiences expected. Consciously, the producers of *The Scottsboro Boys* sought to reinterpret an ugly chapter in American legal and racial history through the employment of the racially denigrating theatrical form of blackface.

The Scottsboro Boys, much like the earlier Kander and Ebb musical based on a sensational American trial, *Chicago*, seeks to instruct as well as to delight. Its satiric tone and gallows humor are meant to provoke thought as they work both to engage and to distance the audience. In addition to blackface, this play uses turn-of-the-twentieth-century black musical conventions such as the cakewalk "to keep audiences dancing nimbly between" what Charles Isherwood calls, "two states of feeling, enticing us to cackle knowingly at the plague of racism at one moment, and arousing sorrow and sympathy for its victims the next."[26] As Karen Sotiropoulos discusses in *Staging Race: Black Performers in the Turn of the Century*, "Black Vaudevillians such as Bert Williams sought to subvert the darky image and to present a 'black political agenda' to their stage productions even though they worked in commercial theatre."[27] Their song and blackface performances were often double-voiced, layered with coded meanings that a black audience would understand, while the white audience would not. Correspondingly, *The Scottsboro Boys* intends to provoke the audience and disrupt the history of injustice dealt upon the nine innocent young men. Bones and Tambo, the conventional stereotypical darkies and comic end men, interrupt the traditional minstrel show format by portraying the boys' white persecutors: "a grisly rogue's gallery of corrupt sheriffs, clueless or opportunistic lawyers and abusive guards, all leering, conniving, pratfalling fools whose ineptitude and immorality are played for low laughs."[28] These over-the-top white characters juxtapose the stereotypical black figures of the minstrel show, the structure of which *The Scottsboro Boys* uses its form to attempt to subvert. In this way, form functions as the inner logic of the content that seeks to bring to light the abuses heaped upon the Scottsboro Boys. Lisa B. Thompson argues:

> *The Scottsboro Boys* brings all that pathos to the stage through a clever use of minstrelsy, a controversial theatrical form from a bygone era, in order to foreground the performance of race. The jovial abandon of the opening number, "Minstrel March," also named "Hey, Hey! Hey!" belies the somber subject matter, yet also keenly illustrates the ways black suffering has served as entertainment.[29]

The notion is, then, that even as the black actors present the liturgy of injustices done to the Scottsboro Boys, they are concurrently commenting on that presentation, and foregrounding the spectacle of black suffering.

However, the risk in presenting blackface, as musical performer Ben Vereen infamously discovered from the critical response to his 1981 blackface tap dance performance before then-president Ronald Reagan, is that the history and cultural power of blackface are already so overdetermined. The mere embodiment of blackface by black actors for the entertainment of white audiences contains the possibility of reinscribing the images and racist representations that they seek to protest. *The Scottsboro Boys* intends to overturn stereotypes by overtly employing these same stereotypes. Josephine Lee maintains in "The Seduction of the Stereotype" that: "The Other invoked in stereotype might turn the tables by accentuating the stereotype's anxiety, its implicit instability. Although stereotypes cannot be reappropriated without invoking their racist history, they can nonetheless reveal in their performances the inner dynamics of this history, which already suggest the potential for disruption."[30] As Lee points out, "stereotypes cannot be reappropriated without invoking their racist history," and herein lies the danger for *The Scottsboro Boys*; even as it tries to disrupt the "inner dynamics of this history," the play cannot escape, and potentially reinvokes, the painful legacies of racism.

Not surprisingly, a group of African American activists sought to close the production soon after its opening. New York City councilman Charles Barron proclaimed in the *Amsterdam News*, "We are going to shut down this so-called play. There are no Black people who should be paying to see this minstrel show. It is an insult."[31] Also in the *Amsterdam News*, a spokesperson for the Freedom Party asserts, "This 'musical comedy' makes a mockery of a historic travesty of justice with total disregard for the humanity and suffering of the judicial lynchings that have marred the history of the United States then and now."[32] Mark Anthony Neal observes of this black backlash that "the backdrop of such claims is the desire to police the images of blackness in a country still exhibiting the growing pains of having its first black president and the seeming increase of popular imagery that depicts President Obama and Black Americans in general as less-than-human."[33] Neal points to an increased pressure on controlling racial images in the age of Obama. This anxiety around and desire to censure representation occurs in direct relation to increased freedom that authors, black and non-black, have experienced in presenting race.

Neighbors, the 2010 play by African American playwright Branden Jacobs-Jenkins, also consciously employs blackface, black actors, and minstrel stereotypes to discomfort and shock the audience. The play concerns the interaction of two neighboring households, an interracial couple – a black classics professor, his white wife, and teenage daughter – and the troupe of blackfaced minstrels that have just moved in next door. At issue in the play is the question of interracial prejudice and self-hatred. The black professor, Richard Patterson, despises all the negative racial images and associations that his neighbors represent, and seeks unsuccessfully to distance himself from them. Such subject matter and its engagement with grotesque and extreme stereotypical images is not novel in Black theatre, but recalls most particularly Adrienne Kennedy's 1964 Obie-Award-winning play *Funnyhouse of a Negro*, with its focus on a racially troubled African American graduate student of English literature. Still, Jacobs-Jenkins's drama seeks to probe how discomfort with the early history of black minstrelsy still colors contemporary African American cultural production as well as the social construction of blackness. *Neighbors* attempts, in its untidy and excessive form, also to confront current questions of mixed race, racialized sexuality, and class. Part minstrel archetypes and yet active figures in the play, the blackface neighbors are a troupe of minstrels, aptly named the Crow family – Mammy; Sambo; Topsy; Zip; and Jim Crow, Jr. – who re-enact historic minstrel performances, but also interact with the Pattersons next door. Here then, not unlike in *The Scottsboro Boys*, the performances within the performance of the play reinforce for the audience the ways in which blackness is and has been performed.

The exceedingly over-the-top interludes performed by the Crow family, with their conflation of distorted sexuality and of racial vulgarity, push against the limits of propriety in order to induce an uneasiness in the audience. In Mammy's interlude, she breastfeeds two white babies from two overly large protruding black breasts, while music from a Leni Riefenstahl African folk documentary plays in the background.[34] Jacobs-Jenkins juxtaposes these moments with scenes in which Richard Patterson delivers lectures from a Greek tragedy class he is set to teach. Patterson's ruminations on the Greeks parallel his own internal struggles with race, class, and self-definition: "Agamemnon, as a military man who was raised among the lowly, ignorant 'soldiers' thinks he is and may just be as good as the 'Gods.'"[35] In addition, the contrast between Patterson's personalized recounting of Greek tragedy and the vulgarized and obscenely exaggerated minstrel enactments highlights the interaction between matters of identity, performance, and progress. The high art of classical Greek is set in relation to the low buffoonery of minstrelsy in ways that question the values we assign to art and how we understand racialized performance. Ultimately these two worlds clash, as Zip Coon, the gay minstrel, and Richard Patterson, the bourgeois professor, physically battle each other. After the violent, chaotic, and noisily discordant climax, Jacobs-Jenkins has the remaining Crow family members onstage stare at the audience in awkward silence as Zip and Richard fight on in the background:

> The CROW FAMILY sans ZIP COON, take their place on the "stage," standing in a straight line. Minstrel music plays, but they don't move. Instead, they look into every face in the audience, as stoically as possible. ZIP COON and RICHARD are still fighting in the half-light, and they are the only sound we hear, as the entire family looks the entire audience over. The minstrel music finishes and there is silence before the entire theatre, stage and all, is ever so slowly completely washed in amber light. It is awkward and goes on forever.[36]

Jacobs-Jenkins requests that his minstrels, as Harvey Young writes in *Embodying Black Experience*, "perform stillness." Such performances of stillness, Young notes, link them with a black past: "we can think of black bodies, throughout history, shackled together, either loosely or densely packed in cargo holds; forced to stand motionless on auction blocks as they were poked, prodded, groped, and inspected by doctors; tied to whipping posts on plantations; placed in jails and prisons in disproportionate rates in the post emancipation period to the present day."[37] This frozen moment with the blackface Crows on stage recalls images of the comic Bert Williams and other blackface African American performers at the turn of the twentieth century, and the painful legacy of early African American cultural production. Stillness functions to reinforce the racialized politics of representation. At the same time, the silence and lack of movement actively make the

audiences uncomfortable. In fact, the silence serves as an assault on the audience – later Jacobs-Jenkins wants his actors occasionally to "point to people
in the audience and whisper to each other,"[38] – that proposes to induce the
spectator's discomfort. Such an amount of audience confrontation recalls Ed
Bullins's 1970 Black Revolutionary theatre pieces, *A Short Play for a Small
Theatre*, *The Play of the Play*, and *It Bees Dat Way*, all of which direct black
performers to antagonize white audience members. Yet, while the agenda
of Bullins's audience assault is explicit in its resistance of white oppression,
the politics of Jacobs-Jenkins's ending is more complex, less accusatory, and
explicitly interracial. The ending of *Neighbors* evidences the complex ways
that blackness signifies in the age of Obama.

Irreverence and mixed race in the post-black moment

The artistic license and racial irreverence of *Neighbors* is representative of
what Mark Anthony Neal terms a "post-soul aesthetic." Neal delineates the
political, social, and cultural experiences of African American communities
since the end of the Civil Rights and Black Power movements as "post-soul,"
and identifies within the post-soul aesthetic a seemingly sacrilegious approach
by contemporary African American artists to sacred icons of the African
American past.[39] Accordingly, Robert O'Hara's satiric play *Insurrection:
Holding History* (1996), which reflects on the omission of a gay presence in
the historic narratives of slavery, features a crazed Nat Turner, the leader of
the most famous slave revolt in 1831 Virginia, dancing the "hokey pokey."
According to Neal, "one of the post-soul strategies is to willingly 'bastard-
ize' black history and culture to create alternative meanings."[40] Through
his reimagining of Nat Turner, and slavery more generally, O'Hara ponders
who has the right to "hold" history or to compose its representation. As a
post-soul artist, O'Hara challenges the lines of traditional racial propriety
and purported historical accuracy not simply in problematizing the image
of Nat Turner, but in positing gay figures into the story of his rebellion.
O'Hara's play asks: how should we tell certain black histories, and why
are certain images of history held too seriously to be considered suitable
subjects for humor? *The Scottsboro Boys* also tests the limits of decorum
by featuring such provocative numbers as "Electric Chair," a tap dance performed as a nightmare by the youngest of the Scottsboro nine. Questioning
the appropriateness of such song and dance, Charles Isherwood writes in
The New York Times, "The spectacle of the same system destroying innocent lives does not make quite such an appealing subject for winking jokes
and soft shoes, particularly when the victims are potent historical symbols.
(And when racism in the American courts has not necessarily gone the way

of segregated lunch counters.)"[41] For Isherwood, the current racial realities make such representations extremely difficult to digest. At the same time, it is these same racial contexts that produce such representations.

A critical factor in contemporary racial politics as well as a subject matter in the works of Branden Jacobs-Jenkins, Eisa Davis, and Marcus Gardley, among others, is the subject of mixed-race identity. As Michele Elam reveals in *The Souls of Mixed Folk*, following the 2000 census in the United States, the term 'mixed race' – defined as biracial individuals born to parents from different racial groups – has gained an increasing "political significance in the national imaginary." Mixed-race figures and organizations have sought to locate mixed race as an identity warranting "separate legal, experiential or soulful" categories. Elam points out that within the history of the United States, "mixed race people are not a recent phenomenon: they have existed in often distinct self-defined communities since the colonial era in the Americas."[42] However, the racial climate of the new millennium – marked by the election of a black president of mixed heritage – has produced an atmosphere in which the politics of mixed race appear an emergent and urgent concern. Elam notes, "If once mulattos stood as testimony of racial inequity, now they are frequently invoked as fleshy confirmation that racial equality has arrived and thereby, fulfilled part of the nation's providential destiny."[43] In *Neighbors*, Jacobs-Jenkins presents Melody, the teenage mixed daughter of Richard and Jean Patterson, as suffering from the angst of trying to belong – an anxiety common in contemporary mixed-race representations. Melody confesses to Jim Crow, Jr. her early struggle with skin color and racial identity:

> And I washed my face so hard until I'd basically rubbed my face raw ... So of course, I run to my mother ... and she has no idea at first but somehow figures it out what's happened, tells me my skin is changing color. But because I'm five, I still think this has something to do with like ... not washing my face, you know. Like it has nothing to do with my father. And the next day, my face was covered in all these weird scabs and everyone in first grade made fun of me, called me scabface, and I was, I guess, I was just so traumatized that I resolved that, rather than wash my face, I'd rather let it get so dirty I was just black. Totally black. Cause it seemed easier.[44]

Melody's childhood racial trauma repeats and revises that of another professor's daughter, Emma Boudreaux in Emily Raboteau's 1997 novel *The Professor's Daughter*, where at a young age the protagonist's skin erupts in a mysterious series of rashes. For Emma, the rashes provide a fortuitous cover to hide her light skin and biracial features from the stares and questions of her classmates. Correspondingly, Melody desires not to stick out and as a result chooses to become "totally black." Notably her response to her mixed identity status is to "get so dirty I was just black." Later she confides in Jim, Jr. that "I don't think I have any issues with my ... you know, my identity or whatever. I don't want you to think that I'm some sort of like ... tragic mulatto."[45] Within this context, the association she makes between dirtiness and blackness is particularly revealing. Melody's father, the professor, does not want her socializing with the "dirty" lower-class black next door. Melody, on the other hand, wants to get dirty. For Melody, in her struggle for racial acceptance and identity, dirtiness is free of negative connotations. However, its sexual meanings are explicit. Melody ultimately rolls in the dirt with Jim, Jr. Their sexual intimacy functions as a racializing act, bringing her closer to blackness and belonging. When Melody returns home after their tryst, her face and body bear some of the black cork that has rubbed off Jim. Melody is literally marked by race and made blacker through this experience.

Bulrusher, the title character in Eisa Davis's 2006 Pulitzer-Prize-nominated play, also struggles to belong. Set in 1955 in Boonville, California, *Bulrusher* operates both within the emergent Civil Rights Movement and outside it. Inside this small town in the Anderson Valley of Mendocino County, north of San Francisco, the predominantly white townspeople speak their own private language, "Boontling." As the play begins, Bulrusher does not know of her mixed race status, only of her difference. She knows she is of color and that there is no one else in the town, save for one black logger, called simply "Logger" in the play, that looks like her. Abandoned by her mother in the bulrushes by the river, Bulrusher has been raised by a white male school-teacher, "Schoolch." Blessed with special powers owing to her association with the river, Bulrusher can "read people's water" and see their future.

For Bulrusher, her sense of self and her world profoundly change with the arrival of Logger's niece, Vera. Her interaction with Vera, the only other dark-skinned woman that Bulrusher has ever known, functions to confirm Bulrusher's awareness of her own racial identity. Bulrusher confides to the river that Vera, for her, "is a mirror ... A mirror. Schoolch never allowed any mirrors in the house ... I always think about touching her skin. It's like mine only smoother."[46] Bulrusher's desire to understand herself through the mirror of Vera is an effort at self-construction; such knowledge of her past has been limited by the conditions of her birth, as well as those of her childhood in which Schoolch, her surrogate father, prevents any discussion of race and difference. Bulrusher, prior to the appearance of Vera, has been cut off from seeing herself.

This trope of the mirror is one that Michele Elam identifies and discusses in terms of Danzy Senna's two novels about mixed-race identity, *Caucasia* and *Symptomatic*.[47] According to Elam, "Less an example of the Lacanian mirror stage of identity formation than a bending of Du Boisian double consciousness, the protagonist looks at an image of herself looking back in an effort to pinpoint the vectors of identity."[48] Famously, for Du Bois, double-consciousness provides African Americans with a special and unique perspective on the American world. At the same time, double-consciousness – "always looking at one's self through the eyes of others"[49] – posits an "ontological dilemma of blackness, as Hortense Spillers calls it, that is over-whelming as it requires not only to be perceived by others but to try to understand what their perceptions mean."[50] The trope of the mirror then – as Elam theorizes in Senna and as the character Bulrusher experiences it in Davis's play – adds a twist to Du Bois. For the protagonist, rather than attempting to understand others' perceptions, seeks to find a space finally to determine her own identity. Accordingly, at the end of the play, as she is about to return home to Alabama, Vera presents Bulrusher with the gift of a mirror, bestowing on her permission to continue to find herself.

Bulrusher's association with Vera ushers her into new racial and sexual awareness. In fact, Bulrusher experiences a series of critical racial awaken-ings in the play. Logger confides to Vera that he was the one that first made Bulrusher aware that she was a person of color: "You know I was the one told Bulrusher she was colored. She was five and didn't even know."[51] This early lack of racial self-knowledge speaks to Bulrusher's lack of, and longing for, familial intimacy – she has no knowledge of her father or her mother, only the uncommunicative surrogate Schoolch. This void is first addressed by the arrival of Vera. Driven by mutual desire, Vera and Bulrusher make love in the river. The moment is a new birth for Bulrusher, a sexual baptism for both women. And yet it does not bring the sense of oneness or spiritual fulfillment that either expected. Davis writes in her stage directions, "They are strangely awkward with each other – their lovemaking wasn't what they thought it would be."[52] For neither Vera nor Bulrusher does the sexual consummation produce answers to their driving questions and uncertainties. Vera cannot escape her past and must eventually return home to her family in Alabama to give birth to the baby she is carrying. Bulrusher must continue her search for self. Vera aids this process by sharing with Bulrusher information about the Civil Rights struggle back in the South, and most specifically about Emmett Till, the fourteen-year-old black boy brutally murdered in 1955 and found floating in a river for allegedly smiling at a white woman. Unlike Bulrusher, the river could not save Till. His vicious torture – brought to national atten-tion when *Jet* magazine displayed his bloated, unrecognizable face – gener-ated unrest and protest and galvanized resistance. Vera shares this same *Jet* photo with Bulrusher as Bulrusher comes into racial consciousness by her exposure to injustice through Vera's tutelage. Bulrusher's own experience of race and racism to this point in Boonville, California has been different. "Why do colored people even live where these things happen?," she asks.[53] Her naïve question still points to the geographic realities that shape black experiences. Significantly, for Bulrusher, the politics of blackness, the experience and response to racialized oppression, are not the product of her biology, nor inherent blood memory, but rather learned behavior.

Bulrusher's radicalization, therefore, is conditioned by her own experience, mediated through Vera and her own desire for Vera. Bulrusher proclaims that she will act out against white hegemony not to end racism but rather to support and protect Vera. When Vera talks of compassion for the white man that raped and impregnated her, Bulrusher responds, "I thought you wanted all white people murdered. I'd do that for you. As many as I could."[54] Interestingly, this line repeats and revises a line spoken by a mixed-race figure in Langston Hughes's 1935 play, *Mulatto*. In a climactic confrontation with his white father, Robert – the mulatto son of the colonel and his longtime black servant Cora – exclaims, "I'd like to kill all the white men in the world."[55] Disinherited and disavowed by his father in the segregated post-World War I South, Robert angrily declares his resistance to the unequal and unjust social system. His desire for racial revenge is at once personal and communal, seeking to right the historical wrongs done to black people. In contrast, Bulrusher's call to arms is not so much an act of racial revolution, but rather a proclamation of her kinship with and determination to protect Vera. Race and its consequences remain personal.

The personal dynamics of race play out for Bulrusher with wider political meanings in the climactic revelation of, and confrontation with, her mother. After orchestrating the return of Vera to Alabama near the conclusion of the play, Madame, the proprietor of the local brothel that both Logger and Schoolch frequent, confesses to Bulrusher that she is indeed her mother and that Logger is her father. Here, then, in another moment of racial awakening, Bulrusher comes to understand that she is the mixed, out-of-wedlock child of a purportedly white brothel-manager mother and a black logger. Yet, for Bulrusher, the potential politics of her racial status are not as important as her experience of neglect. Contemporary mixed-race advocates have argued for an appreciation of the new identity-category "mixed race," which recognizes the significance of both parents, white and black. Too often in the past, they assert, the presence of the white mother is missing and has become subsumed by the capacious identity-category of blackness. In Bulrusher's case, however, it is the matter of the willful disappearance of the passing-as-white mother. In this telling mother–daughter moment, Bulrusher confronts Madame on her rationale for leaving her to die.

This dynamic scene again possesses productive parallels with the father-and-son climactic encounter of Hughes's *Mulatto*. In both plays, the child seeks to understand their abandonment by the parent. The differences between the scenes are highly gendered and also historically contingent. In *Mulatto*, the confrontation centers on patrimony and the contestation over masculinity. Robert wants the recognition of his manhood. He demands of his father his "blood debt," the rights of inheritance he is entitled to as the colonel's son. Bulrusher, on the other hand, pursues no claim to property or civic entitlements. Rather, Bulrusher needs Madame to understand the feelings of natal alienation, the emotional damage and suffering she has experienced, because she has been denied maternal nurturing. Left without any contact with her parents, and with the knowledge that her mother abandoned her at birth, leaving her floating in the bulrushes on the river, Bulrusher needs her mother to appreciate that she has survived in spite of her negligence.

> MADAME: What do you want me to say?
> BULRUSHER: I want you to apologize for trying to kill me.
> MADAME: I didn't want you dead.
> BULRUSHER: Then why did you get rid of me like that? I was floating for an eternity.
> MADAME: You can't remember that.
> BULRUSHER: Yes I can. Yes I can I remember floating into the night, the fog and coyotes … I begged to be found. I talked to the sun with my fingers, kept closing my fist around it every time it went down trying to keep it with me. But the night would always come. And the river was so thin there, deep as a teardrop – but I kept myself alive. Why? To find you.[56]

In language thickly imagistic, Bulrusher conveys to Madame her harrowing ordeal of infancy and learned dependence on her own survival instincts. There is no claim for access to privilege, but rather a plea for her mother's admission of guilt. Madame, however, is in denial. She claims that she never wanted her to die, and instead left her in the river with prayers so that the river god would protect her: "The river's your mother. I throw stones in it every day to thank her for caring for you."[57] Naming the river as surrogate mother, Madame rationalizes abnegation of the role.

Robert, in *Mulatto*, also experiences a critical moment of parental rejection in childhood. When Robert, as a young boy, attempts to address Colonel Tom as his daddy in front of a group of other white men, the colonel severely beats him for this social transgression. As a child, Robert painfully comes to understand racial hierarchies and the pejorative status of blackness. Bulrusher, too, accuses her mother of abandoning her because of her race: "White whore didn't want her colored baby."[58] Still, the politics of race are further complicated by Madame's response, "I ain't white, my ma's a Pomo Indian."[59] Madame, like her daughter, is of mixed race. She has passed as white in order to survive economically and to function as a businesswoman in a social order where, as Logger explains earlier to Vera, "Indians are the colored folk here."[60] Ironically, her business of choice is as a prostitute and proprietor of a whorehouse. Thus, questions of racial hierarchy, of blackness and its meanings, of the relationship between race and class, of the "dirtiness" and intersections of sex and race, are purposefully muddied by their presentation in this complex equation. In *Mulatto*, Robert ultimately kills his father, accidentally, and the play calls out for racial reparations for wrongs done. *Bulrusher* concludes with the mother and daughter left in uneasy and unresolved tension. Madame plans to marry Logger. Logger, the newly aware father, awkwardly tells Bulrusher, "if you need anything, uh family history and so forth, I got a lot of stories, uh, diseases you might be prone to, uh, and the like, of that nature."[61] With fatherhood thrust upon him, Logger fumbles with how to interpret the new terms of their relationship. And so, family biology and history are meant to compensate for parental intimacy and the years Bulrusher has lost without any knowledge of her kin. In its unsettled resolution, Bulrusher exemplifies the contemporary politics of the post-black, blackness, and their meanings: they are not fixed but complicated by the dynamics of lived experience, gender, class, and sexuality.

By way of conclusion

New black content meets with new form within the post-black theatre, constructing new possibilities for Black theatre. Black playwrights – such as Marcus Yardley in *And Jesus Moonwalked the Mississippi* and Robert O'Hara in *Antebellum*, like Eisa Davis – turn to historic subject matter – the Civil War and 1939 Atlanta, Georgia respectively – engaging the past with new eyes and new perspectives from the present. The result is an enlarged and even revisionist understanding of the path of social change as well as that of Black theatre. In his critically acclaimed trilogy *The Brother/Sister Plays*, playwright Tarrell McCraney troubles the intersections of blackness, sexuality, gender, and class. In addition to exploring previously taboo subjects, McCraney's *Brother/Sister Plays* innovatively blend Yoruban cosmology with Greek epic tragedy and poetic verse from African American vernacular. Such hybridizations of form are most representative of contemporary Black theatre. New authors push against the limitations of conventional realism or notions of Black theatre. In fact, it is through form that the new black drama most commonly has reinvested in the question of what constitutes a black play, exploring how form might function as the inner logic of new content.

Still, even as playwrights such as McCraney and Lynn Nottage have garnered productions at regional theatres across the country, the space and places for new black work remain limited. The mechanisms of production, the control over venues, budgets, and artistic selections are for the most part not in black hands. The precarious situation that August Wilson decries for Black theatre in "The Ground on which I Stand" persists. And so, perhaps now more than ever – in this age of Obama with its evolving definitions of race – is a time in need of the establishment of black cultural institutions. And yet, it is precisely the racial politics in the age of Obama that decry the necessity of constructing separate black institutions. It is this space of contradiction and complexity that has proved fertile ground for the emergence of new plays and new debates around the notion of how, where, and what, as Suzan-Lori Parks says, Black theatre "IZ."

NOTES

1 Suzan-Lori Parks, "New black math," *Theatre Journal*, 57.4 (December, 2005): 576–8.
2 W. E. B. Du Bois, "Krigwa Player Little Negro Theatre," *The Crisis*, 32 (July, 1926): 135.
3 Mary Schmidt Campbell, "African American Art in a Post-Black Era," *Women & Performance: A Journal of Feminist Theory*, 17.3 (November, 2007): 317–18.
4 Thelma Golden, "Post-Black," in the exhibition catalog to the "Freestyle" exhibition, Studio Museum of Harlem (2001), 1.
5 *Ibid.*
6 *Ibid.*, 2.
7 Suzan-Lori Parks, "An Equation for Black People Onstage," in *The America Play and Other Works* (New York: Theatre Communications Group, 1995), 20.
8 LeRoi Jones [Amiri Baraka], "The Revolutionary Theatre," in *Home: Social Essays* (New York: William Morrow, 1966), 210–11.
9 Keith Herbert and Matthew Chayes, "Obamas Come to New York to See Broadway Play," *New York Newsday*, May 30, 2009.
10 August Wilson, "I Want a Black Director," in *May All Your Fences Have Gates: Essays on the Drama of August Wilson*, ed. Alan Nadel (Iowa City: University of Iowa Press, 1994), 203.
11 *Ibid.*, 201.
12 Michael Awkward, "'The Crookeds with the Straights': *Fences*, Race and the Politics of Adaptation," in Nadel, *May All Your Fences Have Gates*, 225.

13 Marion McClinton, quoted by Patrick Healy, "Playwright's Race Adds to Drama for an August Wilson Revival," *New York Times*, April 23, 2009: A18.

14 Bartlett Sher, quoted by Mike Glitz, "Theater: 'Joe Turner's Come …' to Broadway and Will Stay for a While," *Huffington Post*, April 22, 2008, available online at huffingtonpost.com/michael-giltz/theater-joe-turners-come_b_189039.html.

15 *Ibid.*

16 August Wilson, "The Ground on which I Stand," *Callaloo*, 20.3 (1998): 493.

17 Bartlett Sher, quoted by Healy, "Playwright's Race."

18 LaTanya Richardson Jackson, quoted in *ibid.*

19 Ben Brantley, "Wilson's Wanderings Searching Home," *New York Times*, April 17, 2009, available online at theater.nytimes.com/2009/04/17/theater/reviews/17turn.html?=pagewanted=all.

20 Joe Dziemianowicz, "Rich B'way Revival is August Occasion," *New York Daily News*, April 16, 2009, available online at articles.nydailynews.com/2009-04-17/entertainment/17921006_1_radio-golf-joe-turner-director-bartlett-sher.

21 Wilson, "The Ground," 502.

22 Costanza Romero, quoted by Healy, "Playwright's Race."

23 Glitz, "Theater: 'Joe Turner's Come.'"

24 Romero, quoted by Patrick Healy, "Playwright's Race."

25 Kenny Leon, quoted in *ibid.*

26 Charles Isherwood, "Revisiting an Outrage with Gallows Humor," *New York Times*, November 1, 2010.

27 Karen Sotiropoulos, *Staging Race: Black Performers in the Turn of the Century* (Cambridge, MA: Harvard University Press, 2006), 4.

28 *Ibid.*

29 Lisa B. Thompson, quoted by Mark Anthony Neal, "Fear of the Blackface Minstrel," *Madame Noire*, May 17, 2011, available online at http://madamenoire.com/109789/fear-of-the-black-face-minstrel.

30 Josephine Lee, "The Seduction of the Stereotype," in *Performing Asian America* (Philadelphia: Temple University Press, 1997), 96.

31 Jeanette Toomer, "Freedom Party Protests Scottsboro Boys at Tony Awards," *New York Amsterdam News*, available online at www.amsterdamnews.com/news/freedom-party-protests-scottsboro-boys-at-tony-awards/article_e2c052-11e0-8df9-001cc4c03286.html.

32 *Ibid.*

33 Neal, "Fear of the Blackface Minstrel."

34 Branden Jacobs-Jenkins, *Neighbors*, unpublished playscript, 99.

35 *Ibid.*, 89.

36 *Ibid.*, 119.

37 Harvey Young, *Embodying Black Experience: Stillness, Critical Memory, and the Black Body* (Ann Arbor: University of Michigan Press, 2010), 118.

38 Jacobs-Jenkins, *Neighbors*, 119.

39 Mark Anthony Neal, *Soul Babies: Black Popular Culture and the Post-Soul Aesthetic* (New York: Routledge, 2002), 8.

40 *Ibid.*, 22.

41 Isherwood, "Revisiting an Outrage."

42 Michele Elam, *The Souls of Mixed Folk: Race, Politics, and Aesthetics in the New Millennium* (Stanford: Stanford University Press, 2011), 6.

43 *Ibid.*, 7.

44 Jacobs-Jenkins, *Neighbors*, 72.

45 *Ibid.*

46 Eisa Davis, *Bulrusher*, in *New Playwrights: The Best Plays of 2006*, ed. D. L. Lepidus (New York: Smith and Kraus, 2007), Act 1, 156.

47 See Elam, *The Souls of Mixed Folk*, 149–55.

48 *Ibid.*, 154.

49 W. E. B. Du Bois, *The Souls of Black Folks* (New York: Penguin, 1969), 45.

50 Hortense Spillers, "All the Things You Could Be by Now, if Sigmund Freud's Wife Was Your Mother: Psychoanalysis and Race," *Boundary 2*, 23.3 (Fall, 1996): 104.

51 Davis, *Bulrusher*, 144.

52 *Ibid.*, 171.

53 *Ibid.*, 175.

54 *Ibid.*, 173.

55 Langston Hughes, *Mulatto*, in *Five Plays by Langston Hughes*, ed. Webster Smalley (Bloomington: Indiana University Press, 1968), 23.

56 *Ibid.*, 181.

57 *Ibid.*, 183.

58 *Ibid.*, 180.

59 *Ibid.*

60 *Ibid.*, 148.

61 *Ibid.*, 183.

Abbott, Lynn, and Doug Seroff. *Ragged but Right: Black Traveling Shows, "Coon Songs," and the Dark Pathway to Blues and Jazz.* Jackson: University Press of Mississippi, 2007.

Adubato, Robert A. "A history of the WPA's Negro Theatre Project in New York City, 1935–1939," Ph.D. dissertation. New York University, 1978.

Anderson, Lisa M. *Black Feminism in Contemporary Drama.* Urbana: University of Illinois Press, 2008.

 Mammies No More: The Changing Image of Black Women on Stage and Screen. Lanham, MD: Rowman & Littlefield, 1997.

Andrews, Bert, and Paul Carter Harrison. *In the Shadow of the Great White Way: Images from the Black Theatre.* New York; St. Paul, MN: Thunder's Mouth Press, 1989.

Association for Theatre in Higher Education (US). *Blackstream: Black Theatre Association Presents Select Papers from the 1995 Association for Theatre in Higher Education's San Francisco Conference.* Chicago: Black Theatre Association of the Association for Theatre in Higher Education (ATHE), 1997.

Baker, Houston A. *Modernism and the Harlem Renaissance.* Chicago: University of Chicago Press, 1987.

Baraka, Amiri. *Black Music.* New York: W. Morrow, 1967.

Baraka, Amiri, and Charlie Reilly (eds.). *Conversations with Amiri Baraka.* Jackson: University Press of Mississippi, 1994.

Bean, Annemarie. *A Sourcebook of African-American Performance: Plays, People, Movements.* London; New York: Routledge, 1999.

Bean, Annemarie, James Vernon Hatch, and Brooks McNamara (eds.). *Inside the Minstrel Mask: Readings in Nineteenth-Century Blackface Minstrelsy.* Hanover, NH; London: Wesleyan University Press, 1996.

Bekka, Abu. "The Black Theatre Movement in the United States, 1960–1975," Ph.D. dissertation. California State University, 1984.

Bigsby, C. W. E. *The Cambridge Companion to August Wilson.* Cambridge; New York: Cambridge University Press, 2007.

Black Theatre Canada. *Black Theatre Canada in Perspective.* Toronto: The Theatre, 1980.

Bloom, Harold. *August Wilson.* Broomall, PA: Chelsea House Publishers, 2002.

Bogumil, Mary L. *Understanding August Wilson.* Columbia: University of South Carolina Press, 1999.

Booker, Margaret. *Lillian Hellman and August Wilson: Dramatizing a New American Identity.* New York: Lang, 2003.

Brooks, Daphne A. *Bodies in Dissent: Spectacular Performances of Race and Freedom, 1850–1910.* Durham, NC: Duke University Press, 2006.

Brown-Guillory, Elizabeth. *Their Place on the Stage: Black Women Playwrights in America.* New York: Greenwood Press, 1988.

Bryant-Jackson, Paul K., and Lois More Overbeck. *Intersecting Boundaries: The Theatre of Adrienne Kennedy.* Minneapolis: University of Minnesota Press, 1992.

Bryer, Jackson R., and Mary C, Hartig. *Conversations with August Wilson.* Jackson: University Press of Mississippi, 2006.

Bullins, Ed. *New Plays from the Black Theatre: An Anthology.* New York: Bantam Books, 1969.

Bullins, Ed, and New Lafayette Theatre. *The New Lafayette Theatre Presents.* Garden City, NY: Anchor Press, 1974.

Catanese, Brandi Wilkins. *The Problem of the Color(blind): Racial Transgression and the Politics of Black Performance.* Ann Arbor: University of Michigan Press, 2011.

Charters, Ann. *Nobody: The Story of Bert Williams.* New York: Macmillan, 1970.

Clark, Keith. *Black Manhood in James Baldwin, Ernest J. Gaines, and August Wilson.* Urbana: University of Illinois Press, 2002.

Craig, E. Quita. *Black Drama of the Federal Theatre Era: Beyond the Formal Horizons.* Amherst: University of Massachusetts Press, 1980.

Curtis, Susan. *The First Black Actors on the Great White Way.* Columbia: University of Missouri Press, 1998.

Davis, Ossie, and Ruby Dee. *With Ossie and Ruby: In This Life Together.* New York: W. Morrow, 1998.

Elam, Harry Justin, Jr. *The Past as Present in the Drama of August Wilson.* Ann Arbor: University of Michigan Press, 2004.

Taking It to the Streets: The Social Protest Theater of Luis Valdez and Amiri Baraka. Ann Arbor: University of Michigan Press, 1997.

Elam, Harry Justin, Jr., and Robert Alexander (eds.). *The Fire This Time: African-American Plays for the 21st Century.* New York: Theatre Communications Group, 2004.

Elkins, Marilyn Roberson. *August Wilson: A Casebook.* New York: Garland, 1994.

Fabre, Geneviève. *Drumbeats, Masks, and Metaphor: Contemporary Afro-American Theatre.* Cambridge, MA: Harvard University Press, 1983.

Forbes, Camille F. *Introducing Bert Williams: Burnt Cork, Broadway, and the Story of America's First Black Star.* New York: Basic Civitas, 2008.

Forte', Patricia, and Ted Lange. *The Cambridge Way: An Intimate Look at Black Theatre.* Los Angeles: Forte', 2009.

Fraden, Rena. *Blueprints for a Black Federal Theatre, 1935–1939.* Cambridge; New York: Cambridge University Press, 1994.

Garry David and the Community Protection Act, film, dir. Mark Shannon. Victoria: RMIT, 1991.

Gates, Henry Louis, Jr., and Gene Andrew Jarrett. *The New Negro: Readings on Race, Representation, and African American Culture, 1892–1938.* Princeton: Princeton University Press, 2007.

Gayle, Addison. *The Black Aesthetic.* Garden City, NY: Doubleday, 1971.

George-Graves, Nadine. *The Royalty of Negro Vaudeville: The Whitman Sisters and the Negotiation of Race, Gender and Class in African American Theater, 1900–1940*. New York: St. Martin's Press, 2000.

Urban Bush Women: Twenty Years of African American Dance Theater, Community Engagement, and Working It Out. Madison: University of Wisconsin Press, 2010.

Gill, Glenda Eloise. *White Grease Paint on Black Performers: A Study of the Federal Theatre of 1935–1939*. New York: P. Lang, 1988.

Glasco, Laurence Admiral, and Christopher Rawson. *August Wilson: Pittsburgh Places in His Life and Plays*. Pittsburgh: Pittsburgh History & Landmarks Foundation, 2011.

Goddard, Lynette. *Staging Black Feminisms: Identity, Politics, Performance*. Basingstoke; New York: Palgrave Macmillan, 2007.

Goodman, Gerald Thomas. "The Black Theatre Movement," Ph.D. dissertation. University of Pennsylvania, 1975.

Graham, Maryemma, and Jerry Washington Ward. *The Cambridge History of African American Literature*. New York: Cambridge University Press, 2011.

Gray, John. *Black Theatre and Performance: A Pan-African Bibliography*. New York: Greenwood Press, 1990.

Haedicke, Susan C, and Tobin Nellhaus. *Performing Democracy: International Perspectives on Urban Community-Based Performance*. Ann Arbor: University of Michigan Press, 2001.

Harrison, Paul Carter, Victor Leo Walker II, and Gus Edwards (eds). *Black Theatre: Ritual Performance in the African Diaspora*. Philadelphia: Temple University Press, 2002.

Hatch, James Vernon, and Leo Hamalian. *Lost Plays of the Harlem Renaissance, 1920–1940*. Detroit: Wayne State University Press, 1996.

Hatch, James Vernon, and Ted Shine. *Black Theatre USA: Plays by African Americans 1847 to Today*, 2 vols. New York: Free Press, 1996.

Hay, Samuel A. *African American Theatre: An Historical and Critical Analysis*. Cambridge; New York: Cambridge University Press, 1994.

Herrington, Joan. *I Ain't Sorry for Nothin' I Done: August Wilson's Process of Playwriting*. New York: Limelight Editions, 1998.

Herrington, Joan, and August Wilson. *August Wilson in an Hour*. Hanover, NH: In an Hour Books, 2010.

Hill, Errol. *Black Heroes: Seven Plays*. New York: Applause Theatre, 1989.

Shakespeare in Sable: A History of Black Shakespearean Actors. Amherst: University of Massachusetts Press, 1984.

The Jamaican Stage, 1655–1900: Profile of a Colonial Theatre. Amherst: University of Massachusetts Press, 1992.

The Theater of Black Americans: A Collection of Critical Essays. Englewood Cliffs: Prentice-Hall, 1980.

The Trinidad Carnival: Mandate for a National Theatre. Austin: University of Texas Press, 1972.

Hill, Errol, and James Vernon Hatch. *A History of African American Theatre*. Cambridge; New York: Cambridge University Press, 2003.

Huggins, Nathan Irvin (ed.). *Voices from the Harlem Renaissance*. Oxford: Oxford University Press, 1995 [1976].

Hughes, Langston. *The Collected Works of Langston Hughes*, ed. Arnold Rampersad, Dolan Hubbard, and Leslie Catherine Sanders, 18 vols, Vol. VI: *Gospel Plays, Operas, and Later Dramatic Works*, ed. and introd. Leslie Catherine Sanders. Columbia: University of Missouri Press, 2004.

Hutchinson, George. *The Cambridge Companion to the Harlem Renaissance*. New York: Cambridge University Press, 2007.

   The Harlem Renaissance in Black and White. Cambridge, MA: Belknap Press, 1995.

Jennings, La Vinia Delois. *Alice Childress*. New York; London: Twayne; Prentice-Hall, 1995.

Jones, James Earl, and Penelope Niven. *James Earl Jones: Voices and Silences*. New York: Scribner; Toronto: Maxwell Macmillan Canada; New York: Maxwell Macmillan International, 1993.

Justice-Malloy, Rhona, and Mid-America Theatre Conference. *African and African American Theatre Past and Present*, Theatre History Studies 30. Tuscaloosa: University of Alabama Press, 2010.

Keppel, Ben. *The Work of Democracy: Ralph Bunche, Kenneth B. Clark, Lorraine Hansberry, and the Cultural Politics of Race*. Cambridge, MA: Harvard University Press, 1995.

King, Woodie. *Black Theatre, Present Condition*. New York: National Black Theatre Touring Circuit, 1981.

   The Impact of Race: Theatre and Culture. New York: Applause Theatre & Cinema Books; Milwaukee: Sales & Distribution, North America, Hal Leonard Corporation, 2003.

   The National Black Drama Anthology: Eleven Plays from America's Leading African-American Theaters. New York: Applause, 1995.

   New Plays for the Black Theatre. Chicago: Third World Press, 1989.

King, Woodie, and Ron Milner. *Black Drama Anthology*. New York: Columbia University Press, 1972.

Kodicek, Susan, and Peter Lang. *Black Theatre for Children*. London: Pelham, 1977.

Kolin, Philip C. (ed.). *Contemporary African American Women Playwrights: A Casebook*. London; New York: Routledge, 2007.

Krasner, David. *A Beautiful Pageant: African American Theatre, Drama, and Performance in the Harlem Renaissance, 1910–1927*. New York: Palgrave Macmillan, 2002.

   Resistance, Parody, and Double Consciousness in African American Theatre, 1895–1910. New York: St. Martin's Press, 1997.

Lindfors, Bernth. *Ira Aldridge, the African Roscius*. Rochester, NY: University of Rochester Press, 2007.

Manuel Pérez, Hely, and Victor Leo Walker II. *Black Theatre's Unprecedented Times*. Gainesville, FL: Black Theatre Network News, 1999.

Marsh-Lockett, Carol P. *Black Women Playwrights: Visions on the American Stage*. New York: Garland, 1999.

Mason, Jeffrey D., and J. Ellen Gainor. *Performing America: Cultural Nationalism in American Theater*. Ann Arbor: University of Michigan Press, 1999.

McAllister, Marvin Edward. *White People Do Not Know How to Behave at Entertainments Designed for Ladies & Gentlemen of Colour: William Brown's*

African & American Theater. Chapel Hill: University of North Carolina Press, 2003.

Whiting Up: Whiteface Minstrels & Stage Europeans in African American Performance. Chapel Hill: University of North Carolina Press, 2011.

Meer, Sarah. *Uncle Tom Mania: Slavery, Minstrelsy, and Transatlantic Culture in the 1850s.* Athens: University of Georgia Press, 2005.

Miller, Henry D. *Theorizing Black Theatre: Art versus Protest in Critical Writings, 1898–1965.* Jefferson, NC: McFarland, 2011.

Mitchell, Koritha. *Living with Lynching: African American Lynching Plays, Performance, and Citizenship, 1890–1930.* Urbana: University of Illinois Press, 2011.

Mitchell, Loften. *Black Drama: The Story of the American Negro in the Theatre.* New York: Hawthorn Books, 1967.

Voices of the Black Theatre. Clifton, NJ: J. T. White, 1975.

Moynagh, Maureen Anne. *African-Canadian Theatre.* Toronto: Playwrights Canada Press, 2005.

Mündel, Ingrid, and Ric Knowles. *"Ethnic," Multicultural and Intercultural Theatre.* Toronto: Playwrights Canada Press, 2009.

Nadel, Alan. *August Wilson: Completing the Twentieth-Century Cycle.* Iowa City: University of Iowa Press, 2010.

ed. *May All Your Fences Have Gates: Essays on the Drama of August Wilson.* Iowa City: University of Iowa Press, 1994.

Nathans, Heather S. *Slavery and Sentiment on the American Stage, 1787–1861: Lifting the Veil of Black.* Cambridge; New York: Cambridge University Press, 2009.

Nathans, Heather S., and David C. Driskell Center. *August Wilson Celebrated.* Hamden, CT: New England Theatre Conference, 2008.

Nemiroff, Robert, and Lorraine Hansberry. *To Be Young, Gifted and Black: Lorraine Hansberry in Her Own Words.* New York: New American Library, 1970.

New Lafayette Theatre. "Black Theatre." *Black Theatre: A Periodical of the Black Theatre Movement,* 1 (1968): n.p.

Nyongó, Tavia Amolo Ochieng'. *The Amalgamation Waltz: Race, Performance and the Ruses of Memory.* Minneapolis: University of Minnesota Press, 2009.

Ogbar, Jeffrey Ogbonna Green. *The Harlem Renaissance Revisited: Politics, Arts, and Letters.* Baltimore: Johns Hopkins University Press, 2010.

Pereira, Kim. *August Wilson and the African-American Odyssey.* Urbana: University of Illinois Press, 1995.

Perkins, Kathy A. (ed.). *Black Female Playwrights: An Anthology of Plays before 1950.* Bloomington: Indiana University Press, 1989.

Peterson, Bernard L. *The African American Theatre Directory, 1816–1960: A Comprehensive Guide to Early Black Theatre Organizations, Companies, Theatres, and Performing Groups.* Westport, CT: Greenwood Press, 1997.

Contemporary Black American Playwrights and Their Plays: A Biographical Directory and Dramatic Index. New York: Greenwood Press, 1988.

Pitts, Ethel Louise. "The American Negro Theatre, 1940–1949," Ph.D. dissertation. University of Missouri–Columbia, 1975.

Robeson, Paul. *The Undiscovered Paul Robeson: An Artist's Journey, 1898–1939.* New York: Wiley, 2001.

Robeson, Paul, and Philip Sheldon Foner. *Paul Robeson Speaks: Writings, Speeches, Interviews, 1918–1974*. New York: Brunner/Mazel, 1978.

Roediger, David R. (ed. and introd.). *Black on White: Black Writers on What It Means to Be White*. New York: Schocken Books, 1998.

Rugg, Rebecca Ann, and Harvey Young (eds.). *Reimagining* A Raisin in the Sun: *Four New Plays*. Evanston, IL: Northwestern University Press, 2012.

Sanders, Leslie Catherine. *The Development of Black Theater in America: From Shadows to Selves*. Baton Rouge: Louisiana State University Press, 1988.

Schiffman, Jack. *Harlem Heyday: A Pictorial History of Modern Black Show Business and the Apollo Theatre*. Buffalo, NY: Prometheus Books, 1984.

Schomburg Center for Research in Black Culture. *Scenes from the 20th Century Stage: Black Theatre in Photographs*, catalog of an exhibition, Schomburg Center for Research in Black Culture. New York: New York Public Library, Schomburg Center for Research in Black Culture, 1983.

Sears, Djanet. *Testifyin': Contemporary African Canadian Drama*. Toronto: Playwrights Canada Press, 2000.

Sell, Mike. *Avant-Garde Performance & the Limits of Criticism: Approaching the Living Theatre, Happenings/Fluxus, and the Black Arts Movement*. Ann Arbor: University of Michigan Press, 2005.

Seller, Maxine. *Ethnic Theatre in the United States*. Westport, CT: Greenwood Press, 1983.

Shakong, Samuel. "A Study of Black Theatre from the 1930's through the 1960's," M.A. dissertation. Adephi University, 1975.

Shannon, Sandra Garrett. *August Wilson's Fences: A Reference Guide*. Westport, CT: Greenwood Press, 2003.

   "Baraka, Black Ethos, and the Black Arts Movement: A Study of Amiri Baraka's Drama during the Black Arts Movement from 1964–1969," Ph.D. dissertation. University of Maryland, 1988.

   The Dramatic Vision of August Wilson. Washington, DC: Howard University Press, 1995.

Shannon, Sandra Garrett, and Dana A. Williams. *August Wilson and Black Aesthetics*. New York: Palgrave Macmillan, 2004.

Silver, Reuben. "A History of the Karamu Theatre of Karamu House, 1915–1960," Ph.D. dissertation. Ohio State University, 1961.

Smethurst, James Edward. *The Black Arts Movement: Literary Nationalism in the 1960s and 1970s*. Chapel Hill: University of North Carolina Press, 2005.

Smith, Eric Ledell. *Bert Williams: A Biography of the Pioneer Black Comedian*. Jefferson, NC: McFarland, 1992.

Snodgrass, Mary Ellen. *August Wilson: A Literary Companion*. Jefferson, NC: McFarland, 2004.

Steen, Shannon. *Racial Geometries of the Black Atlantic, Asian Pacific and American Theatre*. Basingstoke; New York: Palgrave Macmillan, 2010.

Thomas, Lundeana Marie. *Barbara Ann Teer and the National Black Theatre: Transformational Forces in Harlem*. New York: Garland, 1997.

   "Barbara Ann Teer's National Black Theatre Quintessential Community Theatre in Harlem," Ph.D. dissertation. University of Michigan, 1993.

Ugwu, Catherine. *Let's Get It On: The Politics of Black Performance*. London: Institute of Contemporary Arts; Seattle: Bay Press, 1995.

Vogel, Shane. *The Scene of Harlem Cabaret: Race, Sexuality, Performance.* Chicago: University of Chicago Press, 2009.

Washington, Rhonnie Lynn. "The Relationship between the White Critic and the Black Theatre from 1959–1969," Ph.D. dissertation. University of Michigan, 1984.

Waters, Hazel. *Racism on the Victorian Stage: Representation of Slavery and the Black Character.* Cambridge: Cambridge University Press, 2007.

Wetmore, Kevin J. *Black Dionysus: Greek Tragedy and African American Theatre.* Jefferson, NC: McFarland, 2003.

Williams, Bert, Ruth Etting, John Buchanan, *et al. Follies, Scandals, and Other Diversions: From Ziegfeld to the Shuberts,* audio recording. New York: New World Records, 1977.

Williams, Dana, and Sandra Shannon. *August Wilson and Black Aesthetics.* New York: Palgrave Macmillan, 2006.

Williams, Mance. *Black Theatre in the 1960s and 1970s: A Historical-Critical Analysis of the Movement.* Westport, CT: Greenwood Press, 1985.

Wilson, August. *August Wilson Century Cycle.* New York; St. Paul, MN: Theatre Communications Group, 2007.

Wilson, Sondra K., and National Association for the Advancement of Colored People. *The Crisis Reader: Stories, Poetry, and Essays from the NAACP's Crisis Magazine.* New York: Modern Library, 1999.

Witham, Barry. *The Federal Theatre Project: A Case Study.* Cambridge; New York: Cambridge University Press, 2003.

Wolfe, Peter. *August Wilson.* New York: Twayne Publishers, 1999.

Woll, Allen L. *Black Musical Theatre: From Coontown to Dreamgirls.* Baton Rouge: Louisiana State University Press, 1989.

  Dictionary of the Black Theatre: Broadway, Off-Broadway, and Selected Harlem Theatre. Westport, CT: Greenwood Press, 1983.

Young, Harvey. *Embodying Black Experience: Stillness, Critical Memory, and the Black Body.* Ann Arbor: University of Michigan Press, 2010.

INDEX

Cambridge companions to ...